Freedom

A HISTORY of US

JOY HAKIM

Dedication

Someone asked me if *A History of US* (the series I wrote for young readers) was the best thing I've ever done. I answered with a strong "no." The best thing I ever did was to have children. This book is for them, and for the grandchildren, too.

> Ellen and Todd
> Jeff and Haya
> Danny and Liz
> And Natalie, Sam, Casey, Eli, and Miriam

It's also for Sam, who helped create the books (and the kids, too).

And for Peter and Philip Kunhardt and their friends, who turned it all into an exciting television adventure.

And for Barbara Dorff, a Texas teacher of the year, a friend, and an inspiration. She's the author of teaching materials that coordinate with this book.

©2013 Joy Hakim

Social Studies School Service
10200 Jefferson Boulevard, P.O. Box 802
Culver City, CA 90232
United States of America

(310) 839-2436
(800) 421-4246
Fax: (800) 944-5432
Fax: (310) 839-2249

www.socialstudies.com
access@socialstudies.com

Project Coordinator: Dr. Aaron Willis
Editors: Kerry Gordonson, Aarya Chevaillier
Cover: Mark Gutierrez, A.R. Harter
Text Design: A.R. Harter

Title hand-lettering by Iskra Johnson.

The lines on page 193 are excerpted from the poem "American Names" by Stephen Vincent Benét, from *Ballads and Poems, 1915–1930*, by Stephen Vincent Benét. Copyright ©1931 by Rosemary and Stephen Vincent Benét. Copyright renewed ©1961 by Rosemary Carr Benét. Reprinted by permission of Brandt & Brandt Literary Agents, Inc.

Printed in the United States of America.

ISBN 978-1-56004-774-2

Product Code: Z215

Contents

Introduction: Ordinary People v
 1. Independence 1
 2. Revolution 19
 3. Liberty for All? 49
 4. Wake Up, America 73
 5. A Fatal Contradiction 95
 6. A War to End Slavery 123
 7. What Is Freedom? 155
 8. Whose Land Is This? 183
 9. Working for Freedom 205
 10. Yearning to Breathe Free 227
 11. Safe for Democracy? 249
 12. Depression and War 273
 13. Democracy and Struggles 299
 14. Let Freedom Ring 321
 15. Marching to Freedom Land 347
 16. Becoming Free 377
 17. War in Doubles 405
The Declaration of Independence 424
Freedom in the Constitution 427
President Obama's Second Inaugural Address 430
Index 434

In CONGRESS, July 4, 1776.

The unanimous Declaration of the thirteen united States of America,

When in the Course of human events, it becomes necessary for one people to dissolve the political bands which have connected them with another, and to assume among the powers of the earth, the separate and equal station to which the Laws of Nature and of Nature's God entitle them, a decent respect to the opinions of mankind requires that they should declare the causes which impel them to the separation.

We hold these truths to be self-evident, that all men are created equal, that they are endowed by their Creator with certain unalienable Rights, that among these are Life, Liberty and the pursuit of Happiness.—That to secure these rights, Governments are instituted among Men, deriving their just powers from the consent of the governed,—That whenever any Form of Government becomes destructive of these ends, it is the Right of the People to alter or to abolish it, and to institute new Government, laying its foundation on such principles and organizing its powers in such form, as to them shall seem most likely to effect their Safety and Happiness. Prudence, indeed, will dictate that Governments long established should not be changed for light and transient causes; and accordingly all experience hath shewn, that mankind are more disposed to suffer, while evils are sufferable, than to right themselves by abolishing the forms to which they are accustomed. But when a long train of abuses and usurpations, pursuing invariably the same Object evinces a design to reduce them under absolute Despotism, it is their right, it is their duty, to throw off such Government, and to provide new Guards for their future security.—Such has been the patient sufferance of these Colonies; and such is now the necessity which constrains them to alter their former Systems of Government. The history of the present King of Great Britain is a history of repeated injuries and usurpations, all having in direct object the establishment of an absolute Tyranny over these States. To prove this, let Facts be submitted to a candid world.

He has refused his Assent to Laws, the most wholesome and necessary for the public good.

He has forbidden his Governors to pass Laws of immediate and pressing importance, unless suspended in their operation till his Assent should be obtained; and when so suspended, he has utterly neglected to attend to them.

He has refused to pass other Laws for the accommodation of large districts of people, unless those people would relinquish the right of Representation in the Legislature, a right inestimable to them and formidable to tyrants only.

He has called together legislative bodies at places unusual, uncomfortable, and distant from the depository of their Public Records, for the sole purpose of fatiguing them into compliance with his measures.

He has dissolved Representative Houses repeatedly, for opposing with manly firmness his invasions on the rights of the people.

He has refused for a long time, after such dissolutions, to cause others to be elected; whereby the Legislative powers, incapable of Annihilation, have returned to the People at large for their exercise; the State remaining in the mean time exposed to all the dangers of invasion from without, and convulsions within.

He has endeavoured to prevent the population of these States; for that purpose obstructing the Laws for Naturalization of Foreigners; refusing to pass others to encourage their migrations hither, and raising the conditions of new Appropriations of Lands.

He has obstructed the Administration of Justice, by refusing his Assent to Laws for establishing Judiciary powers.

He has made Judges dependent on his Will alone, for the tenure of their offices, and the amount and payment of their salaries.

He has erected a multitude of New Offices, and sent hither swarms of Officers to harrass our people, and eat out their substance.

He has kept among us, in times of peace, Standing Armies without the Consent of our legislatures.

He has affected to render the Military independent of and superior to the Civil power.

He has combined with others to subject us to a jurisdiction foreign to our constitution, and unacknowledged by our laws; giving his Assent to their Acts of pretended Legislation:

For quartering large bodies of armed troops among us:

For protecting them, by a mock Trial, from punishment for any Murders which they should commit on the Inhabitants of these States:

For cutting off our Trade with all parts of the world:

For imposing Taxes on us without our Consent:

For depriving us in many cases, of the benefits of Trial by Jury:

For transporting us beyond Seas to be tried for pretended offences:

For abolishing the free System of English Laws in a neighbouring Province, establishing therein an Arbitrary government, and enlarging its Boundaries so as to render it at once an example and fit instrument for introducing the same absolute rule into these Colonies:

For taking away our Charters, abolishing our most valuable Laws, and altering fundamentally the Forms of our Governments:

For suspending our own Legislatures, and declaring themselves invested with power to legislate for us in all cases whatsoever.

He has abdicated Government here, by declaring us out of his Protection and waging War against us.

He has plundered our seas, ravaged our Coasts, burnt our towns, and destroyed the lives of our people.

He is at this time transporting large Armies of foreign Mercenaries to compleat the works of death, desolation and tyranny, already begun with circumstances of Cruelty & perfidy scarcely paralleled in the most barbarous ages, and totally unworthy the Head of a civilized nation.

He has constrained our fellow Citizens taken Captive on the high Seas to bear Arms against their Country, to become the executioners of their friends and Brethren, or to fall themselves by their Hands.

He has excited domestic insurrections amongst us, and has endeavoured to bring on the inhabitants of our frontiers, the merciless Indian Savages, whose known rule of warfare, is an undistinguished destruction of all ages, sexes and conditions.

In every stage of these Oppressions We have Petitioned for Redress in the most humble terms: Our repeated Petitions have been answered only by repeated injury. A Prince, whose character is thus marked by every act which may define a Tyrant, is unfit to be the ruler of a free people.

Nor have We been wanting in attentions to our British brethren. We have warned them from time to time of attempts by their legislature to extend an unwarrantable jurisdiction over us. We have reminded them of the circumstances of our emigration and settlement here. We have appealed to their native justice and magnanimity, and we have conjured them by the ties of our common kindred to disavow these usurpations, which, would inevitably interrupt our connections and correspondence. They too have been deaf to the voice of justice and of consanguinity. We must, therefore, acquiesce in the necessity, which denounces our Separation, and hold them, as we hold the rest of mankind, Enemies in War, in Peace Friends.

We, therefore, the Representatives of the united States of America, in General Congress, Assembled, appealing to the Supreme Judge of the world for the rectitude of our intentions, do, in the Name, and by authority of the good People of these Colonies, solemnly publish and declare, That these United Colonies are, and of Right ought to be Free and Independent States; that they are Absolved from all Allegiance to the British Crown, and that all political connection between them and the State of Great Britain, is and ought to be totally dissolved; and that as Free and Independent States, they have full Power to levy War, conclude Peace, contract Alliances, establish Commerce, and to do all other Acts and Things which Independent States may of right do. And for the support of this Declaration, with a firm reliance on the protection of divine Providence, we mutually pledge to each other our Lives, our Fortunes and our sacred Honor.

Ordinary People

An Introduction by Joy Hakim

We are of the humble opinion that we have the right to enjoy the privileges of free men. But that we do not will appear in many instances, and we beg leave to mention one out of many, and that is of the education of our children which now receive no benefit from the free schools in the town of Boston, which we think is a great grievance, as by woeful experience we now feel the want of a common education. We, therefore, must fear for our rising offspring to see them in ignorance in a land of gospel light when there is provision made for them as well as others and yet can't enjoy them, and for no other reason can be given this they are black. We therefore pray your Honors that you would in your wisdom some provision might be made for the free education of our dear children. And in duty bound shall ever pray.

That's a petition to the state legislature of the Commonwealth of Massachusetts Bay. It was written in 1787. Consider the hopes and aspirations that must have been in the minds of its authors. We hear a lot about our founding daddies, but, again and again, it was people without fancy pedigrees or privileges, those often dubbed "ordinary," who stood up, shouted out, ignored abuse, and, wanting to expand their freedoms, expanded ours, too. Among the astonishments of the American freedom drama-our experiment in republican government, which has lasted more than 200 years-is that it was conceived and played out in town meetings and state assemblies from Maine to Georgia as well as in Philadelphia's stately chambers. Why, suddenly, did men and women think they could rule themselves? What made them believe they could do without kings and emperors?

Grouchy, acerbic Isaac Newton had a lot to do with it. Newton (who was an old man when young Ben Franklin first arrived in London) had taken the vast universe, which seemed beyond human comprehension, and demystified it. He found that the earth and skies are governed by verifiable laws and regulated by nature's checks and balances. If the universe submits to reason and law, men and women certainly should be able to do so, said the eighteenth-century thinkers. Reason and law? It takes free minds to make the most of them. That

Howard Chandler Christy's twentieth-century view of the *Scene at the Signing of the Constitution of the United States* in 1787.

got poet John Milton (who hated kings) thinking about free speech, and some philosophers (especially John Locke, who agreed with Milton) thinking about political freedom. From them and others came the Enlightenment, also known as the Age of Reason. And that's when we were lucky enough to be born.

In our long row of Atlantic-washed colonies, we were far enough from the traditional seats of power to try new ideas. Besides, the European monarchs, not recognizing our potential, neglected us. They let us run our own affairs. We learned by doing it. Then we broke the mold of history and established a nation where citizens are expected to choose their own rulers and govern themselves. It had never been done before in any sizable country. (At our birth, we were, territorially, the largest nation in the western world.)

To add to our good luck (our timing, our isolation, the richness of our land), we had George Washington, John Adams, Thomas Jefferson, Ben Franklin, James

Madison, Alexander Hamilton, and some other independent thinkers to get us started. They met in Philadelphia and, over the course of several years, were courageous enough to stand up to the world's greatest power, Great Britain, and savvy enough to start us off with a written constitution-and a remarkable one at that.

Moralists all, they placed God—who had always been invoked to explain the divine right of kings—in a personal, spiritual sphere, separate from the mundane world of legislatures and taxes. John Adams, talking about the making of the new nation, had this to say:

> *It will never be pretended that any persons employed in that service had any interviews with the gods, or were in any degree under the inspiration of Heaven.... Thirteen governments thus founded on the natural authority of the people alone, without a pretense of miracle or mystery ... are a great point gained in favor of the rights of mankind.*

Religious wars had racked Europe for centuries. The founders wanted none of that. Why should any government presume to direct anyone's innermost beliefs? "Freedom of conscience" was how they described what we call freedom of religion. "The legitimate powers of government extend only to such acts as are injurious to others. But it does me no injury for my neighbor to say there are twenty gods, or no God. It neither picks my pocket nor breaks my leg," wrote Jefferson in *Notes on Virginia*. Still, a government without a state religion seemed risky. It had never been done before. This was an original American idea. Would the population fall into immorality?

George Washington was skeptical in 1786 when Thomas Jefferson introduced his bill for a statute for religious freedom to the Virginia legislature. In colonial Virginia, all state officials were required to be members of the Church of England. If the statute passed, anyone, even Baptists, could hold state office. Supporting the idea, the Presbytery of Hanover declared, "Religion is altogether personal; and the right of exercising it is inalienable; and it is not, cannot, and ought not to be, resigned to the will of the society at large; and much less the legislature." As it turned out, when the statute passed (after much controversy), Virginians were able to do without a state religion; they were no more sinful than before. So, when the Constitution was written, it was easy to make the separation between church and state: Article VI of the Constitution stipulates: *No religious Test shall ever be required as a Qualification to any Office or public Trust under the United States.* James Madison, writing the First Amendment, made that separation a constitutional guarantee: *Congress shall make no law respecting an establishment of religion, or prohibiting the free exercise thereof.*

Washington became an enthusiast of religious freedom. Writing to the Hebrew

Finally! In 1920 the National Woman's Party celebrates the ratification of the Nineteenth Amendment to the Constitution and the enfranchisement of half the population.

congregation of Newport, Rhode Island, in 1790, he said:

> The citizens of the United States of America have a right to applaud themselves for having given to mankind examples of an enlarged and liberal policy, a policy worthy of imitation.... it is now no more that toleration is spoken of, as if it was by the indulgence of one class of people, that another enjoyed exercise of their inherent natural rights. For happily the government of the United States, which gives to bigotry no sanction, to persecution no assistance requires only that

they who live under its protection should demean themselves as good citizens.

James Madison seemed to think coerced religion was as hard on the church as on individuals. In an 1822 letter to a friend, he said: "Religion and government will both exist in greater purity; the less they are mixed together."

There's a whole lot more to this freedom story, but the thing to keep in mind is that we started a way of governing that speaks to the whole world. Our political process, open to all, will let a farmer's son, Harry S. Truman—too poor to go to college follow a wealthy patrician, Franklin Delano Roosevelt—Groton, Harvard, and Columbia Law—into the nation's top job. It's a position that anyone, of either sex or any ethnic background, can now reach for.

Our founding rebels wore knee breeches and spoke in civilized phrases, but they were tough and uncompromising when it came to their beliefs. They demonstrated that you can fight for freedom and change—and be decent about it. Elsewhere, revolutionaries had no problem acting like thugs, which seems the customary way. Our cherished radicals—people like Henry David Thoreau, Frederick Douglass, Susan B. Anthony, Cesar Chavez, and Martin Luther King, Jr.—use reason, discourse, and peaceful demonstration to right wrongs and broaden rights, do us proud, and establish an American model. They will constantly invoke our founding documents as the basis for their claims.

"There is a natural aristocracy among men," wrote Thomas Jefferson in a letter to John Adams. Abraham Lincoln is proof of it. Lincoln transforms a horrific war into an epiphany—a time of insight and enhanced meaning—and makes us look anew at the founding phrase *All men are created equal.*

One hundred and sixty some years after African-Americans petition the legislature in Boston to get decent schooling for their children, the Reverend Oliver Brown goes to court for the same reason: he wants his daughter to have an education equal to that of the white children in his community. That he has to do it is a shameful part of our history; that it takes so long for the Supreme Court to sanction equal opportunity is dismaying; that many American children still don't get a fair shake in their schools is unconscionable. Our system is far from perfect, but it gives us tools to strive for perfection.

So here we are in the twenty-first century, and still a work in progress. *Liberty and justice for all* is both our legacy and our destination. It's not the wishful thinking of textbook writers or governmental dissemblers. It's not corny; it's not maudlin. It is a special, unique, marvelous American gift to humanity. It's a fairness doctrine. In George Washington's words, it is "worthy of imitation." So come aboard and consider how you can help spread the word: freedom works. It is worth the energy and courage it takes to keep it growing.

Connecticut artist John Trumbull made the first sketch for his painting *The Declaration of Independence* while at Thomas Jefferson's house in Paris in 1786. The men standing on the left (from left to right)—John Adams, Roger Sherman, Robert Livingston, Jefferson, and Ben Franklin—are presenting the Declaration to John Hancock (sitting, right).

PART 1

INDEPENDENCE

In Europe, July 4, 1776, seemed just an ordinary day. But if England's King George III had put an ear to the ground, he would have felt the earth tremble. Because something happened on that July day that was going to change the Americas, and Europe, and, eventually, the whole world. It took place in England's American colonies, but it was several weeks before a ship brought the news to England's King George. And even then he didn't understand it.

It is the people who have settled a narrow band of land along North America's Atlantic coast who will cause the changes that are coming. Most of these newcomers are from England, or from Africa. They have accomplished much in the 150 years since the first of them climbed from their small wooden ships at Jamestown and Plymouth. They have cleared land and planted crops and built towns. They have created colonies where life is freer than it is in the Old World.

But not for the Africans. For them there is no freedom at all. Most of them are enslaved. Slavery exists in much of the world in this eighteenth century. Many people say, "There has always been slavery, and there always will be. Let's not worry about it." These people don't realize it, but their ideas will change.

That July day in 1776 will help break chains from the past. Two hundred years into the future, people will be shocked at the *very* idea of slavery. Yet right now almost everyone seems to think that people are made differently from one another—that some are ordinary and some extraordinary; some are elegant and noble, others simple and dull. Most people living in the eighteenth century believe that birth determines where you fit on the ladder of humans. And that some people are better than others. Oh, a few don't accept that idea—but they are the kind who lead frustrated lives. Yet it is that very idea of aristocrat and peasant that will be blasted away on July 4, 1776.

Do you see why the earth will shake? In some European towns, laws actually prevent men and women of the upper classes from being friends with the lower classes. Much of the world is like that. Poor people don't have a chance. These English colonies are like that, too—but only partly. Many people have come here to escape European ways. In America the son of a Boston candlemaker will become one of the wealthiest and most famous men in the land.

That is what the momentous day in 1776 is about. It is about opportunity for all, and equality, and fairness. Americans will fight a revolution to make those things possible. But the most important part of the revolution will be "in the minds and hearts

Hector St. John de Crèvecœur

of the people." The revolution will change everything-well, almost everything. It won't solve the awful problem of slavery. But it will unleash the idea that will end slavery, and that will bring women's rights, and children's rights, and all kinds of other rights. The idea is so daring that nothing like it has been heard in governments before. This is it: ordinary people are as worthwhile and valuable and competent as anyone, even as worthwhile as kings and queens. Imagine it! No one is better than anyone else. That idea will transform the whole world.

AN AMERICAN FARMER

Michel Guillaume Jean de Crèvecœur was a small man with red hair, freckles, and a cheerful face. He was French, and still a teenager when he headed for Canada to fight the English colonists. The French and Indian War was under way (it was part of a bigger war between the French and the British); Crèvecœur was a mapmaker whose skills were needed. But when he saw the American colonies for himself, and the freedom they offered, Crèvecœur changed his ideas. He decided to move. In 1759, he settled on a farm in what is now New York State. And then he gave himself an English name: Hector St. John.

Hector St. John Crèvecœur fell in love with America. He knew that in Europe the aristocrats—wealthy, privileged people—owned most of the land. In America most people were yeoman Farmers—they owned and worked small farms. Crèvecœur thought farming an ideal life and the English colonies an ideal place, though he also said that some Americans were destroying the land, and others were always "bawling about liberty without knowing what it is." He soon married and had a family. And he wrote about

Edward Hicks (1780–1849) painted *The Residence of David Twining* in 1846, but he meant it to evoke an earlier time: the idyllic memory of an eighteenth-century childhood with his foster parents in Pennsylvania, Quaker farmer David Twining (in hat) and his wife, Elizabeth, with Edward, aged seven (lower right).

what he admired most in his newly adopted country. Something special was happening in this land the Europeans had colonized, and he wanted them to know about it.

Crèvecœur's book, *Letters of an American Farmer,* got published in six countries and was immensely popular. Crèvecœur took his son to Europe to get *Letters of an American Farmer* published. When he came back, his wife was dead, his house was burned, and his two other children were gone. Native Americans had attacked. Now, Crèvecœur, means "broken heart" in French. And his heart was indeed broken. Later he found the children alive, and that mended his heart a bit. But perhaps his name should have been "great heart," because he never lost his faith in the basic decency of all the peoples—Native Americans, English, French, Spanish, Dutch, Africans, Germans, and others—who were forming a new kind of society in a land he loved.

> "The American is a new man, wlon new principles; he must therefore enw ideas and form new opinions.... We have no princes, for whom we toil, starve and bleed. We are the most perfect society now existing in the world. Here man is free as he ought to be.... Here individuals of all nations are melted into a new race of men, whose labors and posterity will one day cause great change in the world."
>
> —Hector St. John Crèvecœur

Print master Nathaniel Currier made this lithograph depicting the Boston Tea Party (1773)—his vision was somewhat romantic, since the raid was carried out secretly and under cover of darkness.

A Taxing King

Crèvecœur was warning Europe. Americans had new ideas and those ideas might even spread beyond the seas. But George III and his ministers weren't interested in warnings. Besides, most historians agree that King George wasn't very smart. He made some big mistakes. His pride was more important to him than the valuable American colonies.

George wanted to be a good king. But to be a good king you need wisdom, and George III wasn't a very wise man. For years he had been taxing the colonists, in an effort to help pay the costs of his empire. Foreign wars had left England with big bills. The British thought the colonies should pay some of those bills, especially the ones from the French and Indian War, which was fought to kick the French out of North America.

Americans knew how European kings taxed the peasants and kept them poor, and they didn't want that kind of treatment. Englishmen had the right to vote on their own taxes in Parliament, they said. But since no colonists could serve in Parliament, no colonists got to vote on taxes. The colonists said, "no taxation without representation." They wanted to vote on their own taxes, in their own assemblies, as they had been doing. It was the Stamp Tax, passed in 1765, that enraged most Americans. The colonists were supposed to buy a British stamp for every piece of printed paper they used. That meant every sheet of newspaper, every document, every playing card—everything. The colonists

In 1774, British customs official John Malcolm was tarred, feathered, and carted through Boston after Tea Party member George Hewes tried to stop him beating a little boy on the street and was beaten in return. The cartoonist shows Malcolm's attackers pouring hated English tea down Malcolm's throat.

On the left, the actual stamp that the Stamp Act required to be reproduced on every piece of printed paper in the colonies—and (right) what some of the colonists thought about it.

wouldn't do it. They got so angry they attacked some of the British stamp agents and put tar all over them and then feathers in the tar. The Stamp Tax could not be collected. It was repealed.

Then the king's minister Lord Charles Townshend (who was known as Champagne Charlie) decided to tax lead, glass, paper, paint, and tea. The colonists got even by not buying anything made in England. The English merchants were angry about that—it cost them a lot of money—and they demanded that the Townshend taxes be repealed. They were, in 1770, except for the tax on tea. It was a small tax, but King George wanted to prove that he and Parliament could tax Americans if they wished to.

To the colonists it was still taxation without representation. (What made it worse was that Parliament gave the East India Company the right to sell tea for less than the tea Boston merchants were selling.) So, in 1773, some Bostonians decided

"It was now evening, and I immediately dressed myself in the costume of an Indian, equipped with a small hatchet ... with which, and a club, after having painted my face and hands with coal dust in the shop of a blacksmith, I repaired to Griffin's Wharf where the ships lay that contained the tea. I fell in with many who were dressed, equipped and painted as I was, and who fell in with me and marched in order to the place of our destination.... We then were ordered by our commander to open the hatches and take out all the chests of tea and throw them overboard, and we immediately proceeded to execute his orders, first cutting and splitting the chests with our tomahawks, so as to thoroughly expose them to the effects of the water."

—George Hewes, a participant in the Boston Tea Party

to show King George and Parliament and Lord Townshend what they thought of the tax on tea.

They dressed up as Indians, climbed on a ship in Boston harbor and threw a whole load of good English tea into the ocean. Americans called it the Boston Tea Party, but the English didn't. Then, to show he was in charge, King George asked Parliament to pass Restraining Acts (the Americans called them Intolerable Acts). They closed the port of Boston, took over the Massachusetts government, and passed a Quartering Act, which meant troops

The Rights of Englishmen

What were those English rights the Americans kept demanding for themselves? There was a time when kings in England could do anything they wanted to do: kill people, or take their land and money, or lock them in dungeons and keep them there. Then, back in the thirteenth century, a wicked king named John began picking on the English landholders, especially barons and other noblemen. He felt kings had been put on earth by God for men and women to serve. At last the barons could stand no more. In 1215 they forced King John to sign an agreement that gave Englishmen basic rights. The agreement said the king couldn't take land and money from people without Parliament's permission. The agreement also said that no person could be put in jail unless he had a fair trial "by the lawful judgment of his peers, under the law of the land." It granted other rights, too. The idea behind that great agreement was that the king's power brought responsibilities. After King John signed his name to that document, kings were no longer free to do anything they wanted—and before long, men and women were saying that kings were meant to serve the people, not the other way around.

That document was written in Latin, and its name means "great charter"; in Latin that is Magna Carta. Another very important right that the English got for themselves at this time also has a Latin name: *habeas corpus*. Those words mean "have the body." That is what the police must do if they arrest you. They can't lose you (and your body) in jail. In the old days someone could get arrested and thrown in jail, and no one would tell him what he'd done wrong. Sometimes the police arrested the wrong person; sometimes a person got put in jail, and everyone forgot he was there; sometimes he died in jail without ever knowing he had been arrested. With habeas corpus, a judge must tell you why you have been arrested. If there is no good reason for it, you can go. That is a very important right. In many countries today, people are still thrown in jail for no good reason.

Another English right guarantees that your own words can't be used against you in court. But why would you say bad things about

must be housed by colonists. housed in the colonies. Unable to fish or go to sea, half of Boston's citizens were out of work, and hungry. Now the other colonies, which had hardly paid attention to one another, were alarmed. "The question is," said one Virginian, Theodore Bland, "whether the rights and liberties of America shall be contended for, or given up to arbitrary powers."

At first, Philadelphia's Benjamin Franklin (who was that successful son of a Boston candlemaker) thought the problem was a family affair. He wrote a poem about "Mother England."

yourself? Well, if you were tortured you might. You might even say you did something you didn't do, just to stop the torture. So that, too, is a very important right. The English kept adding to their rights, and then, in 1688, something big happened: it came to be called the Glorious Revolution. With it, Parliament got King William and Queen Mary of England to sign a bill of rights that made Parliament more powerful than the king and queen. Since Parliament represented the English people, the people were now more powerful than the monarchs. England was on the road to constitutional monarchy. The English people were proud of the rights they had won, and they had a right to be proud. The American colonists expected those same rights, and they were right to insist on them. They thought of themselves as English citizens living in the colonies; they believed English rights were their rights. Then things happened to make them think they were losing their rights, so they went to war. After that war, they wrote a great constitution. It gave the American people basic English rights—and then went even farther and guaranteed freedoms that no country had ever before given its people.

England's Glorious Revolutionaries, King William III and his queen, Mary.

We have an old mother that peevish is grown,
She snubs us like children that scarce walk alone;
She forgets we're grown up and have sense of our own.

But when Franklin and others realized that England was not going to treat them as grownups, they began thinking seriously about breaking away—about being free. In Boston, a pudgy, rumpled-looking man helped spark the action. His name was Samuel Adams, and he was a fiery patriot and an inspired organizer. (The British called him a troublemaker—and worse.) He formed Committees of Correspondence and got colonists to write to each other—and get to know one another. He started Sons of Liberty groups that made plans to be free. In Boston and Annapolis they met under old elms called Liberty Trees.

Samuel Adams wanted more than just separation from England. He was inspired by a grander idea: that America could be a special nation, a beacon, a "city on a hill," where people would be free of kings and princes. A nation where, for the first time in history, people could truly rule themselves.

THE FIREBRANDS

Sam Adams had an ally in the proud colony of Virginia, far south of Boston. His name was Patrick Henry, and he was a man with a way of speaking that left his listeners awed. Henry had been a storekeeper, and then a planter, but when he tried the law he found his calling. He was soon elected to Virginia's House of Burgesses. By 1775 it was no longer safe for the burgesses to meet in Williamsburg (then Virginia's capital), so they assembled in St. John's Church in Richmond. It was there that Patrick Henry gave his most famous speech. "The tendons on his neck stood out white and rigid like whipcords," said one witness to that day. "His voice rose louder and louder, until the walls of the building seemed to shake. Men leaned forward in their seats, their faces pale."

The port of Boston was closed. English soldiers were in the city, and the

VIRGINIA'S HOUSE OF BURGESSES

In 1619, at Jamestown, Virginia (the first permanent English settlement in America), a group of colonists—called "burgesses"—is elected to make laws. They form an assembly called the House of Burgesses. In England laws are made by Parliament. The House of Burgesses gives the Virginians their own form of Parliament. That has never happened in a colony before. Until then, all the laws for colonies were made in the home country, or by appointed governors and their councils. The House of Burgesses changed that. England was letting colonists do their own governing. That was a big first in history (an English governor did have veto power over the burgesses, but he didn't use it very often). The House of Burgesses, formed in 1619, gave America's European colonies representative government. It was just a dozen years since the first ships from England tied up at Jamestown, and the English colonists were doing something astonishing. They were making laws for themselves.

Nineteenth-century artist Peter Rothermel's recreation of Patrick Henry's speech against the Stamp Act to the House of Burgesses. On the floor he has thrown down a gauntlet, the traditional challenge to fight.

Massachusetts Assembly had been dissolved. Would Virginia sit idly by? Henry stepped into the aisle, bowed his head, and held out his arms, pretending that they were chained.

"Our chains are forged, their clanking may be heard on the plains of Boston," he said. "The war is actually begun. The next gale that sweeps from the north will bring to our ears the clash of resounding arms." Then Patrick Henry threw off the imaginary chains and stood up straight. "Our brethren are already in the field," he went on. "Why stand we here idle? I know not what course others may take, but as for me, give me liberty, or give me death!"

Historians say the American Revolution had three firebrands, three men who could light a fire in people's minds and hearts: Samuel Adams and Patrick Henry were two of them. Tom Paine was the other. This war of independence might have happened without them, but it certainly would have been different. Sam Adams was a New Englander from Boston with a Puritan background. Tom Paine came from England and lived in the Middle Colonies, in Philadelphia. Patrick Henry was a southerner, an Anglican, a Virginian, and a country boy. These men were alike in one important way: each understood, before most other Americans did, that a break from England was necessary.

Some colonists found it difficult to think of themselves as Americans. They saw themselves as English. Even those who came from France or Germany or Holland soon thought of English rights as their rights. When they stopped calling themselves English, they began to say they were Virginians, or New Englanders, or Carolinians. It was hard for them to understand that diverse colonies could all be part of one country. To begin, they didn't know each other. Overland travel between colonies was very difficult. There were no good roads and few bridges. But Sam Adams's committees of correspondence helped change that. Men who wrote to each other soon realized they had the same ideas and goals.

Should they consider fighting for freedom? England was a great power; the colonies were scattered and had little military experience. Still, it made sense to be prepared. New Englanders began to stockpile cannonballs and gunpowder in

Tom Paine

Tom Paine was hardly off the boat from England, in 1774, when he became a firebrand of revolution. He didn't plan it that way. "I thought it very hard," he wrote, "to have the country set on fire … almost the moment I got into it." Tom had been apprenticed to a corsetmaker when he was a boy in England. Corsets are tight undergarments that women wore to hold in their stomachs and make their waists look tiny. Being a corsetmaker was not exactly an exciting career-not for a boy with a mind like Tom's. So he ran away and went to sea. But that didn't work out. Then he tried to be a grocer, and a schoolteacher, and a tobacco seller. But nothing seemed to work for him until one day in London he met Benjamin Franklin, who was visiting, and who helped him find a job in Philadelphia. That job, as a writer and magazine editor, was the perfect use of Tom Paine's talents: for he was a magician with words. In January 1776 he wrote a pamphlet called *Common Sense*.

Tom Paine was able to say clearly what people really knew in their hearts. In it he told the colonists three important things:

- Monarchy is a poor form of government and they would be better off without it.
- Great Britain was hurting America's economy with taxes and trade restrictions.
- It was foolish for a small island 3,000 miles away to try to rule a whole continent.

"Everything that is right or reasonable pleads for separation," wrote Tom Paine. "The blood of the slain cries, "'Tis time to part…. Let the crown be demolished. We have it in our power to begin the world again."

Concord, a small Massachusetts town about twenty miles northwest of Boston. When the British heard about those munitions, they decided to get them. Paul Revere, a silversmith and one of those who wanted independence, found out that the British soldiers were heading for Concord. Which way would they go? Revere sent a spy. "If the British go out by water," he said, "show two lanterns in the North Church steeple; and if by land, one, as a signal."

So, on the night of April 8, 1775, when Paul Revere saw two lights in the church belfry, he knew the British were taking the water route across Boston's Charles River. Revere leapt on his horse and rode hard through the night. "The British are coming, the British are coming!" he warned all in the countryside.

A few miles from Concord, at Lexington, the American farmers were ready, and they grabbed their guns. They were called "minutemen" because they could fight on a minute's notice. Captain John Parker was their leader, and what he said on that day is now carved in stone near the spot where he must have stood. "Stand your ground. Don't fire unless fired upon. But if they mean to have a war let it begin here!" And it did begin right there, at Lexington in Massachusetts.

Sixty-two years later, the poet Ralph Waldo Emerson wrote about that moment.

By the rude bridge that arched the flood,
Their flag to April's breeze unfurled,
Here once the embattled farmers stood,
And fired the shot heard around the world.

When the smoke cleared, eight American farmers lay dead. It was April 19, 1775. The American Revolution had begun. It *was* a shot heard round the world. This battle for a people's freedom would echo and re-echo around the globe, introducing the world to some American themes.

Patriot spy and silversmith Paul Revere with a teapot he made himself

"So through the night rode Paul Revere;
And so through the night went his cry of alarm
By the rude bridge that arched the flood,
Their flag to April's breeze unfurled,
Here once the embattled formers stood,
And fired the shot heard round the world.
To every Middlesex village and farm,
A cry of defiance and not of fear,
A voice in the darkness, a knock at the door,
And a word that shall echo forevermore!
For, borne on the night-wind of the Past,
Through all our history, to the last,
In the hour of darkness and peril and need,
The people will waken and listen to hear
The hurrying hoof-beats of that steed,
And the midnight message of Paul Revere."
—from "The Midnight Ride of Paul Revere,"
Henry Wadsworth Longfellow, 1860

Companies of redcoats march through Concord in search of weapons and ammunition stores while their officers (in the graveyard) spy out the land—too late. Word of their arrival had preceded them.

But there is always more to war than winning and losing. Here are words from someone who lived through it:

> Isaac Davis was my husband. He was then thirty years of age. We had four children; the youngest about fifteen months old.... The alarm was given early in the morning, and my husband lost no time in making ready to go to Concord with his company.... He said but little that morning. He seemed serious and thoughtful; but never seemed to hesitate.... He only said, "Take good care of the children." In the afternoon he was brought home a corpse.

"Government, even in its best state, is but a necessary evil," wrote Tom Paine, articulating one of those themes. He also said: "My country is the world, and my religion is to do good."

That day at Lexington and Concord, twice as many redcoats fell as minutemen.

A Continental Congress and a Continental Army

In 1774, the Massachusetts committee of correspondence secretly invited the other committees to a meeting. Leaders from twelve of the colonies (Georgia didn't come) met in Philadelphia. It was the First Continental Congress.

"There is in the Congress a collection of the greatest men upon this continent," Massachusetts delegate John Adams noted in his diary. John, a cousin of Sam Adams, was said to have more learning than anyone in the colonies. The delegates declared that the colonists were entitled to the same rights as Englishmen. They announced an embargo on all trade with Britain. And they respectfully petitioned King George III, urging him to consider their pleas. A year later, when the king hadn't responded, they came back to Philadelphia for a second congress. King George wasn't impressed. He said, "Blows must decide whether they are to be subject to this country or independent." And, on August 23, 1775, the king proclaimed that "a general rebellion exists in the American colonies" and that "utmost endeavors" should be made to "suppress it and bring traitors to justice." The delegates in Philadelphia were now traitors; they knew the punishment was death. What did they do? Most became even more determined to be free.

John Adams's extraordinary wife, Abigail, wrote from Massachusetts reminding him that men were not alone in wanting freedom. "In the new code of laws which you will make," she said, "I desire you to remember the Ladies. Do not put unlimited power in the hands of the husbands. Remember all men would be tyrants if they could."

The women would have to wait. But the ideas formed by this remarkable group of men would help free their future. Ben Franklin was there, and Stephen Hopkins, who came from Rhode Island, determined that his palsy would not slow him. Georgia sent three delegates. Inquisitive Benjamin Rush came from Pennsylvania, and modest Roger Sherman from Connecticut. They were men of mind and manner to make any nation proud. But, of them all, it was the dashing Virginians who were the crowd-pleasers—especially tall, dignified George Washington, who had fought with the British in the French and Indian War and become a hero. When well-respected Peyton Randolph had to leave, his young cousin Thomas Jefferson took his place.

Benjamin Franklin

As the Second Continental Congress began discussions, a letter arrived from Boston Patriots pleading for Congress to take command of their forces. The minutemen who fought at Lexington and Concord were gathered near Boston. Others had come from the countryside with rifles and muskets. If someone didn't take charge they would all go home. John Hancock from Massachusetts believed he was the man for the job. He had done a bit of soldiering, and

As president of the Continental Congress, John Hancock, whose name has entered the language as a synonym for "signature," signed the order naming Colonel George Washington commander-in-chief of the new Continental army (though Hancock had hoped to win the job himself).

Samuel Adams

it was his money that was paying some of Congress's bills. So when John Adams stood up to nominate a general almost everyone thought it would be Hancock. But John Adams always did what he thought best for the nation, not what would make him popular at home.

"There is but one man in my mind for this important command," Adams said. "The gentleman I have in mind is from Virginia." When Adams said that, Hancock's face fell, and George Washington, who realized he was the man from Virginia, rushed from the room. He was unanimously elected commander-in-chief of the new Continental army.

He accepted on one condition: he would take no salary. And that was part of Washington's greatness. He was willing to serve without pay for a cause he thought noble. But he also knew he had an almost impossible job. Before he left to take up his command, he spoke to Patrick Henry. "Remember, Mr. Henry, what I now tell you: from the day I enter upon the command of the American armies, I date the ruin of my reputation."

Washington must have had mixed feelings as he set off to lead the army. And some members of Congress still weren't ready to break with England. Once again, they politely petitioned the king. (This one was called the Olive Branch Petition.) But the king didn't even bother to read their message. John Adams was now determined to convince the delegates to declare themselves free of English rule. He talked and talked and talked some more, and finally he did it. As for Washington, it made his reputation.

WE HOLD THESE TRUTHS

If the delegates were going to take this big risk, they wanted to make it worthwhile. And it would be worthwhile if they could help create a free nation, a great nation, a nation run by its citizens-something that had never before been done. So they thought it important to say exactly why it was necessary to separate themselves from England. They asked Thomas Jefferson to write a declaration that would explain their beliefs about government; tell what King George had done wrong; and announce that the colonies were now free and independent states. Some thought it surprising that Jefferson was asked to write the declaration. One of the youngest members of the Continental Congress, he was a tall, shy redhead who loved to read, run, ride horseback, and play the violin. He had a reputation for writing well. "Jefferson proposed to me to make the draft," said John Adams. "I said, 'I will not. You can write ten times better than I can.'" Ben Franklin agreed. And so it was the bookish Virginia aristocrat, writing on a portable desk he'd designed himself, who would compose the central document of American freedom. Adams was right. Jefferson knew just what to say, and he said it in a way that inspired people all over the world.

Thomas Jefferson

> We hold these truths to be self-evident; that all men are created equal; that they are endowed by their Creator with certain unalienable Rights; that among these are life, liberty and the pursuit of happiness; that to secure these rights, governments are instituted among men, deriving their just powers from the consent of the governed.

John Adams wrote to Abigail: "Yesterday, the greatest question was decided which was ever debated in America, and a greater, perhaps, never was nor will be decided among men…. A Resolution was passed without one dissenting Colony 'that these United Colonies are, and of right ought to be, free and independent states.' It is the will of heaven that the two countries should be sundered forever."

That declaration was built on an idea so daring that nothing like it had been heard

"This was the object of the Declaration of Independence—to place before mankind the common sense of the subject, in terms so plain and firm as to command their assent, and to justify ourselves in the independent stand we were compelled to take."

—Thomas Jefferson

in governments before. Governments are not made to make kings happy. They are for the benefit of the people who are being governed. Governments should have "the consent of the governed." Jefferson's words are worth reading, and rereading, and reading again. Especially the phrase "all men are created equal." What does it mean? Are we all the same? Look around you. Of

This cartoonist has little sympathy for King George III, the hapless rider who wields a whip made of swords, axes, and bayonets and is about to lose his seat on "the horse America, throwing his master." Note the cheerful minuteman in the background.

course we aren't. Some of us are smarter; some are better athletes; some better looking; some nicer. But none of that matters, said the delegates. We are all equal in the eyes of God, and we are all entitled to equal rights. When Jefferson wrote, "all men are created equal," he didn't mention women. Did he mean to include women? No one knows; perhaps not. We do know that in the eighteenth century the words "men" and "mankind" included men *and* women. Did he mean to include black men when he said "all men"? Historians to this day argue about that. Jefferson himself was a complicated man—he said slavery was wrong, yet he owned slaves himself. But this is the important part: The Declaration of Independence has grown with time. Today, when people all over the world read its words, they understand them to mean *all* people—men, women, children—of all colors and beliefs.

It was on July 4, 1776, that the colonies (except New York, which agreed on July 15) voted to adopt the Declaration. Only John Hancock and Charles Thomson, the president and secretary of the congress, signed the first broadside copy. Hancock did it with a big, bold signature: "So the king doesn't have to put his glasses on," he said.

The signing of the others came later, and solemnly, on August 2. All knew that if their army were defeated, they would be hanged. Benjamin Harrison of Virginia (the biggest man there) attempted a bit of humor when he chided Elbridge Gerry of Massachusetts (the smallest): "I shall have a great advantage over you, Mr. Gerry, when we are all hung for what we are now doing. From the size and weight of my body I shall die in a few minutes, but from the lightness of yours you will dance in the air for an hour or two."

But that was a month after copies of the broadside, still warm from the printing press, were stuffed into saddlebags so they could be sped on their way to each of the thirteen colonies. Five days later the Declaration reached New York City and was read to Washington's troops, who shouted hurrah and tossed their hats in the air. That night a metal statue of King George was pulled down from its pedestal to be melted and turned into bullets. On July 19 the Declaration arrived in Boston, and Tom Crafts, a house painter, stepped out on a small square balcony in front of the Massachusetts State House and read it aloud.

"When in the course of human events," he began in his flat New England tones. When he finished a voice rang out, "God save the American states," and the crowd cheered. Abigail Adams, who was among the crowd, wrote to John:

The bells rang, the privateers fired the forts and batteries, the cannon were discharged, the platoons followed, & every face appeared joyful.... After dinner the King's Arms were taken down from the State House & every vestige of him from every place in which it appeared, & burnt.... Thus ends royal Authority in this State. And all the people shall say Amen.

Now there was no turning back.

Tom Crafts stands on the balcony of the Massachusetts State House in Boston to read the Declaration of Independence aloud. The lion and the unicorn on the gables are symbols of royalty.

Some Americans talked of unity back in 1754. That year, delegates from seven colonies and the Six Iroquois Nations met in Albany, New York, to adopt a "plan of union," drafted by Ben Franklin of Pennsylvania. The snake in the cartoon at left tells the colonies they need to "join or die." Above, Molly Pitcher at the Battle of Monmouth, New Jersey, in 1778. There really was a Molly who helped fire a cannon at the battle, and a Molly who brought the troops water. Historians still aren't sure if they're the same person.

Part 2

Revolution

That Declaration of Independence did it. On July 4, 1776, we Americans told the world we were free, and then we had to make it real. England wasn't going to give up valuable colonies without a fight. We had a revolutionary idea: that people could form their own government and rule themselves. That may not seem unusual, but no one had tried it in a big country. Could a democracy really work? Did ordinary people have enough sense to choose wise leaders? What could be done to create safeguards against the tyranny of majorities or minorities? A war had to be fought to take a chance on this experiment; that war was the American Revolution.

It was a people's war. It wasn't only men who would do battle. Women did things they hadn't done before. They ran farms and businesses, sewed clothes for soldiers, and helped make gunpowder and cannonballs. Children were part of it, too, making cartridges and soldiers' bags and army rations. Some women put guns to their shoulders. A British officer told his general that if all the men in America were killed, "We should have enough to do to conquer the women." One redcoat wrote home to England, "Even in their dresses the females seem to bid us defiance … on their shoes [they wear] something that resembles their flag of thirteen stripes." Margaret Corbin was twenty-three when her husband went to war; she went with him. When he was killed, "Molly" Corbin took his cannon and kept firing. Another Molly, Molly Hays, also helped fill her husband's place at cannon, and dodged shells as she carried a water pitcher to thirsty soldiers. She became known as Molly Pitcher. Deborah Sampson disguised herself as a man, served in the army for three years, and was wounded twice, taking care of her own wounds to avoid being found out.

But equal work did not make women really free. They were legally ruled by their fathers or husbands, and they couldn't vote to change things. Abigail Adams wrote to her husband, John: "Whilst you are proclaiming peace and goodwill to men, you insist upon retaining an absolute power over wives." Women weren't the

Abigail Adams gave birth to three sons and two daughters, brought them up (often singlehanded when her husband, John, was traveling as a judge) and threw herself into John's life as a politician and statesman: "These are times in which a genius would wish to live," she wrote. "It is not in the still calm of life, or the repose of a pacific station, that great characters are formed."

only ones who weren't free. In another letter to John, Abigail said, "It has always appeared a most iniquitous scheme to me to fight ourselves for what we are daily robbing from those who have as good a right to freedom as we have." She was talking about slaves and slavery.

What about African-Americans? About 5,000 black men and boys are said to have fought on the American side during the war. A redcoat wrote, "No regiment is to be seen in which there are not Negroes in abundance and among them are able-bodied, strong, and brave fellows."

Some blacks fight with the Loyalists. England's imperious governor in Virginia, Lord Dunmore, proclaims "all indentured servants, Negroes, and others … free if they are able and willing to bear arms and join his Majesty's troops for the more speedily reducing this Colony to a proper sense of their Duty to his Majesty's Crown." Some 300 black men form the Royal Ethiopian Regiment. They wear white sashes with the slogan LIBERTY TO SLAVES. A Virginia officer writes admiringly, "They fought, bled, and died like Englishmen."

In the South, where blacks often outnumber whites, many whites don't want black people to have guns. They fear a slave uprising. So a year after the first battles a rule is made: no blacks, free or slave, in the Continental army. George Washington says that those free black soldiers who have already fought should be allowed to reenlist. Otherwise, blacks are excluded. As the war continues, some people begin to see the nonsense of that policy. By the summer of 1777, New England's militias are using black soldiers again and promising them their freedom. Rhode Island has two black regiments. Some of the southern states use blacks as river pilots, even ships' gunners.

Why would African-Americans fight for a nation that allows slavery? Is this really a war for freedom and equality? The words of the Declaration of Independence are noble, but are they meant to be taken seriously? This is where there is some disagreement.

James Forten

Sailmaker's apprentice James Forten was fourteen years old, there was a war being fought, and he wanted to be a part of it. Like everyone in Philadelphia, he'd seen George Washington and Benjamin Franklin; he'd heard those words, "all men are created equal." They were worth fighting for. So he signed up on the *Royal Louis*, a privateer. The colonies had small navies, but they didn't amount to much against the great English fleet. It was the private ships that were hurting England. Congress allowed them to attack British ships and keep any profits they made. James Forten became a powder boy. It was a dangerous job. Eighteenth-century ships were wooden, and flammable. Cannons were kept on deck, but gunpowder was stored below, where it was more likely to stay dry and be safe from accidents. When fighting began someone had to keep the cannons supplied. Powder boys did that. They had to be small, fast and fearless to keep running up and down the ship's stairs, or companionways, even if cannonballs were falling around them and men were screaming in pain. Which was what happened on James's first voyage. The *Royal Louis* met a British ship, and there was a terrible fight. But when she returned to Philadelphia, her guns were pointed at a captive British ship. It seemed as if the whole city came out to cheer. James Forten knew what it was to be treated as a hero. And he got his share of profits when the English ship was sold. Then he and the other surviving crew members repaired their ship and were soon back at sea. This time they were not lucky. James and his mates were brought aboard a British ship as prisoners. Now James had a special worry. In Philadelphia he was a free person, but he knew that the English often sold black prisoners to slave dealers in the West Indies. What would the captain do with him?

It happened that the British captain had a son who was about James's age. When the English boy saw the young prisoner playing marbles, he asked to play. James beat him, but he was so likable that the captain's son asked his father to take him back to England and set him free. The captain said he would—if James would renounce his country. James Forten wouldn't consider it. He was an American and he said, "I shall never prove a traitor to my country." And that was that. James Forten spent the next seven months in a crowded, stinking prison ship before he was released in a prisoner exchange. Eventually, he returned to his father's trade and became one of Philadelphia's most successful sailmakers, employing people of both races. He helped found an antislavery society and was a leader in the African Methodist Church; he supported women's rights and peace movements; he acted as a bridge between the black and white communities, a citizen respected by all.

Above right, an African-American Patriot solider joins in the fight in *The Death of General Warren at the Battle of Bunker's Hill*, as painted by John Trumbull (1756–1843).

Rattlesnakes and vipers (the human variety) turn up in every war; this one is no exception. The Revolutionary War has its share of horror stories. But for every tale of perfidy and profiteering, there are others of sacrifice and valor. There was a core of Americans (of varying age and sex and hue) who wanted to change things and were willing to fight to do so. They were fighting to create a country based on freedom and fairness.

The world of the eighteenth century was like a ladder, where everyone had a particular rung to stand on, where everyone knew his or her place. You were always looking up, or down, at others. Equality was going to knock that ladder on its side. Most men and women believed that if people didn't know their place, society would fall apart. And they were right. The society they knew—the society of the ladder—was going to be destroyed by that phrase "all men are created equal." No one could tell where it would lead. If equality were taken seriously it was bound to change everything about people's relationships. It was going to happen—but not overnight.

A Long Road to Victory

The war went on and on and on. It lasted for eight years. England had the most feared army in the world. It was amazing that a group of small colonies would even attempt to fight the powerful British Empire. At first, nothing seemed to go well for General George Washington. In the fall of 1776, the British commander-in-chief General Sir William Howe chased the American army into New Jersey and then on to Pennsylvania. But the Europeans didn't like to fight in cold weather, and Sir William settled in New York City for the winter, where he and his officers often partied with Loyalists.

Meanwhile, George Washington was making plans. On Christmas Eve, in bitter cold, he had Massachusetts boatmen quietly ferry his soldiers over the Delaware River from Pennsylvania back to New Jersey. Picture small boats, fog, and a river with huge chunks of ice. In New Jersey, German mercenaries (called Hessians; they had been hired to fight for the British) were celebrating Christmas by getting drunk.

Before the Germans could focus their eyes, they were prisoners of the Americans. A week later, Washington left a few men to tend his campfires to fool the enemy as he marched his army to Princeton, New Jersey. There he surprised and beat a British force.

Those weren't big victories, but they were a huge boost to American morale. Then, in 1777, the British captured Philadelphia, and the Continental Congress had to flee the city. It was humiliating. Washington marched his army to a place eighteen miles from Philadelphia called Valley Forge. They got there in December, when the ground was covered with snow. The men had come a long distance, and many were in rags. Within a few days the nearby river turned ice hard. A cold wind began blowing. There were no

The redcoats at Saratoga were forced to fight when they ran out of food for men and horses. One of the battle's heroes was General Benedict Arnold, a brilliant soldier—but who later defected to the British side; his name became a synonym for "traitor." Arnold, mounted, is front and center in this illustration of the battle.

SARATOGA

When a large English army (9,500 men and 138 cannons) headed south from Canada in June 1777, many observers thought the rebellion would soon be over. The army was led by one of Britain's most colorful officers, General John Burgoyne, known as Gentleman Johnny. He was a wild character, a drinker, gambler, actor, playwright and a pretty good general. "I have always thought Hudson's River the most proper part of the whole continent for opening vigorous operations," he wrote. "Because the river, so beneficial for conveying all the bulky necessaries of an army, is precisely the route that an army ought to take for the great purpose of cutting the communications between the Southern and Northern provinces." Burgoyne could capture the Hudson River area; he would cut off New England and New York from the rest of the colonies. So he barged and marched his army south along Lake Champlain and the Hudson River, heading for Albany, New York. His colleague, General Howe, was supposed to come north from New York City up the Hudson to Albany. Another British force was expected from the west.

Burgoyne planned to trap the American army like an insect squashed between three fingers. But General Howe decided to head for Philadelphia instead of Albany. And the western army never made it east. Nevertheless, Burgoyne went ahead with his plan alone. He sailed down Lake Champlain and recaptured Fort Ticonderoga, which had been taken for the Patriots two years before. Then

General Burgoyne

buildings for the army to use as barracks. The soldiers pitched tents and built huts of sticks, logs and mud plaster. Picture 2,000 dirt-floored, drafty wooden huts lined up in streets like a village, and you have an idea of the architecture at Valley Forge. If you look at the ground, you may see blood. Some of the soldiers have no shoes; their toes freeze and leave bloody tracks. Now add hunger to that scene, grubby clothes, and few blankets. Can you begin to get an idea of that terrible winter? "Dec 12th," wrote Dr. Albigence Waldo of Connecticut, a surgeon who served at Valley Forge. "We are ordered to march over the river—it snows—I'm sick—eat nothing—no whiskey—no baggage—Lord. Lord. Lord.... Dec 14th Poor food—hard lodging—cold weather—fatigue—nasty clothes—vomit half my time. I can't endure it.... Here

Gentleman Johnny went on to Fort Edward. When the Patriots saw him coming, they abandoned the fort-but found another way to fight, cutting down trees and throwing them all over the roads. That slowed the British and the wagons and heavy cannon they dragged with them. The Americans sniped, Indian-style, from the woods. Those small guerrilla attacks kept the redcoats on edge, and scared. Finally, the British army reached Saratoga. Now Burgoyne faced a big decision. Saratoga edges the Hudson just north of Albany. General Horatio Gates was in command of the American forces. placed his men on a high bluff overlooking the road to Albany where it is squeezed between hills and river. Colonel Tadeusz Kosciuszko, a Polish military engineer serving with the Americans, had picked the site and fortified it with cannons.

Burgoyne could march his men down that treacherous narrow road, or he could fight the Americans on their fortified heights. He chose to fight. So did the Americans. Fanners poured into the area; soon the Patriot force was three times the size of Britain's army. The American farmers were sharpshooters; the battle wasn't even close. The British lost about 600 soldiers at Saratoga; American casualties were about 150. On October 17, 1777, the incredible occurred: Burgoyne surrendered with his whole army. The European soldiers were marched to Boston and sent back to England. The Americans were jubilant. And the French decided that the Americans might win if the French helped them out a bit. But the war wasn't over.

General Gates

comes a bowl of beef soup-full of burnt leaves and dirt."

What made the men stick it out? No battles were fought at Valley Forge, but something astounding happened there. A spirit evolved. The men who made it through that winter became a team-strong, confident, and proud of themselves and their country. General Washington stayed with them at Valley Forge, making his headquarters in a nearby four-room stone house. The soldiers were awed by his example. His wife, Martha, could often be seen with a basket in her arms, bringing food and socks and cheer whenever she could. A skilled drill sergeant, Baron von Steuben, who had come from Germany to be an American, began teaching military tactics to a hundred men at a time. Before long the Americans could march and

The artist Emanuel Leutze intended *Washington Crossing the Delaware* (1851) (this is a copy) to be monumental (it's more than 21 feet wide) and emotional: the sky is unnaturally bright and includes a red, white, and blue rainbow. Holding the flag at the general's side is another future president, Colonel James Monroe.

"I could not keep my eyes from that imposing countenance. Its predominant expression was calm dignity, through which you could trace the strong feelings of the patriot, and discern the father, as well as the commander of his soldiers."

—A young Frenchman writing of George Washington at Valley Forge

maneuver, load and fire, use bayonets, and respond to complicated orders.

Washington named Nathanael Greene quartermaster general, in charge of supplies. Greene tramped around the countryside, found caches of food and supplies, and hauled them to Valley Forge. By spring there was plenty of food, and clothing too.

A World Turned Upside Down

The war showed no sign of ending. The British had more men, more guns, more experience. But the Americans had a big advantage: they believed in their cause. In England the war was not popular. It was very expensive, and the longer it lasted, the more unpopular it became. Besides, the military leaders in England were trying to plan a war that was being fought thousands of miles away.

That never works well. Then the Americans won a big victory at Saratoga; after that the war in the North became stalemated. Holding on was a kind of victory for the Americans; but the British had to really beat the Rebel forces in order to win. So, in 1778, the English generals tried a new strategy: they headed south. They believed the Southern Loyalists would help the English soldiers. And, led by an able new commander, Lord Charles Cornwallis, they seemed to be winning. At Charleston, South Carolina, an American described the attack. "It appeared as if the stars were tumbling down, cannonballs whizzing and shells hissing continually amongst us; ammunition chests blowing up, great guns bursting, wounded men groaning."

England thought it had conquered the South, but the Patriots wouldn't let them have it. Americans formed guerrilla bands and fought as the Indians did—with raiding parties. "We fight, get beat, rise, and fight again," said Nathanael Greene. The English kept winning battles, but they seemed to be losing the war. And they couldn't find a way to bring it to an end.

Then, in 1781, troops began gathering in Virginia for what everyone knew would be an important clash. It was at the river port of Yorktown, near the Chesapeake Bay in Virginia. After the victory at Saratoga, the French had joined the war on America's side. They had a grudge against England and didn't want it to keep the colonies. France's Admiral de Grasse set sail for Yorktown with a fleet of twenty-eight ships.

Washington and a French general, the Comte de Rochambeau, were in Rhode Island. They decided to march their troops south to Yorktown, almost 500 miles

"If buttercups buzzed after the bee;
If boats were on land, churches on sea;
If ponies rode men and grass ate the cows;
And cats should be chased to holes by the mouse;
If the mammas sold their babies to the gypsies
    for half a crown;
Summer were spring and the t'other way round;
Then all the world would be upside down."

—"The World Turned Upside Down,"
traditional song

away. As they went, men joined them, swelling their army of 9,600 soldiers to one of 16,000. "An enemy a little bold and able would have seized the moment," wrote a French officer after they crossed the Hudson River in unguarded rafts, barges, and boats. Strangely, there were no attacks. The army speeded the tempo of its march. When they reached Yorktown they were greeted by three military leaders: the Marquis de Lafayette, a dashing young Frenchman; Baron von Steuben, the dedicated professional soldier; and bold General Anthony Wayne, who was nicknamed "Mad Anthony" because he was so daring. They had great news for General Washington.

Admiral de Grasse and his ships had been in Chesapeake Bay, fought the English fleet, and sent it sailing back to New York. That wasn't all. De Grasse had brought extra troops who could fight on land. When Washington heard all that he took off his hat, threw it in the air, and jumped with glee. No one had ever seen the dignified general do anything like

John Trumbull completed his painting of *The Surrender of Cornwallis at Yorktown* in 1797. Brigadier Charles O'Hara, offered Washington (on horseback, back right) his sword, but Washington, perhaps angry that Cornwallis didn't show up in person, directed him to give it to Brigadier-General Benjamin Lincoln.

that before. Then the French-American army moved into Yorktown, dug trenches, and prepared to fight. The British didn't have a chance. They were outnumbered and outflanked. On October 17, 1781, Cornwallis surrendered. The British adventure in America was coming to an end at Yorktown, just twenty-five miles from Jamestown, where it had all begun almost three hundred years earlier.

Two days later, American soldiers stood proudly in a long line; facing them was a line of jubilant French soldiers. Between them marched the British and Germans. The defeated men tried to keep their heads high, but many cried as they laid down their arms. The band played an old English tune, "The World Turned Upside Down." And upside down it was. David had licked Goliath. A superpower had been defeated by an upstart colony. The daring experiment was about to happen. A nation would be founded on ideas of freedom and equality. A nation ruled by laws, not kings. The thirteen new American states would adopt a great seal-which you can see on every dollar bill. On one side are the Latin words *e pluribus unum*—which means "out of many, one," and signifies the uniting of states. On the other side are the words *novus ordo seclorum*. They mean "a new order of the ages."

UNITED STATES?

Revolutionaries—whose job it is to tear down and destroy—rarely make good builders. We were lucky. The American Revolution produced some expert nation-builders. At first, though, it seemed as if the thirteen states would never get along. They certainly weren't united. Each state was printing its own money, making its own rules and writing its own constitution. Each got into the taxing business: New York was taxing goods from New Jersey, and New Jersey was taxing goods from New York. In Philadelphia and New York, newspapers reported a movement to create three separate nations out of the former colonies. In England people were saying that the Americans would soon beg to be taken back. The new country didn't begin with the Constitution we now have. The first constitution of the United States was called the Articles of Confederation. It didn't work well at all.

America's citizens were afraid of political power. They had had a bad experience with kings and parliament. So they went to the other extreme. They didn't give Congress the power to do much of anything. There was no president except the president of the Congress, and he couldn't do much either. In 1781 Americans were facing one of the toughest problems there

The States Have Ideas

While the war was still being fought, few people thought about what would come later. They just knew they wanted to be free. But the men at the Continental Congress understood that someone had to plan for the future, so they suggested that each state write a constitution.

Most of the states had been royal colonies with royal governors and royal charters. Now they needed new rules and new governors. They didn't want anything in America like a too powerful English king or a too powerful English parliament. So they drafted state constitutions that divide power between a state congress (sometimes called an "assembly"), a governor, and law courts. They called it separation of powers.

Think of a tree with three main branches: the assembly is the legislative branch, the governor is the executive branch, the courts are the judicial branch. The state constitution writers tried to balance power so no branch would have more weight than the others. They worried about many details. When Americans wrote their state constitutions they argued about freedom of speech and the press; freedom of religion (they called it "freedom of conscience"); the right of the majority to change the government; voting rights (most states abolished property ownership as a voting requirement); free education; and slavery. It was a warm-up for the future nation's constitution writers.

The discussions were the beginning of a new way of thinking about government. Each state constitution had a bill of rights. Virginia's bill, written by George Mason, was a model for many others. It said that all government power was "derived from the people." Elections were to be free and citizens were not to be taxed "without their own consent, or that of their representatives." Then it guaranteed every free person's right to a jury trial and to protection against unreasonable arrest. And the Virginia bill added something new to those English rights—religious freedom. George Mason wrote a guarantee of

George Mason

religious tolerance. A young friend of Thomas Jefferson, named James Madison, suggested that the word "tolerance" be changed to "the free exercise of religion." The idea that government should guarantee freedom and equal opportunity in written documents was totally new. No nation had tried to do it before. There were no guidelines to follow. James Madison wrote of the state constitutions: "It is the first instance, from the creation of the world … that free inhabitants have been seen deliberating on a form of government." Much of America's history from this point on would be an experiment. We would try new ideas—sometimes making awful mistakes—but the goal would remain: freedom and equality for all.

can be in designing a government. How do you provide freedom for each person, have a government powerful enough to accomplish things, and have laws that safeguard everyone? You do have to give up some freedom and some power when you are part of a society ruled by laws. The question is, how much? The Americans had just fought hard for liberty. They weren't about to give up much at all. They went too far—but they learned.

The national government, under the Articles of Confederation, was just too weak. Everyone seemed to know it. Most of the time the states wouldn't even send representatives to Philadelphia to vote at meetings of the Congress. Then, in 1783, Congress got chased out of Philadelphia by its own army, because it hadn't paid soldiers their salaries. But Congress had no money to to pay salaries and no power to collect taxes to get the money. It would take six years for Americans to create a workable government. At first the former colonists didn't even know what to call themselves. Some called us the American Commonwealth; others said the American Confederation.

Some talked of "united states"; only a few said *the* United States. Most people still thought of themselves first as citizens of the state they lived in. They had a hard time accepting the idea of a nation that might be more important than their beloved states. They didn't even like the word "nation." They called it a "union" of states.

A PHILADELPHIA WELCOME

Everyone agreed that Philadelphia was the most modern city m America, perhaps in the world. Boston's narrow, twisting streets reminded people of Europe's old cities. But Philadelphia had straight, broad avenues that crossed each other, making nice, even, rectangular blocks. Water pumps were spaced regularly on each block, and street lamps—662 of them—lit the city at night. Philadelphia's streets were paved with cobblestones or brick. Some people complained of the noise when horses' hoofs clattered over the stones, but they had to admit it was better than dirt roads that turned dusty or muddy with the weather. Philadelphia even had sidewalks. They were edged with posts to protect pedestrians from the traffic. And there was a lot of traffic; in 1787, Philadelphia, with 40,000 people, was the largest city in North America. It was a city proud of itself. After all, it had 7,000 houses, thirty-three churches, ten newspapers, two theaters, a university, a museum, and a model jail.

When General Washington rode into town on May 13, 1787, to attend the convention that was to write a new constitution for the new nation, it seemed as if all 40,000

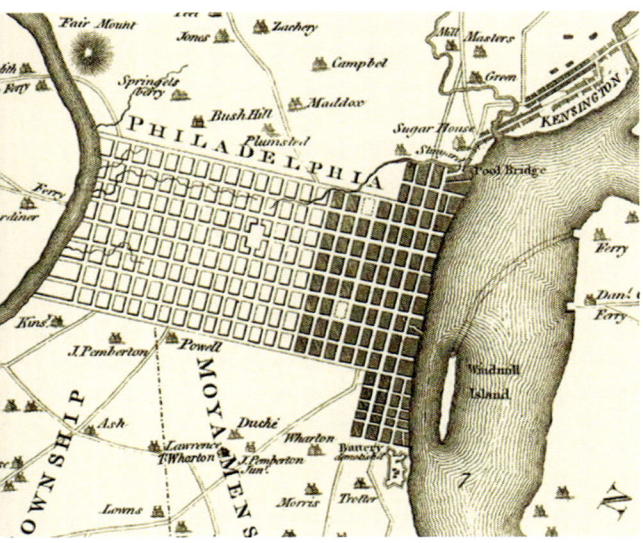
A 1777 map shows Philadelphia's grid system; it was one of the earliest cities designed that way.

townspeople came out to cheer. He was the most loved of the fifty-five delegates to the convention. All were able, determined men; they had to be to make it through that hot summer. There were no window screens, and the heat was awful. The city's flies and mosquitoes bit right through the delegates' silk stockings. Still, Philadelphia was exciting, as big cities often are. One of the sights that summer was frail old Ben Franklin being carried around in a sedan chair because his gout made walking difficult. He had brought the chair from Paris, where he served during the war as Minister to France. A delegate from Georgia, William Pierce, was amazed. "A most extraordinary man, and tells a story in a style more engaging than anything I ever heard," Pierce said. "He possesses an activity of mind equal to a youth of twenty-five years of age."

But it was thirty-six-year-old James Madison from Virginia who would become known as "the father of the Constitution." More than anyone, it was Madison who got the convention organized. Small and soft-voiced—someone once described him as "no bigger than a half piece of soap"—he had one of the finest minds in the country. William Pierce noted: "What is remarkable is that every person seems to acknowledge his greatness. Mr. Madison always comes forward the best informed man of any point in debate. Of the affairs of the United States, he perhaps has the most correct knowledge of any man in the Union." (Thomas Jefferson and John Adams weren't there. Both were serving as ambassadors in Europe.)

The delegates were divided on many issues, but most of all on power: who should have it, and how much they should have. Some delegates wanted the states to be strong; others were for a strong national government; still others hoped for a balance. Alliances and arguments were part of the process.

James Wilson, who had come to America from Scotland during the Stamp Act crisis, was a much respected delegate from Pennsylvania. When South Carolina's governor John Rutledge's ship docked in Philadelphia, a message from James Wilson was waiting for him, inviting Rutledge to stay at his house. Their friendship was surprising; perhaps each admired the lawyerly skills and intelligence of the other. "Interest alone is the governing principle of nations," said Rutledge. By interest he meant property, and property included slaves. Politically, Wilson stood at the other end of the spectrum. People and their individual rights were more important to him than property rights. He opposed slavery and favored democracy. Yet he and Rutledge were friends. Not everyone believed in democracy. That word had a different ring in the eighteenth century from what it does today. Many felt "the people" could not be trusted; they feared mob action and thought only landowners and the educated should vote.

There was something else that made Wilson's thinking different from that of most of the delegates. He cared little for the states. It was the new nation that he thought important.

Alexander Hamilton didn't care about power for the states, either—but for different reasons. He was thirty-five, a New Yorker, and one of the most brilliant of the delegates. He had been a member of Washington's staff during the Revolution. Hamilton wanted a government like England's. He thought it the best possible model. He believed the president should have a lifetime job—like a king or an emperor. Hamilton wanted a strong central government.

John Dickinson of Delaware, who had written the Articles of Confederation, was for strong states. He wanted a confederation. A confederation is a government made

ROGER TO THE RESCUE

It seemed that a constitution would never get written. There was one issue on which everyone was stubborn, and it had to do with the new government's legislative branch—the Congress. The fight was between the big states and the little ones. The original plan said that the number of congressmen for each state should be decided by population. But that meant that the states with the most people would have the most congressmen. The opposing plan said that each state should have an equal number of representatives. That meant that Delaware, with 59,000 people, would have the same number of congressmen as Virginia, with almost 692,000. Was that fair? Neither side would budge. The Constitutional Convention needed a man of good sense and few words. That was Roger Sherman.

This is how Thomas Jefferson described him: "There is Mr. Sherman of Connecticut, who never said a foolish thing in his life." Roger Sherman came up with a compromise. Here it is: one house of the legislature should reflect a state's population—the House of Representatives. One house should have an equal number of representatives from each state—the Senate. That was it. That simple solution meant there would be a constitution.

up of partners who keep all important power for themselves. That's what we had under the Articles of Confederation. There was no higher power. The central government served mainly as an adviser. A federation—which Madison wanted—divides power between a central government and state governments. It isn't easy to do that. The United States is a federation. The central government in Washington has the strongest powers, but not all the power. The states have important powers, too. Our government in Washington isn't as strong as Hamilton wanted. The states' powers aren't as strong as Dickinson wished. The Constitution was a compromise. Both sides gave and both sides got. It may be the best compromise in history.

WE THE PEOPLE

The opening words of the Constitution, called the *preamble,* were the creation of a Pennsylvania man named Gouverneur Morris. When the Constitution was almost finished-it had been argued and reargued and changed and rechanged—it was to Morris that they gave it. He was to polish the words. He wrote with skill and grace, and all knew it. He took twenty-three resolutions and reduced them to seven articles. Morris sometimes talked for hours, but when he wrote the Constitution he wrote just enough and no more.

"We the People of the United States, in order to form a more perfect union, establish justice, insure domestic tranquility, provide for the common defense, promote the general welfare, and secure the blessings of liberty to ourselves and our posterity, do ordain and establish this Constitution for the United States."
—preamble to the Constitution of the United States

One of the first things the delegates decided on was a name for the new country. The Convention officially adopted the name the United States of America. Then the delegates agreed to a three-part government with legislative, executive, and judicial branches. That was part of Madison's Virginia Plan. It was based on the English plan of government. A legislature is a lawmaking body: a congress or parliament. Our congress is divided into two parts, called houses. They are the Senate and the House of Representatives. An executive is a leader: a president or king. The judiciary is the courts. In the United States they go from town courts all the way to the Supreme Court.

Since the delegates were afraid of power, the three branches were planned to check and balance each other. The president was made commander-in-chief of the army and navy, but was not given the power to declare war. Only Congress can do that. The national government controls foreign affairs, business between the states, and the post office. The states control schools, roads, and local government. Congress was given the power to impose taxes. So were the states. Control of money is an important power. Getting things right was a balancing act.

The delegates disagreed on many things, but on some ideas all were agreed: they wanted to guarantee basic human rights and freedom (what Jefferson had called "unalienable rights" in the Declaration of Independence); and they wanted to provide government with laws made "by consent of the governed." They expected the people to govern through their representatives; that makes us a republic. They solved the problem of power in two ways: with those checks and balances and by making the Constitution more powerful than any president, congress, court, or state. They made it the supreme law of the land.

"A Republic, Madam. If You Can Keep It"

When the Framers said, "We the people," did they really mean all the people? Most experts say no. They say the Founders didn't mean women, who were not allowed to vote. And they didn't mean Native Americans, or those enslaved. The Constitution permitted the continuation of slavery in America—even the dreadful slave trade, the business of bringing Africans into the country and selling them. The South was not ready to eliminate slavery, and the citizens of the southern states would not approve the Constitution if it did. (Nor would they stay in the new nation.) So the delegates compromised on the slave trade. They gave the traders another twenty years—until 1808—and then that disgraceful business was to be stopped. It would take a war to end slavery itself.

> "We have the wolf by the ears, and we can neither hold him nor safely let him go."
> —Thomas Jefferson on slavery

Still, some of us believe that when the Founders said "we the people," they did mean all the people. These were idealistic men. They knew they were writing for future generations. But they were also practical. And they knew that some of the citizens of the new United States weren't prepared to do some things that had never been done before. They weren't prepared to accept women as citizens. They weren't prepared to give up property, even human property. And they weren't prepared to be fair to the Indians in the rivalry over land. So the delegates compromised, and some

James Wilson

people were left out. But those three small words, "we the people," were powerful; they would keep pushing the nation to include all peoples. James Wilson was sure of it. "I consider this as laying the foundation for banishing slavery out of this country;" he said of the Constitution, "and though the period is more distant than I could wish, yet it will produce the same kind of gradual change which was pursued in Pennsylvania."

It turned out that Wilson was wrong. Slavery would not disappear gradually. But, in 1787, many wise people thought it was dying. Slavery seemed to be becoming unprofitable. Most white people thought it would fade away naturally. They didn't think it worth a fight. They were wrong. They couldn't know that there would soon be an invention—the cotton gin—that would change farming in the South. It would make slavery profitable again. So they did what was practical, not what was right. Understanding history is hard because it is often paradoxical. So are people and nations. It would be easier but less interesting if people were either all good or all bad, and if the good people never made mistakes. Take South Carolina's John Rutledge, for example. He wouldn't budge an inch when it came to defending his state's interests. He fought harder to keep slavery than anyone in Philadelphia. But while he was arguing in support of slavery at the Convention, he was quietly freeing his own slaves. Rutledge had inherited sixty slaves; he owned only one when he died. His wife freed all her slaves. George Mason and Thomas Jefferson hated slavery and said so. But they owned slaves and kept them. That is a paradox.

All that summer of 1787 the delegates tried to work out their differences and create the best constitution they could. Washington had them keep the windows of the State House closed so no one could stand outside and listen. Some delegates almost fainted from the heat. Finally, on September 17, the need for secrecy was over. The Constitution was finished and ready to be signed. When it came the turn of eighty-one-year-old Ben Franklin to put his name to the document, he paused and pointed to the chair in which George Washington had sat as president of the convention. Carved in the chair's back was a half sun with sunbeams. Franklin said he had often wondered if it were a rising or a setting sun. Now he knew: the sun was rising! And as the old man put his signature on the parchment, tears are said to have streamed down his cheeks: "It astonishes me to find this system approaching so near perfection; I think it will astonish our enemies."

Franklin was right. The Constitution was remarkable. Those Framers made it a flexible document. They came up an amendment process so it could be changed and adapted to new times and new ideas. And right away there were demands for changes. The Constitution, it turned out, didn't spell out some rights clearly enough. Ten amendments were added almost immediately. They made up a bill of rights, which guarantees, in words, freedoms Americans didn't want to be without. James Madison wrote those first ten amendments. (State bills of rights, especially Virginia's, had pioneered the idea.)

Most people agree that the First Amendment is the most important part of the Bill of Rights. It guarantees freedom of religion, freedom of speech, freedom of the press, and freedom to assemble and protest to or petition the government. The Second Amendment says, "A well regulated militia being necessary to the security of a free state, the right of the people to keep and bear arms, shall not be infringed." To "bear arms" means to carry guns. But there is more to it. Most people agree that the First Amendment is the most important part of the Bill of Rights. A farmers' rebellion in Massachusetts, Shays Rebellion, was put down by a citizen's militia. Do we have a militia today? Why is it important for citizens to bear arms in the twenty-first century?

The Third Amendment says that soldiers can't be quartered in your house without your consent. The Fourth Amendment says that the police can't come and search your house unless they have proper legal papers. The Fifth, Sixth, Seventh, and Eighth Amendments all have to do with fair trials. The Fifth Amendment says that no person can be forced to be a "witness

The Bill of Rights, contaning the first ten amendments to the Constitution.

The Case of Peter Zenger

In 1710, long before the Constitution was written, a young man named Peter Zenger came to the American colonies from Germany with his family. He was apprenticed to a printer, and learned that trade. When he went out on his own it was in New York City, where he founded a newspaper called the *New York Weekly Journal*. New York had a rotten governor then; his name was William Cosby. There was an official newspaper that supported the governor. Zenger thought that people should be able to read more than one side of the story. The *Weekly Journal* was full of spicy articles: one said the Governor took bribes, another that he took away people's land, another that he rigged elections. The governor was furious. He wanted the paper to stop publishing; Zenger wouldn't stop. The governor had him arrested and sent to jail.

Zenger had some influential lawyer friends (they had written some of the critical articles). They were ready to be his lawyers, but just before the trial, Governor Cosby had them disbarred, so they couldn't practice law. Things looked bad. Then some of Zenger's friends made a secret trip to Philadelphia.

The trial began on a hot morning in August 1735. An old man in a powdered wig entered the courtroom and stood before the judge. When he said his name there were gasps throughout the courtroom. It was Andrew Hamilton, a Quaker from Philadelphia, and a friend of Benjamin Franklin and William Penn. He was the most famous lawyer in the colonies, and he had come to take Peter Zenger's case. Zenger was being tried for libel.

Today in America, two things are necessary to prove libel. You must publish something you know is a lie, and that lie must hurt a person. Libel laws weren't very clear in 1735. Zenger had printed bad things about Governor Cosby, but most people thought the things he said were true. "So what?" said

against himself." That helps protect us from those who might be tempted to use torture to force confessions.

Finally, the Ninth and Tenth Amendments say that any powers or rights that the Constitution does not give to the federal government belong to the states or to the people. (Recent court decisions have said that the Ninth Amendment gives people the right to privacy. That means we can have secrets—even from the government.)

Alexander Hamilton didn't get the kind of constitution, or the kinglike president, he wanted. But when the Constitution was signed, Hamilton wrote a series of articles supporting it. Those articles, now part of a book called *The Federalist Papers,* helped convince people to vote for the Constitution. Hamilton's the government's lawyer, the attorney general.

It didn't matter if the bad things were true. Truth was no defense, he said. In those days, in England and the English colonies, it was a crime to say anything bad about the king, even if it was true. The attorney general said that the governor was just like the king.

People say that lawyer Hamilton spoke very softly. Everyone had to pay attention to hear what he said. Most seemed to know that history was being made. "Free men have a right to complain when hurt," said Hamilton. "They have a right to oppose arbitrary power by speaking and writing truths … to assert with courage the sense they have of the blessings of liberty, the value they put upon it … and their resolution … to prove it one of the greatest blessings heaven can bestow.… *There is no libel if the truth is told*," he said. The jury decided that Peter Zenger was not guilty. But there is more to the case even than that. "The question before the court and you, gentlemen of the jury, is not of small nor private concern," said Andrew Hamilton. "It is not the cause of one poor printer, nor of New York alone, which you are now trying. No! It may in its consequence affect every freeman that lives under a British government, on the main of America. It is the best cause. It is the cause of liberty."

Andrew Hamilton defending John Peter Zenger in court.

graciousness became the American way. Here, when a candidate loses an election for president, he doesn't try to overturn the decision. He pledges to help the new president. That is the American way. By 1788, every state legislature voted to ratify the Constitution. Now there were thirteen states in a unified nation, and just about everyone-except people in Europe, who still predicted that the country would fall apart and a king or dictator be necessary—was feeling good about it. When Benjamin Franklin came out of the Pennsylvania State House on September 17, 1787, his friend Elizabeth Powel, the wife of the mayor of Philadelphia, was waiting for him. She asked what kind of government the new nation would have. "A republic, madam," Franklin replied. "If you can keep it."

Being President

It was April 14, 1789. At Mount Vernon, his plantation home in Virginia, George Washington was handed a letter telling him he had been chosen as president of the brand-new union of states. He had been elected unanimously (which has never happened since), and that was important: it meant the government could get started without fighting over a leader. Almost everybody admired Washington.

"He is polite with dignity, affable without familiarity, distant without haughtiness, grave without austerity, modest, wise, and good," said Abigail Adams. The general, who was now fifty-seven years old, was sorry to give up his life as a private farmer once again. But he did what his sense of duty told him to do.

It took him eight days to make the 235-mile journey to New York, which was to be the capital until a new one could be built. It should have been faster, but all along the way citizens greeted their president-elect with parades, and bonfires, and fireworks, and speeches, and banquets. In Philadelphia, the famous artist Charles Willson Peale had designed a floral arch for Washington to pass through, adding a surprise. Peale's fifteen-year-old daughter, Angelica, was hiding in the shrubbery. As Washington and his horse passed under the arch she pulled on a lever and a laurel wreath fell right on the general's head. At his swearing-in at New York's Federal Hall, Washington promised to "preserve, protect and defend the Constitution of the United States." He added his own prayer at the end: "So help me God."

No one could tell Washington how to be president, for no one had ever had the job before. He knew he would set an example for all presidents to come. "I walk on untrodden ground," he said. "There is scarcely any part of my conduct which may not hereafter be drawn into precedent." He didn't want to act like a king, but he thought it important that the president be grand. So he traveled in a canary-yellow carriage pulled by horses powdered white with marble dust. And he wore formal attire to his weekly

"About ten o'clock," wrote George Washington of his last day as a private citizen, "I bade farewell to Mount Vernon and to private life, and with a mind oppressed by more anxious and painful sensations than I have words to express, set out for New York."

receptions—knee breeches and a sword strapped to his waist.

As president, Washington was head of the executive branch of our three-branch government. He knew he couldn't make all the executive branch decisions by himself, so he appointed advisers—a secretary of state, a secretary of the treasury, and so on. All together, they were known as the cabinet. Washington picked the very best people he could find. For secretary of state, he needed a man who knew a lot about foreign nations, so he chose Thomas Jefferson. He needed a good financial adviser, so he chose Alexander Hamilton as secretary of the treasury. It just happened that Hamilton and Jefferson had ideas that clashed. Both were brilliant men, and patriots who wanted to do the best for their country. But they disagreed on what was best—especially about power and who ought to have it. Jefferson saw a strong, centralized government as a possible enemy of individual liberty. He feared a too strong president and a too strong congress, and believed that ordinary people could govern themselves—if they were educated. "If a nation expects to be ignorant and free, in a state of civilization, it expects what never was and never will be," said Jefferson.

Hamilton believed the federal government had to be strong if it was to work for all the people and to counter self-interest and greed. The masses often act like sheep, he said, thoughtlessly following a leader.

Alexander Hamilton

"Give all power to the many and they will oppress the few. Give all power to the few, they will oppress the many. Both therefore ought to have power, that each may defend itself against the other."

—Alexander Hamilton

The rich and powerful usually do what is good for themselves, not necessarily for others. The government needed to have power to consider what was best for the nation.

Their differences gave rise to the first American political parties. Hamilton's followers formed the "Federalist" party. Jefferson's sympathizers were the "Democratic Republicans."(They were not like our Democrats and Republicans today—but they were the beginnings of today's party system.)

Washington didn't like the idea of political parties at all. He called them "factions," and warned against them. But James Madison understood that people just don't think alike. One-party governments are usually dictatorships. Madison believed that in a democracy parties should be encouraged. He said they would balance each other, so that no one group could become too strong and take control of the government. The tension and compromises between those points of view are part of our tradition and have helped make this country great. They are still with us today.

MAKING A COURT SUPREME

After eight years as president, George Washington was ready to go home to Mount Vernon and let someone else take over the presidency. His vice president, John Adams of Massachusetts, the man who had helped convince Thomas Jefferson to write the Declaration of Independence, was eager to have the job. When he was younger, and the country needed help breaking away from England, Adams provided crucial leadership. After that he went off to Europe and served his country well as a diplomat.

Perhaps he stayed too long in Europe. He grew to love European ceremony and European ways. While he believed in republican, representative government, he didn't think much of democracy. Like Alexander Hamilton, he thought that the educated and the naturally aristocratic should govern; he didn't trust the mass of people. Once, at a dinner, Hamilton got angry at a Jeffersonian who said that ordinary people could govern themselves. Hamilton pounded the table with his fist:

"Your people, sir," he said, "your people is a great beast!" He and the Federalists feared mob rule. "Men are never good but through necessity," said Adams—which means people are good only if forced to be so. But that wasn't true of either Hamilton or Adams. Adams was a good man even when he didn't have to be—and that means he always did what he thought was right, not necessarily what was popular.

In 1798—while Adams was president—it looked as if there might be war with France. People were fearful of spies and foreigners. Congress approved Alien and Sedition Acts, and President Adams signed them into law. Today, most historians believe these were bad laws, outside American tradition. The Alien Act made it difficult for foreigners to become American

Vermont Representative Mathew Lyon (above right) didn't just attack things he didn't like in the newspapers. He was called "The Spitting Lyon" because he once spat in the face of Connecticut representative Roger Griswold. This 1798 cartoon shows him in a fist fight on the floor of Congress—going at it hammer and tongs (with actual tongs!).

citizens; it allowed the president to throw anyone he wanted out of the country if he thought them dangerous. The Sedition Act may have been even worse. It made it a crime to criticize the government.

Some people got arrested for doing just that. One was Congressman Mathew Lyon of Vermont. Lyon was a hot-tempered man who attacked President Adams in a newspaper. He said the president was trying to act like a king and should be sent "to a madhouse." Because of the sedition law, it was Lyon who got sent away—to jail.

Congress and the president had done something the Bill of Rights said they couldn't do. They had abridged freedom of speech and of the press, contrary to the guarantees in the First Amendment. If Congress were to pass Alien and Sedition Acts today, the Supreme Court would declare them unconstitutional. But the Supreme Court was just getting organized during Adams's presidency. It wasn't very strong.

The men who wrote the Constitution were afraid of too much political power in

As a young congressman, John Marshall voted against the Sedition Act and his own party. That took courage.

"It is emphatically the province and duty of the judicial department to say what the law is."

—John Marshall

one place. So they set up a government with three parts—the executive, legislative, and judicial branches—that were supposed to be partners, ready to check and balance each other. But at first the Supreme Court didn't seem to know what it was to do. It was no check at all. And then, in 1801, in one of the last acts of his presidency, John Adams named John Marshall as chief justice of the Supreme Court. Marshall, from Richmond, Virginia, was friendly and cheerful, with a sense of humor and he had a good brain and used it. It was a brilliant choice. Marshall, a Federalist, believed a strong government would help protect the rights of all the people. He tried to make the federal government stronger than the state governments, and the Supreme Court strongest of all. In 1803, in a very important Supreme Court case called *Marbury* v. *Madison,* Marshall said the Court could throw out any law passed by Congress if the Court thought that law was unconstitutional. *Marbury* v. *Madison* began a process called *judicial review.* It gave the Supreme Court the power to decide if a law passed by Congress meets the requirements of the Constitution. Judicial review made the Court a real check and balance to the two other government branches. Most people (but not all) think it helps guarantee our freedoms. John Marshall wanted to protect our rights even from Congress and the president.

"Nevertheless," wrote the historian Henry Adams (great-grandson of John Adams), "this great man nourished one weakness: he detested Thomas Jefferson." These two brilliant, remarkable Virginians—who happened to be distant cousins couldn't stand each other. Their dispute was all about ideas. Marshall believed the purpose of government was to protect "life, liberty and property." And you know that Jefferson believed in "life, liberty and the pursuit of happiness." They didn't realize it, but their ideas complemented each other. The nation needed them both.

John Marshall and his cousin Tom Jefferson did agree on one thing: the Alien and Sedition Acts. Neither liked them. Most of the country didn't like them, either. When

John Adams ran for a second term in 1800, he was defeated—by Thomas Jefferson, who campaigned with the slogan "Jefferson and Liberty." Chief Justice Marshall had to swear him in as president. Then they both let the Alien and Sedition Acts die.

An Empire for Liberty

Thomas Jefferson did away with the pomp and ceremony of his two predecessors. He walked from a boarding-house to his inaugural. When he had someplace to go, he rode on horseback, without a guard. Sometimes he appeared in the White House in rumpled clothes and old slippers. And he refused to give favors to the rich and powerful. Even so, the Federalists—who had predicted terrible things from the president they described as a radical—were surprised. They had forgotten that Jefferson was a gracious country gentleman with fine taste and a belief in people's natural goodness. The nation didn't fall apart under a Democratic-Republican administration. But, in 1803, when Jefferson went shopping and bought a huge piece of land for the United States, some people thought it extravagant (and Jefferson himself feared that it might be unconstitutional).

He bought all the land that France had claimed in North America (outside Canada), called Louisiana after a French king named Louis. The Louisiana Purchase cost $15 million, about four cents an acre; it doubled the size of the country. Jefferson called it an "empire for liberty."

Now the Mississippi was no longer controlled by a foreign power. And the United States had acquired land that stretched from that great river to the Rocky Mountains and maybe beyond. No one was sure how far it went or what it was like. The West was more unknown in 1803 than outer space is today. So Jefferson organized an expedition to explore its vast reaches and to go on to the Pacific Ocean. He commissioned two men to lead it. One was his personal secretary Meriwether Lewis, a shy dreamer and lover of science. The other was a good-natured, talkative soldier and mapmaker, William Clark.

Meriwether Lewis in full explorer's gear, circa 1800: coonskin cap with tails, fringed deerskin tunic and leggings, with powder horn and rifle. The members of the expedition ate, dressed, lived and traveled much as the Indians they met did.

Lewis and Clark and their team—a kind of dream team—went up the Missouri River on a fifty-five-foot flatboat and two narrow canoes. The boat held bales of gifts for the Native Americans—beads, ribbons, mirrors, cooking pots, tools. They moved slowly, mapping, exploring, and hunting as they went. It was dangerous country, with high mountains, difficult deserts, fierce animals, suspicious Indians. Lewis and Clark had prepared for danger, but they weren't prepared for the beauty and diversity of the country—for the awesome, towering Rocky Mountains, for the rattlesnakes, bears, mountain lions, and endless herds of buffalo, for the colors of the wildflowers, or the brilliance of sunsets on snowy peaks. Here are words from Lewis's log (the spelling and grammar are his) describing the Great Falls of the Missouri River: "I saw the spray arrise above the plain like a collumn of smoke…. the irregular and somewhat projecting rocks below receives the water in it's passage down and brakes it into a perfect white foam which assumes a thousand forms."

They captured four black-and-white magpies and sent them back to Jefferson (it was a kind unknown). They dug up the bones of a forty-five-foot dinosaur. Wherever they went they took careful notes, made maps, wrote down lists of Indian words, and collected samples of strange plants and animals. They added two hundred species to the world's list of known plants. The Native Americans taught them

"Your observations are to be taken with great pains and accuracy, to be entered distinctly and intelligibly for others as well as yourself to comprehend," wrote Jefferson in his instructions to Lewis. "Objects worthy of notice will be: the soil and face of the country, its growth and vegetable productions … the animals of the country generally, and especially those not known in the U.S." Clark kept painstaking, beautifully illustrated journals, and both men worked to create maps depicting the geography they encountered, such as the one below, tracing various bodies of water starting with the Great Lakes and heading westward, towards the Pacific.

to use some of those plants as medicines and foods. They established friendships with the Indians and prepared for trade with them. Their description of the west would bring a rush of others; the world that Lewis and Clark saw would soon be gone forever.

A Dream—and a Nightmare

For the first time in the history of the western world, ordinary people's prosperity and happiness were made the aim of society and government. In 1831, after we'd had almost fifty years to try out our government, a Frenchman named Alexis de Tocqueville came to the United States to see how our democracy was working. He saw us a laboratory for democracy. What was happening here, Tocqueville said, was "interesting not only to the United States, but to the whole world. It concerns not a nation, but mankind." Our Founders set a splendid goal: liberty and justice for all. They wrote an extraordinary plan of government: a great constitution. But they never suggested that good, fair government would be easy to achieve. They left some problems unresolved. (How do you find a balance between individual freedom and the rights of the whole community? It would be a continuing challenge.) When they gave their consent to slavery—the very opposite of liberty and equality—some knew they were making a terrible compromise, while the whole world was watching. Their compromise would make the United States both dream and nightmare. Slavery in the land of the free? It was in-your-face hypocrisy.

In *Liberty as Goddess of Youth,* Liberty symbolically feeds the American eagle. How many stars were on the flag in 1796?

The fight to end that horror was to be the most important battle in all our history. It would test the young nation, and change it, and strengthen it. It would give new meaning to the words "liberty" and "equality." It would create a "new birth of freedom."

PART 3

LIBERTY FOR ALL?

While Meriwether Lewis and William Clark were crossing the Rocky Mountains (it was 1805), a group of Indians was gathered on the other side of the continent, at Buffalo Creek, in the state of New York. They were Iroquois of the Seneca tribe, and their leader was the orator Sagoyewatha. During the Revolutionary War, the Iroquois were divided. Some had fought on the American side, but others, like Sagoyewatha, fought for the British. Because Sagoyewatha wore a red English jacket in battle, the Americans called him Red Jacket. At war's end Chief Red Jacket was forced to sign a treaty that gave much Indian land to the new nation. Now, at Buffalo Creek, the Iroquois were being asked to give up their religion, too. Some preachers had come from Boston to convert the Indians to Christianity. The Senecas listened politely to the ministers. Then Sagoyewatha replied.

> Brothers ... listen to what we say. There was a time when our forefathers owned this great island ... from the rising to the setting sun. The Great Spirit had made it for the use of Indians. He had created the buffalo, the deer, and other animals for food. He had made the bear and the beaver. Their skins served us for clothing. He had scattered them over the country and taught us how to take them. He had caused the earth to produce corn for bread. All this He had done for his red children because he loved them.... But an evil day came upon us. Your forefathers crossed the great water and landed on this island. Their numbers were small. They found friends and not enemies. They told us they had fled from their own country for fear of wicked men and had come here to enjoy their religion.... We took pity on them ... and they sat down among us.... The white people, brothers, had now found our country. Tidings were carried back and more came among us. Yet we did not fear them. We took them to be friends. They called us brothers. We believed them.... At length their numbers had greatly increased. They wanted more land; they wanted our country. Our eyes were opened and our minds became uneasy.

That was all history. It was the past. Sagoyewatha began to talk of the present.

> Brothers, our seats were once large and yours were small. You have now become a great people, and we have scarcely a place left to spread our blankets. You have got our country but are not satisfied; you want to force your religion

In his youth Red Jacket's Iroquois name was Otetiani, which means "prepared" or "ready." As a chief, he took the name Sagoyewathar—"He causes them to be awake."

This painting by John Mix Stanley records a difficult time in the life of Red Jacket (standing in the center). In the 1790s the Iroquois leader tried to negotiate for the United States with western tribes (Miami, Shawnee, and others) who had allied to resist American encroachment on their land. They got angry at Red Jacket for not helping them, and booed and humiliated him.

upon us.... You say there is but one way to worship and serve the Great Spirit. If there is but one religion, why do you white people differ so much about it? ... Brothers, we ... also have a religion which was given to our forefathers and has been handed down to us, their children.... Brothers, we do not wish to destroy your religion or take it from you. We only want to enjoy our own.... Brothers, we have been told that you have been preaching to the white people in this place. These people are our neighbors. We will wait a little while and see what effect your preaching has upon them. If we find it does them good, makes them honest and less disposed to cheat Indians, we will then consider again of what you have said.

"Our system is to live in perpetual peace with the Indians ... by giving them effectual protection against wrongs from our own people.... They will in time either incorporate with us as citizens of the United States or remove beyond the Mississippi."

—Thomas Jefferson

Most Americans didn't care what happened to Red Jacket and his people. The Iroquois had lost most of their land and power. Things would get worse for them.

They were going to be pushed west and pushed again. The new Americans wanted Indian land and they didn't know a fair way to share it. There would be promises and treaties and they would all be broken.

As to religious freedom, that was why many Europeans had come to America—to be free to follow dictates of mind and heart. But some had forgotten their own golden rule: *Do unto others as you would have them do unto you.* Others understood.

Already, this new nation, with its Bill of Rights, had achieved something unprecedented. It had figured out that a unified state does not need a unified religion. We don't all have the same beliefs—that's obvious; but previous governments had ignored that. They thought it necessary to have one national religion. That usually took force and coercion.

All that was changed in America in 1791. What was achieved with the Bill of Rights was more than personal religious freedom; it was the full separation of the government from all churches. It freed citizens to think for themselves, and it freed churches from the national state. It was a clean break with what came before. James Madison, writing to his friend Edward Livingston in 1822, made his thoughts clear on the subject: "Religion and government will both exist in greater purity; the less they are mixed together." The well-meaning preachers of Buffalo Creek didn't understand. They were still living in the past.

Sequoyah revolutionized all Indian languages when he created the first Native American alphabet and began writing in his Cherokee tongue.

A New World

In seventeenth-century England, there was no religious freedom. You belonged to the Church of England or you went to jail. England had been Catholic until King Henry VIII came along in the sixteenth century, had marriage troubles, and founded his own church, the Church of England (also known as the Anglican Church or the "established" church—it was established by the government). The king was head of the nation and also head of the Church. Catholics and others were now out of luck—and in danger.

> "Having undertaken a voyage to plant the first colony in the Northern parts, we covenant ourselves together to enact, constitute, and frame such just and equal laws, ordinances, acts, constitutions, offices … for the general good of the Colony; unto which, we promise all due submission and obedience."
> —from the Mayflower Compact

Their religions were banned in England.

Actually, except for the matter of control and leadership (the head of the Catholic Church is the Pope in Rome), the Anglicans and Catholics were much alike (although they didn't think so). Some Englishmen wanted the differences between Catholics and Protestants to be greater. They didn't want the Anglican service to be at all like the Catholic service.

They said they wanted to "purify" the Church of England, and so they were called Puritans. Others wanted to go even further. They believed people could speak directly to God without a priest or bishop at all. They wanted to separate from the Church of England and form congregations of their own. They called themselves "Saints." Others called them Separatists. Most people called them troublemakers.

James I, who became King of England in 1603 when Henry VIII's daughter Queen Elizabeth died, would not let the Separatists practice their religion. "I will make them conform themselves, or else I will harry them out of the land," said the king.

Their religion was more important to the Separatists than their homes—sometimes even than life itself. When some of them read a book about Virginia by John Smith, they decided to risk the ocean voyage.

So, in 1620, 102 brave souls clamber aboard a little ship, named the *Mayflower*, and begin their sail westward to what they see as a "New World." About half are Saints; the others are called "Strangers." The Strangers are leaving England for adventure, or because they're unhappy, or in trouble. Yet Strangers and Saints have much in common. Most are from the lower classes; most have a trade; they expect to work hard; they are ambitious; they don't like the new ideas that are changing England. All of them want a better life-but the Saints hope to build a society more perfect than any on earth. They call themselves "Pilgrims," because they are on a religious journey.

It is a terrible voyage, taking sixty-six days. The ship is small, wet, and foul. The smells are vile. Fresh food runs out. But the Pilgrims have onions, lemon juice, and beer to keep them from getting the dreaded scurvy. Finally, they sight American land. It is Cape Cod. The Pilgrims thought they were on their way to Virginia; this is not where they expected to be. But they're exhausted; they want to get off the ship. One of them, "William Bradford, writes a description of what they see: "A hideous and desolate wilderness, full of wild beasts and men." Nonetheless, they sail the

Mayflower around the cape to a place they see on John Smith's map. He has called it Plymouth, after a town in England. There they drop anchor. "Being thus arrived in a good harbour and brought safe to land," writes Bradford, "we fell upon our knees and blessed the God of Heaven who had brought us over the vast and furious ocean."

This shipload of diverse people has to find ways to live together peacefully. There has been trouble between Saints and Strangers. So, even before landing, they draw up a plan of government, the Mayflower Compact, which establishes a governing body. These settlers agree to live together under a government of laws. The king doesn't realize what is in the future. This breed of people will not allow others to rule them for long. "As one small candle may light a thousand," says "William Bradford, "so the light here kindled shall shine unto many."

FREEDOM FOR WHOM?

Meanwhile, in England, a new king, Charles I, is making life hard for religious nonconformists—especially Puritans. Between 1630 and 1640, 20,000 Puritans sail for New England. They intend to build a holy community where people live by the rules of the Bible. They expect their colony to be an example for all the world. One of the colony's governors, John Winthrop, says, "We must consider that we shall be as a city upon a hill. The eyes of all people are upon us."

The Puritans come to America to find religious freedom—but only for themselves. That individuals should be free to decide their own beliefs is unthinkable to them and to almost anyone of their time. Souls are at stake. And souls are too precious to leave to ordinary folks. The Puritans have taken a big step; they have decided their souls are too precious to leave to the king. These are

Puritan ministers like John Cotton preached the Golden Rule (do to others as you want them do to you) but did not tolerate other religions.

rebels willing to abandon their homes and much that they love in order to save their souls. Unlike the Pilgrims, the Puritans are often prosperous, educated, and landed. Sailing to an unknown world takes astonishing courage and dedication.

They are exchanging the authority of the king for that of Holy Scripture (as their ministers interpret it). But religious freedom? Each Puritan interpreting the Bible for himself? That doesn't make sense to them. Nor does it make sense to allow anyone into the colony who follows a different faith. They have come to this cold, hard region seeking purity. To let in other voices, other practices, would, in their minds, pollute and threaten their quest. The historian Perry Miller says: "Every respectable state in the Western world assumed that it could allow only one church to exist within its borders, that every citizen should be compelled to attend it and conform to its requirements, and that all inhabitants should pay taxes for its support." The Puritans are forming a "respectable state." In those days each nation had its own church, and everyone was expected to pay taxes for its support. If you believe you

At Puritan church services women sat at the back or upstairs. At a Quaker meeting like this one, everyone sat together. There was no minister or sermon; as Quakers do today, members of the congregation sat in silence unless moved to stand and speak.

know "the true religion," as Puritans are sure they do, then it is wrong to practice any other. It is helping the devil, they say. Tolerance, says the Reverend John Cotton, a New England Puritan, is "liberty to tell lies in the name of the Lord."

Democracy is another strange idea to Puritans. "If the people be governors, who shall be governed?" asks the Reverend Cotton. John Winthrop, the beloved Puritan governor, calls democracy the "meanest and worst" form of government. And yet Puritans do practice a kind of democracy—for male church members. Once a year these men get together, form a General Court, and vote to elect the governor and council. The General Court is a lot like the House of Burgesses in Virginia, or Parliament in England.

Today, some people describe the Massachusetts Bay Colony as a theocracy—government by church officials in the name of God. That's not quite true.

Though the ministers are the most important people in the colony, they are not allowed to hold political office. They do not govern. This is a step, however small, toward the idea of the separation of church and state. One day that idea will be a foundation of American liberty.

Newe and Dangerous Ideas

Roger Williams's reputation had preceded him to New England. When he arrived in Boston he was asked to be a teacher and minister. It was the best job he could have been offered. He turned it down. The ways of the congregation were not sufficiently pure for him. So off he went to Salem, Massachusetts, where people were more separatist in their outlook. But the intensity of his beliefs began to lead him—one step at a time—into a relationship with God that he could share with no one. Wanting extreme purity, he found himself forced to discard the layers of human distractions that stood between him and his God. It also led him to understand that others might have beliefs that were different from his, but appropriate for them. Williams's intellectual honesty forced him to ask questions.

- Is it possible that there can be more than one path to God?
- If there is only one path, can any human be sure he is on it?
- How can it be right to kill in the name of God? (The Puritans hanged heretics.)
- How could the king charter and sell land that didn't belong to him?

That last question was threatening to the king and to the colonists. No matter if it was logical and ethical too; if the king heard that, he might revoke the charter of the Massachusetts Bay Colony and order everyone home. There seemed no way

> "We may praise him for his defense of liberty and the separation of church and state. He deserves the tribute, but it falls short of the man. His greatness was simpler. He dared to think."
>
> —Edmund Morgan, writing about Roger Williams

around it. Kind, pious Roger Williams was found guilty of holding "newe and dangerous ideas." The Massachusetts court decided to ship him back to England.

When Williams's wife heard the news, she cried. Williams said, "Fifty good men did what they thought was just." But he wasn't about to go back to England. So he ran off, to the wilds of Rhode Island, in the January snow. In Rhode Island, he bought land from the Narragansett Indians and founded a colony he called Providence. Its charter said no one should be "in any wise molested, punished, disquieted, or called in question for a difference in opinion on religion." In other words, governments should stick to civil matters. Providence soon attracted many who were not wanted elsewhere. Williams welcomed everyone—Quakers and Catholics, Jews and atheists. As   Americans, he loved and res   em as they would love and respect him. He learned the Narragansett language and wrote a guide to it so others could learn, too. Williams, despite his innate goodness, was surprised that non-Christians could be ethical. "Whence cometh the morality of the atheist?" he asked. Others of his time never asked.

In England the established religion went from Catholic to Protestant, to Catholic and Protestant, to Protestant again. Each swing came through government power. Roger Williams understood the hypocrisy of it all. He knew people could be made to go to church, but no one's mind can be made to believe. "Since the commonweal cannot without a spiritual rape force the consciences of all to one worship, oh, that it may never commit that rape … which a stronger arm and sword may soon (as formerly) arise to alter." "Spiritual rape"—it was a powerful phrase. "Stronger arm and sword may … alter"? Williams was talking about that back-and-forth English church history. His ideas were unacceptable in Massachusetts, where the leaders were trying to work out their independent ways without antagonizing the English authorities. But Williams wouldn't stop. This is what he said about forced worship: "It is against the testimony of Christ Jesus for the civil state to impose upon the souls of the people a religion. Jesus never called for the sword of steel to help the sword of spirit." The Separatist churches-all of them-thought there should be one religion; they just disagreed on which it should be. Williams questioned what had previously been unquestioned without losing his faith. He was a devout Puritan who cared deeply about the purity of his church. But he understood the irony, and evil, of killing and coercion "for cause of conscience." The historian Edmund Morgan, writing about Roger Williams, said, "We may praise him … for his defense of religious liberty and the separation of church and state. He deserves the tribute … but it falls short of the man. His greatness was simpler. He dared to think."

CONSCIENCE AND FRIENDSHIP

In Virginia, where the scenery was different and the Anglican Church (the Church of England) was established, laws said you had to attend church services. To deny the truth of the Trinity (the Christian belief in God as father, son, and Holy Spirit) was punishable by death. Freethinkers (which meant Methodists, Baptists, and atheists) might have their children taken from them. Nonetheless, freethinking preachers, attempting a religious revival, rode a circuit preaching at tented meetings. And they often found themselves in jail.

By the second half of the eighteenth century, more than a few people appreciated the folly of locking up the devout. Young James Madison, who went off to Princeton with a solid Anglican upbringing, came under the tutelage of the college president, Calvinist John Witherspoon. Witherspoon had brought a hatred of church establishments with him from Scotland, along with Enlightenment ideas. This is what he said about education: "In the instruction of the Youth, care is to be taken to cherish the spirit of liberty, and free enquiry, and not only to permit, but even to encourage their right of private judgment, without presuming to dictate with an air of infallibility, or demanding an implicit assent to the decisions of the preceptor."

Madison's best friend at college was William Bradford of Massachusetts. In a letter written in 1774, after they graduated, Madison told his friend of persecuted Baptists in Virginia. "This vexes me the most of any thing what ever. There are at this time in the adjacent county not less than 5 or 6 well-meaning men in close Gaol [jail] for publishing their religious

Some Calvinists believed that displays of beauty and wealth in church were heretical or sacrilegious and should be destroyed.

Edward Hicks painted a peacemaking ideal in *Penn's Treaty with the Indians* (above). William Penn agreed to exchange land voluntarily with the Susquehannock, Shawnee, and Leni-Lenape in 1682, the year he arrived from England to launch his colony of Pennsylvania. "No one," he wrote, "can be put out of his estate … without his consent." He learned Indian dialects so he could negotiate without interpreters.

Sentiments which in the main are very orthodox.… I have squabbled and scolded and abused and ridiculed for so long about it, to so little purpose that I am without common patience. So I leave you to pity me and pray for Liberty and Conscience to revive among us." Madison kept scolding and squabbling. Between the pillars of Virginia and Massachusetts sat an anomaly: vibrant, diverse, religiously tolerant Pennsylvania. It had been founded by William Penn, who was born a rich Anglican with a silver spoon in his mouth and servants at his feet. His father was a friend of King Charles II; the king owed a debt to Penn's father; he wanted to pay it; he had land in America, and Penn got a colony.

Like a lot of kids, Penn didn't do what his father expected of him. Instead of treading the Anglican path, he became a member of a radical, hated, outcast sect, the Society of Friends, also known as Quakers. Being a Quaker got Penn kicked out of college when he refused to attend Anglican prayers. It led him to jail—more than once. It gave him a faith he carried through his life. And it gave him a reason for founding that American colony. Because the Bible says, "Thou shalt not kill," Quakers believe all war is wrong. They won't fight even when drafted into the army. They are called "conscientious objectors," because their conscience tells them not to fight. And they won't swear allegiance to a king or government or flag or anyone but God. That was a problem in England, where people were expected to swear their loyalty to the king.

William Penn wanted to create a haven for Quakers and Quaker ideas in America. That meant a place where all people and all religions were treated with respect. Penn's Charter of Liberties for Pennsylvania established a government "free to the people under it, where the laws rule, and the people are a party to those laws." Penn really believed in brotherly love. As long as he was in charge, he tried to treat all people fairly. (Later, things would change.) And when Penn said all people he meant all people. Quakers were among the first to protest against slavery and to deal with Indians as equals.

Still, Penn didn't believe in democracy. It was a big mistake. The men he chose to run his colony fought among themselves and cheated him. (He would have been better off with democracy.) But Penn did prove that freedom and fairness work.

Philadelphia, the capital of Pennsylvania, designed and laid out by William Penn himself, was soon the largest, most prosperous city in the colonies.

MAKING FREEDOM THE LAW

By the mid-eighteenth century, there was a significant group of educated Americans, born and bred here. One of them put a question to the members of Virginia's House of Burgesses. "Has the state a right to adopt an opinion in matters of religion?" Thomas Jefferson asked. Then he answered his own question with a loud "no." Religion tied to state power is always oppressive, he said. The Virginia legislators were all members of the Anglican Church. According to law, they had to be. Jefferson wanted to persuade them to let anyone—of any Christian sect, or any other religion, or no religion at all-join what had been their exclusive club. So he wrote a bill—a Statute for Religious Freedom—intended to do something never done before: to legally keep church and state separate. Virginians would be able to worship, or not worship, as they wished. And religion would have nothing to do with citizenship or public service. "The legitimate powers of government extend to such acts only as are injurious to others," Jefferson wrote. "But it does me no injury for my neighbor to say there are twenty gods or no god. It neither picks my pocket nor breaks my leg."

That idea of separation of church and state was too much for many Virginians. Patrick Henry, who had so eloquently denounced taxation without representation, argued against it. So, at first, did George Washington and James Monroe. The bill was easily defeated. Patrick Henry wanted a tax to support all Christian churches, which seemed an innovative thing to do. (After the Revolution, with the Baptists increasingly feisty, and many Anglican ministers gone back to England, something had to be done.) Henry's bill passed its first two readings. Passage on its third and final reading seemed certain. Writing to James Madison from France, where he was now ambassador, Jefferson said, "What we have to do is devotedly pray for his death." Jefferson was talking about Patrick Henry.

Madison was more pragmatic. He wrote an attack on religious tyranny that

The Reverend James Blair—minister of Williamsburg's Bruton Church, founder of the College of William and Mary (where Jefferson studied), and a force in the colonies for fifty years was an intolerant and "very vile old fellow," according to a contemporary; the Virginia Statute for Religious Freedom might not have happened had he lived a little longer.

Patrick Henry

became a widely signed petition (especially by Baptists). Then he helped kick Henry upstairs into the governor's office, where he had no veto. Finally, in 1786, two years before the Constitution was ratified, the statute became law. When Jefferson heard the news he wrote Madison, "It is honorable for us, to have produced the first legislature with the courage to declare, that the reason of man may be trusted with the formation of his own opinions." Later, he said, "it was the severest contest in which I have ever been engaged."

For Jefferson the statute did more than just guarantee the freedom to choose a church (or to choose not to go to a church). It said, officially, that governments have no business telling their citizens what to believe. Its concern was with freedom of the mind. "Truth is great and will prevail, if left to herself," wrote Jefferson in that ground-breaking document.

Some genuinely feared that without a law enforcing religion, Virginians would become sinners. It didn't happen. People were no more sinful than before. So, five years later, when Madison wrote the first amendments to the Constitution—the Bill of Rights—he had no trouble making the ideas of the Virginia statute the law of the land. "Congress shall make no law respecting an establishment of religion, or prohibiting the free exercise thereof," says the First Amendment.

And what about George Washington, who had feared that a country without an established church might become a country without faith? He became one of the biggest champions of religious freedom. Writing to the Hebrew Congregation of Newport, Rhode Island, in 1790, he said:

The Citizens of the United States of America have a right to applaud themselves for having given to mankind examples of an enlarged and liberal policy, a policy worthy of imitation.... It is now no more that toleration is spoken of, as if it was by the indulgence of one class of people, that another enjoyed exercise of their inherent natural rights. For happily the government of the United States, which gives to bigotry no sanction, to persecution no assistance, requires only that they who live under its protection should demean themselves as good citizens, in giving it on all occasions their effectual support.

The Pull of the West

On the frontier, no one cared if you were Puritan or Anglican or Catholic. It didn't matter if your father was a lord or a pauper. Could you be depended on? Did you shoot straight? Were you brave? That's what mattered on the frontier.

George Boone was a weaver and an independent-minded Quaker who moved his whole family to the New World in 1717 because he wanted them to be free and own land, too. Land meant everything in a society that lived by farming. Boone's grandson Daniel was just as fierce in his devotion to land and freedom. Sitting at a campfire in 1755, he heard tales of a region across the mountains from North Carolina that the Indians called *kentake*—which means "meadowland." It was said to be land filled with high grasses, birds, buffalo, deer, and beaver. Boone wanted some of that land. So he went searching for a way to get over the mountains, and finally found an Indian trail that led through a gap into the rich grasslands of Kentucky.

The trail went for 300 miles. Boone came back east and told others of it. By 1790, almost 200,000 people had gone west along what they named the "Wilderness Road."

Some daring travelers kept going. Some went all the way to the Rocky Mountains. A German-born trader described the mountain men who went to explore and trap beaver for the fur market: "In small parties, they roam through the mountain passes," he wrote. "No rock is too steep for them; no stream too swift. Danger seems to exercise a magic attraction over most of them."

By the 1820s, soon after Mexico became independent of Spain, wagonloads of hopeful traders began heading southwest, cutting deep ruts in a path that was called the Santa Fe Trail. In 1831 Josiah Gregg took a hundred wagons west. He described what happened when he reached Santa Fe. "The arrival produced a great deal of bustle and excitement among the natives," Gregg said. "'¡Los Americanos! los carros!' was heard in every direction; and crowds of women and boys flocked around to see the newcomers."

The Santa Fe traders were entrepreneurs, and part of an American tradition that Ben Franklin had exemplified. But for most of those who climbed into covered wagons and onto pioneer trails, it was land that was the lure. Like their ancestors who had hugged parents and grandparents, wiped away their tears, and set out for a New World—they, too, were leaving homes and families, often never to see

"Do not ask me to analyze this sentiment; it must be felt. It enters into hearts prepared to receive it; it fills them; it enraptures them."

—Alexis de Tocqueville, *Democracy in America*

George Caleb Bingham was born in 1811 near Charlottesville, Virginia (Thomas Jefferson's home), but moved to Franklin, Missouri—the wild West of those days—as a boy with his family. Between 1852 and 1855 he painted a series of pictures—this one is *The County Election*—about the rough-and-tumble of politics on America's frontier.

them again. For some it would be a great adventure; some would not live to finish the journey. One Missouri farmer wrote home to explain why he was taking the Oregon Trail.

> Out in Oregon I can get me a square mile of land. And a quarter section for each of you all. Dad burn me, I am done with the country. Winters it's frost and snow to freeze a body; summers the overflow from Old Muddy drowns half my acres; taxes take the yield of them that's left. What say, Maw, it's God's Country.

They were going for the reasons that usually make people move: because they wanted a better life for themselves and their children, or because they were adventurous or restless. And the farther west they went, the freer they felt. In 1835 a young Frenchman named Alexis de Tocqueville wrote of the "holy cult of freedom" he encountered everywhere he traveled in America.

A People's Government

America's new concept of freedom had implications that few people understood. One who did was John Quincy Adams, the son of the second president. "Let us not be unmindful that liberty is power," he said in 1821, when he was James Monroe's secretary of state and wrote the Monroe Doctrine, which told European states to keep their hands off the Americas. John Quincy—who may have been the best prepared of our presidents—had other prophetic things to say. "The nation blessed with the greatest portion of liberty must in proportion to its numbers be the most powerful nation on earth." But no one much listened. JQA didn't have a way with people.

The electorate was broadening. Until now, in many states, only men who owned property had been able to vote. That was changing. The vote was being extended to citizens whether they owned land or not, and that would transform American politics. In 1824, when Adams was elected president number six, 356,038 Americans voted. Four years later, 1,155,340 white men went to the polls—an increase of 224 percent. That democratic surge overwhelmed the patrician Adams when he ran for reelection.

The first few presidents of the United States were all from Virginia or Massachusetts. They were all born into successful, prosperous families, with the time and opportunity to be well educated. But what if you were living in nineteenth century America in Tennessee and you were poor? Would you have a chance to be president? After Andrew Jackson was elected the seventh president, you knew you had a chance. If Andy Jackson could be president, then any white man born in the United States could be president. Jackson was born in a log cabin on the border between North and South Carolina. His parents were Scotch-Irish farmers. His father died just before he was born. But nothing could stop Andy. A born leader, he became a judge and a military hero. His soldiers called him "Old Hickory," because, they said, he was as strong as a hickory tree. A college professor named Woodrow Wilson (who would become a president) described him as "a cyclone from off the western prairies." Jackson formed a new political party: the Democratic Party.

"Oh this is a life I would not exchange for a good deal! There is such independence, so much free uncontaminated air, which impregnates the mind, the feelings, nay every thought, with purity. I breathe free without that oppression and uneasiness felt in the gossiping circles of a settled home."

—Susan Magoffin, a bride traveling west along the Santa Fe Trail in 1846

John Quincy Adams couldn't abide him. "He is a barbarian and a savage who can scarcely spell his own name," said Adams. That old Federalist, Chief Justice John Marshall, had to swear Jackson in as president; he would as soon have sworn in the devil. But Jackson took that word *democracy,* which scared some people, and glorified it. He called his presidency a revolution, and he was right. He made people's government—democracy—respectable. When Jackson was elected, it seemed to those in Washington as if everyone in the West came to town to take part in the inauguration. The people—ordinary people—had elected one of their own. And they all

Looking Northwest

King George III, back in 1763, drew an imaginary line down the Appalachian spine of mountains that make for a natural barrier to the West. The king issued a proclamation saying that settlers were forbidden west of that line. Those lands to the west were reserved for the Indians. Some people in England were bothered by the idea of taking Indians' lands; for them this seemed the right thing to do. The line was also meant to keep settlers and Indians apart and save England the worry and cost of keeping peace between them. Besides, most people in England didn't think the region was worth much. The learned Samuel Johnson, who wrote the first English-language dictionary, said that the western land that England got as a result of the French and Indian war was "only the barren parts of the continent, the refuse… which the French, who came last, had taken only as better than nothing."(We're talking about the future states like Ohio, Indiana, and Wisconsin. Dr. Johnson should have stuck to his dictionaries.)

When the British left America, after the Treaty of Paris ended the Revolutionary War in 1783, the new Unites States claimed all their western land—which went to the Mississippi River and doubled the size of the new nation. What should be done with it? New immigrants were panting for farmland. They weren't going to worry about the Native Americans who happened to be there. Or about some British traders who weren't ready to give it up. There was another problem: a few big states, like Virginia and New York, had old claims on that land. Smaller states, like Maryland and Rhode Island, weren't going to let them hog it. They finally got the large states to give up all claim to western lands. That land was now like a colony belonging to the thirteen states. Before this, colonies have always existed for the benefit of the mother country—but, because of their bad experience with Great Britain, Americans didn't want to take advantage of others. So, in 1787 the Articles of Confederation Congress wanted to get into the White House—at the same time. They poured in through the mansion's doors in buckskins and muddy boots. They climbed on the satin chairs and broke the glasses and spilled orange punch. Ladies fainted, men got bloody noses, people pushed and shoved, and some had to scramble out the windows to leave.

Many remembered President Washington's receptions, where men wore gloves and silver shoe buckles and talked softly. This world of Andrew Jackson's would be the end of the United States, some said. Mobs would take over the government. But it didn't happen. It helped that Jackson had good manners, natural manners. People who thought they

passed a Northwest Ordinance based on equal rights for the territories. It was agreed that those lands would eventually become states. (Once again, Native Americans were going to be pushed from their lands. Disease and guns killed many; some joined white society; most fled farther west. The ordinance had a bill of rights, so settlers who moved into the territory were guaranteed freedom of religion, habeas corpus and trial by jury. Based on a document written by Thomas Jefferson, the ordinance said (take note of this): "There shall be neither slavery nor involuntary servitude in the said territory." It also said (note this, too): "Religion, morality and knowledge, being necessary to good government and the happiness of mankind, schools and the means of education shall forever be encouraged. "If people were to govern themselves—as Americans were doing— they had to be educated. How can you govern yourself if you can't read or write? How can you take part in government if you don't know about current events—and history, too? So the ordinance required towns to set aside land for public schools. Finally, it said, " the utmost good faith shall be observed towards the Indians."

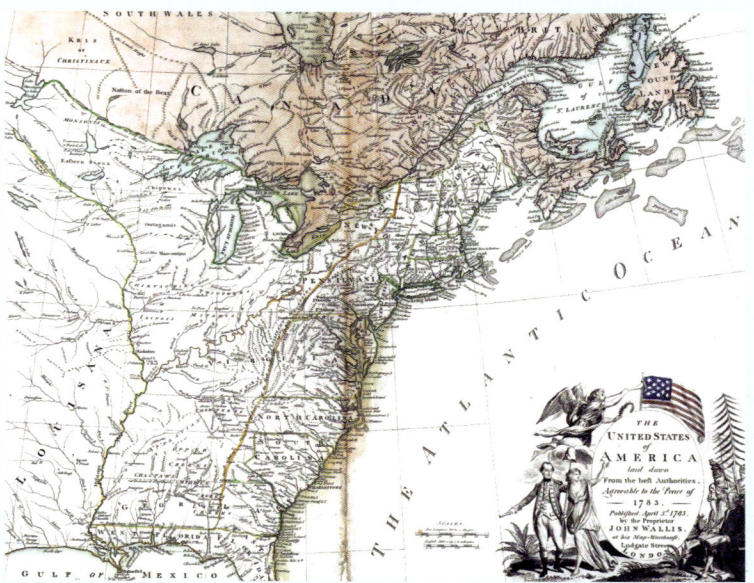

This 1783 map recorded the boundaries of the new United States. Most land west of the Appalachians was Indian but the Indians were soon pushed farther and farther back.

In 1844, Josiah Gregg, one of the traders who blazed the Santa Fe trail between Missouri and New Mexico, wrote a book about his adventures called Commerce of the Prairies. This picture of the caravan of covered wagons on the trail was one of the illustrations.

would be appalled by him ended up being charmed. Andrew Jackson did change the presidency—it was never the same again. Most people think he made it stronger. For the earlier presidents, democracy had meant government *for* the people. For Jackson, democracy meant government *by* the people.

A Trail of Tears

The immigrants who were pouring into the country from Scotland and Ireland and Germany had been told there was land enough for everyone. But most of the frontier land belonged to the Indians. The immigrants didn't care; they pushed west. Cherokee land stretched across the mist-covered southern Appalachian Mountains in a semicircle that reached from Kentucky to Alabama. Some newcomers built cabins on that land. The Cherokees had a warrior tradition. They didn't know which white people were friendly and which weren't. They just knew their land and lives were being threatened, so they raided and killed and burned cabins and farms. The settlers retaliated. And, though many died, it was mostly the Indians who lost out. The white people's diseases, weapons, and numbers were too much to withstand. Some national leaders tried to find ways to protect the Indians, but it wasn't easy to do. Settlers began saying that all Indians should live west of the Mississippi. Most white Americans—including Andrew Jackson—agreed. They said the Indians could live there in peace. But the Cherokees didn't want to move. They loved their land. It didn't matter.

In 1830 Congress passed an Indian Removal Act. That law made it legal for the president to move the tribes west. President Jackson was eager to do so. Then gold was

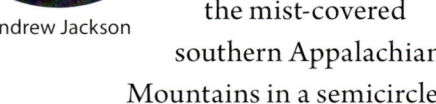

Andrew Jackson

"Those tribes cannot exist surrounded by our settlements. They have neither the intelligence nor the moral habits. Established in the midst of a superior race, they must disappear."

—Andrew Jackson

discovered on Cherokee land in Georgia, and gold hunters came by the thousands. The Georgia government held a lottery and gave the Cherokee land to white settlers. Soldiers helped those settlers take the Cherokee farms and orchards. President Jackson said there was nothing he could do about it. The truth was, he didn't want to do anything about it.

The problem with the Indians, said many white men and women, was that they were "savages" and "uncivilized." By that they meant that the Indians did not do and think as white people did. But tribes such as the Cherokees confounded the whites. Many did live as whites did. Some married white people. Some combined the two ways of life. They cleared the land, built big farms, planted apple and peach orchards, and raised cattle and hogs. Some lived in European-style houses. Many owned slaves. Missionaries moved into Cherokee territory and converted some to Christianity. One great Cherokee, Sequoyah, created the first Indian alphabet, so that the Cherokee language could be written. The Cherokees formed a government, wrote a constitution, founded schools, and built a capital city with broad avenues and solid buildings. They became very prosperous. But the wealthier the Cherokees became, the more anxious others were to have their land.

Samuel Worcester was a Congregational missionary who had come to Cherokee territory in Georgia to teach school and preach Christian doctrine. He was soon convinced that the Cherokees had a right to their land, and he said so. The Georgia legislature passed a law saying all white men in the Indian portion of the

Sod dugout houses like this one in Nebraska territory were made of prairie earth and sod, or turf. They were warm in winter and cool in summer, but when it rained, the floors turned to mud. This family brought out their most valuable possessions for the camera.

Tempting Texas

Texas was tempting. All that beautiful land ... land that seemed made to grow cotton. That land was part of Mexico and controlled by Spain. It had been so since the sixteenth century, when explorers like Cabeza de Vaca and Coronado had searched for the seven cities of Cibola and the gold and riches they were sure they would hold. By the early nineteenth century the vast land of Texas was almost empty; diseases carried by Europeans had killed most of the Native American population. Spain had hoped some of its citizens would settle in Texas—as other Europeans had settled in the United States—but few did. Gold had not been found in Texas. And there was no freedom, either. In the Spanish colonies everyone was expected to be Catholic and subject to the monarchy.

As a young man, before Sam Houston was the hero of Sanra Anna and a Texas senator, he was adopted by a Cherokee tribe and lived as an Indian for three years.

That didn't bother Stephen Austin. In 1821, he led a group of 300 settlers to Texas from Missouri. They said they would become good Mexican citizens and Catholics. That same year, Mexico rebelled against Spanish rule and became independent. Three years later, in 1824, the Mexicans approved a fine constitution and formed a republic. Unfortunately, there was no tradition of self-government in the Spanish colonies, as there had been in the English colonies. People weren't used to running things themselves. That made it easy for a strong, ambitious dictator named Antonio López de Santa Anna, to take power. He

state had to be licensed. They wouldn't give Worcester a license. He was arrested, tried, found guilty, and sentenced to four years in prison at hard labor. He appealed his case to the Supreme Court. It was called *Worcester* v. *Georgia*.

The case went beyond Samuel Worcester. The court ruled on the issues of Indian ownership of land and their right to govern themselves. Chief Justice John Marshall, now an old man, wrote a famous opinion in *Worcester* v. *Georgia*. That opinion is still cited as a statement of fairness on human rights. "The Cherokee nation," wrote Marshall, "is a distinct community, occupying its own territory ... in which the laws of Georgia can have no force, and which the citizens of Georgia have no right to enter, but with the assent of the Cherokees themselves." The Cherokees had won the right to their land. The Supreme Court said that the Indians "have a present right of possession." In other words, it was unconstitutional ignored many of the freedoms the constitution had promised.

By now other people from the United States were settling in Texas. Some of them didn't want to be Mexican citizens or Catholics. They wanted schools and freedom of religion. They wanted to build towns and run those towns themselves. Some brought slaves—which was against Mexican law. Most didn't want to share the land with Indians. By 1830, there were more English-speaking Americans in Texas than Spanish-speaking Mexicans. Santa Anna said no more Americans would be allowed in—but that didn't stop them. People from the States crossed the border illegally and demanded the rights of the Mexican constitution.

In 1836, some Texas rebels attacked Mexican forts. Then Santa Anna massacred one group, bunkered in a San Antonio mission and fort called the Alamo. Inside were Jim Bowie and Davy Crockett, who'd been a congressman and frontiersman. A few months later another group of rebels, led by Sam Houston, captured Santa Anna at San Jacinto and got him to sign a treaty that made Texas an independent nation. Texas was now a republic, with Houston as its president and a lone star on its flag. But Houston wanted Texas to be part of the United States.

There should have been no problem with that, except that some Texans wanted to own slaves. By this time, the Unites States was divided; according to an 1820 law, called the Missouri Compromise, there were slave states and free states, and they were equal in number. If Texas became a state, and a slave state, the southern slave states would have more votes in Congress than the northern free states. That would create trouble. So Texas stayed independent for almost ten years, until 1845, when it became the twenty-eighth state and Sam Houston a U.S. senator. By then, slavery was a hot issue. And not just in Texas.

to push them from their land. Only it didn't matter. The president—Andrew Jackson—refused to enforce the law. Our system of government under law failed. It was a shameful moment in United States history.

And so the Indians had no choice. They went west on a Trail of Tears—a long trail—that they were forced to walk. As they went, they wept. They were leaving their homes, their farms, their hunting grounds, the land of their fathers and mothers. The Choctaws were first; they moved in 1831. Three years later the Chickasaws trudged west. The Creeks had signed a treaty that said "they shall be free to go or stay, as they please." It didn't matter. In 1836 they were sent west—some with chains around their necks. The Cherokees set out in 1838. They walked—the children, their parents, and the old people—on hot days and cold. They walked in rain and windstorm. Often there was not enough food; often there was no shelter. One of every four of them died on the journey. The government said the new lands would be theirs forever. But when new settlers moved west, they forgot those promises.

In 1786, Thomas Jefferson wrote: "It may be regarded as certain that not a foot of land will ever be taken from the Indians without their consent." Forty-four years later, the Indian Removal Act was the law of the land.

Manifest Destiny

In 1844 James K. Polk of Tennessee was elected president. Like his hero, Andrew Jackson, Polk thought the country had a God-given right to lands in the West. Polk wanted Oregon and Mexican-owned California, and so did most Americans. The land was inviting, and there was something that helped convince people that the United States should take it. It was an idea called *manifest destiny*. Those high-falutin words were first used in 1845 by a reporter named Jane Cazneau, writing for editor John L. O'Sullivan (many people ascribe her words to him—but they're wrong). Manifest Destiny meant that Americans had the right and duty to spread democracy across the continent. Soon that phrase was on everyone's tongue. "Nothing less than a continent," wrote Ignatius Donnelly, a politician of the time, "can suffice as the basis and foundation for that nation in whose destiny is involved the destiny of mankind."

In 1846 Polk signed a treaty with Great Britain. England got western Canada, and the United States got what is now Oregon, Washington, Idaho, and parts of Montana. Then Polk went to war against Mexico. When the war ended, the border between Texas and Mexico was set at the Rio Grande River. And the United States got California—which at that time meant land stretching from Texas to the Pacific and as far north as Wyoming. Nine days before the end, something had been discovered in California on land belonging to a Swiss man, John Sutter. Something the Spanish conquistador and explorer Coronado had searched for in North America and couldn't find. Gold!

Gold fever spread across the country like an epidemic. Farmers left their plows, blacksmiths left their forges, tailors left their needles, sailors left their ships, and doctors left their patients. They were all off to California. Once you got there, people said, your cares would be over. Why, you could bend down and pick up gold in the

"It is our manifest destiny war's to overspread the continent allotted by Providence for the free development of our yearly multiplying millions."
—Jane Cazeau, reporter, 1845

John Gast painted his portrait *American Progress* a quarter-century after John Sullivan promoted manifest destiny—but it sums up that relentless drive west of U.S. empire. The imperial goddess tows the telegraph wire behind her, while in front Indians and buffalo are in desperate retreat.

streams. Nothing to it. Sell everything you have and head west. You'll be rich in no time at all. Sure. Some miners did strike it rich. But not many. Louisa Clappe, one of the few women in the mining camps, knew that: "Goldmining is nature's great lottery scheme. A man may work a claim for many months, and be poorer at the end of the time than when he commenced; or he may take out thousands in a few hours. It is a mere matter of chance." It was the stories of lucky miners that filled newspapers around the globe, and that kept people coming. The lure of gold and land and freedom was hard to resist. Immigration soared. There was something else; in 1845 the Irish potato crop failed. For five years there was almost nothing for poor people to eat in Ireland. People were arriving in America from all over the world. Most of these immigrants knew very little about the United States except that it was a land of freedom. But that was all they wanted: freedom and a chance to work.

PART 4

WAKE UP, AMERICA

"I am an independent farmer, don't owe five guineas in the world," says the hero of William Ioor's play *Independence,* staged in South Carolina in 1805. Ioor's farmer exults in his land, which he says yields "every necessary comfort for me and mine." He boasts that "an honest farmer knows of no dependence, except in heaven." It's a popular theme of the time: the idyll of independent agrarian life. Thomas Jefferson (a planter with slaves to do his bidding) sees the yeoman farmer as the model American. Freedom and land—what more could anyone want?

Thirty years later an industrial revolution is in the making, transportation innovation is opening new vistas, and subsistence farming on your own land—which had seemed splendid to the landless Europeans who flocked to the new nation—is no longer enough.

When the writer James Fenimore Cooper comes back to the United States in 1833, after a long stay in Europe, he is horrified by an attitude that seems to have taken hold in his country. "The desire to grow suddenly rich has seized on all classes," one character complains in Cooper's novel *Homeward Bound.* Are Americans losing

After 1825, when the Erie Canal linked the Great Lakes and the Hudson River, New York City gained a huge share of the nations shipping: 62 percent of imports came through its splendid deep-water harbor in 1836. On one day that year 921 vessels were counted lining the East River (shown here in 1883, with the famous Brooklyn Bridge connecting the boroughs of Manhattan and Brooklyn).

This picture of one area of Slater's mill in Pawtucket, Rhode Island, was made in 1836 to illustrate Sam Slater's memoirs, published the year after he died worth $1.2 million, one of the richest men in America. By then Slater's textile empire had expanded; he owned factories all over New England, and even a bank.

their souls in a search for riches? Cooper thinks so. But the drive to make money has surprising consequences. It will make the whole country rich, providing better food, clothing, and shelter to more people than in any nation before. It will spawn ideas, and poetry, and songs.

Playwright Ioor's independent farmer grew or raised most of what he ate; his wife made his clothes and baked his bread, his neighbors helped him build a barn, and he bartered for shoes and some other necessities. He rarely saw cash. A few decades into the nineteenth century, and things once made at home—like cloth—are being made faster, and often better, in factories. Cash money is becoming an essential and technology is about to seduce the independent farmers' children: some will be lured to the city, but those who stay on the farm will not be satisfied with life as it was. Children of illiterate European peasants are becoming educated citizens in these "united states." That combination of freedom and education is empowering. For everyone, even those trapped in slavery, the promise of the nation—liberty and justice for all-provides hope and impetus and a destination.

In England, an industrial revolution (although no one called it that for a while) has been germinating since the 1760s; it is based on new technology and new methods of organizing labor and capital. It is machinery that makes most of the innovation possible. Americans want those machines. The English aren't about to share them. They want to keep the industrial revolution in England. No one who works in a cotton mill is allowed to leave the country.

In the United States, a reward is offered to anyone who can build a cotton-spinning machine. In England, Samuel Slater takes notice. He works in a mill in Derbyshire, where he uses Richard Arkwright's state-of-the-art machinery. In eight years, Slater has gone from apprentice to superintendent; he knows how to build and operate the machines. Slater runs off to London (it is 1790), pretends to be a farm worker, and sails for America. The key to the industrial revolution is in his head. Financed by Rhode Island businessman Moses Brown, in 1793 Slater builds a small cotton-spinning mill next to a waterfall on the Blackstone River at Pawtucket, Rhode Island. Waterpower turns the machines that spin cotton fibers into yarn. Soon there are spinning mills—and, later, weaving mills—beside many New England streams. The textile mills, foundries, and factories produce more than goods: they churn out a new economic stratum of people—what is called a "middling class."

Slater does something else. He gets entire families—including children—to work in his mill. Big, poor families are his chief source of labor. Slater builds housing for them. Then he builds company stores, and churches, and pays his workers with store credits. By 1830, 55 percent of all millworkers in Rhode Island are children younger than thirteen. They work from sunup to sundown, usually for less than one dollar a week. Before the mills came, many of these children would probably have been working long hours on farms.

Industry brings wealth to many, but it is an uneven affair, and for the workers it frequently means only long working hours and terrible factory conditions. Thomas Jefferson, who has seen the squalor and misery in England's new industrial cities, is alarmed, and wants no part of it. "I view cities as pestilent to the morals, the health, and the liberation of man," he scolds. But most Americans aren't listening. The country is now doubling its population every two decades. It is still overwhelmingly rural, but cities hold excitement and jobs. Many of the immigrants find themselves in the burgeoning cities; there they create both the ethnic enclaves and the ethnic mixes that enliven the new nation.

Eli Whitney

At left, slaves operate a cotton gin. To figure out how to build his gin, Eli Whitney watched a man clean cotton. One hand held a seed while the other teased out the strands of lint. Whitneys machine duplicated this. In place of a hand holding the seed, he made a sieve of wires. A drum rotated past the sieve, almost touching it. On the drums surface, hook-shaped wires caught at the lint, and the sieve held the seeds back. A rotating brush cleaned the lint off the hooks. That was it.

In 1831, a ready-to-wear clothing factory opens in America. Imagine clothes made in uniform sizes to fit more than one person! Will the idea work? Amazingly well. In the first factory, seamstresses do all the sewing by hand. The market is ready for a sewing machine. Walter Hunt develops one for "sewing, stitching, and seaming cloth" in 1838; then, believing his machine will throw seamstresses out of work, he abandons it as immoral. (Hunt invents the safety pin and has no problem promoting that.) Meanwhile, Elias Howe tries to duplicate his wife's sewing motions on a machine. He finds an answer in the shuttle motion of a loom. In 1844, at age twenty-five, he perfects his machine, and productivity soars. Now that factories can turn cotton into yarn quickly and easily, there is great demand for raw cotton. But the cotton that grows best in America—short-staple cotton—is full of seeds, and those seeds stick to the cotton bolls. It takes a worker all day to remove the seeds from just one pound of cotton. Eli Whitney hears all about that problem when he comes to Savannah, Georgia, to take a job as a teacher. He thinks and fiddles and, in 1793, comes up with a simple machine that easily removes seeds from cotton. He calls it a "cotton engine"; the name is soon shortened to cotton gin.

A worker with a gin can clean fifty pounds of cotton in one day. The South has been having economic problems. Tobacco has used up the soil; indigo and rice production are faltering. Some say slavery is no longer economically viable. Then the cotton gin comes along. If you can grow a lot of cotton you can get rich. Southerners look for land for cotton and workers to plant and harvest it. Suddenly, slaves are more valuable than ever. Whitney didn't intend it, but his invention helps turn the South into a slave empire.

Until you've been in a factory it's hard to understand how loud they can be. The noise and commotion of the New England spinning machines were difficult to get used to—"the buzzing and hissing and whizzing of pulleys and rollers and spindles and flyers."

The Dark Side of Industry

Those who go into the mills as children are often dead in their thirties. In the cotton mills the air is full of tiny cotton fibers that get into lungs, which can sometimes lead to cancer or other ailments. The noise of the heavy machines makes heads ache and ears go deaf. Factory lighting is usually poor, and so, quickly, is the mill-workers' eyesight. The work is mind-numbingly dull. And anyone who loses a finger or an arm to a voracious machine loses his job, too. The writer Herman Melville, author of the great American novel *Moby-Dick*, visits a paper factory in 1855. This is what he sees:

> At rows of blank-looking counters sat rows of blank-looking girls, with blank, white folders in their hands, all blankly folding blank paper.... Not a syllable was breathed. Nothing was heard but the low, steady, overruling hum of the iron animals. The human voice was banished from the spot. Machinery—that vaunted slave of humanity—here stood menially served by human beings … as the slaves serve the Sultan. The girls did not so much seem accessory wheels to the general machinery as mere cogs to the wheels.

Herman Melville

Many millworkers don't have a choice. They have to work. Most Americans hardly know they exist. A shy young woman named Rebecca Harding, from Wheeling, West Virginia, changes that ignorance. In 1861, she writes an anonymous article called "Life in the Iron Mills" for the *Atlantic Monthly*, the most prestigious magazine of the day. It is the workers of Wheeling of whom she writes, people whose lives are so different from hers they might as well live in a different galaxy.

Masses of men, with dull, besotted faces bent to the ground, sharpened here and there by pain or cunning; skin and muscle and flesh begrimed with smoke and ashes; stooping all night over boiling cauldrons

Sending a Message

In 1850 the thirty-first star is sewn on the American flag. It is there for the state of California. Most places in the West are territories for years and years before they become states. California leapfrogs into statehood. That's because a whole lot of people move to California lickety-split, after a carpenter named James Marshall discovers gold at Sutter's Mill in 1849. Those people want to know what is happening to their loved ones back in Ohio, or New Hampshire, or Alabama. And the people back home are often frantic.

Have their fathers and brothers made it to the goldfields? Sometimes a year goes by without letters or news. The United States Post Office wasn't prepared for the thousands and thousands of letters that came in 1849. There aren't enough postal workers, and those doing the job keep quitting to work in the goldfields. So some enterprising Americans found private postal services. The fastest is the Pony Express. In St. Joseph, Missouri, the freighting firm of Russell, Majors, and Waddell hires eighty riders, buys 500 horses, and sets up 190 stations ten to fifteen miles apart on a route nearly 2,000 miles long. Mail carriers gallop as fast as they can, switching to a fresh horse at each station. After eight stations, a new rider takes over. An ad for Pony Express riders says: WANTED: YOUNG SKINNY WIREY FELLOWS, NOT OVER 18.

of metal, breathing from infancy to death and air saturated with fog and grease and soot, vileness for soul and body.

Rebecca Harding writes of the smells and the dirt-laden air:

Smoke rolls sullenly in slow folds from the great chimneys of the iron foundries, and settles down in black, slimy pools on the muddy streets. Smoke on the wharves, smoke on the dingy boats, on the yellow river;—clinging in a coating of greasy soot to the house-front, the two faded poplars, the faces of the passersby.... Smoke everywhere! A dirty canary chirps desolately in a cage beside me. Its dream of green fields and

MUST BE WILLING TO RISK DEATH DAILY. ORPHANS PREFERRED.

The Pony Express is a great idea, and it works. So why does it only last eighteen months? Samuel R B. Morse is to blame for that. He is an artist, who goes off to study painting in England, where he gets caught up in the scientific excitement of the time, especially the experiments in the new science of electricity. Morse wonders if electrical pulses can be sent along a wire in dots and dashes, short bursts and longer ones. If so, those dots and dashes could be used as a code to carry messages. Starting with that simple idea, Morse devises the telegraph. It takes twelve years to work out the details and get wires strung on poles, but it happens. In 1844 the first message goes—by Morse code—from the Supreme Court in Washington to Baltimore. "What hath God wrought?" asks Morse with dots and dashes. A few seconds later, his message is answered. At first people thought the telegraph was an amusing toy.

When someone says that Maine can now talk to Florida, the writer Ralph Waldo Emerson asks, "Yes, but has Maine anything to say to Florida?" Soon, some people—especially newspaper editors—begin to see that the telegraph is more than a toy. After Senator Henry Clay is nominated in Baltimore as the Whig candidate for president, people in Washington, D.C., learn about it seconds later. Seventeen years after Morse sends that first message, telegraph wires reach from coast to coast, and the Pony Express is out of business.

Samuel Morse (above, in a daguerreotype, an early form of photography) was a better ideas man than engineer. Assistants helped him perfect his telegraph key; one of them probably devised the dotdash code that bears Morse's name. By 1854 there were 23,000 miles of telegraph wire in operation.

Children in textile mills had fingers nimble enough to mend broken threads and bodies small enough to crawl under machines that needed fixing. In the 1850s Lowell millgirls worked six days a week, twelve hours a day.

sunshine is a very old dream,—almost worn out, I think.

People weep when they read her story and learn—often for the first time—of the wage slaves who tend the scalding pots of liquid metal that become the iron and steel needed to build the railroads and machines the nation is demanding. Does Harding's story help those workers? Probably not, for no one knows how to smelt iron, or dig minerals, or make steel or paper or textiles without hard, monotonous, backbreaking labor. Someday the problem will be solved by other machines, and by legislation. (But in 1910, less than half of Rhode Island's children attend school. And Rhode Island isn't alone. In 1938 a Fair Labor Standards Act finally eliminates child labor.)

Taking the High Road

One thing leads to another: if you start making cloth, thousands of yards of it, you can't keep it all in New England. You have to send it to other markets. Americans have no problem with that. They develop a world class merchant fleet. Ships from ports like Salem and New Bedford can be seen in China and Sumatra and the Netherlands. But how can you get cloth from Boston to Buffalo? In the early days of the nineteenth century, roads were no answer. Picture this: ruts, holes, stones—and when you come to a river, no bridge. In rainy weather the mud can be deep enough to tickle a horse's belly. It can take almost a week to get from Boston to New York by stagecoach. What is badly needed are better forms of transportation. Americans—who are becoming known for their ingenuity—soon come up with answers to that problem.

South Carolina's powerful spokesman John C. Calhoun says (in 1816), "Let us bind the republic together with a perfect system of roads and canals. Let us conquer space." Roman roads cemented an empire. The Aztecs built good roads in America, but their skills were lost. In this era of economic dynamism, access to markets is essential. So it's not surprising that road building gets reinvented as a science. Engineers begin to construct stone roads with drainage and a slope, or camber, for water runoff. Around 1806, some Americans with big ideas envision a road that will cross the country (well, at least from the East Coast to the Mississippi) and be called the National Road. Part of its route will follow a trail blazed by the Delaware Indian Nemacolin, and widened by General Braddock and Colonel Washington in the French and Indian War. The National Road is to be paid for by the federal government. That annoys a lot of people. If a road doesn't go anywhere near a state, should that state have to pay for it? How far should federalism go? What about states' rights? (The road is begun—but the issue doesn't go away.) By 1833 the road

The Erie Canal in 1839, fourteen years after it opened. By 1829, the population of the little village of Buffalo, where the canal began, had tripled; by 1840, it was 18,000 and Buffalo was on its way to becoming New York's second city. By steamboat and packet from New York City via Albany, the trip to Buffalo took six days—ten days faster than the stagecoach.

"I've got a mule and her name is Sal,
Fifteen miles on the Erie Canal.
She's a good old worker and a good old pal,
Fifteen miles on the Erie Canal.
We've hauled some barges in our day,
Filled with lumber, coal, and hay,
And we know every inch of the way
From Albany to Buffalo.

CHORUS:
Low bridge! Everybody down.
Low bridge! We're a-coming to a town.
You'll always know your neighbor,
You'll always know your pal,
If you've ever navigated
On the Erie Canal."

reaches Columbus, Ohio; by 1850 it is at Vandalia in central Illinois. Before the National Road is built it takes four weeks to travel from Baltimore to St. Louis. On the road, if you travel without stopping, you can make it in four *days*.

But even good roads are expensive to build and maintain. There have to be better and cheaper ways to move goods and people. Some think canals are the answer. They are quieter, smoother, and more reliable than roads. In New York, Governor DeWitt Clinton proposes a canal that could go from Albany, on the Hudson River, to Buffalo, on Lake Erie. It will be named the Erie Canal. Admirers dub it "Clinton's dream"; others snort and call it "Clinton's folly." The great ditch will have to traverse

On October 26, 1825, New York Governor DeWitt Clinton boarded the Seneca Chief in Buffalo to make the ceremonial trip on the Erie Canal to the Hudson River and, finally, to New York City. There he poured a barrel of Lake Erie water into New York harbor.

360 miles. There are steep hills to climb. Boats will have to get over those hills. And it's a long haul-through rough land. When Thomas Jefferson heard of the project he said to a canal booster, "Why, sir, you talk of making a canal of 350 miles through the wilderness—it is little short of madness to talk of it at this day!"

It takes eight years, from 1817 to 1825, and $7 million, but somehow a giant ditch four feet deep and forty feet wide gets dug. The canal is an engineering marvel—with eighty-three locks to raise and lower boats, and an aqueduct to carry them across the Mohawk River. It opens with a bang-actually, a whole chain of bangs. First, a cannon is fired in Buffalo, and when that is heard down the canal, another is fired, and then another—in Rochester, Syracuse, Rome, and Utica—until they hear the blast in Albany, where they just keep the cannons going and going, and on down the Hudson River. It takes an hour and twenty minutes until the last cannon blasts in New York. Then, just for fun, they shoot the cannons again, all the way back to Buffalo. Soon everyone is singing a song called "The Erie Canal."

Before the canal is built, it costs $100 to ship a ton of grain from Buffalo to New York. On the Erie Canal, in 1855, it costs only $8. People pack their belongings and take the Erie Canal west; they move to places like Indiana, Michigan, and Wisconsin. Some go east; the canal helps make New York the country's largest city.

Full Steam Ahead

Canals are easy to navigate; they have no current. You can pole your craft or get a horse with a tow line to pull it. Rivers are a different story. Boats float easily downstream, but there is no easy way to go upriver against the current. You can row (hard work), sail (if there's enough wind), or be pulled by horses from the shore (many problems). On the Mississippi, boats sometimes make one mile an hour going upriver. In England, several people figure out that the energy generated by boiling water—steam—can be a source of power that will move a boat or a train. Robert Fulton (like Samuel Morse, an artist as well as an inventor) does something with

Peter Cooper died in New York in 1883 at age ninety-two; huge crowds turned out to see his coffin transported to Green-Wood Cemetery in Brooklyn. He founded an art and design school in New York, the Cooper Union, which still gives full scholarships to all its students.

Peter Cooper's steam locomotive *Tom Thumb*.

that idea. He puts an engine inside a sleek hull and adds paddle wheels on each side. In 1807, his steamboat *Clermont* chugs 150 miles *up* the Hudson River, from New York to Albany, in an astonishingly fast thirty-two hours. But the real need for steamboats is out west. Fulton's *New Orleans* runs aground in shallow water near Natchez. Henry Miller Shreve designs a flat-bottomed steamer and, eventually, a grand steamboat (a prototype for the "floating palaces" to come). By 1820 there are sixty steamboats on the Mississippi; by 1860 there are about a thousand. And steam power is being used on land as well.

When the Baltimore & Ohio Railroad opens thirteen miles of railroad track in 1830, horses pull carriages on wheels. On a track, one horse can pull as heavy a load as ten horses off the track. But the railroad's directors are not satisfied. They are forward thinkers, and want to put a new steam engine on a railroad. A Baltimore inventor named Peter Cooper tells them he can do it. He builds a little steam locomotive he names *Tom Thumb*, and invites the directors for a ride. "We started—six on the engine, and thirty-six on the car," Cooper wrote afterward. "It was a great occasion. We made the passage to Ellicott's Mills in an hour and twelve minutes."

The next year, Robert Dale Owen, editor of New York City's *Free Enquirer*, sets off to see this new wonder for himself. Near Albany he climbs aboard a railroad ("one of the noblest triumphs of human ingenuity," he calls it). He finds "the steam engine already smoking, and six or eight stages—*cars* they are usually termed though scarcely differing except for their wheels from ordinary stages- ready to receive passengers." The engine starts off unattached to the cars; it needs to get up steam. "As one would walk a racehorse about, before starting," Owen explains. Finally, the nine-seat passenger cars are hooked on, "and the next minute we were off at the rate of twenty miles an hour, whistling past surrounding objects pretty much in the same style as if mounted on a fleet horse at full gallop.... No one can enter a rail-road car … without feeling that a new era in the annals of locomotion has commenced," Owen exults.

But even the best inventions can be risky business. A twenty-two-year-old politician, proud of his service in the Black Hawk War (a war about Indian removal), runs for election to the Illinois legislature in 1832, praising railroads as "a very desirable object" and a "never-failing source of communication, between places of business remotely situated from each other." But he thinks laying railroad tracks is expensive and he recommends that the state spend its resources on river transportation. (He has built a barge himself.) Abraham Lincoln loses that election. He will become a champion of railroads and a railroad lawyer.

Unlike canals, which freeze in winter, trains can be used year-round. Unlike horses, they can carry very heavy loads, and they don't get tired. Trains are the future. By 1840, about 3,000 miles of track have been laid, and by 1860, there are 30,000 miles. Traveling by train, at an unbelievable thirty miles an hour, you can go from New York to Chicago in two days. In 1854, the first railroad train makes it from the East Coast to the Mississippi River, at Rock Island, Illinois. The builders of the Rock Island Line intend to take the railroad right across the broad Mississippi to the town of Davenport, Iowa. They begin building a bridge, and, in 1856, a newspaperman is on board when the first train crosses the river.

> Swiftly we sped along the iron track-Rock Island appeared in sight—the whistle sounded and the conductor cried out, "Passengers for Iowa keep their seats." There was a pause-a hush, as it were, preparatory to the fierceness of a tornado. The cars moved on-the bridge was reached—"We're on the bridge—see the mighty Mississippi rolling on beneath"—and all eyes were fastened on the mighty parapets of the magnificent bridge, over which we glided in solemn silence. A few minutes and the suspended breath was let loose. "We're over," was the cry. "We have crossed the Mississippi in a railroad car."

Back east, an article in the *Philadelphia Bulletin* proclaims, "civilization took a railroad trip across the Mississippi."

It is a head-over-heels affair. Technology has captured us. We Americans, in the nineteenth century, become fascinated with machines and scientific advances. We fall in love with speed—with locomotives and steamboats and clipper ships. We fall in love with inventions—with John Deere's steel plow,

A Rock Island locomotive around 1880.

Cyrus McCormick's reaper, Elias Howe's sewing machine, and Samuel Morse's electric telegraph. And we put our energy behind our ideas.

Do Girls Have Brains?

In 1850, a larger percentage of children go to school in the United States than in any European country. The census that year shows that fifty-six of every hundred white children attend school (but only two of every hundred black children). Some children who never get to school learn to read in Sunday school, and just about everyone reads Bible stories or hears them read. Many parents teach their children at home.

The public-school idea begins to catch on in the 1840s and '50s. American democracy is growing—more men can vote—and the voters are demanding schools for their children. The Constitution doesn't mention education. That isn't because the Founders thought education unimportant; it's because they expected the states to control schooling. Thomas Jefferson believed the American experiment in government—that new idea called "self-government"—would only work in a country where every citizen was educated. How can you vote and make decisions if you can't read? "If a nation expects to be ignorant and free, in a state of civilization, it expects what never was and never will be," wrote Jefferson in a letter to a friend. George Washington said, "a plan of universal education ought to be adopted in the United

By the 1870s, some schools, like this one in New York City, were teaching girls and women serious subjects. As the population grew, women were needed more and more as teachers—so they had to be better educated.

Mary Lyon

States." And he also said, "Knowledge is, in *every* country, the surest basis of public happiness."

Sarah Pierce agrees. She starts the Litchfield Female Academy in the dining room of her Connecticut house. Most people think girls should concentrate on needlework and music and painting—but not Sarah Pierce. In her school, girls are taught grammar, reading, composition, history, philosophy, and logic—as well as needlework. Harriet Beecher Stowe, a famous author, is a student at the Litchfield Academy.

But few girls get a chance to go to a high school, and girls can't go to college. "Women's brains are smaller than men's. Girls can't learn as much as boys." That's what some nineteenth-century male experts actually say. Mary Lyon doesn't believe them. She knows she is as smart as any boy. One day, when she was little, her mother finds her fiddling with an hourglass. "What are you doing?" she asks. Mary says she is trying to invent more time. Mary Lyon never seems to have enough of it. Sometimes she studies eighteen hours a day. But she can't go to college, because there are no colleges for women.

So Mary Lyon founds Mount Holyoke College, in Massachusetts, in 1837, with four teachers and 116 students. Lyon insists that it be a democratic school and

"I maintain that men and women are equal. But we are much in the situation of the slave. Man has asserted and assumed authority over us."

—Sara Grimké

The Grimke sisters, Angelina (left) and Sarah (right), both became fervent abolitionists and women's rights activists. Sarah signed her *Letters on the Equality of the Sexes* "Thine for the oppressed in the bonds of womanhood."

Ain't I a Woman?

Some men and women are beginning to agitate for equal citizenship for women. In the 1840s and '50s women's rights conventions are held in Indiana, Massachusetts, Pennsylvania, New York City, and elsewhere. One man, who speaks at a convention in Ohio, in 1851, thinks he is telling the truth when he says that women are by nature weak and inferior to men. But a lean, stately woman who hears him doesn't agree. She is almost six feet tall and she wears a gray dress with a white shawl and a white turban wrapped around her head. When she walks, it is with the dignity of a queen. The tall woman is the only black person in the room—all eyes are upon her. Finally she can bear no more. Her name is Sojourner Truth, and she stands up and speaks in a voice like rolling thunder.

Ain't I a woman? Look at me. Look at my arm. [She showed powerful muscles.] I have ploughed, and planted, and gathered into barns, and no man could head me! And ain't I a woman? I could work as much and eat as much as a man—when I could get it—and bear the lash as well! And ain't I a woman? I have borne thirteen children, and seen them most all sold off to slavery, and when I cried out with my mother's grief, none but Jesus heard me! And ain't I a woman?

The story of Sojourner Truth's address is published twelve years later, in 1863, by a feminist reformer named Frances Gage. Some people argue about whether Sojourner Truth actually used those famous words "Ain't I a woman," but there is no argument about the power of her speech. Frances Gage says, "Amid roars of applause she returned to her corner.... She has taken us up in her arms and carried us over the slough of difficulty, turning the whole tide in our favor."

Sojourner Truth was named Isabella when she was born a slave in New York State. She was treated harshly, as slaves often were. In 1826, the year before New York frees its slaves, she runs away. She is a young mother and she plans to buy her children. But before she can do so, one of them is sold to

that the women do their own cooking and cleaning, to keep the tuition price low. Emily Dickinson, who will become one of America's finest poets, is a student at Mount Holyoke. "The school is *very* large," she writes to a friend, "quite a number of girls have left, on account of finding the examinations more difficult than they anticipated, yet there are nearly 300 now.... Miss Lyon is raising her standard of scholarship a good deal." A few other colleges begin opening their doors to women—and to African-Americans as well.

Still, in the nineteenth century, there are many people who really believe that women and blacks aren't meant to learn. So, with rare exceptions, there is no way for most women to become doctors, or lawyers, a buyer in the South. That is against New York law. With the help of a Quaker family Isabella goes to court and wins the child. That says much for her determination, and for the fairness of the court. Later, she helps other blacks fight for their rights in court. Isabella's Quaker friends tell her, "Before God, all of us are equal." No one has ever said that to her before. They read to her from the Bible. She memorizes large parts of the Bible (she has never had a chance to learn to read). She is deeply religious and has visions of God. She decides to live a godly life and help others; she a new name to celebrate her freedom and new life. It is Sojourner Truth. A sojourner is a traveler who stops somewhere for a short time and then continues on. For the next forty years she will travel and speak out for truth and justice.

Perhaps it is her dignity, or her sincerity, or that mighty voice, but when Sojourner Truth talks, people listen. She works for women's rights, black people's rights, prison reform, and temperance. On her chest she wears a banner that says PROCLAIM LIBERTY THROUGHOUT ALL THE LAND UNTO ALL THE INHABITANTS THEREOF. Those words from the Bible are written on the Liberty Bell in Philadelphia.

Sojourner Truth

or skilled workers. If a woman does get a job, she knows her pay will be half that of a man doing the same work. Her salary, along with the rest of her possessions—even money from her parents—belongs to her husband. Women can't vote, so they can't change the laws. A husband can whip his wife and the law is on his side. The law makes it almost impossible to get a divorce, and when a woman does manage it, many people consider such a thing shameful. If a wife runs away from her husband, the law says he has rights to the children—even if he is an alcoholic who beats them. And yet many good men are horrified at the idea of a woman standing up and speaking her mind. "It's a man's world," they say, and in the nineteenth century it is.

Susan B. Anthony (left) and Elizabeth Cady Stanton (right). Stanton died in 1902 and missed seeing her life's goal, women's suffrage, by just eighteen years.

But Sarah and Angelina Grimké have something to say and they say it to audiences of men and women. The sisters set out on a lecture tour in 1837 to tell what they have seen of slavery. "What kind of women would speak out in front of men?" people ask. "Monster women!" That is what some people say of the Grimké sisters. Ministers say it is wrong for women to speak when men are there to hear:

> *Woman depends on her weakness which God has given her for her protection. But when she assumes the place and tone of a man as a public performer, our care and protection of her seem unnecessary. If the vine ... thinks to assume the independence of the elm, the vine ... will fall in shame and dishonor into the dust.*

Those who come to hear the Grimkés see two women dressed in simple gray Quaker garb. Southern women they are, women who can no longer live in their slave-owning families, who have come north and who tell why. They tell of black children being sold away from their families, they tell of whippings with lashes, they tell of other horrors. And their audiences are astonished, for they do not know these things. Angelina went before the Massachusetts legislature with tens of thousands of antislavery petitions that have been collected by women. She is the first American woman to address a legislative body. "Men may reject what I say because it wounds their pride," says Sarah Grimké, "but I believe they will find that woman as their equal is unquestionably more valuable than woman as their inferior."

ALL MEN ... AND WOMEN

Elizabeth Cady Stanton reads the nation's great Declaration, and it bothers her. *All men are created equal,* it says. But what about all women? Elizabeth's father, Daniel Cady, is a judge; she spends hours in his office listening and learning. "If only you had been a boy," he tells her. "You could have been a lawyer." Elizabeth doesn't want to be a boy. She just wants to use her mind. She decides to learn everything the boys are learning. At school she is a top student. She is determined to use her intelligence to help women. In 1848, Stanton and her friend Lucretia Mott gather some 300

An 1869 man's nightmare of *The Triumphs of Woman's Rights*: women smoke, vote, abandon babies, and generally take charge.

women and men at Seneca Falls in upstate New York for a women's rights convention. There they write a declaration: it is known as the Seneca Falls Declaration, and it says, *We hold these truths to be self-evident: that all men and women are created equal.*

The women and men at Seneca Falls go on from there, telling of all the ways they feel women are being wronged. In the Declaration of Independence Thomas Jefferson had accused King George III of tyranny; Elizabeth Stanton accuses "man." "The history of mankind is a history of repeated injuries on the part of man towards woman, having in direct object the establishment of an absolute tyranny over her," she writes. One hundred people sign the Seneca Falls Declaration; thirty-two of them are men. Does anyone pay attention? Yes, indeed. This is what Elizabeth Cady Stanton writes in her autobiography:

No words could express our astonishment on finding, a few days afterward, that what seemed to us so timely, so rational, and so sacred, should be a subject for sarcasm and ridicule to the entire press of the nation.... So pronounced was the popular voice against us that most of the ladies who had attended the convention and signed the declaration, one by one, withdrew their names and influence and joined our persecutors.

Nonetheless, the reform movement spreads. Elizabeth Cady Stanton has started something that will grow and grow. Amelia Bloomer, the editor of a temperance newspaper, is one of the reformers. She wears long pantaloons, known as bloomers, under her short dresses, and tries to talk other women into that fashion. But people

throw stones at the "bloomer girls," or laugh at them.

One day in 1851 Amelia Bloomer introduces Elizabeth Cady Stanton to a teacher named Susan B. Anthony. It is a momentous meeting. Stanton and Anthony form a team—like Lewis and Clark—that will leave a big mark on American history. In 1853 Anthony gets permission to speak at a teacher's conference in Rochester, New York. No woman has done that before. This is part of what she says:

Wake Up, America 93

Cartoons made fun of the participants in women's rights conventions such as this one, in 1857. Elizabeth Cady Stanton wrote of Seneca Falls: "All the journals ... seemed to strive with each other to see which could make our movement appear most ridiculous."

"The childhood of woman must be free and untrammeled. The girl must be allowed to romp and ploy, climb, skate, and swim; her clothing must be more like that of the boy—strong loose-fitting garments, thick boots, etc., that she may enter ... freely into all kinds of sports."
—Elizabeth Cady Stanton, 1851

Stanton and Anthony understand that the American experiment in democracy is based on that promise contained in the words of the Declaration of Independence: that all are created equal and should be equal before the law. It is something new for a government to make that kind of promise—something new and wonderful and special. But it has created a paradox, because the reality is different from the promise. As Stanton says,

> To you, white man, the world throws wide her gates. But the black man and the woman are born to shame. The badge of degradation is the skin and the sex. Man is born to do whatever he can; for the woman and the Negro there is no such privilege.

How can a nation founded on the idea of liberty keep its brothers and sisters in chains? How can they allow slavery? More and more, fair-minded people are beginning to ask that question.

Do you not see that so long as society says a woman has not brains enough to be a doctor, lawyer or minister, but has plenty to be a teacher, every man of you who chooses to teach admits that he has no more brains than a woman?

This 1863 set of card illustrations, based on images by Henry Louis Stephenson, shows the a slave's journey as he progresses through life, eventually dying in battle while fighting for the Union.

PART 5

A Fatal Contradiction

Proclaim liberty throughout the land unto all the inhabitants thereof? Bells are meant to celebrate, to make known, to ring in triumph. But from Texas to Alabama to Virginia bells were chained to contentious slaves. If the slave attempted to run away—to find freedom—the bell tolled, making him or her easy to track.

How could this have happened—slavery in the land of the free? People treated as commodities, like items of farm equipment? It was shameful, inhuman, awful; some justified it, pretending it was otherwise, but those who thought at all knew they wouldn't trade their freedom for a minute of slavery. So how did it happen? How did we get there? How did we, proclaiming liberty, become a land whose wealth was in good part dependent on slave labor?

Workers were needed. In the beginning, in the English colonies, it was cheaper to buy servant indentures than to buy the enslaved—especially in Virginia, with its appalling death rates. But when the British economy had an upsurge and jobs in England became plentiful, few servants wanted to risk an unknown future in a wild land across the sea. Slaves filled a void. Besides, there was money to be made selling laborers into the English colonies. American slavery happened without much thought.

Slavery itself had an ancient and worldwide lineage. Estimates vary; some experts say that two thirds of the Roman Empire lived in some form of bondage. After Rome fell, European slavery evolved into serfdom (although it didn't completely disappear). It was in the European

James Martin was born a slave in Virginia in 1847. In 1937, aged ninety, Martin described a slave auction: "When the slaves is on the 'block,' the overseer yells, 'Tom or Jason, show the bidders how you walk.' … The overseer … makes 'em hop, he makes 'em trot, he makes 'em jump. 'How much,' he yells, 'for this buck? A thousand? Eleven hundred?' Then the bidders makes offers accordin' to size and build."

colonies—whose mission was to make money—that a new kind of slavery flourished. Slaves provided the labor for developing international agribusiness. Slavery became racial; not from original intent—it just happened. After that, skin color made it easy to suggest other differences, and to help justify oppression.

The largest slave plantations were in the sugar colonies pioneered in the Canary Islands, the Madeiras, Brazil, and Barbados. Sophisticated business ventures, they used advanced technology and demanded huge investments. In the fields, a gang work system based on time-and-motion studies (with rewards for achievement and whips for slackers) made for efficiency. Large, well-equipped plantation factories processed the cane into refined sugar, molasses, and rum. Return on investment was high (about 10 percent), creating some of the world's greatest fortunes.

In three and a half centuries, some 9.9 million Africans got hauled forcibly across the ocean—more than half of them to work in sugar fields. About 41 percent went to Portuguese Brazil, and 47 percent to the Spanish-American colonies (especially those on the Caribbean islands). A surprisingly small 7 percent was transported to what became the United States.

Blacks are isolated on the big plantations in Latin America and have little contact with whites. Their culture, though displaced, remains overwhelmingly African. Not so in North America. Here, as late as 1725, the median slave plantation in the Chesapeake Bay region has ten slaves. Blacks are in constant contact with whites; both are participants in a multiracial society. Despite their enslavement, the Africans become Americans—giving and taking in a cultural exchange.

So, from the beginning, American slavery includes a dichotomy. Blacks are not just victims; they are participants in American life. They are farmers, trailblazers, mountain men, cowhands, pioneers. They pan for gold, dig canals, and help

Self-taught surveyor and mathematician Benjamin Banneker corresponded with Thomas Jefferson and published a popular almanac in which he argued against the idea of black inferiority.

To make a profit, colonial tobacco planters had to cultivate huge areas of land, using many workers. When the supply of free labor wasn't enough, they turned to slavery. By 1750 there were more Africans in Virginia than any other single group of people.

build railroads. They soldier at Concord, Bunker Hill, and Yorktown. Most interact with whites daily, and, like all Americans, they long for liberty; for their country and for themselves. African-Americans want, and are willing to fight for, the same rights as other Americans. In an article published in a Maryland newspaper not long after the Revolution, a black man writes:

> Though our bodies differ in color from yours; yet our souls are similar in a desire for freedom. [Difference] in color can never constitute a [difference] in rights. Reason is shocked at the absurdity! Humanity revolts at the idea! … Why then are we held in slavery? … Ye fathers of your country; friends of liberty and of mankind, behold our chains! … To you we look up for justice-deny it not—it is our right.

And yet, for most, justice is denied. A few are free, but most are slaves.

Big-time cotton production, arriving in the South in the nineteenth century, changes the demographics. Using the sugar plantations as a model, the cotton planters establish giant business enterprises that segregate, isolate, and dehumanize workers. In 1800, about 11 percent of those enslaved in the United States toil on cotton plantations. By mid-century that number has risen to 64 percent. That leap tells a tale of wrenching dislocation—of the destruction of families and communities and established ways of life. Slavery makes sense economically; the morality of it is another issue.

A Growing Problem

In 1776, when Thomas Jefferson wrote the Declaration, he included a section describing slavery as a "cruel war against human nature." Jefferson was born into a slave society and owned slaves himself. Yet he thought slavery was wrong, and said so. "Nothing is more certainly written in the book of fate than that these people are to be free," he wrote. John Adams spoke out strongly against slavery. Benjamin Franklin founded the first antislavery society in the New World. But South Carolina and Georgia would not sign the Declaration if it contained Jefferson's antislavery section.

So those words were cut out. The delegates compromised. Should they have gone ahead without the southern colonies? That would certainly have meant defeat for the proposed union of states. Jefferson, Franklin and the others thought the Union more important than the slavery issue. They believed slavery could be dealt with later.

When it came to writing the Constitution, the Framers didn't outlaw slavery then, either. The problem was the same: a way of life depended on slavery. The citizens of the southern states threatened to stay independent. Abraham Baldwin

Slavery and the Constitution

Exactly what does the Constitution of the United States say about slavery? Here are its words:

From Article I, Section 2:

Representatives and direct taxes shall be appointed among the several States which may be included within this Union, according to the respective numbers, which shall be determined by adding to the whole number of free persons, including those bound to service for a term of years, and excluding Indians not taxed, three-fifths of all other persons.

The number of members of the House of Representatives allotted to each state is based on its population. "All other persons" means slaves. The southern states wanted to count slaves in order to have more representatives in Congress. Northerners felt that slaves should not be counted. The three-fifths clause was their compromise. A slave could not vote—but counted as three-fifths of a person for population purposes.

From Article I, Section 9:

The migration or importation of such persons as any of the States now existing shall think proper to admit, shall not be prohibited by the Congress prior to the year one thousand eight hundred and eight; but a tax or duty may be imposed on such importation, not exceeding ten dollars for each person.

This has to do with the slave trade.

From Article IV, Section 2:

No person, held to service or labour in one State, under the laws thereof, escaping into another, shall, in consequence of any law or regulation therein, be discharged from such service or labour; but shall be delivered up, on claim of the party to whom such service or labour may be due.

Fugitives are to be returned. Later, the Fugitive Slave Law strengthened this clause, making it a crime not to hand over slaves. Note that nowhere in the Constitution are the words *slave* or *slavery* used. Was it because the Founders looked forward to the end of slavery? Was it just a natural tendency to employ euphemisms for nasty practices? No one is sure what they had in mind. Did these constitutional mentions strengthen slavery, giving it legitimacy? Historians argue about that.

of Georgia said he "could not avoid the recollection of the pain and difficulty which the subject [slavery] caused in that body." He was clear that the agreement reached at Philadelphia in 1787 would not have happened if slavery had been outlawed in the Constitution.

But the issue would not go away. In 1790 Congress debated both the abolition of the slave trade and of slavery itself. There was no way to avoid it. A petition came from the Pennsylvania Abolition Society, signed by the august Benjamin Franklin. No one ignored Dr. Franklin. James Jackson of Georgia invoked the Bible in defense of slavery, and then admitted "rice

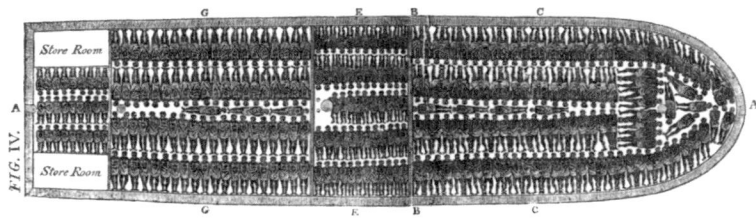

This famous diagram of a slave ship was a rough indicator of the number of slaves it was possible to stow on a deck. Often ships were overloaded; in 1788 one slaver, built to hold 451 people, was found to be carrying more than 600 from Africa to the Americas.

cannot be brought to market without these people." Thomas Scott of Pennsylvania said it was the Declaration of Independence, not the Constitution, that was the new nation's defining document, and it "was not possible that one man should have property in the person of another." Elbridge Gerry of Massachusetts, attempting conciliation, said the slave owners had been "betrayed into the slave trade by the first settlers." He came up with a plan to buy slaves at their market value (he thought the money could come from the sale of western lands). In the end, the house voted to refer the petitions to a committee and that ended it. They were willing to put the issue aside, in good part because they believed slavery was dying as an institution.

They were wrong. Statistics from modern scholars tell us slave imports kept rising (except in the war years) until 1808, when the slave trade was legally abolished. After that, an illicit trade was established, but its numbers were limited. And yet the black population grew explosively. In 1800 there were almost one million slaves in the country (actually 893,602); sixty years later there were close to four million (3,953,760). That increase came mostly from longer life expectancy and a phenomenal birth rate. Abolitionists attributed the birth rate to the horrendous practice of "slave breeding." Some modern historians argue about that, citing statistics that show it to be less important than previously thought. But in Latin America something else was happening: the death rate was high, the birth rate low, and the enslaved population fell dramatically.) By mid-century, the South was the center of slavery in the Americas.

A Terrible Triangle

It was called the "triangular trade," a pretty name for an awful practice. It made some people rich. This is one way it worked. Yankee skippers would take salted cod from Massachusetts to Barbados and trade it for cane sugar. Then they'd go to Virginia to pick up tobacco. They'd take the tobacco and sugar to England and trade those goods for cash, guns, and English cloth. Then on to Africa, where they exchanged the guns and cloth for men, women, and children. From there it was back across the Atlantic Ocean to the West Indies, where the people were sold into slavery in exchange for more sugar and molasses. Finally the merchants sailed home to New England (or New York or Annapolis), often criss-crossing the triangles. While the Constitution didn't outlaw the slave trade, it gave the slavers twenty years—until 1808—and then legislation could be passed ending the trade. Which is what happened. It became illegal to bring Africans into the United States as slaves. In 1820 the penalty for breaking that law became death. But the profits in slave trading were huge, and some people thought it worth the risk. Others agitated for its renewal. Southerner William Fitzhugh said that slavery was "the natural and normal condition of laboring men;" he thought the slave trade should be made legal again.

Freedom Fighters

Santo Domingo, on the island that the Arawak natives had called "Haiti" (meaning *place of mountains*), was, with its sugar and coffee plantations, the richest of France's colonies. Most of its population was African-born and enslaved. Its rulers were French and Creole (whites born in Haiti). The slaves rebelled. They fought for their freedom under a brilliant leader, a former slave-turned-general named Toussaint L'Ouverture. As to the details: a lot of whites were murdered; President Thomas Jefferson sent unexpected aid to the rebels; slavery was abolished; Toussaint was killed; Haiti became the second nation in the western hemisphere to win independence. Other details depend on who is telling the story. But in the United States, especially in the South, the tale that was most told was of slaves rising up and killing their masters. How would you react if you were a slave owner? They talked of it in whispers-but slaves heard and passed it on.

Nat Turner was brilliant; that was clear from his earliest years. His master liked to show off the little slave boy who had taught himself to read and could recite long Bible passages. Turner was smitten by the Bible; he preached its message and had a compelling way that made others listen. He even baptized a white overseer. He seemed

Thomas Gray, the writer who said he took down Nat Turner's story, reported that "this 'great Bandit' was taken by a single individual ... without attempting to make the slightest resistance."

to have psychic abilities—he knew things he shouldn't have been able to know—and he had visions. In 1831, in February, a major eclipse darkened the skies. Turner's visions grew more intense. His personal world was awry. His father had run away to freedom, his mother was sold no-one-knew-where, his master had died, and he was now owned by a nine-year-old. Even in Virginia's backwater Southampton county (west of Norfolk and south of Richmond), Nat Turner heard the story of Toussaint L'Ouverture. Turner believed he was meant to lead a revolution in Virginia, freeing slaves and overturning the power structure. He picked July 4 as the day to do it.

But it wasn't until August that the skies and his visions converged. He explained that "on the sign appearing in the heavens, the seal was removed from my lips, and I communicated the great work laid out for me to do." With axes and knives, Turner and some followers killed sixty-two white people (beginning with the nine-year-old slave owner and his parents) in an orgy of terror and butchery. Some hundred slaves were slaughtered in the search for Turner that ensued, with many of their heads ending up mounted on pikes. Turner finally turned himself in—he hadn't gone far and dictated his story to a newspaperman, who said he wrote it down as it was told (it's called *The Confessions of Nat Turner*). The shocking killings—on both sides—were too much for decent people to accept. A Virginia legislator said, "We talk of

"The teaching of slaves has a tendency to excite dissatisfaction in their minds. Therefore, any free person who shall teach any slave to read and write shall be liable to indictment. If any slave shall teach, or attempt to teach, any other slave, he or she shall receive thirty-nine lashes on his or her back."

—North Carolina law

THE PRICE OF A PERSON

America has a kind of civic religion based on both the idea of freedom and justice and on the sanctity of private property. So what do you do when the natural rights of the enslaved infringe on the natural right of slave owners to keep their property safe from seizure? That was the dilemma no one had been able to solve. It wasn't a dilemma for the abolitionists. To them it was clear: slavery was morally wrong. It would have to go. (They didn't own slaves, so it wasn't their own property they were talking about.) There were those in both North and South who wanted to gradually free the slaves and even pay the slave owners—but most abolitionists wanted to do away with slavery at once. They didn't think anyone should be paid for owning someone else. (As it turned out, it would have been cheaper to pay the slave owners than to go to war.)

Frederick Douglass

What was it like to be a slave? Few white Americans—especially in the North—had any idea. But in 1841, a tall, handsome man, a runaway slave whose name was Frederick Douglass, stood up at an abolitionist meeting on Nantucket Isand. "I felt strongly moved to speak," Douglass wrote later. But he hesitated; his legs shook. "The truth was, I felt myself a slave, and the idea of speaking to white people weighed me down." Yet he found the courage to speak out. Frederick Douglass just told his own story: how he had lived and what he had seen. When he started an abolitionist newspaper, *The North Star*, whites and blacks subscribed. Then he wrote a book and called it *Narrative of the Life of Frederick Douglass, an American Slave*. Here is an excerpt:

I never saw my mother … more than four or five times in my life…. She made her journeys to see me in the night, travelling the whole distance on foot [twelve miles], after the performance of her day's work. She was a field hand, and a whipping is the penalty of not being in the field at sunrise…. I do not recollect of ever seeing my mother by the light of day. She was with me in the night. She would lie down with me, and get me to sleep, but long before I waked she was gone…. She died when I was about seven…. I was not allowed to be present during her illness, at her death, or burial.

Young Frederick was sent to Baltimore to be a companion to a little white boy. For a slave, that was a lucky break. That chance, he said, "opened the gateway to all my subsequent prosperity." His new mistress was young and kindly. She began to teach the eager boy to read—until her husband saw her doing it and ordered her to stop. Reading, said the master, "would forever unfit him to be a slave." It was too late for Frederick. He'd been bitten by the learning bug. He became determined to learn to read and to write, too. He traded bread with white boys for reading lessons. But then he was sent away to a cruel

freedom while slavery exists in the land." Thomas Jefferson's grandson presented Jefferson's plan for gradual emancipation to the Virginia General Assembly. It suggested that slave owners be paid for their slaves. The legislators argued freedom versus slavery, and came close to freeing the slaves (the vote was 73 to 82). They wouldn't get another chance to do it. Nat Turner was hanged, but he wasn't finished. His small rebellion fomented a national debate on slavery and helped kindle the abolitionist movement.

Southern white slaveholders were now scared of slave uprisings. Toussaint L'Ouverture's rebellion had left 60,000 people dead. New laws, called black codes, made life even more difficult for slaves.

new master, beaten with a whip until he was bloody and scarred, and not given enough to eat. He was sent into the fields to work long hours. He saw all the terrible things than can happen when one person has complete power over another. "But for the hope of being free," Douglass wrote later, "I have no doubt but that I should have killed myself."

Frederick Douglass kept repeating this simple truth: Justice to the Negro is safety to the nation. He also said, "You may rely on me as one who will never desert the cause of the poor, no matter whether black or white." He never did. He fought to get the vote for blacks and for women; he spoke out against mistreatment of Chinese immigrants and American Indians; he worked for better schools for all. Always he had the courage to stand up for his beliefs—well, not always; once it took all his strength to sit for those beliefs. He was in a railroad car and was asked to leave because he was black. He wouldn't budge. Some white men tried to make him go. Douglass held on while they pulled the seat out of the floor of the car. He kept his seat.

"People in general will say they like colored men as well as any other, but in their proper place. They assign us that place; they don't let us do it ourselves nor will they allow us a voice in the decision. They will not allow that we have a head to think, and a heart to feel and a soul to aspire.... That's the way we are liked. You degrade us, and then ask why we are degraded—you shut our mouths and then ask why we don't speak—you close your colleges and seminaries against us, and then ask why we don't know more."

—Frederick Douglass

Laws could have been passed to prevent the selling of children and the separating of husbands and wives. They were not. Laws could have been passed to make sexual abuse of slaves a crime. They were not. Those who beat or murdered blacks could have been brought to trial. They were not. After 1831, slavery became more and more brutal. The revolutionary generation had been clear about it—they knew slavery was wrong, but they didn't know how to get rid of it. The generations that followed saw what they dubbed their "peculiar institution" differently. They began to believe it was morally right and God-given. It wasn't hard to do that. If the slaves could be seen as truly different—and inferior—then it seemed clear that it was ordained that they be enslaved. It was easy to make them seem inferior; just keep them from schools, learning, and equal opportunity. Slave laws in the South grew more and more restrictive. Southern states passed laws saying it was a crime to teach black people to read and write. One white woman in Norfolk, Virginia, who taught some free blacks in her home, was arrested and spent a month in jail. The black codes made it clear: slaves were property, not people.

Only about one fourth of the 1.55 million white families in the South owned slaves. Of the slave owners, just one in seven had more than ten slaves. Some Southerners were mountain folk who hardly knew any black people. The big plantation owners—who had hundreds of slaves—were few in number. But they dominated the South and controlled the legislatures. Most were sure that whites were superior—and they convinced others. It was that same racism that made the settlers treat Indians so cruelly. And it made those blacks who were free much less than full citizens. The whole idea of races was one that was just being considered in intellectual circles, and there was much disagreement. (1831 was the year Charles Darwin first boarded the *Beagle* on his historic voyage.) Believing that blacks were inferior—a kind of subhuman—Senator Albert Gallatin Brown of Mississippi said slavery was "a blessing for the slave, and a blessing to the master." If the world *liberty* was to be bandied about incessantly, as it then was, then racial inferiority was a necessity. It gave white supremacy reason. For some, it explained slavery in the land of the free.

In 1820, Missouri asked to enter the Union as a slave state. Northerners were alarmed. As long as Congress was divided evenly between slave states and free states, there was stability in Congress. If Missouri became a state, the North would be outvoted. What might happen next? Suppose Congress passed a law allowing slavery in all the states! Northern congressmen couldn't risk that. Speaker of the House Henry Clay, soon to be known as "the Great Compromiser," found a solution. Maine was carved from Massachusetts and made into a free state. That kept the balance of free

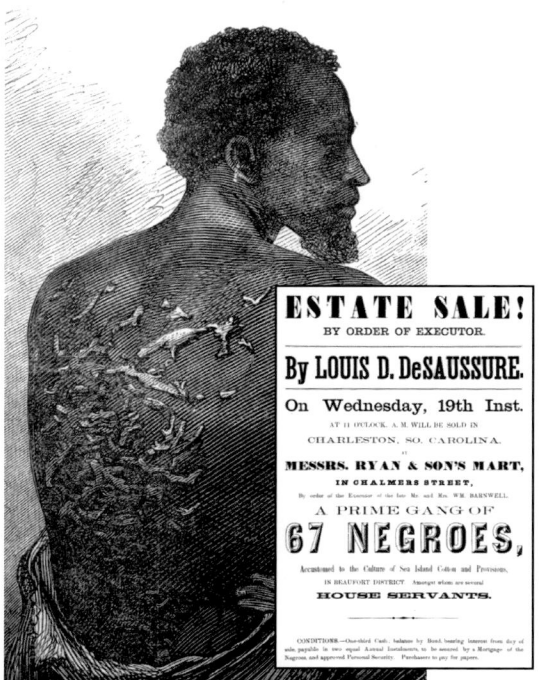

This slave, Gordon, escaped from a Mississippi plantation; he said he'd received his scars from his master "Christmas Day last." Inset: A notice of a slave sale. Estate sales like this (when an owner died) could be especially painful for families, who might be sold in lots (together) or "separate"—i.e., broken up.

and slave states. That action was called the Missouri Compromise. The compromise also said that the rest of the Louisiana Purchase territory north of Missouri's southern border (except for Missouri) was to remain free. The Missouri Compromise managed to cool some of the anger between North and South. Meanwhile, Canada, with less of an economic stake in slavery, abolished the practice. In 1826, when he was John Quincy Adams's secretary of state, Henry Clay asked that blacks who had run away to Canada be returned. The Canadian government said, "It is utterly impossible."

ABOLITION!

William Lloyd Garrison's hard-drinking sailor father abandoned his family, leaving his wife, Fanny, to raise three children on a housekeeper's earnings. Fanny Garrison got her son an apprenticeship with a newspaper publisher; she also gave him the intensity of her Baptist belief. After his apprenticeship ended, Garrison edited a series of newspapers in Vermont and Massachusetts, and never lasted long at any of them. His uncompromising attacks on politics and politicians won him few friends. And then he moved to Baltimore and got lucky—he landed in jail. It changed his life.

Garrison had written an editorial calling a slave trader a "murderer." He was sued for libel, convicted, and hauled off to jail. It was a transforming experience. In jail he got to know blacks and listen to a slave auction. For forty-nine days Garrison wrote editorials from his prison cell demanding "immediate emancipation" of all slaves. The abolition movement had been timid; Garrison gave it a strong voice.

On January 1, 1831, Garrison began publishing *The Liberator,* soon to be the leading abolitionist newspaper. In the first issue he wrote these words:

> *I do not wish to think, or speak, or write with moderation. No! No! Tell a man whose house is on fire, to give a moderate alarm ... but urge me not to use moderation in a cause like the present. I am in earnest—I will not equivocate—I will not excuse—I will not retreat a single inch—AND I WILL BE HEARD.*

The next year Garrison helped found

The Liberator's motto was "Our country is the world—our countrymen are Mankind." William Lloyd Garrison was so hated in the South that the state of Georgia offered a $5,000 reward for his arrest. In 1854 he publicly burned a copy of the Constitution to protest its failure to forbid slavery.

> **CAUTION!!**
> **COLORED PEOPLE**
> OF BOSTON, ONE & ALL,
> You are hereby respectfully CAUTIONED and advised, to avoid conversing with the
> **Watchmen and Police Officers of Boston,**
> For since the recent ORDER OF THE MAYOR & ALDERMEN, they are empowered to act as
> **KIDNAPPERS**
> AND
> **Slave Catchers,**
> And they have already been actually employed in KIDNAPPING, CATCHING, AND KEEPING SLAVES. Therefore, if you value your LIBERTY, and the *Welfare of the Fugitives* among you, *Shun* them in every possible manner, as so many *HOUNDS* on the track of the most unfortunate of your race.
> **Keep a Sharp Look Out for KIDNAPPERS, and have TOP EYE open.**
> APRIL 24, 1851.

After 1850 and the passing of the Fugitive Slave Act—which forced Northerners to return runaway slaves to their owners—abolitionists put out notices like this one, reminding free blacks that they and those they knew might also be in danger.

the New England Anti-Slavery Society. It attacked racism head on. African colonization, which many (including James Madison) had thought of as an answer to the "black problem," was denounced as racist. (That wasn't the terminology then, but it was the concept.) Garrison demanded nothing less than complete equality for blacks, socially and educationally. Equality is equality, and, for Garrison, there could be no compromises. When the Quaker abolitionist Prudence Crandall opened an integrated academy for women, he supported her. It only added to the outrage of his critics.

It was a time of religious revivalism. Evangelical Christians became the mainstay of the abolitionist movement. Holding a vision of human perfectibility, believing in the urgency of moral reform, and in the importance of fighting sin, they were unbending. Gerrit Smith, a wealthy upstate NewYorker with a long list of benevolent activities, was one of them. A Presbyterian, Smith thought politics should be used to bring about an "evangelical moral revolution."

The abolitionists were brilliant propagandists. They printed newspapers, pamphlets and books that soon filled the postman's backpack. Philanthropists like Gerrit Smith paid the bills. Former slaves began to speak out, tell their stories, and see them printed. Southerners talked of their "benevolent institution." But tales of beatings and sexual abuse—which were widely circulated—hardly seemed benevolent. Abolitionist petitions to end slavery in the District of Columbia flooded Congress. The abolitionists got angrier and angrier. Some were so outraged by slavery that they suggested New England secede from the Union and form a separate country. The anger was returned. Abolitionist presses were burned; one abolitionist editor was murdered; mail was destroyed, undelivered. Congress instituted a "gag rule," blocking consideration of abolitionist petitions.

To those who owned slaves, or to those (North and South) just content with life as it was, the abolitionists were religious zealots and meddling busybodies. It was Southerners' lives that would be changed if slavery were abolished. They didn't think it was the Yankees' business, and they said so. They didn't want to be told they were sinners. It was their liberty and property that were being threatened by outsiders (few of them worried about black people's liberty and property).

Meanwhile, abolitionists like Garrison were insisting not only that African-Americans be freed, but that they have full rights as citizens. They were extending the American idea of freedom. Race was not to be an issue in the United States, they said. And while they were at it, they said, women hould have equal rights, and drinking was sinful and should be outlawed. The abolitionists believed passionately in American democracy and in the perfectibility of society. They were willing to wage a holy war for the souls of the enslaved. Their intensity scared away the less committed. "Demagogues," "religious fanatics," was the way they were often described. By 1840 there were said to be about 2,000 abolitionist societies in the North. Few were fanatics, but they were very determined.

SAVE THE UNION

"A dissolution of the Union is inevitable.... Slavery will be the medium & great agent for rescuing and recovering to freedom and civilization all the vast tracts of Texas, Mexico &c.... [and that] secures the perpetuation of slavery for the next thousand years," said South Carolinian W. Gilmore Simms in a letter to his friend James Henry Hammond on April 2, 1847. Jefferson Davis, of Mississippi, was more cautious. That same year he wrote, "That it might be necessary to unite as southern

This Massachusetts anti-slavery poster ran the text of the Fugitive Slave Act and questioned the law's constitutionality and its un-Christian character—"that the Cardinal Virtues of Christianity shall be considered … as CRIMES."

"I shall know but one country. The ends I aim at shall be my country's, my God's, and Truth's," said Daniel Webster (shown at left giving his final oration to the Senate). "I was born an American; I will live an American; I shall die an American."

men, and to dissolve the ties which have connected us to the northern Democracy, the position recently assumed in a majority of the non-slaveholding states has led me to fear." The country is being pulled apart—everyone can see that. Each time a new state enters the Union, the balance in Congress between North and South is threatened. California's constitution prohibits slavery. If California enters the Union, free states will outnumber slave states. The free states might pass a law outlawing slavery. Before that happens, says John Calhoun, the South would rather secede-leave the Union. Calhoun has been a powerful voice in politics since he served as Andrew Jackson's vice president. He is slavery's spokesman. "Ours, sir, is the government of the white race," he says. Now an old man, he is more vehement than ever. Calhoun calls slavery a "positive good"—good for slaves and good for masters. He is part of a triumvirate that has dominated Congress for more than a decade: Calhoun, Henry Clay, and Daniel Webster. Few legislatures have seen their like.

Calhoun has convinced many, but he hasn't convinced Henry Clay. Clay, now a senator, is a slave owner who has worked for gradual emancipation. "All legislation, all government, all society, is formed upon the principle of mutual concession, politeness, comity, courtesy; upon these, everything is based," says the much loved Kentuckian, who is working on another compromise. California is to be admitted to the Union as a free state—but, to mollify Calhoun, a fugitive slave law will make it illegal for anyone to refuse to return runaway slaves. (In 1850, there are about 30,000 fugitives in the North-worth about $15 million.) That law still isn't enough for Calhoun. The North must "cease the agitation on the slave question." If the abolitionists are not silenced, he says, "Let the states agree to separate." Calhoun dies while debate over the Compromise of 1850 rages.

It is now the turn of eloquent Senator Daniel Webster of Massachusetts. He will give his last Senate oration, and there isn't an empty seat in the chamber. "I wish to speak today, not as a Massachusetts man, nor as a Northern man, but as an

With his Kansas-Nebraska bill, Stephen Douglas (far left) pitted himself against those opposed to letting slavery into the territories. "The spirit of '76 and the spirit of Nebraska," said Abraham Lincoln (lef), "are utter antagonisms."

American," he says.. "I speak today for the preservation of the Union. Hear my cause." Webster has been Henry Clay's opponent and the abolitionists' darling—now he is agreeing with Clay! He will go along with a fugitive slave law. The abolitionists are horrified. The law makes all Americans a party to slavery. They must agree to return runaway slaves or be lawbreakers. But Webster will do almost anything to save the Union.

There can be no such thing as a peaceable secession…. Is the great Constitution under which we live, covering this whole country; is it to be thawed and melted away by secession, as the snows on the mountain melt under the influence of a vernal sun—disappear almost unobserved and run off? No sir! No sir! I will not state what might produce the disruption of the Union; but, sir, I see it as plainly as I see the sun in heaven. What that disruption must produce [is] … such a war as I will not describe.

Webster knows that if the South secedes now, the North will not be able to stop it. There will be two nations—one slave, one free—and perhaps war between them. His speech does what it is meant to do. It holds the Union together. Congress votes to accept Henry Clay's compromise. The real problem is that no one knows how to end slavery, and still hold North and South together.

A Little Giant

Senator Stephen A. Douglas of Illinois is known as the Little Giant. Just over five feet tall, he is so full of energy he is also called "a steam engine in breeches." His suits are well tailored, his friends influential. In 1854, in part to benefit himself as a western landowner, Douglas writes a bill that divides the Indian territory west of Missouri, Iowa, and Minnesota (which was guaranteed to the Indians "as long as grass shall grow and water shall run") into two new regions: Kansas and Nebraska (both are much bigger than today's states with those names). Called the Kansas-Nebraska bill, it ignores the ban

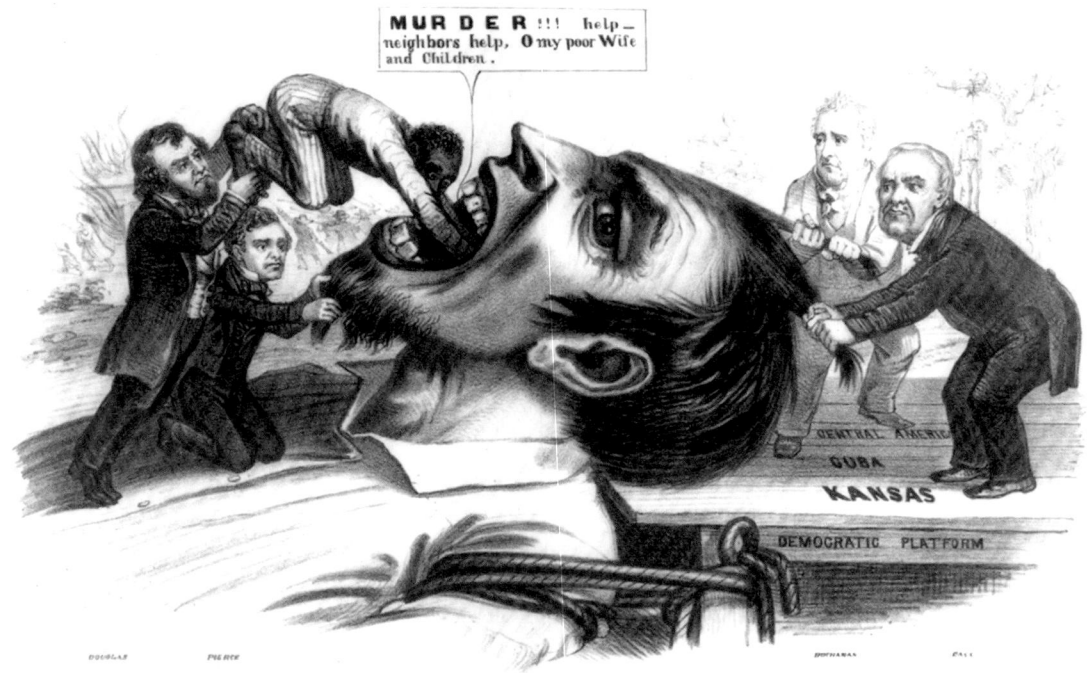

In this 1858 antislavery cartoon, President James Buchanan and former president Franklin Pierce hold down an antislavery Kansas settler while Stephen Douglas tries to shove a helpless slave down his throat

on slavery in those territories that was part of the Missouri Compromise. Instead, it will be left to the free residents of each territory to decide for themselves whether or not to have slaves. Douglas calls it "popular sovereignty."

Among those dismayed by the bill is an Illinois lawyer named Abraham Lincoln."It is wrong, wrong in its effect, letting slavery into Kansas and Nebraska," he says. The growing conflict now includes a new issue: slavery in the western territories. Douglas has completely misjudged most Northerners' feelings. Henry Clay's 1820 Missouri Compromise has kept the peace between North and South for thirty-four years. The Founders hadn't approved of slavery; they looked forward to the end of the slave trade; they prohibited slavery in the Northwest Territory; they talked about gradual emancipation. The Kansas-Nebraska Act is a break with that tradition. If the Missouri Compromise is abandoned, what will be next? It seems clear: some slave owners want to make the whole nation accept slavery. Many Northerners who hadn't agreed with abolitionist tactics now join their ranks. Fiery speeches denounce the Kansas-Nebraska Act. One congressman calls it an "atrocious crime"; another says it is a "gross violation of a sacred pledge." The turmoil helps create a new political party,: the Republican party—out of the Whigs (the party of John Quincy Adams and Henry Clay). That Illinois lawyer, Abraham Lincoln, becomes a Republican. This is what he has to say about the Kansas-Nebraska Act in a speech at Peoria, Illinois, a few years later:

> *The spirit of '76 and the spirit of Nebraska, are utter antagonisms.... Little by little... we have been giving up the old for the new faith.... we began declaring that all men are created equal; but now from that beginning we have run down to the other declaration, that for some men to enslave others is a "sacred right of self-government." These principles cannot stand together. ... Let us readopt the Declaration of Independence.... If we do this we shall not only have saved the Union; but we shall have so saved it, as to make, and to keep it, forever worthy of saving.*

An Infamous Decision

It is March 4, 1857. James Buchanan has been elected president, and the Supreme Court is considering a very important case—a case that deals with slavery. Buchanan knows though it is improper that he does—what the court's decision will be. So he stands before the nation on this inaugural day and says that slavery is a question that "belongs to the Supreme Court of the United States, before whom it is now pending, and will, it is understood, be speedily and finally settled."

The slavery issue finally settled-how wonderful that would be! The case, *Dred Scott* v. *Sandford,* deals with a slave living in Missouri, a slave state. That slave, Dred Scott, lived for several years in Wisconsin, a territory, not yet a state. Does his residence in Wisconsin territory (now Minnesota) make him a free man? There is legal precedent in Missouri saying that it does.

Scott sues his owner, Irene Emerson, for his freedom and that of his wife. It seems a clear case, but the legal papers are filed incorrectly and the case is set aside—for three years. Meanwhile, Scott and his wife have been hired out. Their salaries are held by the sheriff. Do they go free and get their earnings? Does Irene Emerson get them? She is getting married and has other things on her mind; she hands her affairs to her brother, John Sanford (the court misspells the name of the case). Because he is a New Yorker, the case goes to a federal court and then to the Supreme Court. (Mrs. Emerson's new husband is an abolitionist. When he learns what has happened he tries to free Scott, but he can't while the matter is in litigation.)

Seventy-nine-year-old Roger Taney is chief justice, appointed by Andrew Jackson to replace the renowned John Marshall.

Left, an anti-abolitionist cartoon suggesting that all politicians danced to those who played the slavery litigation tune. But in the end power remained in the establishment's hands. Right, Dred Scott; he could not read or write, yet he kept going through eleven years of legal appeals.

Taney is well respected. So is the court. Two days after Buchanan's inauguration, the Supreme Court issues its decision. All nine justices write opinions, so different are their views. This is what Chief Justice Taney has to say in his majority opinion in the case of *Dred Scott* v. *Sandford*:

> The question before us is, whether Negroes compose a portion of the American people and are constituent members of this sovereignty. We think they are not. On the contrary, they are a subordinate and inferior class of beings, who have been subjugated by the dominant race. They can therefore claim none of the rights and privileges which the Constitution provides for citizens of the United States.

"An inferior class of beings … subjugated by the dominant race…. none of the rights and privileges which the Constitution provides." It couldn't have been stated more clearly: slaves are property, and the Fifth Amendment protects property. Taney says that the Missouri Compromise, which prohibits slavery in the territories north of latitude 36° 30′, is unconstitutional. Because of that, Wisconsin wasn't free territory when Dred Scott lived there. Furthermore, says the court, blacks have no right to citizenship. Even free blacks have "no rights which the white man was bound to respect; and that the Negro might justly and lawfully be reduced to slavery for his benefit." In Springfield, Illinois, Abraham Lincoln says, "We think the decision is erroneous." He also says slavery is "an unqualified evil to the Negro, the white man, and the State."

President Buchanan thought this decision would settle the slavery question! What it settles is the question of war. It makes war almost certain.

THE FREEDOM TRAIN

John Price was a slave in Kentucky. We don't know much about him, but we do know he must have hated being a slave. He was willing to risk his life to run away. He got a chance to do it one cold winter when the wide Ohio River froze over. Price and two friends-a woman named Dinah and a man named Frank-decided to cross the river. In the dark of night they took two of their master's horses and headed out onto the slick ice. When they got to the Ohio side of the river there was no way to get onto the land. The riverbanks were too steep, and the horses kept slipping. Soon the three runaways feared they might freeze to death. Then, as morning came, they saw where a road cut through the hilly bank. They were out of Kentucky—a slave state—and had made it to the free state of Ohio.

But that doesn't mean that they are free. According to the Fugitive Slave Law, anyone who finds them has to send them back to their owners, or face jail, be fined, or both. John, Dinah, and Frank are lucky: the first person they meet is a Quaker who will not obey that law. He is willing to risk a jail sentence. He feeds them and gives them a place to rest. Then he sends them off on the Underground Railroad.

The fugitives travel at night, following the North Star (for which Frederick Douglass's abolitionist newspaper is named). John Price makes it to Oberlin, an abolitionist town in northern Ohio. There he stops and finds work as a laborer. One day, a boy named Shakespeare Boynton tells Price someone has a job for him. Shakespeare, who has been

In Charles Vebber's influential painting *The Underground Railroad*, the Quaker abolitionists Levi and Catherine Coffin welcome runaway slaves to their home outside Cincinnati—across the river from slave state Kentucky. Coffin helped finance the Railroads work through a store that sold goods made only by freed slaves.

paid to lie to Price, leads him to some slave catchers—sent from Kentucky.

Price is handcuffed and put in a wagon. His captors head to a nearby town. On the way, their horse and wagon pass two Oberlin men. Price shouts out, "Help, help!" The men rush to Oberlin and tell others what they have seen. Meanwhile, Price's captors take him to a hotel to wait for the next train south. Soon the street in front of the hotel is filled with angry people from Oberlin. Price is recaptured and put on a train heading for Canada. It is September of 1858, and he is not heard of again. But that isn't the end of his story. The men who freed Price have broken the Fugitive Slave Law. The rescue in Oberlin is the talk of the nation. Those who believe in slavery see it as a test case. Will the

Harriet, Also Known as Moses

Harriet Tubman was born a slave on Maryland's Eastern Shore, in about 1820, but there was none of the spirit of an enslaved person in her. She was tiny—just five feet tall—but stronger than most men. She could lift great weights, withstand cold and heat, chop down big trees, and go without food when necessary. She had been trained, in childhood, to take abuse. That was part of what it meant to be a slave. She put that training to good use. When she was still very young and small, she was sent to work in the fields, where she worked hard. No one ever taught her to read and write, but she learned to listen and to remember, and she soon had an unusual memory. She listened to the slaves who whispered about freedom. She learned that a few slaves were freed by their masters. She learned that others ran away north, and found freedom. She learned that if a slave tried to escape and was caught, he would be whipped, branded, and sold. He would be sold far south, to cotton plantations where life was even harder for blacks than it was in Maryland and there was little chance of escape.

Harriet also learned that some people—white and black—helped slaves to escape. They were part of an Underground Railroad. Harriet thought it was a real railroad when she first heard of it. It was actually a secret way of travel, with conductors and stations and passengers. The passengers were enslaved black people.

Harriet Tubman

government enforce the Fugitive Slave Law, they ask? The people who are against slavery also see it as a test case. Will the government send the leading citizens of a community to jail for helping someone become free? An editorial in the *Ohio State Journal,* an abolitionist paper, says:

> It is not so much a violation of the Fugitive Slave Law which is to be punished by the United States as the anti-slavery sentiment. That is the thing.... It is freedom of thought which must be crushed out.

The accused men of Oberlin are tried, convicted of violating the Fugitive Slave Law, and fined. It happens, though, that they are not the only ones who have broken the law. John Price was not taken legally.

The conductors—both blacks and whites—helped them along the way to freedom. The stations were places where people could be trusted to feed and house the runaways. Some of those places were houses with special hidden rooms; some were barns; some were even riverboats. But no one who escaped ever came back. No one really knew what became of them. Harriet would be different: she would escape and she would come back. But before that, something happened to her. She was hit in the forehead by a lead weight thrown by an overseer. For months she lay unconscious. Everyone thought she would die. For the rest of her life she had fainting spells and times when she would just fall asleep and no one could wake her.

So she was sent to work with her father, who taught her the ways of the woods. He taught her to walk softly, as the Native Americans did. He showed her the plants she could eat, and the ones that were poisonous. Then she met a white woman who said she could help her. Harriet guessed that the woman was part of the Underground Railroad.

After she escaped north, to freedom, she came back and got her brothers and sisters and her parents. It took many trips. And she didn't stop with her family. She became the most famous conductor on the Underground Railroad. She is said to have led 300 African-Americans to freedom. Southerners like South Carolina's Senator John Calhoun kept saying that slaves were well treated and loved their masters and mistresses. But people who are well treated don't risk everything—sometimes their lives—to run away. Those who escaped on the Underground Railroad told of children being taken from their parents; they showed scars from whippings; they told of abuses that made many Northerners change their minds about slavery. Harriet Tubman became the most wanted runaway in the nation.

The abolitionist poster on the right tells the story of fugitive slave Anthony Burns, arrested in Boston in 1854. On June 2, as Burns was put on a boat heading south, 1,000 police had to guard him from outraged Bostonians howling "Shame, shame!" His capture and return to slavery cost the government almost $100,000.

"A house divided against itself cannot stand. I believe this government cannot endure permanently half slave and half free. I do not expect the Union to be dissolved—I do not expect the house to fall—but I do expect it will cease to be divided. It will become all one thing, or all the other."
—Abraham Lincoln, quoting from the Gospel of St. Mark at the Republican convention in Springfield, Illinois, July 17, 1858

The slave catchers had to show the proper papers. That wasn't done. The Oberlin lawyers have the catchers arrested and jailed. Jail is not fun for slave catchers in an abolitionist town. They agree to drop their case if the Oberlin men do the same thing. So, finally, it is over. Except, of course, that it isn't at all. The issue of slavery hasn't been solved. The conflict is accelerating.

Big Debates

In 1858, Abraham Lincoln is picked by the newly formed Republican party to run for the U.S. Senate in Illinois. His opponent is the Little Giant himself, Stephen Douglas. They couldn't be more different from each other. Born in a dirt-floored Kentucky cabin, Lincoln grows up in Indiana and Illinois, where he educates himself to become a lawyer. He is friendly, he is honest, and he has a deep hatred of slavery. In the summer of 1858 Abraham Lincoln and Stephen Douglas

It's true that Lincoln was about a foot taller than Douglas, but this cartoonist has definitely exaggerated the difference in their height. Behind the fence, a slave urges on Lincoln in the 1860 presidential race.

get on a train and travel across Illinois. Douglas has a private railroad car. Lincoln rides coach. They speak to large crowds at train stops and in meeting halls. At seven stops they appear together and debate issues. They are called the Lincoln-Douglas debates, and no political contest in American history has ever been as impressive.

Douglas talks about popular sovereignty, the right of the people to govern themselves. He says that means the right of white voters to decide if they want to have slaves. "I hold that the signers of the Declaration of Independence had no reference to Negroes at all when they declared all men to be created equal," he says. "They did not mean the Negro, nor the savage Indians, nor the Fiji islanders, nor any other barbarous race. They were speaking of white men."

Lincoln says Douglas is hiding from the real issue—slavery itself. "The doctrine of self-government is right, absolutely and eternally right," says Lincoln, but that is not the point. "When the white man governs himself, that is self-government; but when he governs himself and also governs another man, that is more than self-government; that is despotism." Lincoln puts the issue in words that everyone can understand. He has none of the anger of the abolitionists; he can see both sides. He was born in a slave state; his wife is a Southerner; but he believes slavery is wrong, and says so.

> *Our fathers left slavery in the course of ultimate extinction. Judge Douglas and his friends wish it to become national and perpetual. He is blowing out the moral lights around us! I want every man to have a chance—and I believe a black man is entitled to it.*

In this 1861 antisecession cartoon, some of the eggs in the eagle's nest (the Union) are a nasty brown or green; they are the Southern states, gone bad and hatching into vipers, alligators, and other loathsome beasts.

Stephen Douglas is elected senator from Illinois. But the Lincoln-Douglas debates have made the tall, gangling country lawyer known across the land.

Splitting Apart

There is civil war in Kansas. Those who believe in slavery are killing those who do not—and vice versa. It is called "Bleeding Kansas," and the nation should be taking warning. In May 1856, a tall, fierce-eyed, Bible-quoting white man and some of his followers brutally murder five proslavery Kansans. The tall man is named John Brown, and he believes he is acting for God. He leaves war-torn Kansas and grows a bushy white beard. It is a disguise; he intends to start a revolution. He expects slaves to rise up and join him. Three years later, on a dark, rainy night, he and twenty-one others put rifles over their shoulders and march quietly into the pretty little town of Harpers Ferry in Virginia. It is at a strategic spot: a gap in the mountains where two rivers, the Potomac and the Shenandoah, come together. Brown plans a guerrilla war, and the mountain setting seems right. A railroad runs through the town. Even more important, Harpers Ferry is the site of a government arsenal and armory. Guns are made and stored there. Brown and his men easily capture the armory.

But the slaves who John Brown said would rise up and join him never come. He has kept all his plans a great secret. Brown is caught and brought to trial. He pleads not guilty to treason and murder. The fiery abolitionist has he skills of a brilliant actor, and, thanks to the telegraph, his captors give him a worldwide audience. Reporters write of his every word and action, and Brown puts on a performance that few will forget. Often he lies, but he knows how to make people believe in him, and there is truth in the cause he argues.

> *I deny everything but … a design on my part to free slaves.… Had I interfered in the manner I admit … in behalf of the rich, the powerful, the intelligent, the so-called great … every man in this court would have deemed it an act worthy of reward rather than punishment.*

The abolitionists say the trial isn't fair. Brown becomes their martyr hero. Southerners are outraged. They see Brown as a terrorist and are scared of a slave uprising. They want John Brown convicted-quickly. They get their wish. Brown sits on his black walnut coffin in a furniture wagon, and rides to his death. "This is a beautiful country," he tells the driver. Then he gets down from his coffin, holding his head high, and mounts the steps of the gallows. He hands his jailer a slip of paper. It says: *I John Brown am now quite certain that the crimes of this guilty land will never be purged away, but with blood.* Then Brown sticks his head in a noose made of South Carolina cotton.

His ghost will soon haunt both North and South, though only a few people are able to talk of John Brown with any sense. One of them is Abraham Lincoln, who says, "Old John Brown has been executed for treason against a state. We cannot object, even though he agreed with us in thinking slavery wrong. That cannot excuse violence, bloodshed, and treason." That winter, Lincoln, who is now campaigning for president against Stephen Douglas, says:

> *One-sixth of the population of the United States are slaves, looked upon as property, as nothing but property. The cash value of these slaves, at a moderate estimate, is two billion dollars. This amount of property value has a vast influence on the minds of its owners, very naturally. The same amount of property would have an equal influence upon us if owned in the North. Human nature is the same—people at the South are the same as those at the North, barring the difference in circumstances.*

John Brown, right (pre-beard) and below, in one of the hagiographic illustrations of his last moments, perpetuating legends such as the one that said he kissed a slave child on his way to the scaffold. "You may dispose of me very easily," he said in his final moments. "But this question is still to be settled—this negro question … the end of that is not yet."

And so it comes to that. Slaves represent money, and few people will give up their wealth without a fight. Americans must choose. They can't have a free nation where some people are owned by others. The moral issue won't go away. It is no longer just a paradox. It is hypocrisy. It is mean-spirited. It is evil.

In 1860 Abraham Lincoln is elected president of the United States. Before he even takes office, states begin to leave the Union. South Carolina is first to secede. Mississippi, one of the richest states in the nation, follows eagerly. So do Florida, Alabama, Georgia, Louisiana, and Texas. Virginia, Arkansas, North Carolina, and Tennessee hesitate until President Lincoln calls for volunteers to fight in the South. That decides it for them. They will not fight their sister states. These eleven form the Confederate States of America. Maryland, Delaware, Kentucky, and Missouri—slave states on the border between North and South—remain, tentatively, in the Union.

Alexander Stephens, who will become vice president of the Confederacy, says what everyone is now thinking. "All efforts to save the Union will be unavailing. The truth is our leaders and public men do not desire to continue it on any terms." In February 1861, Jefferson Davis of Mississippi is elected president of the CSA. "All we ask is to be left alone," he says at his inauguration.

People on both sides claim they aren't fighting over slavery. But they are fooling themselves. There would be no war if there were no slavery. There are other issues: the Southerners—now "Rebels"—believe in "states' rights." They think any state should have the right to pull out of the

Dramatic portrayals of scenes by artists, like this Currier & Ives print of the 1861 bombardment of Fort Sumter that began the war, weren't very realistic. Northerners especially were made far more aware of the bloodshed by the battlefront photographs of Matthew Brady and Alexander Gardner.

Union, and that it is tyranny to keep them in against their wishes. They say they are doing the same thing George Washington and the other revolutionaries did against King George: fighting for their freedom. But it is white freedom they are fighting for, and the North won't let them do it. Revolution is only right, says President Lincoln, "for a morally justified cause." The South has no just cause. So, said Lincoln, secession is "simply a wicked exercise of political power."

The American nation is still an experiment. Will a people's government survive? Lincoln says Americans need to prove "that popular government is not an absurdity." Then he adds, "We must settle this question now, whether in a free government the minority have the right to break up the government whenever they choose."

Abolitionists scream for him to free the slaves—at once. But to win a war, Lincoln says, he needs to hold on to the slave states that border the South. If he frees the slaves in the border states, loses the war, and destroys the Union, he won't help the slaves or anyone else. He offers hope that "the weights [will] be lifted from the shoulders of all men, and that all [will] have an equal chance." But he will not start a war. "The government will not use force unless force is used against it," he says. In April 1861, young Theodore Upson is working in a cornfield when he hears the news: "Father and I were husking out ... corn ... when William Corry came across the field. He was excited and said, 'Jonathan, the Rebels have fired upon Fort Sumter.' Father got white, and couldn't say a word."

Fort Sumter is a United States government fort in the harbor at Charleston, South Carolina. Those shots are intended as an act of war. One eyewitness writes, "A perfect sheet of flame flashed out, a deafening roar, a rumbling, deadening sound, and the war was on."

During the Revolutionary War, most fighting was eyeball to eyeball, and many deaths were from bayonet wounds. But by 1860, the new rifled muskets and even newer breechloading rifles such as the Sharps carbine or Spencer repeater could kill a man up to half a mile away. Their accuracy made hand-to-hand bayonet fighting—as at Chattanooga (above), the November 1863 battle that secured one of the Union army's most important supply bases in the South—quite rare.

PART 6

A WAR TO END SLAVERY

It was going to be a heroic adventure. Both sides thought it a fight for freedom. In North and South, most people believed the war would last a few months. Southerners liked the idea of soldiering. It seemed bold and brave. Besides, they were sure the Yankees were all cowards. Just wait until they met on the battlefield, they boasted to their wives and girlfriends as they marched off in their handsome gray uniforms. The Northern men were just as confident. One big battle, they said, and the war would be over. They were sure the Southern soldiers were lazy. Why, without their slaves they wouldn't be able to do a thing. They'd run for the hills at the first shots—or so the Northerners boasted to their wives and girlfriends as they marched off in their handsome blue uniforms.

It turned out to be the worst war in American history. It was called the Civil War, but there was nothing civil about it. More than 620,000 Americans died; cities were destroyed, farms burned, and homes leveled. On one bloody day at a place called Antietam, more men were killed than on any other day in our history. The total deaths were almost as many in all of our other wars combined.

It was more than a war that split the nation. It was a war that split families. Major Clifton Prentiss, Union army, and his younger brother, William, Confederate army, fought and died in the same battle at Petersburg, Virginia. Four of President Abraham Lincoln's brothers-in-law fought for the Confederacy; three died for it. Three grandsons of Henry Clay fought for the Union, four for the Confederacy. In one battle, Confederate cavalry general J.E.B. Stuart was chased by Union cavalry general Phillip St. George Cooke, who

A Southern paper announces secession.

Drilling the 26th New York infantry. Union private Oliver Norton wrote a friend: "The first thing in the morning is drill, then drill, then drill again. Then drill, drill, drill, a little more drill. Then drill, and lastly, drill." Left, top to bottom: two Union soldiers, also brothers; a Rebel soldier from North Carolina; a private in a Georgia regiment, Edwin Jennison. He was killed in 1862 at Malvern Hill, Virginia, aged sixteen.

was Stuart's father-in-law. (General Stuart said General Cooke would regret being a Union man "but once, and that will be continuously.") Most men went to war for their region. But some believed in the cause of the other part of the nation and fought for those beliefs. Admiral David Farragut was a naval commander on the side of the North, though he was from Alabama. Samuel P. Lee, a cousin of Confederate general Robert E. Lee, commanded the Union naval forces on the James River. Generals Winfield Scott and George H. Thomas, both Virginians, fought for the Union.

Did they hate each other, Northerners and Southerners? Often they thought they did, but when they got to know each other it wasn't so. It wasn't unusual for Northerners to camp in trenches facing Southern soldiers while both sides waited for orders to fight and that could take weeks or months. At first they taunted each other, then they talked, occasionally they even sang together. Sometimes they traded things, or exchanged letters. Then, when the orders came, they would settle down to the business of killing, which is what war is about. But they did have beliefs, and most of them knew in their hearts that they were fighting for things that were important. They knew it had to do with slavery, and where they lived, and whether a state has a right to nullify acts of Congress and to secede. This was a defining war. Who were they? Were they Virginians, or North Carolinians, or New Yorkers first? Or were they Americans?

The future of the nation was at stake. Would the grand American experiment last? Or would this union of states—this federal republic—end up in history books as an idealistic scheme that failed? If so, then the skeptics would be right: ideas like equality, self-government, and justice for all don't work long in the real world. The French political philosopher Montesquieu championed political freedom and advocated separation of powers—but he also said that large republics can't work. Would he be proved prophetic? We were trying something that was outside the chain of history. Born of an idea, not of ancient peoples and established procedures, it had taken hubris, and a bit of luck, to establish the American nation. There was nothing inevitable about our continued existence. All we had was the power of an idea.

The Northern soldiers knew that. Henry Clay and Daniel Webster had given speech after speech on the Union and what it stood for. In an age that cherished oratory, schoolboys memorized their speeches. The Yankees could recite the lines by heart. "I know no South, no North, no East, no West, to which I owe any allegiance.... The Union, sir, is my country," said eloquent Senator Clay. "When my eyes shall be turned to behold for the last time the sun in heaven, may I not see him shining on the broken and dishonored fragments of a once glorious Union," said mighty Senator Webster. But his most quoted line was "Liberty and Union, now and forever, one and inseparable." Northern soldiers were willing to die to preserve "liberty and Union."

Except for the abolitionists. Mostly they didn't care that much about the Union one way or the other. They were fighting for the ideas of freedom and decency and equality. They would do everything in their power to achieve them and spread their blessings. But holding on to the Union—or overthrowing it—wasn't where their passion lay. Abraham Lincoln was not an abolitionist—although he shared many (but not all) of their goals. When the war began, Lincoln said, "I have no purpose, directly or indirectly to interfere with slavery in the States where it exists." Like the founding generation, he put the great experiment first. "We must settle

"We all declare for liberty, but in using the same word we do not mean the same thing. You think slavery is right and ought to be extended, while we think it is wrong and ought to be resisted."
—Abraham Lincoln

this question now," said Lincoln in 1861, "whether in a free government the minority have the right to break up the government whenever they choose."

The Rebels—inspired by John Calhoun—said that individual liberty comes first. That meant their liberty to be white and dominant. That liberty was more important than holding on to a Union that, they believed, didn't represent them. They quoted the Declaration of Independence, citing the phrase about "governments … deriving their just powers from the Consent of the Governed."

So the word *liberty,* which was on everyone's lips, meant different things in North and South. This nation, precocious at birth, was still a work in progress. From the first there were those skeptical of the shared, federal form of government. "I smell a rat," said Patrick Henry about the Constitution, which took some of his beloved Virginia's autonomy. The argument had not gone away. White Southerners wanted the security of Old World values, the continuity and comfort of what they knew, and the "liberty" to do as they wished. They feared domination by the North, and a loss of power and prestige. "The surrender of life is nothing to sinking down into acknowledgment of inferiority," said Senator Calhoun. Secession was in the American tradition. After all, the Revolution was a grand secession. Why couldn't the South do its own thing?

Besides, the Southern way of life was different from the Northern way. The Rebel soldiers believed they were fighting for that, too. Northern cities were facing all the problems that come with industry and change. They seemed crass, and often were. In the South, life was pastoral, conservative, and orderly. It was where the old European class society had taken root in the New World. The South offered great opportunity and ease for a small number of white people. For many other whites, living was comfortable and secure. But for poor whites and blacks it was neither comfortable nor fair. In some Southern states, like South Carolina, more than half the population was black. Most lived the lives of prisoners, though they had committed no crime.

Virginia senator James M. Mason understood the differences between North and South. He said, "I look upon it [the Civil War] … as a war of … one form of society against another form of society." It was certainly that, and much more.

Getting Down to Business

The first big battle of the war was fought at a place called Manassas, not far from the city of Washington, near a muddy stream known as Bull Run. It was a place where two railroad lines met. The Northern generals planned to take Manassas and

A War to End Slavery 127

The war began when Rebel guns fired on U.S. troops in Fort Sumter, an island fort in the harbor at Charleston. Safely on shore, the citizens of Charleston watched. "I had a splendid view," wrote Emma Holmes. "I saw the shots as they struck the fort, and the masonry crumbling."

> "There is nothing in American military history quite like the story of Bull Run. It was the momentous fight of the amateurs, the battle where everything went wrong, the great day of awakening for the whole nation, North and South together. It . . . ended the rosy time in which men could dream that the war would be short, glorious and bloodless. After Bull Run the nation got down to business."
>
> —historian Bruce Catton

then to march south, to the Confederate capital at Richmond, Virginia.

When that July day in 1861 began, war seemed a bit like a performance. And hundreds of Washingtonians didn't want to miss the show. They came to Manassas with their picnic baskets and settled down near Bull Run stream to watch the fighting. But it didn't turn out to be a picture-book battle; it was real, and disorderly. Both sides fought for hours. It was a hot, *very* hot, humid summer day. By afternoon, bodies littered the ground, and the bloody earth was beginning to smell. The Northerners did seem to be winning. Then fresh Southern troops arrived—by train. (This was the first war where troops were transported by trains.) The Rebels attacked with bloodcurdling shouts; they called it the "rebel yell." It was too much for the Yankees. They dropped their guns and ran.

The Northern soldiers, who had expected to fight on to Richmond, now went the other way, back to Washington. Cavalry, infantry, artillery, hospital wagons, and families in their carriages squeezed together on the narrow road north when a stray shell exploded and upset a wagon. That blocked a bridge, and soldiers, horses, and civilians were all stuck, and scared. Someone shouted that the Southern cavalry was attacking (it wasn't). That started a panic—a shoving, pushing, screaming panic. Lieutenant Colonel W. W. Blackford of the Virginia 1st Cavalry described it:

> They plunged through Bull Run wherever they came to it, regardless of fords or bridges, and there many drowned.... We found ... along the road, parasols and dainty shawls lost ... by the frail, fair ones who had seats in most of the carriages of this excursion.

It didn't take long for people to realize that war is no picnic.

Southern Generals

The South had a wealth of good generals. Of them all, Thomas J. Jackson and Robert E. Lee were the most venerated. At Bull Run, when things were at their worst for the rebel forces, General Barnard Bee rallied his Alabama troops by pointing to Jackson standing soldier-straight with his troops. "There is Jackson standing like a stone wall," said Bee. The nickname stuck as tales of the man grew. Stonewall Jackson kept doing things that couldn't be done. He marched his men farther and faster than armies could march, beat forces much larger than his, and won battles that were said to be unwinnable.

An orphan child who grew into a strange, brooding man, Jackson, like many of the officers, North and South, had gone to the U.S. military academy at West Point and fought in the Mexican War. He was a teacher at the Virginia Military Institute when this war began. He wasn't popular—he was strict, deeply religious, and had no sense of humor. The boys called him "Tom Fool" behind his back. Awkward and rumpled, he liked to sit on his dumpy horse, Sorrel, sucking a lemon. But when he took command, he knew what he was doing. Nothing scared him. In Virginia's Shenandoah Valley, he marched a small army 400 miles at a brutal pace, kept a large Union army off balance, seized needed supplies, inflicted heavy casualties, and inspired legends. "Boys," said one Union general, "he's not much for looks, but if we had him, we wouldn't be in this trap."

Robert E. Lee was different. He sat erect, aristocratic, and unruffled on his beautiful horse, Traveller, and looked as a general should look: handsome, gray-haired, and dignified. He commanded as a general should command: with fairness, audacity, and courage. His soldiers were awed by him, and rushed into battle and died for him. He had a gambler's instincts, he took big chances, and, again and again,

Robert E. Lee

Thomas "Stonewall" Jackson

his daring paid off. He wasn't troubled putting men in battle; if you fought for him, chances were good you wouldn't make it home. Yet if ever there was a born leader, it was General Robert E. Lee. His wife was a granddaughter of Martha Washington. His father was "Light Horse Harry" Lee, a Virginia planter and Revolutionary War cavalry hero. Light Horse Harry was said to be fearless in battle, and Patrick Henry didn't scare him either. When Henry was trying to get Virginians to vote against ratification of the new Constitution, Harry Lee spoke up.

> *The people of America, sir, are one people. I love the people of the North, not because they have adopted the Constitution, but because I fought with them as my countrymen.... Does it follow from hence that I have forgotten ... my native state? In all local matters I shall be a Virginian: in those of a general nature, I shall not forget that I am an American.*

Robert E. Lee, too, loved America and its Constitution. He didn't like slavery, and he freed his slaves before the war started. He didn't think much of states' rights, either. In a letter to his son, he wrote:

> *Secession is nothing but revolution. The framers of our Constitution never exhausted so much labour; wisdom and forbearance in its formation, and surrounded it with so many guards and securities, if it was intended to be broken by any member of the Confederacy at*

> "I have fought against the people of the North because I believed they were seeking to wrest from the South its dearest rights. But I have never cherished toward them bitter or vindictive feelings, and I have never seen the day when I did not pray for them."
>
> —Robert E. Lee, commander in chief, Confederate army

> *will.... Still, a Union that can only be maintained by swords and bayonets, and in which strife and civil war are to take the place of brotherly love and kindness, has no charm for me. If the Union is dissolved, the government disrupted, I shall return to my native state and share the miseries of my people. Save in her defense, I will draw my sword no more.*

When the war began, President Lincoln offered Lee command of the Union army. It was hard to turn that job down. Lee's wife said he stayed up all night walking back and forth trying to decide what to do. He had been a loyal United States officer. Still, when he had to make a choice, he chose Virginia. Few generals have inspired men as Robert E. Lee did. Few people have conveyed the integrity and intelligence that Lee did. On the battlefield he was cool and daring, but it was in defeat that he showed the best of himself. When the war was over he refused to be bitter, or angry, or anything but noble.

President Davis's Problems

President Jefferson Davis, like President Abraham Lincoln, was born in a log cabin. His father, Sam Davis, fought in the Revolutionary War and then headed west on Daniel Boone's Wilderness Trail, to Kentucky. There he claimed land, felled trees, and built a house. He and his wife had ten children. They went to the Hebrew Bible to name their first sons: Joseph, Samuel, Benjamin, and Isaac. The tenth child, born in 1808—the year before that other Kentucky baby, Abraham Lincoln—was named for the president, Jefferson, with Finis as a middle name. It means "the end" in Latin. The Davises meant to have no more babies, and they didn't.

Soon after Jefferson's birth, Sam Davis and his family moved, first to Louisiana and then to Mississippi. In Mississippi they found what they were looking for: prosperity. They grew cotton and became rich. Joseph, the oldest son, became the richest planter in the state. He was a lawyer, and kindly, and he owned the finest library in Mississippi. Joseph helped raise his younger brother Jefferson and saw that he went to the best schools and to the military academy at West Point. When Jefferson grew up he fought in the Mexican War and was a hero. After the war, he entered the U.S. Senate, came under the sway of South Carolina senator John C. Calhoun, and was soon arguing for the extension of slavery into the western territories. When the Confederate nation looked for a president, it could find no one more qualified than Jefferson Davis.

Davis moved into the Confederate White House in the

Above, the White House of the Confederacy in Richmond. Left, Jefferson Davis; most portraits disguised the Rebel president's appearance, which, a journalist said, combined "the face of a corpse, the form of a skeleton."

Confederate capital—Richmond, Virginia. The Confederate constitution harked back to the Articles of Confederation. So President Davis began with the kind of government that many Southerners had wanted all along. And he had those superb generals to help protect it. What he didn't have enough of was food, clothing, weapons, and ships. Slavery had kept the South feudal and agricultural while much of the world was becoming industrial. The South's transportation system was out of date. Weapons and ammunition were in short supply. Under the confederate system of government, President Davis couldn't get the Southern states to pay taxes or do anything they didn't want to do. When farmers hoarded crops, he couldn't do much about that, either. So soldiers in the Rebel army often went hungry in a land of plenty. The Confederates were sure their long-time friends in England would help out. They believed England depended on Southern cotton and tobacco. They were wrong. When the Union navy blockaded Southern ports, the British navy didn't interfere. Some British politicians wanted to help the South, but most English people wouldn't hear of it; they had become abolitionists.

GENERALS AND BATTLES

When the war began, General Winfield Scott was in charge of the Union Army. Known as "Old Fuss and Feathers," he was a hero of the War of 1812 and, in 1846, had waged a victorious campaign in the Mexican War. He'd even run for president on the Whig ticket. But Scott was in terrible physical shape. "For more than three years," he said, "I have been unable, from a hurt, to mount a horse or to walk more than a few paces at a time." Still, there was nothing wrong with General Scott's mind. While most people thought it was going to be a quick war, Scott figured it would take at least two or three years for the North to win against the South. He came up with a plan—called the Anaconda Plan—that began with a blockade of Southern ports. If the Confederacy could be kept from trading with Europe it would be in trouble. Everyone knew the South was depending on cotton sales to get cash to fight—so a blockade would really hurt. Scott also intended to control the Mississippi River. That would cut off Louisiana, Texas, and Arkansas from the rest of the South. Then the Union could send armies from the east

General Winfield Scott

The Soldiers

Their median age was twenty-four. That means that half of the Civil War soldiers were younger than twenty-four, and half were older. Many were eighteen or nineteen. Some were even younger. Eleven-year-old Johnny Clem was a drummer boy in a Michigan regiment. When a Confederate colonel tried to take him prisoner, Johnny picked up a musket and killed the colonel. He was made a sergeant.

Union rules said a soldier was supposed to be at least eighteen years old. But boys eager to fight found a way around that. They wrote the number 18 on a piece of paper and put it in a shoe. Then, when asked, they could say, "I'm over eighteen." One young volunteer, Ned Hunter, didn't lie, and was taken anyway: "When the recruiting officer asked my age, I told him the truth: sixteen next June. When my father said, 'He can shoot as straight as any who has been signed today,' the officer handed me the pen and ordered, 'Sign here.'"

Young men weren't the only ones anxious to fight. Iowa had a famous Graybeard Regiment. Everyone in it was older than forty-five. "So old were these men, and so young their state," wrote historian Bruce Catton, "that not a man in the regiment could claim Iowa as his birthplace. There had been no Iowa when these

Confederate colonel Nathan Forrest advertised for recruits like these Rebel volunteers as follows: "I wish none but those who wish to be actively engaged.... Come on, boys, if you want a heap of fun and to kill some Yankees."

Iowans were born." At first there were so many volunteers that neither army could handle them all. Later, when the volunteers wrote home about the battles and the deaths and the conditions, fewer came willingly, so the governments paid cash rewards for volunteers, and finally both sides had to draft men.

Some people called it "a rich man's war and a poor man's fight"—because, if you were rich enough, you didn't have to be in the army. Confederates who owned twenty or more slaves could be excused, although many fought anyway. And Northerners who could afford it were allowed to pay someone to fight for them. Many did.

Most soldiers were farmers, because it was a country of farmers. Some were small town boys; few had ever been far from home. Soldiering sounded like an adventurous thing to do, and for a while it was a bit like boys' camp. One Illinois recruit wrote in a letter home, "It is fun to lie around, face unwashed, hair uncombed, shirt unbuttoned and everything un-everythinged." There were new friends and uniforms and parades and drills—but that soon changed. Then, often, there were long marches, long, boring encampments, homesickness, bad food, hunger, and disease. For every man who died in battle, two died of sickness.

and west to squeeze the Confederacy, as an anaconda squeezes its prey.

And, eventually, that's what happened. But when people heard of Scott's plan, they laughed. The war lasting two or three years? Why, that was the nonsense of an old, has-been general. This was a war that would be over in a few months. Scott's Anaconda Plan caused so much dismay that President Lincoln was forced to look for a new general. "It is with deep regret that I withdraw myself, in these momentous times," said General Scott, "from the orders of a president who has treated me with distinguished kindness and courtesy."

The president found a man who was handsome and intelligent and popular with the troops. Thirty-five-year-old General George McClellan was an excellent organizer. A general has to feed, house, and equip his armies. He has to move them long distances. He has to inspire them. He has to train them. McClellan was good at all those things. He'd fought in the Mexican War, and he'd been a railroad executive. He was brash and full of confidence. "I found no army to command," he said, "just a mere collection of regiments cowering on the banks of the Potomac." McClellan did have a problem. He didn't like to fight. He kept hesitating, making excuses, and pulling back. "If we had a million men," said Lincoln's secretary of war Edwin Stanton, "he would swear the enemy had two millions, and then he would sit down in the mud and yell for three."

> "What would happen if no cotton were furnished for three years? England would topple headlong and carry the whole civilized world with her, save the South. No, you dare not make war on cotton. Cotton is king."
>
> —M. B. Hammond, South Carolina senator

General McClellan made plans to capture Richmond. That city was not only the capital of the Confederacy, it was one of the few industrial cities in the South. If Richmond fell, the Confederacy might collapse and the war be over.

It is spring 1862. McClellan intends to sail an army to the Virginia Peninsula (the land between the York and James Rivers that juts into Chesapeake Bay). Once the army is in place, it is to march north up the peninsula to Richmond. There it will meet another Union army marching south from Washington. It is that anaconda, squeeze—the enemy strategy. McClellan lands his army on the Virginia Peninsula, as planned, and then he sits. He is cautious by nature. That gives the Confederate

General George McClellan

army plenty of time to get ready. It rains (which it often does in Tidewater Virginia) and the peninsula turns into mud. Marching is difficult, especially with wagons and cannons. The Union army is way behind schedule. The Rebels use the time to send Stonewall Jackson and his men toward Washington—so the Union army that is supposed to march south and meet McClellan has to stay and protect the capital instead.

McClellan's army takes Yorktown and Williamsburg and keeps marching until it is twenty miles from Richmond. Then the general decides to wait for reinforcements. The Confederates have managed to convince McClellan that their army is much larger than the Union army (the opposite is true). He hesitates. Robert E. Lee is a man who rarely hesitates. He attacks. For seven days (it's called the Seven Days' Battle), the two armies fight ferociously. Both suffer terrible losses. In the end, it is a draw.

But McClellan's confidence is gone. He orders his army to retreat. Months of planning, transporting, marching, and fighting, and nothing gained. The Union army sails back North. The Yankees have lost a chance to capture Richmond and end the war. It will be two years before it comes again.

And so it went. One horrific, man-eating battle after another, and not much gained for either side. The war raged in

FRIENDLY FIRE

In the spring of 1863, in an area so dense and thick with trees that people called it the Wilderness, both sides fight with awful ferocity amid burning trees; the scene is a blinding inferno. Rebel forces are outnumbered almost two to one in this battle near Chancellorsville, Virginia, but they win the day. It may be Lee's most brilliant victory. He doesn't think it worth the cost. In the thick smoke and confusion, Stonewall Jackson is wounded by one of his own men. (It isn't unusual for soldiers to be hit by shots from their own companions—it's known as "friendly fire.") After Jackson's left arm is amputated he seems to be getting better; then pneumonia sets in. General Lee sends a message: "Tell him to make haste and get well, and come back to me as soon as he can. He has lost his left arm, but I have lost my right arm."

The message pleases Jackson, and he tells it to his wife, Anna. Stonewall never talks much about his private life, but he loves Anna and is proud of their new baby, Julia. They have come to be with him. Jackson is in terrible pain and often delirious. "Prepare for action," he calls out, and "Let us cross the river and rest under the shade of the trees." And then he dies. In Richmond, 20,000 hushed, tearful people line the streets as four white horses pull his coffin in a solemn military cortege. When his body is brought home to the Virginia Military Institute, no one talks of Tom Fool. He is now a hero, and will remain so.

Antietam became an example of the waste of war: at Antietam Creek, for instance, Union forces under General Burnside tried to storm the bridge, as depicted here. Rebels defended the bridge stubbornly; yet Burnside went on throwing men at the site rather than sending them to ford the creek nearby, where they could have waded across with little opposition.

Tennessee and Mississippi and Louisiana and Missouri as well as in Virginia and Maryland. In the West the Union forces often seemed to be ahead. In the East it was the Confederacy. For both North and South, deaths piled on deaths. It was the youth of a nation, and yet, overall, there was no winner.

Forever Free

President Lincoln wanted to do something important. He wanted to make an announcement that would change the purpose of the war, and he didn't want to do it as the leader of a discouraged, defeated army. He needed a victory, and finally he had it. Not the kind of victory the president had hoped for—too many men were killed; more than ever before—but on September 17, 1862, the Union army stopped Lee's forces at Antietam Creek, and that, Lincoln decided, would have to do. Both sides suffered terrible losses; Antietam, which

"The flowers in bloom upon the graves at the Cemetery were shot away. Tombs and monuments were knocked to pieces, and ordinary gravestones shattered in rows."

—Union Army Private Uilrren Goss

was near the little farm town of Sharpsburg, Maryland, was the scene of some of the most savage fighting of the war. By the time the day ended, 4,710 were dead and more than 18,000 wounded. But things were

A slave learns news of the Emancipation Proclamation—as painter Henry Louis Stephens imagined it in his somewhat romanticized watercolor rendering

worse for the Confederacy than the Union. Lincoln took a train to Sharpsburg and urged McClellan to go after Lee. McClellan had two divisions of fresh soldiers. "I came back thinking he would move at once," said Lincoln. "I … ordered him to advance." McClellan sat for nineteen days; then he moved slowly. He let the Confederate army get away. Lincoln was enraged. He believed he had lost another chance to end the war.

He wasn't the only one. Northern soldier Elisha Rhodes wrote a letter home saying, "Oh, why did we not attack them and drive them into the river? I do not understand these things. But then I am only a boy." (Soon after, Lincoln replaced McClellan; McClellan did not go willingly. He said, "They have made a great mistake. Alas for my poor country!") Still, Antietam was a victory for the North. Lee had been on his way to Pennsylvania. He had intended to cut railroad lines at Harrisburg. He had hoped to find shoes and supplies for his men. Now a discouraged Confederate army was back in Virginia. Lincoln could make his announcement. On September 22, 1862, this is what he said:

> *On the first day of January, in the year of our Lord one thousand eight hundred and sixty three, all persons held as slaves within any State, or designated part of a State, whereof shall then be in rebellion against the United States, shall be then, thenceforth, and forever free.*

It was an Emancipation Proclamation. It didn't free slaves in the North—there were no slaves there to free. It didn't free slaves in the border states that were still in the Union—Maryland, Delaware, Kentucky, and Missouri; that could only be done by a constitutional amendment, or by the state legislatures. It did free slaves in the Confederate states—where Lincoln had no power at all. So what was its purpose? People in 1862 understood that when the president signed that document there was no going back. When the war was over, slavery was finished.

The president no longer thought it enough just to save the Union. He had come to realize that slavery was like a worm in a good apple—it was making the whole apple rotten. The nation could not allow an evil practice and believe in itself. And thus the Civil War became a war to make the United States what it had meant to be from

Harriet and Uncle Tom

Harriet Beecher grew up in Litchfield, Connecticut, in a houseful of children: seven boys and four girls. Her father, Lyman Beecher, was a Congregational minister known throughout New England for his fine sermons. Congregationalists were descendants of the Puritans: serious and moral in their religion. All Lyman Beecher's boys became ministers. One of them, Henry Ward Beecher, said to be the greatest preacher of his day, inspired many abolitionists. Another son, Edward, was a college president. Catharine and Isabella, two of the Beecher daughters, were pioneers in the fight for women's rights. Harriet became the most famous Beecher of them all. In fact, she was the most famous American woman of her day.

Lyman Beecher moved his family to Cincinnati, Ohio, where he became head of a college to train ministers. In New England, slavery had seemed far away. Now it was close by in Kentucky, just across the Ohio River, was a slave state. Harriet stood on the banks of the river and watched boats filled with slaves being shipped south to be sold. Harriet learned a lot about slavery, and what she learned made her very angry.

Then she married Calvin Stowe and had babies; there never seemed to be enough money, so Harriet wrote stories to earn money. Her brother Edward's wife said to her, "If I could write as well as you do, I would write something to make this whole nation feel what an accursed thing slavery is." And that was just what Harriet did. She wrote *Uncle Tom's Cabin*.

It may be the most influential book ever written in America. Within a week of its publication in 1852 as a book (it was first printed in a newspaper), 10,000 copies were sold. Before the Civil War began, two million copies were bought in the U.S. It was translated into many languages and distributed around the world. People wept over the story of Uncle Tom and Eliza. Even the Queen of England was said to have wept. *Uncle Tom's Cabin* is the first American novel to make real people of African-Americans; it made people care. And it changed people's ideas about slavery. (In much of the South it was against the law to buy or sell the book.) When President Lincoln met Harriet Beecher Stowe during the Civil War, he said to her, "So this is the little lady who wrote the book that made this great war."

Harriet Beecher Stowe wrote *Uncle Tom's Cabin* at her kitchen table with her children running in and out. Above are early illustrations of two of its characters—Uncle Tom himself, and Topsy, who "jus' growed."

Harriet Beecher Stowe

its beginnings: a fair nation. A great nation. A nation that fulfilled the best ideas of its founders and went on from there. A nation that would set equality of opportunity as a goal. A nation that could promise "life, liberty and the pursuit of happiness" and mean it for all its peoples.

Usually the president signed government bills with a simple *A. Lincoln.* But when he signed the Emancipation Proclamation, Abraham Lincoln wrote his name in full.

"Gentlemen," he said to the cabinet officers standing near him, "I never, in my life, felt more certain that I was doing the right thing than in signing this paper."

WHO SHOULD FIGHT?

Neither army, North or South, would accept black soldiers. "What upon earth is the matter with the American people?" asked Frederick Douglass. "The national edifice is on fire. Every man who can carry a bucket of water … is wanted…. [Yet government leaders] refuse to receive the very class of men which has a deeper interest in the defeat and humiliation of the rebels than all others…. Such is the pride, the stupid prejudice and folly that rules the hour."

In the South, African-Americans—thousands of them—ran from plantations to Yankee army camps, calling it a freedom war, meaning freedom from slavery. The runaways were known as *contrabands—property,* seized from the enemy. Soon the contrabands were doing useful work for the Northern armies. But they, and free blacks North and South, really wanted to fight. They wanted to fight because they knew—long before most white people—that this was a war about slavery. They wanted to fight because they cared about America as much as anyone else. They wanted to fight because they knew that fighting men would never be thought of as slaves again. President Lincoln had announced after Antietam, in October 1862, that the Union would begin enlisting black soldiers.

The president, in July, made some impromptu remarks to a crowd come to serenade him at the "White House. He talked of the Declaration of Independence and of those who would topple it. The republic, he said, was facing "a gigantic Rebellion, at the bottom of which is an effort to overturn the principle that all men are created equal." Not everyone is pleased with his thoughts.

This war had begun as a fight to save the Union; the Emancipation Proclamation had made it a war to end slavery; was it to be something else, too—a war to foist equality on the land?

This was still a land of classes, and not just in the South. The immigrants who were marching hopefully off the ferries from Castle Garden on to New York City's streets usually found themselves near the lowest rung of society's ladder.

They hadn't come to America to go to war, especially a war that didn't seem to be about anything that was important to them. They didn't have a choice. Many were drafted. "What made it worse was the exemption given to the rich. That was hardly equality. Immigrants who had fled hunger and failed potato crops in Ireland, bringing their Catholic heritage with them, were often greeted with taunts about "popery." Religious prejudice often kept them out of mainstream institutions. On top of that, jobs were scarce. The Irish were usually at the bottom of the list when it came to hiring workers. Now they were hearing that Negroes were about to be freed and would flood the city, work for low wages, and take their jobs. On July 13, someone threw a stone through the window of an army office as a clerk was drawing names for the draft. That set things off. For four days, uncontrolled mobs pillaged, lynched, burned, and fumed. The anger was mostly directed at African-Americans. It was explosive. It was racist. It was shameful. It was called the New York draft riots.

Fighters Against the Odds

The Union army had a debt to settle at Fort Sumter. More important, they wanted to take Charleston. To get to that city they had to pass Fort Sumter in Charleston harbor. Ironclad ships had tried but been unable to destroy the fort. So plans were made to capture Morris Island, a sandy spit a mile and a half away. The idea was to plant artillery there and pound Sumter into oblivion. Morris Island was not unoccupied. Fort Wagner, a massive structure of sand, logs, and earth, with twenty-foot-high sloping walls studded with sharp tree branches, stood on the island. Tides complicated access.

The first attack was beaten back. So the fort was bombarded by heavy cannon fire. Finally, Wagner's guns fell silent and the Yankees prepared to attack. A deep, dry moat stood on one side of the fort; access was across a bit of land that forced would-be attackers to squeeze together in a tight mass, making them easy targets. But, with the guns quiet, the Federal troops thought the fort might have been abandoned. Two federal brigades lined up to find out. The

54th Massachusetts, a regiment of black soldiers under the command of a patrician Bostonian, Colonel Robert Gould Shaw, headed the assault. They learned quickly that the bombardment had done little damage. The sand seemed to have absorbed the shells. The Confederate defenders aiming guns from behind the walls had an easy shot at the men as they charged. For the riflemen, shooting down, it was like picking off ducks in a shooting gallery. Still, some of the black Yankees gained the fort's parapet, where they fought hand-to-hand before finally being beaten back. Shaw and 272 of his 650 men were killed. Union casualties (dead, wounded and missing) totaled 1,515. Confederate casualties were 174. Following that, Union general Quincy A. Gillmore initiated a siege. Fifty-seven days later, the Confederates slipped away and the fort was in Union hands. But somehow Charleston was still out of reach.

After Fort Wagner, no one asked if black men could fight. "Prejudice is down," wrote a man who was there. "It is not too much to say," ran an article in the *New York Tribune*, "that if this Massachusetts 54th had faltered when its trial came, 200,000 troops for whom it was a pioneer would never have been put into the field.... But it did not falter. It made Fort Wagner such a name for the colored race as Bunker Hill has been for ninety years to the white Yankees."

Confederates who found Colonel Shaw's body threw it into a common grave, reporting that he had been buried "with his niggers." Those who knew him said he would have wanted to be buried with his men. Confederate officers announced

When the 54th Massachusetts' flag bearer fell at Fort Wagner, Sergeant William Carney (left) saved the colors despite several bullet wounds. He was later awarded the Congressional Medal of Honour. Below, the military band of the 107th Colored Infantry, which helped defend Washington, D.C.

Why Fight the Rebels?

Almost everyone is fed up with this war. It has been neither heroic nor adventurous. An Ohioan, Clement Laird Vallandigham, leading a group of "Peace Democrats" (called "Copperheads" by their opponents), is relentless in criticizing Lincoln and the government. Why fight the Rebels? Give them what they want. War isn't worth it, says Vallandigham (using words to that effect). He cites defeat after defeat for the Union army. He wants the carnage to end. In May 1863, Vallandigham is arrested by the military governor of Ohio and charged with "publicly expressing … sympathies for those in arms against the Government of the United States." He is tried by court-martial, found guilty, and placed in a military prison. His lawyer petitions for a writ of habeas corpus, which is denied. The U.S. Supreme Court says no law gives it jurisdiction to hear appeals from a military commission. The president orders the army to release Vallandigham and banish him to the Confederacy. He stays there for a month and then flees to Canada.

that any captured white Northern officers leading black troops would be put to death as criminals. Captured black soldiers knew they would be sold into slavery. Nonetheless, African-Americans kept volunteering. Before the war was over, more than 200,000 fought for the Union. Lincoln said they made victory possible.

In 1864 black troops marched in New York City. A *New York Times* reporter said that the marching soldiers were a sign of the "marvelous times" and that there had been a "revolution [of] the public mind."

> Had any man predicted it last year he would have been thought a fool…. Eight months ago the African race in this City were literally hunted down like wild beasts. They fled for their lives…. How astonishingly has all this been changed. The same men … now march in solid platoons, with shouldered

The 54th Massachusetts, led by Colonel Robert Gould Shaw, make their gallant assault on Fort Wagner.

muskets, slung knapsacks, and buckled cartridge boxes down through our gayest avenues ... to the pealing strains of martial music and are everywhere saluted with waving handkerchiefs, with descending flowers.

Abraham Lincoln said, *In giving freedom to the slave, we assure freedom to the free.*

GETTYSBURG

Robert E. Lee knows there are strong peace movements in the North. If his soldiers can win some Northern territory, if they beat the Yankees on their own home ground, he believes the North will soon beg for peace. He decides to march his army north. It is an enormous gamble, but Lee's daring has made him successful in the past.

It is early summer of 1863. Lee meets the Union army, led by hot-tempered General Meade, at a quiet Pennsylvania college town named Gettysburg, where roads come together like the spokes of a wheel. It is postcard-pretty land: green and peaceful, a gentle valley with hills and ridges and knolls. In 1863, Gettysburg is twelve blocks long, six blocks wide, and has 2,400 inhabitants. A wooden sign on Cemetery Hill says that anyone firing a gun in the area will be fined five dollars. If, on the first three days of July in 1863, the town could have collected those five-dollar fines, it would have been the richest place in America.

When the fighting begins, on July 1, neither army has all its soldiers in place—many are still marching toward Gettysburg—but that doesn't stop these armies. They are eager to fight. They want to finish this war; it has gone on too long. At first, it looks as if it will be another Union defeat. The Rebels push the Union forces through the town. Casualties are high. But fresh soldiers are pouring in. Union General Buford sends a message to General Meade: "Get soldiers here at once. This is a good location for a fight." Buford's cavalry has discovered that Gettysburg sits on a series of ridges with a shallow valley between. Whoever holds the high ground will have a big advantage. The Yankees have fewer men than the Rebels, but Buford and his men are on Cemetery Ridge, south of the village. It is a good place to be. Any attack by the Confederates will have to come uphill.

July 2 comes, and the fighting begins early and is even more murderous than

General George Meade

the day before. That the day is blazing hot doesn't make a difference. Men fight and die with a frenzy that is still hard to believe. A Northern regiment—the 1st Minnesota—has 262 men when the day begins; forty-two survive. "The blood stood in puddles in some places on the rocks," says Confederate Colonel William Oates, commander of the 15th Alabama.

And then July 3 dawns, and the battle that some say will decide the war. General Lee now has fewer men than General Meade. That doesn't scare Lee; he has been outnumbered before. He begins by blasting the Union line with two hours of nonstop artillery fire. "The very earth shook beneath our feet, "wrote a soldier later," and the hills and rocks seemed to reel like drunken men."

Major General George Pickett, CSA, gets ready to lead the most famous charge in American history—across three-fourths of a mile of open fields. It is an awesome sight. Line after line of gray-uniformed men march out of the woods. Elbow to elbow, like a grand parade, 15,000 fighters step forward in an incredible, orderly, moving rectangle almost a mile wide and half a mile deep. Lee has gambled everything on this old-fashioned military charge. It is eerily quiet. It is also crazy. What does he have in mind? He is sending these men marching on a sunshine-filled day with no cover at all.

For two hours shells have been exploding over the heads of the Yankees crouched behind stone walls on Cemetery Ridge. Now they watch as the Rebels march

Augustus Buell, who became known as the "Boy Cannoneer," recalled the first day at Gettysburg: "Up and down the line men reeling and falling … in rear, horses tearing and plunging, mad with wounds of terror; drivers yelling, shells bursting, shot shrieking overhead … smoke, dust, splinters, blood, wreck and carnage indescribable."

toward them. The noise, the July heat, the smoke, and the tension of waiting for battle have been almost more than the men can bear. Luckily for them, much of the shot has gone too high and fallen behind the lines. The Confederates don't know this. They march on cheerfully across the open field in their bright uniforms. Later, Confederate Captain W. W. Wood will remember, "We believed the battle was practically over, and we had nothing to do but march unopposed to Cemetery Hill and occupy it."

The Union commander says, "Let them come up close before you fire, and then aim low and steadily." When the order finally comes for the artillery to fire, the cannons shoot more than cannonballs. The new firepower includes cans that explode and send off a hail of metal that murders the oncoming

On July 5, 1863, a Union cavalryman wrote in his diary (this is his own spelling): "We went into the village this morning and commenc buring our ded and it was a dredjul site to behold our ded sogers lay all over the ground as thick as they could lay."

"Foot to foot, body to body, and man to man they struggled and pushed and strived and killed. The mass of wounded and heaps of dead entangled, hatless, coatless, drowned in sweat, black with powder, red with blood."
— A Massachusetts Union soldier

General George Pickett

soldiers. Bravely they close ranks and keep coming. The Confederates, a tight mass of men in light gray uniforms, are caught with nowhere to go but forward. The Yankees are shooting at them from different angles all along Cemetery Ridge. The Rebels keep coming, stepping over the bodies of those who have fallen before them, and then falling themselves. This is a massacre. When the charge is over, the Confederates have lost (killed, wounded, or missing) one third of their army; that's 28,000 men. General Lee blames no one but himself. This was a gamble, an arrogant gamble with men's lives. It didn't pay off.

News of the victory at Gettysburg arrives in Washington on the Fourth of July. In a few days people will learn that on this same July 4, General Ulysses S. Grant has also won a major victory at Vicksburg, in Mississippi. Control of Vicksburg means control of the Mississippi River. Those two victories—Gettysburg and Vicksburg—turn the war around." The men behaved splendidly—I really think they are becoming soldiers," writes General Meade to his wife, savoring the moment. The only one who has reservations about Vicksburg is Grant. "I intended more from it," he says.

As for Lee, he turns to Colonel Fremantle and says, "This has been a sad day for us, Colonel—a sad day; but we can't expect always to gain victories." Lee's greatest victories are behind him.

A New Birth of Freedom

The war is not yet over, but eighteen Northern states have agreed to share the costs of a national cemetery on Cemetery Hill at Gettysburg. The dead soldiers will rest in peace. A ceremony is planned for November 19, 1863, to honor them. Edward Everett, who has been a teacher of Greek, president of Harvard, and secretary of state, is expected to give a funeral oration in a grand tradition going back to Pericles of ancient Greece. He will speak for two hours, and he never uses notes. Fifteen thousand people will hear him. The president is asked to make a few remarks.

Lincoln doesn't want to miss this occasion. He has come a day early to work on his speech. He will try to explain the meaning of the war. Many Northerners are crying out for peace. They no longer care about the Union, or the slaves. Lincoln knows the nation can have peace any time it wants. But that would end the United States as it was conceived. Lincoln believes this terrible war has a purpose.

A Philadelphia journalist, John Russell Young, is among the crowd.

The procession from town was a ragged affair, we all seemed to get there as best we could. A rude platform looked out over the battlefield. On one side sat the journalists; the eminent people had the other side. When the President arose, he stood an instant waiting for the cheers to cease, slowly adjusted his glasses, and took from his pocket what seemed to be a page of ordinary paper, quietly unfolded it, and began to read.

Lincoln's Kentucky voice sounds countrified after the polished tones of orator Everett, but Lincoln has given many speeches; he knows how to make his voice carry. He speaks for three minutes.

Four score and seven years ago our fathers brought forth on this continent, a new nation, conceived in liberty, and dedicated to the proposition that all men are created equal. Now we are engaged in a great civil war, testing whether that nation, or any nation, so conceived and so dedicated, can long endure. We are met on a great battlefield of that war. We have come to dedicate a portion of that field, as a final resting place for those who

The president (in red box) snapped at Gettysburg during his address. Lincoln's private secretary John Hay wrote in his diary for November 20, 1863: "The President, in a fine free way, with more grace than is his wont, said his half dozen words of consecration, and the music wailed and he went home through crowded and cheering streets."

here gave their lives that the nation might live. It is altogether fitting and proper that we should do this. But, in a larger sense, we cannot dedicate—we cannot consecrate—we cannot hallow this ground. The brave men, living and dead, who struggled here, have consecrated it for above our poor power to add or detract. The world will little note, nor long remember, what we say here, but it can never forget what they did here. It is for us the living, rather, to be dedicated here to the unfinished work which they who fought here have so nobly advanced.

It is rather for us to be here dedicated to the great task remaining before us—that from these honored dead we take increased devotion to the cause for which they gave the last full measure of devotion—that we here highly resolve that these dead shall not have died in vain; that this nation, under God, shall have a new birth of freedom—and that government of the people, by the people, for the people, shall not perish from the earth.

The president has not mentioned North; he has not mentioned South. This speech has no names in it at all. He means to transcend this time and spot. His audience is here to mourn, both for their sons and for their country. Lincoln takes them back to the founding moment (*fourscore and seven years ago*), to the Declaration of Independence (*dedicated to the proposition that all men are created equal*). Lincoln intends that it be that document that sets the moral tone for the future (*that this nation, under God, shall have a new birth of freedom*).

And he pulls it off. This address will take its place with the founding documents as an expression of the nation's purpose. Before the Gettysburg Address, the United States was always a plural noun; afterwards, we became singular. The United States, *one nation, under God, indivisible.*

THE FINAL YEAR

President Lincoln can't find a general he can trust. Then he looks out west and there is a leader who is winning battles. The general who trapped a whole Confederate army. That general is Ulysses S. Grant, and Lincoln calls him "the quietest little fellow you ever saw." Grant had been at West Point, where he was nicknamed "Uncle Sam" because of his initials. His army friends called him Sam Grant. At West Point, Sam Grant was too small to excel at any sport but riding. He fought in the Mexican War, then left the army; he wasn't much of a success at civilian life. He was poor, really poor, when he inherited a slave. He could have sold the slave for $1,000, but he didn't do it. He gave the man his freedom.

It didn't look as if Grant would amount to anything until the Civil War came along and trained officers were needed. He was the kind of general who didn't worry much about military theories. He just outkilled or outlasted the enemy.

General Grant and his friend, red-bearded General William Tecumseh Sherman, are just the generals Lincoln has been looking for. Grant knows that the longer the war goes on, the more likely it is that Northerners will tire of supporting it. He is anxious to fight it out as quickly as possible. So Grant attacks, and attacks, and attacks. The Confederates still win battles—they lose fewer men than the Yankees—but the losses hurt them more; they have fewer men to lose. The Union army is back on the

The story goes that some politicians tried to get General Ulysses S. Grant fired for drinking too much. To which President Lincoln replied: "Find out the brand of whiskey he drinks and send every general in the field a barrel of it."

Virginia Peninsula, getting closer and closer to Richmond. Grant decides to besiege Petersburg, the supply center for Lee's army and for Richmond, too. That siege goes on for ten long months. Ten boring, nerve-racking, tense months.

It is 1864, and all the fighting is now in the South. Much of the Southern land is in ruins. General William Tecumseh Sherman marches the U.S. Army of the West from Tennessee, through Georgia, and on to the Carolinas. Breaking the rules he learned at West Point, Sherman leaves his supply lines. He gambles that he can find enough food on the land. He is right. Before long, the Northern soldiers are out of control. They steal, burn, and destroy the country as they cut a forty-mile-wide path through the Deep South. Sherman believes in total war. He says that the Southern ability to make war—its food and arms production—must be destroyed. He may be right. He probably shortens the war. But he leaves devastation, hatred, and anguish in his wake. Those who still think of war as a patriotic adventure with rules of decency will never forgive him.

In 1864, the tide began to turn. General Sherman (left) was marching on Atlanta, leaving a path of ruin behind him. In the Shenandoah Valley in northern Virginia, a Union army under General Philip Sheridan (below, center) destroyed farmland whose crops were meant to feed the Confederate troops.

WITH MALICE TOWARD NONE

"I'm a tired man," says President Abraham Lincoln to a visitor. "Sometimes I think I am the tiredest man on earth." He has reason to be tired. He has shouldered the cares and anguish of four years of war, along with the death from typhoid fever of his beloved son Willie, and a fight for the presidency.

In 1864, General George McClellan runs against him as a peace candidate. McClellan says he will end the war quickly. He doesn't think slavery should be allowed in the western territories, but he had no intention of prohibiting slavery in the South. His supporters call him a great general who has been misunderstood by the president. A leading Southern paper says McClellan's election will "lead to peace and our own independence." By now everyone is tired of the war. It looks as if Lincoln will lose. He is sure of it. "I am going to be beaten," he says, "and unless some great change takes place, badly beaten." And then a great change does take place. General Sherman captures the city of Atlanta, Georgia.

It is clear now that the North is winning and the war may soon be over. Abraham Lincoln is reelected by a big margin. The American people are beginning to appreciate the tall man who is their president. Four years earlier, when he was first elected, he hoped to prevent war. He was willing to do almost anything to keep the country from splitting apart. He was even willing to allow slavery to continue in the South. Now he feels differently. The war has been ghastly, much worse than anyone ever imagined it could be; but now he sees a purpose in the war. Slavery will be ended. It might not have happened without the war. Lincoln thinks it is all part of God's mysterious way, and that is what he says in his second inaugural address. The abolitionist and former slave Frederick Douglass is there. "I was present at the inauguration of Mr. Lincoln, the 4th of March, 1865," he says. "At the time the Confederate cause was on its last legs as it were, and there was deep feeling. I could feel it in the atmosphere here. I heard Mr. Lincoln deliver this wonderful address. It was very short; but he answered all the objections raised to his prolonging the war in one sentence—it was a remark-

At his second inaugural, Lincoln asked both sides to be generous to each other: "With malice toward none, with charity for all; with firmness in the right ... let us strive on to finish the work we are in ... to do all which may achieve and cherish a just, and lasting peace."

able sentence."

This is what the president says: "Fondly do we hope, profoundly do we pray, that this mighty scourge of war shall soon pass away, yet if God wills it continue until all the wealth piled up by two hundred years of bondage shall have been wasted, and each drop of blood drawn by the lash shall have been paid by one drawn by the sword, we will still say … the judgments of the Lord are true and righteous altogether."

Planning for Peace

On March 14, 1865—ten days after his second inauguration—the president is so tired he holds a cabinet meeting in his bedroom. He is in bed, propped up with pillows. His secretaries and those who knew him are alarmed. Maybe a change will help. He needs to get away from Washington. Perhaps General Ulysses S. Grant hears of his fatigue. He sends the president a message by telegraph wire: *Can you not visit City Point for a day or two? I would very much like to see you, and I think the rest would do you good.*

A few days later, on March 23, Lincoln and his wife, Mary, and young son Tad are aboard the yacht *River Queen* on their way to Grant's headquarters at City Point, thirteen miles from Petersburg, Virginia, where the siege continues. City Point may be the busiest place in the nation that April. Lincoln watches as ships and people stream in. General Sherman has left his army in North Carolina to consult with General Grant. Lincoln talks of peace with the two military leaders. All agree: the war has been harsh but the peace should be gentle. The three of them know that Lee and his army will soon be starved out of Petersburg and the Confederate government starved out of Richmond, the Rebel capital. Will the Rebels then surrender? Or will they choose to fight on?

The Confederate leaders do not feel they have a choice. Many fear they will be hanged as traitors if captured. Many have such a strong belief in their cause they cannot imagine surrendering. Of course they will fight. But they, too, know the siege has worked. Lee plans to leave Petersburg, march south, join with a Rebel army there, and continue the war, perhaps as a guerrilla force. Things could go on that way for years. Lee believes he has a few weeks to get ready. But that is before General George Pickett fights a battle at Five Forks, Virginia, where roads come together near a railroad line. Lee tells Pickett he has to hold Five Forks. Food and supplies for Petersburg and Richmond come down those roads and go through Five Forks. The army and the city are starving; this is their lifeline. Pickett, the man who led the famous charge at Gettysburg almost two years earlier, wins the battle. But when it is over he goes off to a shad bake a few miles away. While he is

Richmond, a reporter wrote, had "no sound of life, but the silence of the tomb.... We are under the shadow of ruins." Yet an abandoned Richmond meant that the war was ending. "Thank God I have lived to see this," said Lincoln. "It seems to me that I have been dreaming a horrid nightmare for four years, and now the nightmare is gone."

gone, the Yankees counterattack. This time they win. They capture Five Forks. It is April Fool's Day, and when some Union soldiers are told of the victory, they can't believe the news; they think they're being fooled.

Now there is no hope that the Confederates can survive the siege. Robert E. Lee tells President Jefferson Davis to leave Richmond. Rebel troops set fire to the city, creating an inferno of destruction. When news of the fall of Richmond reaches Washington, its citizens go wild with excitement. Cannons boom, banners fly, people hug and kiss and cry with happiness. After four years the Confederate capital is finally captured. On April 4, a tall man wearing a tall black hat steps off a small military boat at the foot of one of Richmond's seven hills. He is escorted by ten sailors. He has been told not to go to Richmond. It is too dangerous. He goes anyway.

The men climb two miles: past the governor's mansion, past Thomas Jefferson's capitol, to the "White House of the Confederacy. Once, when they stop to rest, an old black man with tears running down his cheeks comes up to the tall man, takes off his hat, bows, and says, "May the good Lord bless you, President Lincoln." The president takes off his hat and silently bows back.

All along the way black people come to touch Lincoln and cheer and sing to him. The white population stays inside, watching through shuttered windows. Later, one of the president's sailor guards writes of "thousands of watchers without a sound, either of welcome or hatred." Most of Richmond's whites are terrified. They have fought this man for four terrible years. Will he exact revenge? Lincoln enters the three-story brick mansion that has been the "White House of the Confederacy. It is a fashionable house with columns at the entrance, newfangled gas lamps on the walls, and the latest in wallpaper. He sits in Jefferson Davis's chair, grins, and says he now feels like the president of all the United States.

But the war still isn't over. Grant will have to capture or defeat Lee's army before it can end. That tired, shoeless army is now racing west. Expected supplies have not come. Grant wants to surround Lee's army so there will be no way out. And finally he does that, near Appomattox Court House.

We Are All Americans

Ely Parker knew that we aren't all the same. Our skins are different colors, our religions are different, our abilities are different, our backgrounds may be different. So what is it that makes us all the same? What is it that makes us all Americans?

An idea. We share an idea. That's what makes us alike. Other nations didn't begin with ideas; most began with barons and kings. We started with a declaration that said all men are created equal. That new and powerful idea excited people all over the world. But our Constitution had not guaranteed that equality. This Civil War—terrible as it was—will cause the Constitution to be changed for the better. Three constitutional amendments—the 13th, 14th, and 15th—will soon be passed. They will make sure that we are all Americans. They will give the nation a new birth of freedom.

Mr. McLean's Parlor

Remember Manassas Junction in Virginia, where the first big battle of the war was fought, near Bull Run stream? Much of the land there was owned by a retired businessman, Wilmer McLean. The Confederates used his farmhouse as a meeting place. After the battle, soldiers stay around, and, a year later, another battle is fought at Manassas. McLean has had enough. He decides to find someplace very quiet. He wants to be as far from the war as possible. So he moves to a tiny, out-of-the-way village—called Appomattox Court House.

Wilmer McLean may have magnets in his blood; he seems to attract historic occasions. In 1865, the two armies—North and South—find themselves at Appomattox Court House. A Confederate officer is looking for a place to have an important meeting. Wilmer McLean shows him an empty building. It won't do. So McLean takes him into his comfortable brick house. That turns out to be just fine. On April 9, 1865, Robert E. Lee—proud, erect, wearing his handsomest uniform, with a gleaming sword strapped to his waist—walks into Wilmer McLean's parlor. He has come to surrender to General Grant.

Grant writes out the official surrender terms. They are kinder than anyone expected. The Southern soldiers can go home, and—as long as they give their promise not to fight against the country again—they will not be prosecuted for treason. They must surrender their guns, but they can take their horses and their sidearms. Everyone knows that means Lee will not have to surrender his sword. Lee, noticing one of Grant's aides—copper-skinned Lieutenant Colonel Ely Parker, a Seneca Iroquois-says, "I am glad to see one real American here." Parker replies firmly, "We are all Americans." Robert E. Lee, with all his intelligence and dignity, still doesn't seem to understand why so many men and women have been willing to fight and die in this terrible war. *We are all Americans.* It is in those words.

Lee (seated, left) signed the surrender in McLean's parlor. Grant sits beside him, accompanied by various Union generals. Sheridan stands between them, while at the far left stands George Custer, graduated bottom of his West Point class and would die ingloriously at Little Bighorn.

The allegory of *Bateman's National Picture*, full of earnest patriotism and religious references, represents the reconciliation of North and South. The huge pavilion is the national government; the thin drum just below the dome, the legislature, the Supreme Court, and the cabinet. Below, the outer pillars stand for the state governments, undergoing "reconstruction"— the 'foundations of slavery," the former Confederate states, are being replaced with new ones: Justice, Liberty, Education.

Part 7

What Is Freedom?

Abraham Lincoln is in a good mood. It is April 14, 1865, and he is meeting with his cabinet. General Grant, now a war hero, is a guest at the meeting. The president tells Grant and the cabinet members of a dream he had the previous night. He was on a boat heading for a distant, misty shore. He has had this dream before. Each time, it has been followed by big news. He is sure the nation will hear something important before the day is over.

The cabinet members are in a good mood, too. They laugh about Lincoln's dream and go on to other matters. There are still Southern armies in the field, and Jefferson Davis is somewhere on a well-provisioned railroad train exhorting his people to "fight on." Despite this, and despite the real danger of continuing guerrilla warfare, the cabinet believes the war is almost over. How will the South be brought back into the Union? What should be done to help the newly freed men and women? The process of remaking the nation—without slavery—is already being called "reconstruction."

The president and his cabinet are not agreed on how Reconstruction should go. Many in the cabinet are known as "Radical Republicans." They have been uncompromising abolitionists. Some want nothing less than full citizenship for former slaves; that means the vote and equal rights. Lincoln believes that much of the nation is not ready to go that far. As for the defeated Confederate leaders, are they traitors? If so, the punishment for treason is death. After four years of terrible war, many Northerners are in no mood to forgive.

After the shot and John Wilkes Booth's (inset) leap onto the stage, a doctor named Charles Leale, who was in the audience, struggled to the president's box, laid Lincoln on the floor, and gave him artificial respiration until he was breathing on his own. "His wound is mortal," Leale said, "it is impossible for him to recover."

Lincoln has already forgiven. He made that clear at his recent second inaugural. "With malice toward none," he said. And "let us strive to finish the work we are in; to bind up the nation's wounds ... to do all which may achieve and cherish a just, and lasting peace, among ourselves, and with all nations." The president has not laid out detailed ideas on Reconstruction, but his general thoughts are known. Southerners are still part of the family, he says. Meeting Grant and Sherman on the presidential yacht, the *River Queen,* he says, "Let them all go, officers and all, I want submission, and no more bloodshed.... I want no one punished; treat them liberally all around. We want those people to return to their allegiance to the Union and submit to the laws."

It was after that meeting that Grant surprised everyone with the generosity of his terms of surrender. When the proceedings in Wilmer McLean's house were done, Grant stepped outside, where soldiers were watching, and, as Robert E. Lee mounted his horse Traveller, tipped his hat to his former foe. It was a moment filled with symbolism, respect, and grandeur. Lee will, in the days ahead, be equally gracious.

The president has encouraged a liberal Reconstruction plan already under way in Louisiana. He is eager for that state to resume its place in the Union. But Congress has refused to seat a new Louisiana delegation. Lincoln thinks that is a mistake. He wants the South back as part of the Union as soon as possible. At this cabinet session the president listens. He will announce his Reconstruction plans soon, he says. Lincoln knows that while the cabinet is meeting, an American flag is being raised at Fort Sumter in the harbor at Charleston, South Carolina—the very flag that was lowered exactly five Aprils earlier, when the war began. Now there are cheers for the flag, and hopeful words spoken by two of the nation's foremost abolitionists: the flamboyant Reverend Henry Ward Beecher, and the writer and editor William Lloyd Garrison. Beecher announces that the doctrine of natural rights "shall be applied to all men, without regard to race, or color, or condition."

Northerners are going south again—and not as soldiers. Some have already opened schools for the newly freed men, women, and children. Some intend to teach the white community how to behave. The former rebels, with their land devastated and their families decimated, are less than welcoming. Reconstruction will not be easy.

At the cabinet session, someone hands General Grant a note from his wife. She says they are to go to Philadelphia to see their sons as soon as this meeting adjourns. President Lincoln was looking forward to spending the evening with the general—the Grants and the Lincolns have been invited to a performance of *Our American Cousin* at Ford's Theatre, the popular playhouse located between the White House and the Capitol. Lincoln enjoys the theater, though this is said to be a silly play. When he hears that Grant isn't going, the president says he doesn't want to go either. But he knows Mrs. Lincoln has been looking forward to an evening out, and he doesn't want to disappoint her. So they go with some other guests. When they arrive, the orchestra plays "Hail to the Chief," and the audience stands and cheers. The president

> "There will never be anything like it on earth. The shouts, groans, curses, smashing of seats, screams of women, shuffling of feet and cries of terror created a pandemonium that through all the ages will stand out in my memory as the hell of hells."
> —Helen Truman, a member of the audience at Ford's Theatre when Lincoln was shot

settles into a special rocking chair placed in the flag-covered president's box. He and Mrs. Lincoln hold hands and laugh at the play's nonsense.

Then the audience hears a sound like a muffled clap of thunder. A handsome young man, wearing a black felt hat and high boots with spurs, climbs out of the president's box, leaps onto the stage, and shouts Virginia's Latin motto: *"Sic semper tyrannis!"* ["Thus ever to tyrants."] Some recognize him. He is an actor, a twenty-six-year-old matinee idol, John Wilkes Booth. He falls, breaking his leg, and is gone. A woman screams, and a voice cries out, *The president has been shot*. For a moment it all seemed part of the play, but this is no act. The audience panics, not knowing if more is to come. Later they will learn that Secretary of State William Seward, along with four others, has been stabbed in his house. The vice president, Andrew Johnson, escapes assassination when the plotter, with cold feet, gets drunk instead of killing him.

Abraham Lincoln dies the next day in the place he is carried to—a small house across the street from the theater. It is April 15, 1865. This awful war, begun with a madman's violence at Harpers Ferry, has come to an end with another act of madness. As the news spreads, there is disbelief and then terror and anguish and weeping. After all that the nation has gone through, this is almost too much to bear. Outside the White House, a crowd, mostly of African-Americans, gathers in a rain that seems to weep with them. Meanwhile, Booth has galloped off, sure people in the South will cheer this, his final dramatic performance. He is wrong. Robert E. Lee calls it "a crime that was unexampled," and one that "must be deprecated by every American." Booth is hunted down, trapped, and shot in a Virginia tobacco barn.

In Norfolk, Virginia, on the day of Lincoln's funeral, a long procession marches through the streets while a military band plays a dirge. Many of the marchers are former Rebel soldiers. Standing at attention are former slaves. In Washington, Philadelphia, New York, Albany, Buffalo, Chicago, wherever his funeral train passes on its way home to Springfield, Illinois, tens of thousands line up to pay last respects. One is six-year-old Theodore Roosevelt. Another, a tearful Walt Whitman, will write a poem about the season and the nation's loss.

A Wounded Nation

All anyone had to do was look in the history books. Whether it was Ireland, or France, or Scotland, or China—after a rebellion you find bloodbaths, guerrilla war, and decades or more of violence. Lincoln knew that. So did Lee. Was there any reason to expect the United States to be different? North and South were almost two separate countries; the hatreds were intense. There was nothing inevitable about our continued existence as a nation. And yet those two leaders and some of their peers imagined "a just and lasting peace," and made it happen.

At war's end, white Southerners are angry, confused, hurt, and miserable. Their lovely, elegant, aristocratic South is in ruins. A visitor to Charleston, South Carolina, writes of "vacant houses, of widowed women, of rotting wharves, of deserted warehouses, of weed-wild gardens, of miles of grass-grown streets." And the countryside? "We had no cattle, hogs, sheep, or horses or anything else," a Virginian wrote later. "The barns were all burned, chimneys standing without houses and houses standing without roofs, or doors, or windows." Across the South, there is no government, no courts, no post offices, no sheriffs, no police. Guerrilla bands loot at will.

Those who come home bring wounds with them. In 1866, the year after Lee's surrender, Mississippi spends one-fifth of

The remains of Columbia—the capital of South Carolina and the original "cradle of secession"—devastated by a huge fire after Sherman's army occupied the city on its march to the sea.

its revenues on artificial arms and legs for veterans. Southerners have to blame someone for their misery, and the former Rebels blame the Northerners. All they tried to do, they say, was form their own nation. How can they forgive the North for stopping them? But it isn't only Southerners who have lost sons and brothers. Many Northerners are bereaved. The South started the war, they say. The South should be punished. The Rebel leaders should be hanged.

President Lincoln had felt differently. "Enough lives have been sacrificed," he said. "We must extinguish our resentments if we expect harmony and union." Fierce General Sherman, who showed little mercy in his march through the South, had talked to the president on the *River Queen* about plans for peace.

I inquired of the President if he was all ready for the end of the war. He said he was all ready; all he wanted of us was to defeat the opposing armies, and to get the men composing the Confederate armies back to their homes, at work on their forms, and in their shops. I was more than ever impressed by his kindly nature and his deep and earnest sympathy with the afflictions of the whole people. His earnest desire seemed to be to end the war speedily, and to restore the men of both sections to their homes.

It is the soldiers and their officers who will make this peace work. Robert E. Lee fought as hard as he could, he lost fair and square, and now he refuses to look back. Again and again he will counsel Southerners to get on with their lives, to make the nation

> "It seemed like it took a long time for freedom to come. Everything just kept on like it was. We heard that lots of slaves was getting land and some mules to set up for theirselves. I never knowed any what got land or mules nor nothing."
>
> —Millie Freeman, a former slave

whole again. Embossed on the sword that Lee wore to Wilmer McLean's parlor are these French words: *Aide-toi et Dieu t'aidera* ("God helps those who help themselves"). Those words seem his guide. His wife's beloved family home in Arlington, Virginia, has been confiscated and turned into a cemetery for—and this must have really hurt—the Union dead. His other properties are all seized. Lee never complains. When a cavalry scout comes to him in Richmond, sent by daring John Mosby, asking if Mosby's Raiders should fight on, Lee says: "Go home, all you boys who fought with me. Help to build up the shattered fortunes of our old state." Of the end of slavery, he says, "The best men of the South have long been anxious to do away with this institution." And he promises "to make any sacrifice or perform any honorable act that would tend to the restoration of peace."

But what of the four million black Southerners who are now free men and women? What are they to do? Where will they go? Should they be paid for all their years of work? Should the government give them land of their own and mules, as Lincoln once promised? Most former slaves can't read or write. Who will their teachers be? Someone needs to do some organizing. Someone needs to maintain law and order. Reconstruction, the time in the South after the war, when the president, Congress, and many individuals attempt to remake the region and answer those questions, begins as a promising, idealistic, hopeful, moment in our history. It turns heart-wrenching. Then nasty. It is a lost opportunity. A time that cries out and says: leadership matters.

MAKING AMENDMENTS

Andrew Johnson is sworn in as seventeenth president. Lincoln had left the choice of a vice president up to the nominating convention in 1864. (Hannibal Hamlin was vice president in Lincoln's first term.) Johnson, a Democrat and a slave owner (Lincoln was a Republican who hated slavery), was picked because he was a Southern politician who opposed secession. The Republican Party was calling itself a "national Union" party. No one thought Johnson would actually become president. Lincoln saw Johnson only once after their inauguration, on the day before he died. They did have things in common. Johnson was a poor boy without much education

Andrew Johnson

who made his own way in life. He started out as a tailor, but when he got up at a political meeting and began speaking, he found he had a talent. He could captivate and hold an audience. In his home state, Tennessee, he became governor, representative, and senator. But he refused to follow his state into the Confederacy. "I love my country," he said. When Union forces captured Tennessee during the war, President Lincoln made him military governor. With the war over, people hoped he might be the right person to bring the country together again. Some who knew him weren't so sure. He had courage, no doubt about that. He was also stubborn and uncompromising.

The Radical Republicans hope to influence Johnson. They believe he will be more malleable than Lincoln. Some expect nothing less than a freedom revolution in the South, with blacks playing a role equal to whites'. Even before the war's end, Congress creates a Freedmen's Bureau. It is to help the newly freed find food, clothing, and shelter, as well as tools to help them lead independent lives. The Freedmen's Bureau begins opening schools. Slaves are starved for learning. In Mississippi, when a Freedmen's Bureau agent tells a group of 3,000 former slaves they are to have schools, he reports, "Their joy knew no bounds. They fairly jumped and shouted in gladness." Parents often sit in classrooms with children. As soon as they can read and write, the newly literate teach others.

Many of the teachers are whites sent by Northern churches. Others, like Mary Peake, who founds the first school for African-Americans in Hampton, Virginia, are educated Northern blacks. Those who go south often feel as if they are in a foreign land. One teacher in Georgia says, "Our work is just as much missionary work as if we were in India or China." (Old-guard Southerners—feeling that they are the true Americans—are less than enthusiastic about this reaction.)

By 1877 more than 600,000 Southern blacks had enrolled in school. The Freedmen's Bureau also ran "industrial schools" like this one, where practical skills such as sewing were taught.

Ku Klux Klansmen used terror tactics such as burning crosses, flogging or murder. Their aim was to stop blacks voting, holding political office, or otherwise exercising their new constitutional rights.

It's hard to learn if you are hungry, and Southern farms are in terrible shape. In 1865 the wheat crop fails. It doesn't do much better the next year. The Freedmen's Bureau keeps most people from starving. And people help each other. One former house slave with a job brings five dollars to his old mistress each week. A few Southern whites are ready to live with racial harmony, but many can't accept the idea of a society where people were equal—not after the hard-fought war. It seems to make the deaths meaningless. Thousands leave the country for Mexico and South America. Some Confederates go to Brazil, where slavery still exists (abolition is soon to come there, too). General Lee is not pleased. "Virginia has need of all her sons and can ill afford to spare you," he writes one man. To others he says, "Abandon all these local animosities and make your sons Americans."

But many whites turn, once again, to short-sighted leaders. Often they have no choice. Right after the war, in 1865 and 1866, the same old Southern establishment takes charge. Every Southern state passes laws that discriminate against blacks. The laws, called black codes, give whites almost unlimited power. It becomes a crime for a black person to refuse to sign a contract to work on a white plantation. No Southern state will establish public schools for African-Americans. Former slaves have no voice in government. Race riots erupt. In New Orleans, thirty-four blacks and three whites who stand with them are killed. General Philip Sheridan, who is there, calls it a massacre. Some whites put masks over their faces, burn black churches and schools, and terrorize and kill black people. They are members of a newly formed hate organization, the Ku Klux Klan, and they don't have the courage to show their faces. President Johnson urges the Southern states to protect the freedmen and freedwomen's rights, but he didn't do anything to see that they are protected. He turns against Southerners who backed the Union (as he did himself). He is taking sides at a time when what is needed is a leader of all the people.

Expanding Civil Rights

On December 6, 1865, Congress ratifies the Thirteenth Amendment to the Constitution which states: *"Neither slavery nor involuntary servitude, except as a punishment for crime whereof the party shall have been duly convicted, shall exist within the United States, or any place subject to their jurisdiction."*

That ends slavery. The Emancipation Proclamation is now the law of the land. But is being free of slavery enough? If you are free but can't vote, are you really free? If you are free but laws say you can't quit your job or leave your plantation—as the black codes said—are you really free?

The war has been fought to end slavery, and slavery is finished. But the black codes are there to do the same old thing: to keep African-Americans from their inalienable rights. So, in 1866, a small group of leaders within the Republican Party (the Radical Republicans) gets Congress to pass a Civil Rights Act. It is designed to nullify the black codes. Johnson vetoes the Civil Rights Act. Although he no longer believes in slavery, he does not believe in equality. He thinks it is up to the states, not the central government, to protect individual rights. He says the act is unconstitutional. After a presidential veto, two-thirds of both houses of Congress must vote for a bill for it to become law—and two-thirds do. It is the first time in American history that an important piece of legislation is passed over a president's veto. Johnson is furious. "I am right. I know I am right," says the president. "And I am damned if I do not adhere to it."

In the *Dred Scott* case, the Supreme Court said that African-Americans were not citizens and held none of the rights of citizens. The Radical Republicans are determined to overturn that decision. They start with the Civil Rights Act, but they know that future legislation may reverse it. They decide to expand the Constitution itself. They have already begun with the Thirteenth Amendment (ending slavery); now they write a Fourteenth Amendment. It includes a definition of citizenship: "all persons born or naturalized in the United States" are "citizens of the United States and of the State wherein they reside." Blacks are now citizens. The Fourteenth Amendment is meant primarily to address issues relating to the newly freed African-Americans, but a key clause turns out to do much more than that.

> *No State shall deprive any person of life, liberty, or property, without due process of law; nor deny to any person within its jurisdiction the equal protection of the laws.*

In other words, no state can take away any citizen's rights. We are all entitled to the safeguards provided by the Constitution and the Bill of Rights. In a controversy between a state and an individual, the individual is to have the protection of the Constitution. As interpreted by succeeding courts, that "due process" clause will expand freedom for all Americans.

Back in 1787, the Constitution makers had worried about protecting citizens from abuses by Congress, or the president, or the central government—not from abuses by their states. Each state was expected to protect its own citizens. But some didn't. In a landmark case, *Barron* v. *Baltimore,* in 1831, John Barron, who owned a dock put out of use by city dredging, sued the city of Baltimore under the Fifth Amendment for destroying his property without "just compensation." Chief Justice John Marshall and his court said the Constitution offered Barron (who was acting for ten wharf owners) no protection from state injury. That was solely in the hands of state agencies. Under the ruling, states might censor, take property, legalize slavery, do whatever they wanted—limited only by their own constitutions.

The Fourteenth Amendment makes the federal government superior to any state. The South had fought for states' rights. Many Southerners think each state should be free to make its own decisions. If a state wants an aristocratic society with layers of privilege and unfairness—well, if that's what the majority of its people want (or that those in power can legislate)—why shouldn't they have it? This powerful amendment sets limits. It helps turn a collection of diverse states into a nation. In the twentieth century it will become an instrument for protecting of individual freedom in ways totally unanticipated by its authors. Before the amendment, the United States *are* a collection of semi-independent states. After the amendment, the verb actually changes: the United States *is* a federal nation. Andrew Johnson doesn't like it a bit. He isn't alone.

Reconstruction Means Rebuilding

Laws aren't enough to guarantee freedom to the former slaves. Laws have to be enforced. So, in 1867, Congress divides the South into military districts to help restore order and do something about the black codes. Soldiers are sent south to organize and run the districts; they stay for about ten years. This time is called "congressional" or "military" Reconstruction (in contrast to the initial period of "presidential" reconstruction). Other Northerners go south to teach, to work with aid programs, to help the state governments get going again—and sometimes to make money for themselves. Those Yankees are known as carpetbaggers, from the traveling bags of the time made of carpet material. Most white

What Is Freedom? 165

Some Southern planters, producing crops like "Reconstruction tobacco," hoped for quick profits after the war, but in 1866 and 1867 crops failed and economic recovery was slow.

Southerners hate them. Congress passes a Reconstruction Act. President Johnson vetoes it. And, once again, enough votes are gathered in Congress to pass it over his veto. The act says that each state must write a new constitution that is in keeping with the U.S. Constitution. It must ratify the Fourteenth Amendment. As to voting: the act says that all males over the age of twenty-one can vote, except for convicted criminals and those who participated "in the rebellion." That means that many former Confederate soldiers can't vote, but that black men can. Northern soldiers make sure that black men are able to vote. Men who were slaves a few years earlier soon line up at the polls. Many are illiterate (about one-fifth of the South's white population is illiterate, too). Being illiterate doesn't mean being stupid. The new voters do exactly what James Madison expected them to do. They vote for what they believe to be their own interests. Senator Timothy Howe of Wisconsin says, "We have cut loose from the whole dead past, and have cast our anchor out a hundred years." Soon blacks are being elected to office. Mississippians Blanche K. Bruce and Hiram R. Revels become United States senators. Both are college men. Revels takes Jefferson Davis's old seat in the Senate. The day he is sworn in, the Senate galleries are packed, and everyone stands as he walks down the aisle. Some observers burst into cheers to see a black senator. "Never since the birth of the republic," says an editorial in the *Philadelphia Press*, "has such an audience been assembled under one single roof. It embraced the greatest and the least American citizens."

It is difficult for some white people to accept the changes. Blacks in Congress! Blacks in the state legislatures! Many whites believe the racist myths; they are sure blacks can't handle the legislative process.

Come along to Charleston, South Carolina, and see what is happening. It is January 14, 1868, and we are at the

This 1867 cartoon is meant to show that the wealthy support black voters while poor farmers stand behind Andrew Jackson's vetoes. The real story was more complex.

fashionable Charleston Clubhouse, on Meeting Street. The members of the state legislature are about to write a new constitution so that South Carolina can again send representatives to Washington. Since most of South Carolina's citizens are black, and they can now vote, they have elected black lawmakers to their legislature. Seventy-six black men and forty-eight white men are gathered in the ballroom. Outside, a noisy crowd surges through the streets. Most are former slaves, and they are full of hope. They believe a new era has begun. In their handsome, shuttered homes overlooking Charleston harbor, the city's white aristocrats wait and worry. Some of the old plantation families are terrified. Will the assembly demand revenge for the years of slavery? There are rumors that say it will.

At the Clubhouse, a few of the delegates wear rough clothing, but most are dressed in long, tailored frock coats. They wear fashionable whiskers and beards. A Charleston newspaper can't help remarking that "many of the colored delegates are intelligent and respectable looking." Twenty-five-year-old Robert Brown Elliott is as well educated as anyone who is here. He has studied at Eton, a famous school in England. Trained in the law, he is fluent

The Right to Vote (Part 1)

The war is hardly over when the black community of New Orleans holds a mock election to show their desire to vote. In Wilmington, North Carolina, former soldiers, ministers, and newly freed African-Americans—members of an Equal Rights League—parade through the streets to press for "all the social and political rights." High on their list is the right to vote. Many whites concur. Henry Ward Beecher says, "Every man has a right to have a voice in the laws … that take care of him. That is an inherent right; it is not a privilege conferred." When some whites fear enfranchising "ignorant" blacks, Beecher responds: "To have an ignorant class voting is dangerous, whether white or black, but to have an ignorant class and not have them voting, is a great deal more dangerous.… The remedy for the unquestionable dangers of having ignorant voters lies in educating them." The Fourteenth Amendment deals with voting rights only obliquely; more needs to be done to settle this issue. Congress passes a bill to end racial qualifications for voting in the District of Columbia. Congressmen cite black sacrifices on the battlefield. President Johnson vetoes the District of Columbia measure. Congress overrides the veto.

in French and Spanish. He will sit in this convention for fourteen days without speaking. Then he will stand and become known as a great orator. Elliott hopes to become South Carolina's governor. But first he will go to Washington and enter the House of Representatives as a congressman from South Carolina. Arguing for civil rights legislation, he will say:

> It is a matter of regret to me that it is necessary at this day that I should rise in the presence of an American Congress to advocate a bill which simply asserts equal rights and equal public privileges for all classes of American citizens. I regret, sir, that the dark hue of my skin may lend a color to the imputation that I am controlled by motives personal to myself.… Sir, the motive that impels me is restricted by no such narrow boundary, but is as broad as your Constitution. I advocate it sir, because it is right.

But it is still 1868 and we are in Charleston. Notice a tall, distinguished man with side whiskers. He is Francis Louis Cardozo, the son of a Jewish economist and a free black woman. Cardozo, thirty-one, was graduated from the University of Glasgow, in Scotland, with honors in Latin and Greek. He has come to Charleston to be a school principal and a minister. A brilliant administrator, Cardozo will save millions of dollars for South Carolina when he exposes corrupt businessmen who are taking advantage of the state. The man he is talking to also has a Jewish father and a black mother. He is Robert Smalls, and

Robert Brown Elliott of South Carolina (inset) addressed the House of Representatives in support of a civil rights bill intended to end discrimination against African-Americans in hotels, railroads, and other public places. The bill passed in 1875, but was rarely enforced.

he stunned both North and South a few years ago when, all by himself, he piloted a Confederate steamer through the guns of Charleston harbor and handed it over to the U.S. Navy. The third man in the group is six-foot-two-inch William Beverly Nash. Nash, a former slave, has taught himself to read. He quotes Shakespeare with ease. Nash is known for his sharp, quick wit. And there are others to watch here. One is Daniel Henry Chamberlain, a white man, a graduate of Harvard and Yale, and ambitious. During the war, Chamberlain was a Union officer who led a black regiment. Robert Brown Elliott hates Chamberlain. Both are carpetbaggers. Chamberlain will become governor of South Carolina.

Some say this session in Charleston is the beginning of America's "second revolution." It is an attempt at a genuine interracial society. Poor whites are represented here, and former slaves, and wealthy white men who are accustomed to rule. No question about it, this is government by the people. These men are making history—and they know it. All across the South,

Reconstruction legislatures are at work. Six men in the Florida legislature cannot read or write. (Four of those six are white.) Jonathan C. Gibbs, a black minister and a graduate of Dartmouth and Princeton, is said to be the most cultured man at the Florida convention.

Most Southerners are small farmers. This is a terrible time for them. Cotton prices have fallen to low levels. As if that is not bad enough, the weather is poor and so are the harvests. White farmers are exhausted and fuming: their sons are dead—killed in the war—their savings are gone. They have no money to hire workers or buy equipment or seeds. The black farmers are mostly without land. It is an impossible situation. The lawmakers ask themselves: Should they take land from the Confederates who rebelled against their nation? Should they give it to the slaves who have worked the land and made others rich? Can they divide the land and be fair? How do you provide opportunity and justice for all?

These Reconstruction legislatures will vote for free public schools; almost none have existed in the South before. They will vote for roads. They will not demand revenge on the white aristocracy. They will do as well as most legislatures and far better than the U.S. Congress, which, right now, is shockingly corrupt. But they won't solve the land problem, and they will fall. When the U.S. soldiers leave the South, "Redeemer" politicians—mostly former Confederates—will take their place. Intimidation and fear—for their lives and their jobs—will soon keep blacks from the polls. Restrictive legislation will finish the job. The hopeful crowds who swirled about the Charleston Clubhouse in 1868 will not see a new era. They will not get to live in a fair interracial society. Robert Brown Elliott will not be governor of South Carolina.

> "All free governments are managed by the combined wisdom and folly of the people.... No government can be free that does not allow all its citizens to participate in the formation and execution of her laws. Every other government is a despotism."
> —Thaddeus Stevens

IMPEACHING A PRESIDENT

President Johnson doesn't like the Fourteenth Amendment. He believes in states' rights. And he doesn't like Radical Republican Thaddeus Stevens, the man behind the Fourteenth Amendment, at all. Abraham Lincoln believed in compromise. He asked questions, listened, and changed his mind when he thought it

AWKWARD COLLISION ON THE GRAND TRUNK COLUMBIA R. R.

A. J. (Driver of Engine "President")—"LOOK HERE! ONE OF US HAS GOT TO BACK."
Thaddeus (Driver of Engine "Congress")—"WELL, IT AIN'T ME THAT'S GOING TO DO IT—YOU BET!"

Two stubborn politicians cast as railroad engineers: Andrew Johnson (left) and the leader of the Radical Republicans, Thaddeus Stevens. Neither would give way on his Reconstruction plans.

needed changing. Stevens is incapable of compromise, and so is Andrew Johnson. He doesn't ask for advice, or listen when it is given. He came into office with much good will. Everyone wanted him to succeed. But he has a stubborn, narrow-minded streak that makes him a poor leader. He goes on a speaking tour and says wild, derogatory things about Congress. Often his actions are undignified, unpresidential. But his beliefs are sincere. He is convinced it is *not* the responsibility of the nation to help the newly freed men and women get fair and equal treatment before the law. He thinks that is the states' job.

Thaddeus Stevens knows the states have not done that; he believes they won't. Johnson calls Stevens a traitor and says he should be hanged. Stevens says the president be impeached.

WHO SHOULD HAVE THE RIGHT TO VOTE?
Two Founders and a Modern Commentator Speak

The same reasoning which will induce you to admit all men who have not property, to vote, with those who have ... will prove that you ought to admit women and children; for, generally speaking, women and children have as good judgments, and as independent minds, as those men who are wholly destitute of property; these last being to all intents and purposes as much dependent upon others, who will please to feed, clothe, and employ them, as women are upon their husbands, or children on their parents.... Depend upon it, sir, it is dangerous to open so fruitful a source of controversy and altercation as would be opened by attempting to alter the qualifications of voters; there will be no end of it. New claims will arise; women will demand the vote; lads from twelve to twenty-one will think their rights not enough attended to; and every man who has not a farthing will demand an equal voice with any other, in all acts of state. It tends to confound and destroy all distinctions, and prostrate all ranks to one common level.
—John Adams, 1776

Today a man owns a jackass worth fifty dollars and he is entitled to vote; but before the next election the jackass dies. The man in the meantime has become more experienced, his knowledge of the principles of government, and his acquaintance with mankind, are more extensive, and he is therefore better qualified to make a proper selection of rulers but the jackass is dead and therefore the man cannot vote. Now, gentlemen, pray inform me, in whom is the right of suffrage? In the man or in the jackass?
—Benjamin Franklin, *The Casket, or Flowers of Literature, Wit and Sentiment*

At its birth, the United States was not a democratic nation—far from it. The very word democracy had pejorative overtones, summoning up images of disorder, government by the unfit, even mob rule. In practice, moreover, relatively few of the nation's inhabitants were able to participate in elections; among the excluded were most African-Americans, Native Americans, women, men who had not attained their majority, and adult white males who did not own land.
—Alexander Keyssar, *The Right to Vote*, 2000

Impeachment is a process borrowed from the English system of government. Thaddeus Stevens says it is "a moral necessity" to impeach President Johnson. Stevens isn't the only one who wants the impeachment. Many who are concerned about Reconstruction, and where it is leading, seem to want it. Will the president be impeached? And if he is, will he then be convicted of "high crimes and misdemeanors" and thrown out of the "White House? The nation holds its breath, waiting to find out.

In 1867, Congress passed the Tenure of Office Act; it prevented the president from firing his cabinet members. Loyal Secretary of State William Seward tries to comfort the stabbed president.

It is 1868. The impeachment debate in the House of Representatives has lasted more than two months. Finally, the House votes. President Andrew Johnson is impeached. Now it is time for the members of the Senate to try the president. Nothing like this has happened before in the United States; a president is on trial. A thousand tickets are printed for admission to the Senate galleries; people do everything they can to get them. One Washington woman wakes a congressman at night and won't leave his house until he promises her a ticket. Reporters cover the trial as if it were a murder case. All over the country, day after day, newspaper headlines scream the details. Saturday, May 16, the day of the trial, comes. The chief justice of the Supreme Court administers an oath to each senator "to do impartial justice." Two-thirds of the senators must vote for conviction in order to remove the president from office. The vote begins. As expected, all the Democrats vote "not guilty." Republican after Republican votes "guilty." Thaddeus Stevens, by now an

A Radical Republican

The word *radical* is rarely used as a compliment. Those dubbed Radical Republicans are often disliked—in the North as well as the South. They are seen as extremists. They have been intense abolitionists; now they refuse to compromise on Reconstruction. The Radical Republicans want full equality for all. They believe that freeing blacks is not enough; the newly freed need a fair chance to achieve. Land and a mule for each black family seems reasonable. The radicals are not very popular. And it doesn't help that they are apt to be self-righteous. Many support the idea of votes for women. They are ahead of their times, which is never easy. Thaddeus Stevens speaks for their ideas in Congress.

Stevens grew up in Vermont, a poor boy with a handicap: he has a clubfoot that makes him limp badly. But he has an amazing mind, and he is unwaveringly honest. Like most Vermonters, he says what he thinks and doesn't waste words. When he is twenty-four, in 1816, he moves to a pretty little Pennsylvania town called Gettysburg. He is soon the best lawyer in Gettysburg, and then the best in Pennsylvania. The richest, too. He owns an iron foundry (it is destroyed by Lee's army during the battle of Gettysburg) and he is a shrewd investor. His Gettysburg neighbors think well of him; they send him to Congress, and keep him there. White Southerners call him the vilest of Yankees. African-Americans see him as a hero, and rank him close to the angels. Those who know him either admire or hate him. Stevens does what he wants, says what he wants, and doesn't seem to care what others think. He can't be bribed or tempted-everyone agrees about that. In 1838, way before the Civil War, he refused to sign the Pennsylvania constitution, because it gave the vote only to white men. When fugitive slaves needed help, he was their lawyer, and never charged a fee. His Yankee mind tells him that all men are created equal means all men—not all white men. So, starting in the 1830s, he begins battling for abolition, and then emancipation, and then equal rights. He never stops fighting; he never keeps quiet. When it comes to the South, you can call him a hardliner. After the war he sees the South as conquered territory over which Congress can rule at its discretion. He is the chief author of the Fourteenth Amendment, and he lays the foundations for the Fifteenth. "We are building a nation," he says, intending that his ideas help change a collection of states into a cohesive nation. He says the Southern states should not be admitted back into the Union until blacks are given the vote, given land, and given guarantees of equality under the law. President Andrew Johnson loathes him. Stevens despises Johnson.

When Thaddeus Stevens dies, in 1868, thousands walk past his casket in the Capitol. He is buried in a cemetery where blacks and whites rest side by side. Chiseled on his tombstone are these words.

I repose in this quiet and
  secluded spot,
Not from any natural
  preference for solitude
But, finding other Cemeteries
  limited as to Race by
  Charter Rules,
I have chosen this that I might
  illustrate in my death
The Principles which
  I advocated
Through a long life.

ailing old man, is carried in on a chair. He votes "guilty."

But a few of the Republicans have had second thoughts. Some have been given assurances that if they vote to acquit President Johnson he will no longer interfere with Reconstruction. Six Republican senators decide to vote for the president. A seventh, newly elected Edmund Ross of Kansas, is having a hard time making up his mind. The Republicans are one vote shy of conviction. Ross holds the deciding vote. A former newspaperman who fought in the Union army, Edmund Ross hates slavery—and he doesn't like President Johnson. He has voted with the Radical Republicans on every issue. Shortly before the trial, he gets a telegram from home:

> KANSAS HAS HEARD THE EVIDENCE AND DEMANDS THE CONVICTION OF THE PRESIDENT. SIGNED, D. R. ANTHONY AND 1,000 OTHERS.

Kansas is a Radical Republican state. Ross answers:

> TO D.R. ANTHONY AND 1,000 OTHERS: I HAVE TAKEN AN OATH TO DO IMPARTIAL JUSTICE ACCORDING TO THE CONSTITUTION AND LAWS, AND TRUST I SHALL HAVE THE COURAGE TO VOTE ACCORDING TO THE DICTATES OF MY JUDGMENT AND FOR THE HIGHEST GOOD OF THE COUNTRY.

On the day of the trial, it is Ross's turn to vote. His is the deciding ballot. The chief justice says, "Mr. Senator Ross, how say you? Is the respondent Andrew Johnson guilty or not guilty of a high misdemeanor as charged in this article?" Later, Ross remembered it this way:

> *Not a foot moved, not the rustle of a garment, not a whisper was heard.... hope and fear seemed blended in every face. The Senators in their seats leaned over their desks, many with hand to ear.... I almost literally looked down into my open grave. Friendships, position, fortune, everything that makes life desirable to an ambitious man were about to be swept away by the breath of my mouth, perhaps forever.*

Softly, Edmund Ross says, "Not guilty." The final result of the Senate vote is 35 to 19, exactly one vote short of the required two-thirds needed for conviction. The president is saved. D. R. Anthony writes to Ross, *Kansas repudiates you as she does all perjurers and skunks*. Others accuse him of taking bribes (he hasn't). Ross is never elected to political office again. When Thaddeus Stevens hears the vote he says, "The country is going to the devil." But the Constitution says that conviction is intended for "high crimes and misdemeanours."

Andrew Johnson has encouraged racial bigotry. He slowed the process of achieving "justice for all." His mulishness was a disaster for the nation. But he committed no "high crimes." It is his ideas that were on trial. Ideas aren't meant to be impeached or tried. The Founders intended for voters to vote bad ideas out of office. Thaddeus Stevens is bitterly disappointed. He knows that President

Above, Republican Senator Edmund Ross (foreground) casts his vote at Johnson's impeachment (top right, a ticket to the trial). Inset: Radical Republican Ben Butler reads evidence. Senator Charles Sumner said, "This monstrous power [of slavery] has found a refuge in the executive mansion, where, in utter disregard of the Constitution and laws, it seeks to exercise its ancient, far-reaching sway …. Andrew Johnson is the impersonation of the tyrannical slave power."

HOW TO IMPEACH

The President, Vice President and all civil Officers of the United States, shall be removed from Office on Impeachment for, and Conviction of, Treason, Bribery, or other high Crimes and Misdemeanours. The writers of the Constitution didn't make it easy to remove a president from office. According to the Constitution: *The House of Representatives shall … have the sole power of impeachment.* If a simple majority in the House of Representatives votes to impeach a president, he is impeached. That means he is charged with misconduct or crimes—it doesn't mean he is convicted of those crimes. He doesn't leave office. The next step is to bring the official to trial. The scene shifts to the Senate. It takes a two-thirds vote to convict. In the words of the Constitution: *The Senate shall have the sole Power to try all impeachments.… When the President of the United States is tried, the Chief Justice shall preside and no Person shall be convicted without the Concurrence of two thirds of the Members present. Judgment, in cases of impeachment, shall not extend further than to removal from office, and disqualification to hold and enjoy any office of honour, trust or profit, under the United States; but the party convicted shall nevertheless be liable and subject to indictment, trial, judgement and punishment, according to law.*

The Right to Vote (Part 2)

The Radical Republicans believe that only an amendment can guarantee broad male suffrage. In 1869 they come up with one. Its first version gives the vote to all male citizens (except Native Americans) without restrictions about ownership of land or literacy. The congressional debate, dealing with the meaning of democracy, is eloquent and impassioned. The issues are complex—the Republicans can sense power slipping away. Adding black votes is in their interest. It is also in the interest of the Southern states—with black voters counted as whole persons (rather than as three-fifths of persons, as in the original Constitution), the South will gain representatives (and votes) in Congress. But many Southerners don't see it that way. And there is much hypocrisy in the North on equal rights. Western representatives worry about giving the vote to the Chinese (even though the Chinese cannot become citizens at this time). Some New England states fear Irish enfranchisement (if there are no property qualifications or literacy tests). Others worry about women wanting to vote. The Fifteenth Amendment is narrowed to deal only with "race, color or previous condition of servitude." It becomes part of the Constitution in February 1870. Frederick Douglass is elated; he says that the amendment "means we are placed upon an equal footing with all other men.... that liberty is to be the right of all." His words are premature. But, for a few Reconstruction years, African-Americans in the South do have the right to vote.

Johnson's policies are destroying the promise of Reconstruction. Stevens has only a few weeks to live. He uses his final days to work on plans for free schools in the District of Columbia. He helps write the Fifteenth Amendment to the Constitution. It gives African-American men the constitutional right to vote. The Fifteenth Amendment says: *The right of citizens of the United States to vote shall not be denied or abridged by the United States or by any State on account of race, color, or previous condition of servitude.*

A Failed Revolution

Black-dominated Southern legislatures appropriate money for schools, roads, and railroads. These are all important to ordinary people. However, you need to levy taxes to pay for them, and taxes cost big landowners more than they cost ordinary people. The landowners are not happy about some of the new appropriations. By 1870, black boys and girls are enrolled in 4,000 new schools in the South. At least nine black colleges are opened. In 1875, Congress passes a civil rights bill prohibiting discrimination in hotels, theaters, and amusement parks. It is a civil rights revolution.

But there is a problem at the bottom of all this. If African-Americans can be congressmen and responsible citizens, if they can be educated, then the whole idea of black inferiority doesn't make sense. So slavery must really have been wrong. Many white Southerners still can't accept that idea. They have been through a ghastly war. One of every five Southern men died. If slavery is wrong, their sons and fathers died for nothing. How can they believe that? White Southerners are not monsters; they are not angels; they are human beings. They need help understanding what has happened to their beloved South. They do not get it. Hate groups, like the Ku Klux Klan, begin waging war on former slaves. Before the Civil War, there was no lynching of blacks—slaves were valuable possessions. Now black lynchings become common. In 1871, the black citizens of Frankfort, Kentucky, send a petition to Congress.

> *We the colored citizens of Frankfort and vicinity do this day memorialize upon the condition of affairs now existing in this state of Kentucky. We would respectfully state that life, liberty, and property are unprotected among the colored race of this state. Organized bands of desperate and lawless men, mainly composed of soldiers of the late Rebel armies, armed, disciplined, and disguised, and bound by oath and secret obligations, have by force, term; and violence subverted all civil society among the colored people.... We believe you are not familiar with the Ku Klux Klan's riding nightly over the country, going from county to county, and in the county towns spreading terror wherever they go by robbing, whipping, ravishing, and killing our people without provocation.... We would state that we have been law-abiding citizens, pay our tax, and, in many parts of the state, our people have been driven from the polls—refused the right to vote. Many have been slaughtered while attempting to vote; we ask how long is this state of things to last.*

Most of the South's big landowners are Democrats. Those Democrats are determined to bring back as much of the old South as possible, using whatever it takes: black codes, murderous Klansmen, or poll taxes that stop poor blacks from voting. The Democrats who oppose Reconstruction call themselves Redeemers. In the 1870s they are busy redeeming one state after another, driving Republicans from power.

In Washington, the Civil War hero General Ulysses S. Grant becomes president. He is popular, but unprepared for the job. As an honorable man, he trusts those around him; they turn out to be untrustworthy. Millions of dollars in public lands and resources are stolen. Grant, and the American people, are victims. The Grant years are a time of appalling government corruption.

Rutherford B. Hayes, looking upright and presidential. But he got the job through voter fraud.

> "What is freedom? Is it the bare privilege of not being chained? If this is all, then freedom is a bitter mockery, a cruel delusion."
>
> —James Garfield, congressman, former clergyman, future president

By the time Grant enters the final year of his presidency, political sleaze is widespread and a rapidly changing economy is bringing social and financial chaos to the nation. Northern citizens are tired of hearing about the need for a just society in the South. They have problems of their own. In the 1876 presidential election, Democrat Samuel Tilden seems to be ahead of Republican Rutherford B. Hayes in the total vote count. But if Hayes can carry three Southern states where the electoral college count is still incomplete, he can win. Strange things begin to happen to the ballots. In Louisiana, 15,000 votes—almost all of them Democratic—are suddenly pronounced invalid. Less than a week before the date of the inauguration, Hayes says that if he is elected, he will pull federal troops out of the South. He gets the Southern electoral votes. On March 5, 1877, Hayes stands on the steps of the Capitol, takes the oath of office, and says, "Only a local government, which recognizes and maintains the rights of all, is a true self-government." He means state governments, unsupervised by the federal army. Hayes keeps his promise. Soldiers leave the South; the hated occupation is over; but no one is left to enforce civil rights for blacks. Reconstruction is over.

The Southern old guard—the Redeemers—take power. They pass laws that make voters pay a poll tax or take a skewed test: that means most blacks can no longer vote. New laws and policies make it impossible for African-Americans to get a decent education, or to buy land. Blacks don't have access to fair trials. Armed hooligans intimidate and sometimes murder those who seek the franchise, proving—if it needs proving—the importance of individual votes. Soon many Southern blacks are not much better off than they were when they were slaves. Some are worse off.

Jim Crow

Reconstruction is finished. The do-good carpetbaggers are hounded out of the South. Some just become discouraged and leave. Some are lynched. Southern whites who try to be fair to blacks are ridiculed—and they too are sometimes lynched. In Arkansas, men with guns force black lawmakers out of the state. Segregation, which has long existed in the North, now heads south. Blacks (and Indians, and Asians, and Latinos) are not welcome in white hotels, restaurants, schools, or theaters. They cannot get good jobs. Segregation gets a name. It comes from a character in a song—a song about a black man who sings and dances and never gives anyone trouble. It's "Jim Crow."

Wheel about, turn about, dance jest so,
Every time I wheel about I shout Jim Crow.

Before the Civil War, in the South, there was slavery but not segregation. Segregation cannot coexist with slavery. Masters and their slaves must live and work in close proximity. After the war, things in the North stay much the same. Segregation by habit continues. But in the South, nothing is the same. Jim Crow dances across the land. Soon blacks and whites ride in separate railroad cars, go to separate schools, get buried in separate cemeteries, pray in separate churches, eat in separate restaurants. There is nothing blacks can do about it—now that they can't vote. State and local laws are passed that make these things possible. A few white Southerners try to stop these laws; they are ignored. An editorial in a Charleston newspaper about seating on railroad trains says:

Reconstruction was a hopeful experiment that died. Jim Crow, here illustrating the song that was written about him (and unsubtly paired with a monkey), was a poor fool who lived way too long.

> *The common sense and proper arrangement, in our opinion, is to provide first-class cars for first-class passengers, white and colored.... To speak plainly, we need, as everybody knows, separate cars or apartments for rowdy or drunken white passengers far more than Jim Crow cars for colored passengers.*

But common sense has fled from the South. Are the states defying the Constitution? Of course they are. The Fourteenth Amendment says:

> *No State shall make or enforce any law which shall abridge the privileges or immunities of citizens of the United States ... nor deny to any person within its jurisdiction the equal protection of the laws.*

But no one in power cares enough, or is strong enough, to do anything about it.

Separate but Equal

In 1890, the Louisiana General Assembly passes a bill that says railroads must "provide separate but equal accommodation for the white and colored races" on passenger trains. Everyone knows that separate is never equal. Six years later, some Louisiana citizens go to the Supreme Court to see what they can do about it. They ask Homer Plessy if he will help. Plessy's great-grandmother was African. Everyone else in his family has a European background. Plessy's skin is white. But, according to the racists, anyone with any African blood at all is black. So Homer Plessy is considered black. His friends in New Orleans want to show the ridiculousness of the whole idea of racial categories. That's why they choose white-skinned Homer Plessy for a test case.

They ask Plessy to sit in the white section of a railroad car. When the conductor is told that he is black, Plessy is arrested, charged with breaking the law, and put in jail. Plessy and his attorneys say that the "separate but equal" law is unconstitutional. New Orleans judge John H. Ferguson says they are wrong. Plessy's case makes it all the way to the Supreme Court. There Plessy loses. And the case—*Plessy* v. *Ferguson*—takes its place, beside *Dred Scott* v. *Sandford,* as one of the worst decisions the Court has made. One lone Supreme Court justice, John Marshall Harlan, disagrees with his peers. This is his dissenting opinion:

> *In view of the Constitution, in the eye of the law, there is in this country no superior, dominant ruling class of citizens. There is no caste here. Our Constitution is colorblind, and neither knows nor tolerates classes among citizens.*

"Our Constitution is colorblind"—but it will be almost sixty years before the Supreme

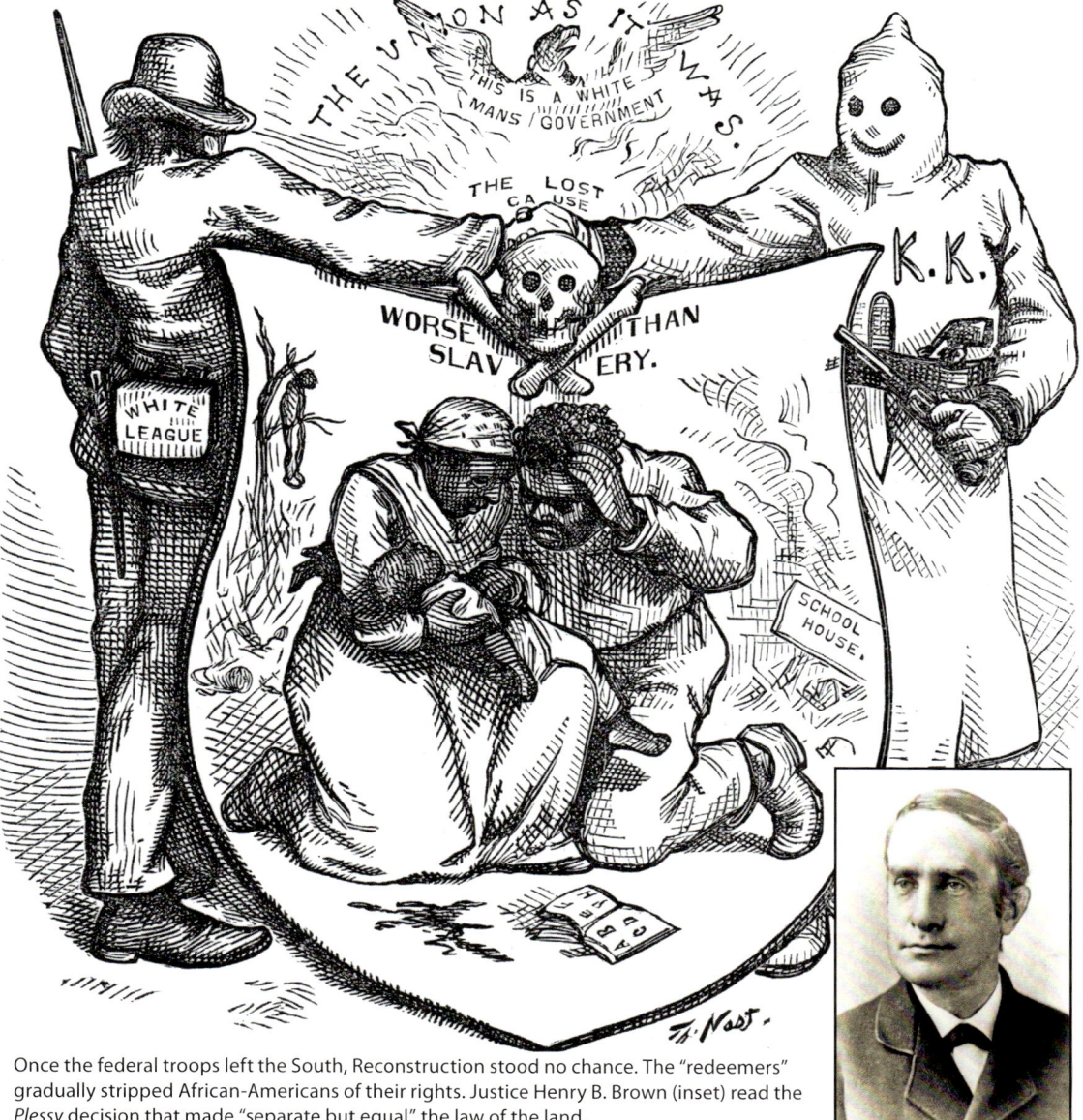

Once the federal troops left the South, Reconstruction stood no chance. The "redeemers" gradually stripped African-Americans of their rights. Justice Henry B. Brown (inset) read the *Plessy* decision that made "separate but equal" the law of the land.

Court understands that and, finally, kicks Jim Crow off the stage. Until then, Mr. Crow dances and sings with abandon. "Separate but equal" becomes the way of the South. In 1893, three years before *Plessy* becomes law, Frederick Douglass, speaking at the Chicago World's Fair, says this:

> *Men talk of the Negro problem. There is no Negro problem. The problem is whether American people have loyalty enough, honor enough, patriotism enough, to live up to their own constitution. We Negroes love our country. We fought for it. We ask only that we be treated as well as those who fought against it.*

George Catlin was born in Wilkes-Barre, Pennsylvania, in 1796; fascinated with Indian life and lore, he traveled thousands of miles—from Missouri to the southwest—between 1830 and 1836, portraying almost forty tribes in 470 paintings.

Part 8

Whose Land Is This?

For two hundred years, the Native Americans have been promised, in treaty after treaty, that if they move, just once more, they will be left alone. First they were pushed across the Appalachians; then west of the Mississippi; now they are being asked to move off all the good land left in the West. They aren't given a choice—or, at least, not much of a choice: it is move or fight. And so, for some thirty years after the Civil War, there are Indian wars in the West. It is the U.S. Army pitted against Indian tribes. The wars, no matter what people say, are all over the same thing: land, and who will control it. "We were at their hearths and homes … and they were fighting for all the good God gives anyone to fight for," says an officer to a court of inquiry that is trying to understand the warriors' ferocity. The horrors on both sides defy reasonable explanation.

The whites who are taking Indian lands are just ordinary people who have been told there is free land in the West. So they come to settle on it. They have heard stories about Native Americans—mostly that they are cruel, bloodthirsty savages, not "civilized" like themselves. Many settlers would rather have stayed in the East, but by 1873 there is an economic depression there; farms are failing and thousands are out of work. So they head west, filling in the lands west of the Appalachians, and then going on across the Mississippi. They're in for surprises. Farming on the prairie is different from farming back East. About a third of the people who head west turn around and go back where they came from. IN GOD WE TRUSTED, IN KANSAS WE BUSTED, say signs on the covered wagons returning home.

That vast American plain—stretching from Texas to Canada—is one of the world's great savannahs, grassland rich in flora and fauna, like the Russian steppes, or Argentina's

Cyrus McCormick, inventor of the reaper.

pampas. Those who have come from regions rimmed with fjords, or forests, or alps, or just fenced New England farms, are unprepared for an open panorama like this. It is almost like landing on another planet. These adventurers, used to trees and mountains in their visual background, are often lost without somewhere to tether their eyes. But a few feel a freedom unlike anything they have known before. The unconstrained vistas may make humans seem small, but it also makes them a part of an awesome, endless universe. This is not a region for everyone, but some who take to it come to love its vastness, its silence, its possibilities.

Others find it unforgiving. The prairie is not empty land, but to those who trudge beside covered wagons with high expectations, it seems bleak, barren, and achingly lonesome. It takes time to adjust; many never do. The soil is wonderfully rich and fertile, but the weather is blisteringly hot or frigidly cold, with tornadoes thrown in for excitement. Invasions of grasshoppers eat the crops, droughts dry them up, and the aloneness of the open plains drives some people mad.

But the dream of most Americans is to have a farm. Even with problems, those vast plains are inviting to people who want land of their own. In 1862, while the Civil War is still going on, Congress passes a bill called the Homestead Act. It says that for ten dollars, any citizen (that includes women), or anyone who has filed papers to become a citizen, can have 160 acres of public land. (Later, the historian Paul Johnson will write: "Never in human history, before or since, has authority gone to such lengths to help the common people to become landowners.") As soon as the war is over, a lot of people head west. Some say a quarter of a million widows and single women are among them. Many homesteaders are immigrants, right off the boat. Some western settlements become all German, or all Swedish, or all Norwegian.

A new kind of agriculture developed on the Plains. There is little precipitation, so farmers dig wells and use the abundant winds to turn metal windmills that pump water and soon punctuate the landscape. Many farmers become specialists who grow only one or two crops. For thousands and thousands of years men and women have used the same methods of sowing and harvesting. Then a few inventions come along and change everything. One is John Deere's plow.

Plains land is grassland, held together by thick tangles of roots, and firm; so firm you can dig it up in blocks, called "sod," and build a house with the blocks. Try plowing that hard land. The old wooden plows break. Iron plows don't work well, either; the soil sticks to the iron. Deere designs a steel plow. It is strong, and the soil falls away from it. It changes agriculture. But that is nothing compared to what Cyrus McCormick's reaper did. More than anything else, it's that reaper—and the railroads—that brings people west and changes the way they farm. A reaper cuts and harvests grain. In the old days, farmers cut wheat with a scythe, which is a hand tool. That is hard, back-breaking work. It took a good worker all day to reap an acre. If he had forty acres to cut, that meant forty days. In forty days a crop could be overripe and rotten. McCormick's machine—pulled by horses or mules—can harvest a huge field in an afternoon. The mechanical reaper does to wheat farming what Eli Whitney's cotton gin did to cotton growing. It makes big farms practical. Before Cyrus McCormick came along, the Industrial Revolution was mostly a city phenomenon. McCormick brings that revolution to farm life. He is more than an inventor. He is also a business and marketing genius. He guarantees his machines: if they break down he sees that they are repaired—no one has done that before. He trains experts to show farmers how to use them; no one has done that before, either. The machines are expensive, more than most farmers can afford, so McCormick lets farmers take several months to pay for them. It is called "installment buying"—and that is another

Getting Wired

Picture this: you're settled on a farm in Kansas. You've worked hard, your crops are thriving, you're pleased with yourself. Then a cowpuncher decides to drive his herd to market—right across your land. Wham—you have no crops. Nothing left of a year's work. And maybe no farm, because without a crop to sell you don't have money to buy seed and supplies. That is just one of the things that discourages farming in the Plains states. The conflict between Native Americans and farmers is matched by that between farmers and ranchers. Farmers can't fence their land as they do in the East because there aren't enough trees to make fenceposts. Then Joseph Glidden solves their problem. He experiments in his backyard with an old coffee mill and a big grindstone that turns. He uses them to twist two wires together, and then he coils sharp barbs around the wires. With barbed wire, farmers can fence in miles and miles of property at a relatively low cost. By 1874, Glidden is turning out 10,000 pounds of barbed wire a year. Farmers are pleased; cattlemen aren't. They can no longer take the direct route; now they have to find their way around the fences.

of his ideas. He adds a research department to his factory, and he keeps improving the models. That, too, is something new for a businessman to do.

In the thirty years between 1860 and 1890, more land is turned into farmland in the United States than in all the years from 1607 to 1860. In 1879 the McCormick factory produces 18,760 reapers; two years later it makes nearly 49,000 machines. And it keeps growing. Farming is becoming an industry. Expensive farm equipment becomes essential. The new equipment makes huge, businesslike farms common. Bank loans and capital are now an important part of farming. The farmer who can't raise money is usually squeezed out. More and more small farmers sell out and head for cities to take jobs in manufacturing and industry. By 1900, the lone, self-sufficient farmer whom Jefferson admired hardly exists in the lands beyond the Appalachians. The new farmer is part of a huge system. His wheat, cotton, beef, and wool are sold around the world. He has to worry about markets and prices in London and Chicago instead of in his neighborhood.

Because the land seems limitless, American farmers farm wastefully. When a farm wears out, they just moved on to better land on the frontier. But, by the end of the nineteenth century, there isn't any frontier left. In addition, poor farming methods have destroyed more than 100 million acres of the land (that's about the size of Ohio, North Carolina, Maryland, and Illinois combined). On the prairie, grasses are cut, pulled up, and plowed under, and then there is nothing to hold the soil in place; good land turns to dust and is gone with the wind. Rain takes much topsoil, the fertile part of the earth, and washes it into streams. Land that once supported buffalo, tall grasses, and a rich variety of wildlife becomes barren.

The Trail Ends on a Reservation

The new Americans and the Native Americans are sharing the same land, but they have different ways of living. And neither wants to change—why should they? The problem is that the two ways of life can't exist together on the same land. And they both want that land. The Plains Indians are mostly hunters. The new settlers are mostly farmers and ranchers. Hunters and farmers have a hard time living together. Hunters need land free and uncultivated so that herds of buffalo, deer, and antelope can move about. Farmers need land cleared of wild animals so their crops won't be trampled, eaten, and destroyed. Ranchers need grazing land free of buffalo and other wild animals, so their domestic herds can munch without competition.

When Lewis and Clark explored the West, vast herds of buffalo stretched as far as the eye could see. By 1865, there are still about 12 million buffalo. One observer writes of a herd, moving at about fifteen miles an hour, that is so big it takes five days to pass him by. A few years later, the buffalo are just about all gone. Millions are killed for meat and hides, sometimes just for the sport of it, or to clear the land. Hunters like Buffalo Bill Cody leave herds where they fall. The land stinks with the smell of dead buffalo. The plains, which once vibrated with the sound of animal hoofs, become quiet as a desert. (But not for long; cattle soon replace the buffalo.)

To better understand what happens to the Native Americans, it helps to realize that after the Civil War there are many former soldiers who have learned, during the war, how to kill people. They are used to doing it, and some of them don't know quite what else to do. So they go west and kill Indians. Peaceful settlers who move west to farm are sometimes innocent victims of angry Indians. On both sides the hatreds are intense, and so is the desire for revenge.

"The white men hired hunters to do nothing but kill the buffalo," said Old Lady Horse, a Kiowa. "Behind them came the skinners. Sometimes there was a pile of bones as high as a man stretching a mile along the track." This particular bone pile contains only skulls.

In 1875, the United States government decides that all remaining Plains Indians must be confined to reservations (which are almost always on unwanted land, too poor to grow crops). Those who resist are to be captured or shot. Soldiers are sent west to move the Native Americans onto reservations; the Indians fight for their land and their way of life. "The only good Indian is a dead Indian," said Philip Sheridan in a widely quoted phrase. Sheridan, a Civil War Union general, becomes an Indian fighter. His boss, William Tecumseh Sherman, has this to say: "All who cling to their old hunting grounds are hostile and will remain so till killed off." Sherman talks of a "final solution" to the Indian problem. Sherman's middle name is that of a great Indian hero, but Sherman doesn't brag about that. John Pope (who commanded the Union forces at the second battle of Bull Run, and lost) announces that he will deal with the Sioux "as maniacs or wild beasts, and by no means as people with whom treaties or compromises can be made." In Colorado,

"Your people make big talk, and sometimes make war, if an Indian kills a white man's ox to keep his wife and children from starving. What do you think my people ought to say when they see their buffalo killed by your race when you are not hungry?"

—a Cheyenne chief

One of numerous imagined renderings of the last stand of Custer (left) against Sioux chief Crazy Horse, who said: "All we wanted was peace and to be left alone.... Then Long Hair [Custer] came.... They say we massacred him, but he would have done the same thing to us had we not defended ourselves."

> "The more Indians we can kill this year, the less will have to be killed the next year, for the more I see of these Indians, the more convinced I am that they all have to be killed or be maintained as a species of paupers."
>
> —General William Tecumseh Sherman, 1867

Colonel John M. Chivington, a former minister, slaughters 150 Cheyenne who have gone to the governor for protection. Most are women and children. Chivington calls it "an act of duty to ourselves and civilization."

One of the men ordered to accomplish the new goal is Lieutenant Colonel George Armstrong Custer. Custer, who has long blond hair that hangs in ringlets to his shoulders, is a Civil War hero about whom legends are told. He is brave and daring, but also reckless and vain. On June 26, 1876, after ignoring his orders and his scouts' reports, Custer leads 266 soldiers in an attack on 2,000 Cheyenne and Sioux. The Indians, led by Sioux chief Crazy Horse, are gathered at the Little Bighorn River in central Montana. What happens comes to be known as "Custer's Last Stand." The only U.S. Army survivor is a horse called Comanche. Back east, as the tale is told, Custer becomes a heroic figure facing death on a hilltop.

The fact is, most Native Americans want nothing to do with the white Americans' world. They want to be left alone to pursue their own way of life. Here are some words from a Minnesota chief:

> *The whites were always trying to make the Indians give up their life and live like white men—go to farming, work hard and do as they did—and the Indians did not know how to do that, and did not want to.... If the Indians had tried to make the whites live like them, the whites would have resisted, and it was the same way with many Indians. The Indians wanted to … go where they pleased and when they pleased; hunt game wherever they could find it, sell their furs to the traders, and live as they could.*

The chief and his people are herded onto a reservation where the land is poor and there isn't enough to eat. They have to buy food and supplies from government agents who usually cheat them.

> *Many of the white men often abused the Indians and treated them unkindly. Perhaps they had excuse, but the Indians did not think so. Many of the whites always seemed to say by their manner when they saw an Indian, "I am much better than you," and the Indians did not like this.... the Dakota did not believe there were better men in the world than they.*

Even those, like Christian missionaries, who mean to help Native Americans, usually end up destroying tribes because they are sure their way of life is better than the Native American way. They think they are doing right when they take Indian children and put them in missionary or government boarding schools. The Native Americans are forced to wear white men's clothes, eat white men's food, and learn white men's ways. Lone Wolf, a Blackfoot Indian boy, describes his experience:

> *It was very cold that day when we were loaded into the wagons. None of us wanted to go, and our parents didn't want to let us go. Once at the school at Fort Shaw our belongings were taken from us, placed in a heap, and set afire. Next to go was the long hair, the pride of all the Indians. The boys one by one would break dawn and cry when they saw their braids thrown on the floor.*

The new Americans talk of "conquering" the land and its ancient peoples. And that is what they do. The West of traditional Indians, mountain men, and buffalo is coming to end. A new and different West emerges: a land of farmers, ranchers, miners, city dwellers, and Indians who adapt to new realities. But before the final act in the drama, a great leader tries to save his people.

The Carlisle Indian School was founded in Pennsylvania in 1879. The school was part of the government's first efforts to "civilize" Native Americans. Students—like these Sioux boys, photographed before (left) and after (right) entering school—had to cut their hair, wear uniforms, speak only English, and convert to Christianity.

I Will Fight No More Forever

The Nez Perce Indians live in a region that is a kind of paradise. Their land—where today Idaho, Washington, and Oregon come together—holds lush valleys, grassy prairies, steep mountains, and canyons that seem to have been cut by a giant's steam shovel. The Nez Perce share that land with elk, deer, antelope, rabbits, fowl, and mountain goats (along with some predator enemies: bears, wolves, foxes, and coyotes). Fish, especially the lordly salmon, splash in their streams. The Nez Perce are mighty hunters. They are known for their strong bows fashioned of cherrywood or yew, although the best are made of the horns of the mountain sheep, which are boiled and bent and backed with layers of sinew.

Other tribes trade their most precious goods for those bows. When horses arrive in this northern region, the Nez Perce quickly become skilled riders, among the best in the land. Horses thrive on the high, abundant pastureland, and the Nez Perce learn to breed the animals for strength and beauty and fleetness.

Even before they see the first outsiders, the Nez Perce hear tales of them from other tribes. They learn of Spaniards to the south, Russians in Alaska and on the West Coast, and French to the north and east. Still, the Nez Perce must be surprised when Meriwether Lewis and William Clark stumble into one of their camps. It is late September in 1805, and the members of the expedition sent to explore the West by President Thomas Jefferson have been caught in a mountain snowstorm. They are starving. The Indians feed Clark and his men buffalo steak and camas roots and probably save their lives. They like each other. Lewis and Clark convince the Native Americans to stop the warring between tribes; that will make it safe for white men to open trading posts where they plan to sell guns, mirrors, and other goods. The Indians want those goods; they hold a council and promise "to cultivate peace." Until gold is found on their land in 1860, that is easy to do. But gold-seeking miners can't be kept off the land. Settlers follow. It is the beginning of troubles.

President Grant tries to solve the problem. He sets aside a section of land "as a reservation for the roaming Nez Perce Indians." Settlers aren't allowed there. But that doesn't stop the miners and homesteaders. They defy the president and move onto the land. Some Nez Perce sign treaties giving up part of their land, but others won't do it. One of the "no treaty" tribes is led by a man most Americans called Chief Joseph. His real name was Hin-mah-too-yah-laht-ket, which means "thunder rolling in the mountains." Joseph tells his people to be patient. He doesn't want to fight the white settlers. In 1876, the U.S. government sends three commissioners to meet with Chief Joseph. They want to persuade him to move from his land to a reservation. Joseph will not agree to move. "We love the land," he says. "It is our home." The commissioners lose patience. The Indians must go, and quickly, they say, even though the weather is awful. One angry young Indian, whose father was murdered by white settlers, kills some of the white men. Now the whites have an excuse to call the Indians savages. Now they can attack.

The first battle begins when Indians, carrying a white flag of truce, approach the soldiers. A shot rings out and the Nez Perce returned the fire. The fight is over quickly. Thirty-four troopers died, and no Indians. The fleeing soldiers drop their weapons—sixty-three rifles and many pistols. It is a

Chief Joseph. "Straight and towering, he seemed strangely amicable and gentle," writes historian Alvin M. Josephy, Jr., "yet he bore himself with the quiet strength and dignity of one who stood in awe of no man."

bonanza for the Indians. But they are few in number, and they know that an alarm will go out. Other soldiers will soon be after them. So they race for the place where they think they will be free. They head for Canada.

It is a thousand-mile journey. First one army, then another, and another, and another, follow and fight this remnant of Nez Perce. Most of Chief Joseph's small band are children and old people. Everywhere they are outnumbered and outgunned. Yet over and over again they outwit their pursuers. But they are fighting the telegraph as well as an army. Fresh troops are summoned by wire. Finally, just thirty miles from Canada, facing new soldiers, the Nez Perce are surrounded. They can go no farther. Chief Joseph speaks.

> *I am tired of fighting. Our chiefs are killed.... The old men are dead.... The little children are freezing to death. My people, some of them, have run away to the hills, and have no blankets, no food; no one knows where they are ... my heart is sick and sad. From where the sun now stands I will fight no more forever.*

"Understand me fully with reference to my affection for the land. I never said the land was mine to do with it as I chose. The one who has the right to dispose of it is the one who has created it. I claim a right to live on my land, and accord you the privilege to live on yours."
—Chief Joseph

That day, promises are made to Chief Joseph, but they will not be kept. In Washington, those who want Indian land tell false stories. The Nez Perce Indians are sent from their lush mountain lands to a barren reservation. Many sicken and die. Chief Joseph pleads for justice:

> *All men were made by the same Great Spirit Chief They are all brothers. The earth is the mother of all people, and all people should have equal rights upon it. You might as well expect the rivers to run backward as that any man who was born a free man should be contented when penned up and denied liberty to go where he pleases. We only ask an even chance to live as other men live. We ask to be recognized as men. We ask that the same law shall work alike on all men. If the Indian breaks the law, punish him by the law. If the white man breaks the law, punish him also. Let me be a free man—free to travel, free to stop, free to work, free to trade where I choose, free to choose my own teachers, free to follow the religion of my fathers, free to think and talk and act for myself—and I will obey every law, or submit to the penalty.... Whenever the white man treats the Indian as they treat each other, then we will have no more wars. We shall all be alike—brother of one father and one mother, with one sky above us and one country around us, and one government for all.*

Bury My Heart at Wounded Knee

The Chiricahua Apaches roam the land of the tall saguaro cactus: Arizona. Expert horsemen and warriors, they live mostly on wild game and the spoils of raids on the pueblos and on Mexicans. In 1851, Mexican soldiers murder the mother, wife, and three children of one of them: Goyakla (his name means "One Who Yawns"). He vows revenge and, after that day, often takes it. The Mexicans give him a nickname, Geronimo. The Treaty of Guadalupe Hidalgo (which ends the Mexican War in 1848) cedes Arizona, Texas above the Rio Grande, California, New Mexico, Nevada, Utah, and parts of Colorado and Wyoming to the United States. When the Americans arrive in the region (mostly after the Civil War), they claim Apache land. The U.S. government orders the natives onto reservations. Geronimo refuses to go. For some thirty years he fights with guerrilla bands against the U.S. Army; his exploits are the stuff of legend. He gets captured, put on a reservation, escapes, raids, is captured again, put on a reservation, escapes, raids—and so it goes. He's known as the "human tiger." Finally, a big contingent of soldiers is assigned to get the wily Apache. He evades

"If I die in bondage," Geronimo said, "I hope that the remnant of the Apache tribe may be granted the one privilege which they request—to return to Arizona."

> "I have fallen in love with American names,
>   The sharp names that never get fat,
>   The snakeskin titles of mining claims,
>   The plumed war bonnet of Medicine Hat,
>   Tucson and Deadwood and Lost Mule Flat.
>   I shall not rest quiet in Montparnasse.
>   I shall not lie easy at Winchelsea.
>   You may bury my body in Sussex grass,
>   You may bury my tongue at Champmedy.
>   I shall not be there. I shall rise and pass.
>   Bury my heart at Wounded Knee."
>
> —Stephen Vincent Benét, "American Names," in *Ballads and Poems, 1915–1930*, 1931

The 7th Cavalry open fire at Wounded Knee in Frederic Remington's version of the scene. He focused on the soldiers, not their unarmed victims.

them for months, but eventually Geronimo surrenders with the understanding that his men will be sent to join their families in Florida. It is 1886. "I will quit the warpath and live in peace hereafter," he says, and means it. (He and his men are imprisoned and then sent to a reservation in Oklahoma.) Later he dictates *Geronimo's Story of His Life*.

At a place near Wounded Knee Creek, in South Dakota, a group of Hunkpapa Sioux—mostly women and children—are gathered for their ritual Ghost Dance. Five hundred soldiers from the U.S. Seventh Cavalry appear. Confrontation turns to violence and then to massacre. A Sioux leader named American Horse is a witness. "The soldiers turned their guns upon the women who were in the lodges," he says. "Women fleeing with their babies were killed together, shot right through. Little boys were butchered." Black Elk, a Sioux medicine man, arrives soon afterward: "Men and women were heaped and scattered all over the flat at the bottom of the little hill where the soldiers had their wagon guns. All the way to the high ridge, the dead women and children and babies were scattered. When I saw this, I wished that I had died too."

It is 1890 and the Indian wars in the West are at an end. On September 21, 1904, Chief Joseph dies. The doctor at the Colville Indian reservation in the state of Washington lists the cause of death as "a broken heart."

Geronimo, now a tiger tamed, is exhibited at the 1904 St. Louis World's Fair. He rides in Theodore Roosevelt's inaugural parade. In World War II, Native American paratroopers shout "Geronimo" as they leap into the sky. After that war, it becomes a popular expression of delight.

COMING TO AMERICA

Nineteenth-century immigrants to America come from across the globe, but more from Europe than anywhere else, and more from Germany than from any other European nation. Carl Schurz is one of them. Here he tells his story:

> It is one of the earliest recollections of my boyhood.... One of our neighboring families was moving far away across a great water, and it was said that they

would never again return. And I saw silent tears trickling down weather-beaten cheeks, and the hands of rough peasants firmly pressing each other, and some of the men and women hardly able to speak when they nodded to one another a last farewell. At last the train started into motion, they gave three cheers for America, and then in the first gray dawn of the morning I saw them wending their way over the hill until they disappeared in the shadow of the forest. And I heard many a man say, how happy he would be if he could go with them to that great and free country, where a man could be himself.... That was the first time I heard about America, and my childish imagination took possession of a land covered partly with majestic trees, partly with flowery prairies, immeasurable to the eye, and intersected with large rivers and broad lakes-a land where everybody could do what he thought best, and where nobody need be poor, because everybody was free.

In 1848, Schurz fought in a freedom movement in Germany, but, when the freedom fighters lost, he was in trouble and had to flee to Switzerland. Then, being uncommonly brave, he went back to Germany to help his college professor escape from jail. But he knew if he stayed in Germany he too would be jailed. Schurz was twenty-three, and he set out for the land of freedom.

When Schurz arrives in America, before the Civil War, he finds that some people aren't free. He is horrified, and he says so. He realizes there is no freedom of speech in the slave states. Without free speech, says Schurz, no one is free, neither slave nor master. "I am an antislavery man, and I have a right to my opinion in South Carolina just as well as in Massachusetts.... If you want to be free, there is but one way," says Schurz. "It is to guarantee an equally full measure of liberty to all your neighbors."

In his new country Carl Schurz can speak out and say the things he believes. Just ten years after his arrival in the United States, President Abraham Lincoln names him American minister to Spain. Then he serves as a general in the Union army. After the war Schurz becomes a newspaper correspondent, an editor, a U.S. senator from Missouri, and secretary of the interior. He talks of conservation of the wilderness and fairness to Indians when hardly anyone else thinks of those things. "Equality of rights ... is the great moral element of true democracy," writes Carl Schurz. Like so many other immigrants, he falls in love with America's ideals.

Immigrant and Radical Republican Carl Schurz was made secretary of the interior in 1877 by President Hayes. Schurz reformed the civil service and began conserving the environment.

Freedom and a Chance to Work

In Ireland the potato crop fails in 1845 and keeps failing. More than a million Irish starve to death. In the years leading up to the Civil War, one-fourth of the entire population of Ireland (1.7 million men, women, and children) comes to America. On the European continent, the population doubles between 1750 and 1850. All those extra people need food, homes, and jobs—and there just don't seem to be enough of them in Europe.

Many immigrants come to America to find work and avoid hunger. Many come to be free of religious oppression. Religious dissenters arrive from Holland; Jews, who are often persecuted for their beliefs in the Old World, come from Germany, Poland, and Russia. Still others come to escape political wars that are leaving parts of Europe in turmoil. In the half-century after the Civil War, some 26 million immigrants arrive in the United States. Many of the newcomers begin life in the cities—in overcrowded apartment buildings called tenements. Sometimes eight families share one bathroom—if there is a bathroom. Often there is just an outhouse out back. Few immigrants know much about America except that it is a land of freedom. But that is what they want: freedom and a chance to work.

They come on steamships. Most are crowded into belowdecks areas called steerage, where the trip costs thirty dollars. It takes ten days. Many of the immigrants land in New York harbor, at a place called Castle Garden, and after 1892 at Ellis Island.

Jacob Riis sails from Denmark. He has read books about America and thinks he knows something about the country. What he has read in Denmark is cowboy books. He expects to find buffaloes and cowboys in New York. The first thing he does when he arrives is to take half his money and buy a gun. Later he said he was surprised to find New York "paved, and lighted with electric lights, and quite as civilized as Copenhagen." A friendly policeman sees the boy with a pistol tucked in his belt and tells him to leave it home. "I took his advice and put the revolver away, secretly relieved to get rid of it. It was quite heavy to carry around." It takes Riis seven years to find a decent job. Then he gets hired as a newspaper reporter and writes about the life of the poor in America's cities. He learns photography. Most photographers take pictures of beautiful scenery or prosperous people. No one is taking pictures of the poor. Riis does. He shows exactly how some immigrants are forced to live. Riis's pictures and words (one book of his is called *How the Other Half Lives*) help get laws passed that change some things. "I have aimed to tell the truth as I saw it," he writes. "If my book shall have borne ever so feeble a hand in garnering a harvest of

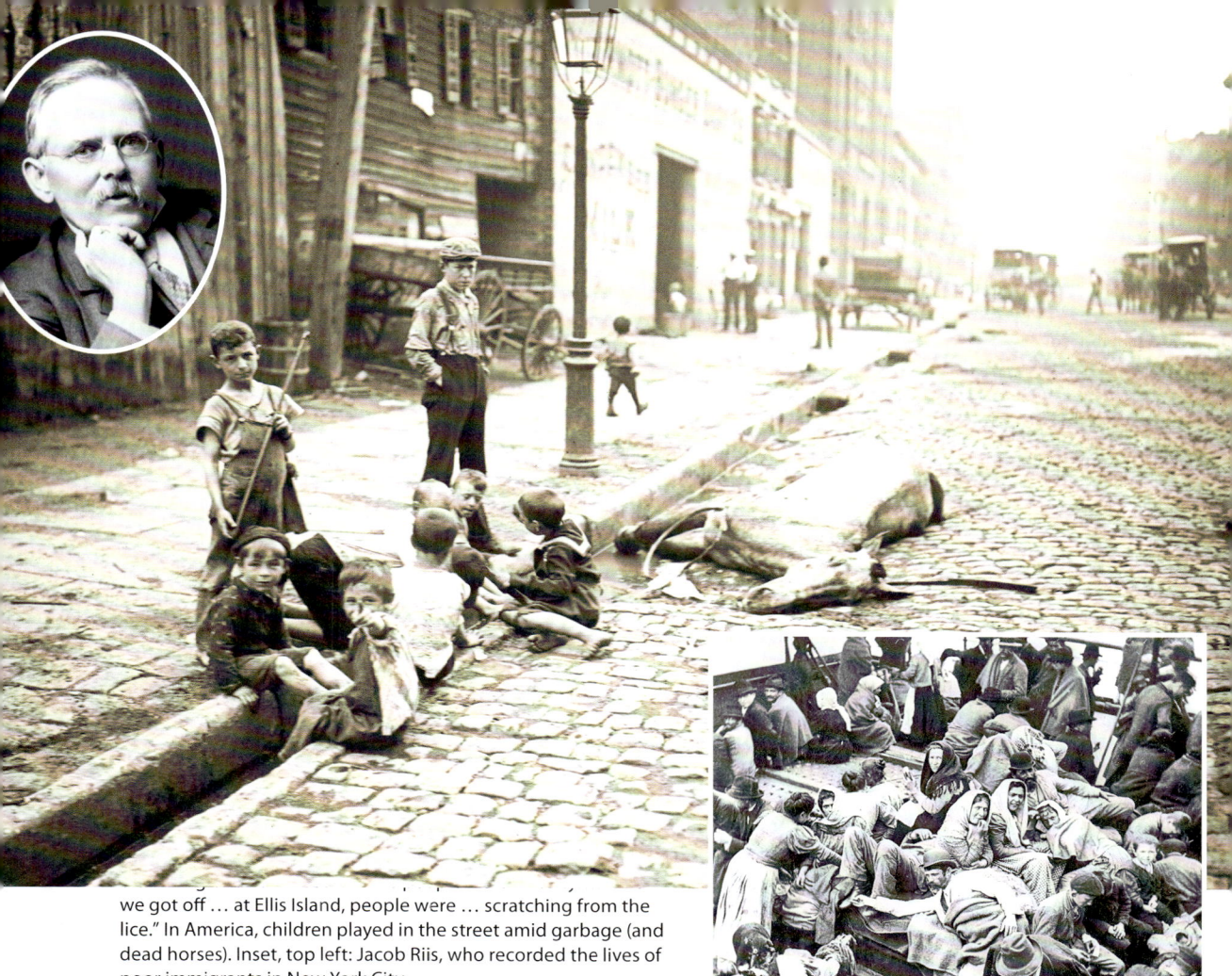

we got off … at Ellis Island, people were … scratching from the lice." In America, children played in the street amid garbage (and dead horses). Inset, top left: Jacob Riis, who recorded the lives of poor immigrants in New York City.

justice, it has served its purpose." Jacob Riis, like Carl Schurz (whom he knows), and some others of the time, is a reformer. He wants to make the world a better place.

WHO WANTS IMMIGRANTS?

Some Americans don't want newcomers in the country; and some of the newcomers, as soon as they get settled, don't want any other immigrants to come after them. Usually the newest immigrants are poor, and willing to work hard and for less money than those who arrived earlier.

So some people want to stop immigration because they fear competition for jobs. There are other reasons, too. Because most newcomers can't speak the language, they need extra help in school. That costs money—tax money. The cities where many newcomers live are overcrowded and filled with crime, so there is a need for extra police and extra city services. That costs money—tax money. Some people say, "Why should we have to pay for the problems of those poor people?"

Meanwhile the newcomers are doing jobs no one else wants to do-washing dishes, scrubbing floors, or building railroads. No one can foresee that their sons and daughters will become some of the most productive citizens any country has ever known. But the times are different, and some philosophers and scientists believe that some people are superior to others—it's a seductive idea (and turns out to be hogwash). But it leads to discrimination—sometimes vicious discrimination, especially against Catholics, Jews, blacks, Irish, Asians, and Hispanics.

One group of prejudiced people actually forms a political party. Officially it is the American Party, but most people call it the "Know-Nothing Party." The Know-Nothings are anti-Catholic and anti-foreign. They manage to destroy a stone block sent from Rome by the Catholic Pope, intended as part of the Washington Monument. Another group of haters, the Ku Klux Klan, is fiercely anti-black and anti-Semitic. On the West Coast, the Workingmen's Party's slogan is THE CHINESE MUST GO.

By 1882, there are just over 50 million people in the United States; of those, only 300,000 are Chinese. Most American workers want high wages to work in the

The Know Nothings (officially called the American Party) were "nativists" and anti-immigrant. The images of Native Americans and soap in this ad symbolize the "purity" they said they aimed for.

> "It is an old dodge of the advocates of despotism throughout the world, that the people who are not experienced in self-government are not fit for the exercise of self-government.... [But] liberty is the best school for liberty, and self-government cannot be learned but by practicing it. This, sir, is a truly American idea; this is true Americanism, and to this I pray the tribute of my devotion."
>
> —Carl Schurz

More than 4.1 million Italians entered the United States between 1890 and 1920, more than any other ethnic group in such a short time. Some traveled as far as California, founding farms and vineyards. This 1890 illustration by W.A. Rogers depicts Mulberry Street, in the Italian quarter of New York City.

fields or to build railroads. If they head for California they expect to hit gold. In China, times are hard. Chinese men are willing to work for very little money. Some companies send ships to China (and then Japan and India) to find workers.

Some say the employers are exploiting the workers. But the process works both ways. When the Asians take their earnings and go home, as many do, they are exploiting the land of opportunity. Many immigrants to the East Coast do the same thing. They come, work hard, save money, and go back—to Greece, or Italy, or Poland, where their American earnings make them seem rich. And that is all right. America has opportunities to share. Besides, most take more than money back to their old worlds. They take American ideas and ideals with them, too. People from China keep coming to the land they call the Golden Mountain—as long as they can.

In the 1860s and '70s, when times are difficult in China, they aren't easy in the United States. Jobs are scarce. Since the Chinese are willing to work for low wages, they usually find work. That infuriates many white working men. Mobs attack and kill Chinese people; hoodlums burn Chinese homes and laundries. The Workingmen's Party demands a law to end Chinese immigration. Congressmen in the East, needing political support from Californians, help pass that law. Most Americans on the East Coast don't know any Chinese. The concept of race is being taken seriously, along with the idea that some races are better than others.

A law passed back in 1790 says that only white people can become naturalized citizens. That old law is now applied only to Asians. So the Chinese are not citizens unless they're born in the United States; and they can't become citizens by naturalization. In 1882, a Chinese Exclusion Act is passed and signed into law by President Chester A. Arthur. It puts a stop to all further immigration from China; it comes after many Chinese have died building railroads, dig mines, and laboring on farms.

The Strange Case of the Chinese Laundry

There is a San Francisco ordinance that says that all laundries must be housed in brick buildings. It makes sense. San Francisco grows quickly after gold is discovered at Sutter's Mill in 1848. Houses and stores are crowded together, and most are built of wood. Fire can be a serious problem. It's used to heat and cook and heat water in almost every building in the city. San Francisco has 320 laundries; 310 of them are in buildings made of wood; 240 of the laundries are owned by citizens of China. (San Francisco has the largest Chinese population in America; most Chinese, unable to become naturalized, are citizens of China.)

In 1886, just four years after the Chinese Exclusion Act, Sheriff Hopkins enters the Yick Wo laundry in San Francisco. He has a warrant for the arrest of the owner. The Yick Wo laundry is in a wooden building. Sheriff Hopkins has warrants for the arrest of all the Chinese owners of laundries in wooden buildings. He arrests only one white laundry owner (that laundry is owned by a woman). The Chinese laundry owners are convicted and fined. If they don't pay their fines, they go to jail. Their businesses are closed. The discrimination is clear, and they are angry. What can they do? Remember, they aren't citizens.

To get some perspective on this, imagine you're living in the nineteenth century. Now, go to China and try to become a Chinese citizen. You'll find that you can't do it—unless you are Chinese. You can't become a citizen of Japan—unless you are Japanese. You can't even get working papers in those countries. The same thing is true in most European nations. In the nineteenth century there is hardly a country that will allow you citizenship except the land of your ancestors' origin. Even today, many

President Rutherford Hayes vetoed the Chinese Exclusion Act in 1882, but it passed anyway. Senator George Hoar of Massachusetts said it represented "the legalization of racial discrimination"; he was right, but few others cared.

countries do not let people of other ethnic backgrounds become citizens. In the nineteenth and twentieth centuries Americans struggled with the idea of citizenship. What makes a citizen? The freedom and openness of the United States was and is unusual. Most people thought that made our country special—but some didn't like the idea at all.

Now, back to Sheriff Hopkins and the Chinese laundrymen. White laundry owners were running laundries in wooden buildings. Why was the city picking on Chinese laundrymen? The Chinese launderers thought the city of San Francisco was being unfair. They went to court. Their case, called *Yick Wo* v. *Hopkins*, made its way to the U.S. Supreme Court. As it happens, there was no Yick Wo. Sheriff Hopkins just assumed that the man who owned the Yick Wo laundry was named Yick Wo. Actually, his name was Lee Yick. We don't know much about Lee Yick, except that he came to California in 1861 and operated a laundry for twenty-two years. We also know that he was willing to fight for his rights. But what were his rights? He wasn't a citizen. Did he have the same rights as if he had been an American citizen? No one was sure.

The Supreme Court doesn't listen to all the cases that people want it to hear. It attempts to pick cases that will test important issues, especially constitutional issues. There were two issues in this case. The first was this: do the police have the right to

Advertisements could be racist, too—because many Chinese people, especially on the West Coast, ran laundries, the Magic Washer company unashamedly exploited anti-Asian sentiment and urged Americans to get along without Chinese labor.

enforce a law arbitrarily? The second has to do with the rights of noncitizens. Should the law treat aliens the same way it treats American citizens? This was a significant case. Police departments in many states were interested. They didn't want their power limited. They wanted the power to treat aliens as they wished. Briefs—written legal arguments that are rarely brief—were presented to the Supreme Court by the states of Nebraska, Iowa, Indiana, Mississippi, New Jersey, Wisconsin, and Florida. All supported Sheriff Hopkins.

This is what the Supreme Court said:

> For no legitimate reason this body by its action has declared that it is lawful for eighty-odd persons who are not subjects of China to wash clothes for hire in [wood] frame buildings, but unlawful for all subjects of China to do the same thing.

The law was applied "with an evil eye and an unequal hand." That, said the justices, is wrong. And, said the court:

> The Fourteenth Amendment to the Constitution is not confined to the protection of citizens. It says: "Nor shall any state deprive any person of life, liberty, or property without due process of law; nor deny to any person within its jurisdiction the equal protection of the laws."

This was a groundbreaking interpretation of the Fourteenth Amendment. It said that all persons in the United States, citizens or not, are entitled to the same fair treatment. Lee Yick and his friends had won a momentous victory. The Chinese laundrymen beat the sheriff of San Francisco.

THE PROMISED LAND

Mary Antin came to Boston in 1894 from a little village—called, in her Yiddish language, a *shtetl*. Its roads were of dirt and some of its houses had dirt floors, too. Mary was thirteen. It was as if they had come from the Middle Ages into the modern world.

> I began life in the region of Russia known as the Pale of Settlement. Within this area the Czar commanded me to stay, with my father and mother and friends, and all people like us. We must not be found outside the Pale, because we were Jews.

The name of the shtetl was Polotzk. Its people were pious, and set in their ways, for they lived just as others had for generations before them. Mary's family was poor, very poor, and had hardly enough to eat. Even if they had been rich, Mary could not do what she wanted to do. She had a good mind, and she loved to read, but schools in Russia were closed to most jews and there were no public libraries inside the Pale of Settlement. Because her parents cared about learning, they paid a *rebbe*—a teacher—to teach their daughters. Their brother went to religious school, which was only for boys. In Polotzk, once a girl learned to read her Hebrew prayers, she was supposed to be content with sewing and household chores. And Jewish boys who wanted to study something beside religious books had no way to do it. Mary's father had been that kind of boy: a scholar, but not of religion. Perhaps that was why he wanted to bring his family to America. Perhaps it was because he was a failure in the Old World.

On the evening of the first day after Mary and her family arrived at their new home in Boston, they went out to the public baths—there was no bathtub in their apartment. When they came home it was evening, and—this was amazing—the streets were bright.

> So many lamps, and they burned until morning, my father said, and so people did not need to carry lanterns. In America, then, everything was free, as we had heard in Russia. Light was free; the streets were as bright as a synagogue on a holy day. Music was free…. we had been serenaded, to our gaping delight, by a brass band of many pieces, soon after our installation on Union Place. Education was free. That subject my father had written about repeatedly, as comprising his chief hope for us children, the essence of American opportunity, the treasure that no thief could touch, not even misfortune or poverty…. On our second day I was thrilled with the realization of what this freedom of education meant. A little girl from across the alley came and offered to conduct us to school. My father was out, but we five between us had a few words of English by this time. We knew the word school. We understood. This child, who had never seen us till yesterday, who could not pronounce our names … was able to offer us the freedom of the schools of Boston! The doors stood open for every one of us.

It was May, almost the end of the school year, so the Antin children had to wait until September to begin school.

> That day I must always remember, even if I live to be so old I cannot tell my name. To most people their first day of school is a memorable occasion. In my case the importance of the day was a hundred times magnified, on account of the years I had waited, the road I had come, and the conscious ambitions I entertained.
>
> Father himself conducted us to school. He would not have delegated that mission to the President of the United States. He had awaited the day with impatience equal to mine, and the vision he saw as he hurried us over the sun-flecked pavements transcended all my dreams…. The boasted freedom of the New World meant to him far more than the right to reside, travel, and work wherever he pleased; it meant the freedom to speak his thoughts, to throw off the shackles of superstition, to test his own fate, unhindered by political or religious tyranny.

Mary Antin became the best student in her elementary school. When she wrote a poem about George Washington, it was published in a Boston newspaper and the whole school cheered. When she grew up she wrote her autobiography, calling it *The Promised Land*. In it she wrote of what she most loved about her adopted nation: it was the freedom and opportunity that let even the poorest immigrant—like herself—become rich in learning.

Inset, a Wobbly (Industrial Workers of the World) meeting, c.1910–1915. The IWW was a giant open union, unlike the craft organizations such as the Women's Auxiliary Typographical Union, whose float ran in the 1909 Labor Day parade in New York City (above). The Labor Day holiday itself came about in the wake of President Clevelands brutal suppression of the Pullman railcar strike in 1892; trying to appease workers and unions, Congress hastily voted in a national holiday dedicated to labor; nonetheless, Cleveland was not reelected in 1894.

Part 9

Working for Freedom

Eighteen seventy is a big year for freedom. The Fifteenth Amendment, intended to give African-Americans the right to vote, becomes law. It says: *The right of the citizens of the United States to vote shall not be denied or abridged by the United States or by any state, on account of race, color or previous condition of servitude.* Finally, African-American men, whose labor built so much of the young nation, are (officially, at least) self-governing citizens.

But half of the population is still left out. Susan B. Anthony and Elizabeth Cady Stanton, who are the nation's leading women's rights advocates, wanted that amendment to read "race, color, *sex* or …". It didn't happen. Even sympathetic congressmen said they'd never get the amendment passed if they raised the sex issue. So it was purposely not specific. Now the question is: Can women vote? In 1871, in Washington, D.C., seventy-two women are turned away at the polls. But that same year, three women in Nyack, New York, and one woman in Detroit, Michigan, do vote. The *New York Times* writes in an editorial, "No evil results followed."

In Rochester, New York, Susan Anthony does a lot of thinking about the Fifteenth Amendment. It says citizens can vote. Is she a citizen? Her friend Henry Selden, a lawyer and judge, believes the answer to that question is yes. On November 1, 1872, Anthony and fifteen other women march into a barbershop in Rochester's Eighth Ward, where voter

"Well, I've gone and done it!—positively voted the Republican ticket, straight, this morning. I'm awful tired—but to splendid purpose."
—Susan B. Anthony, November 5, 1872

Susan B. Anthony

registration takes place. The women ask to be registered to vote. The three registrars—who are men—don't know what to do. They argue a bit, but finally they agree. They see no harm in women voting. The next day, the Rochester newspaper is full of the story. So are papers in other parts of the nation. Many of them call the women lawbreakers. But on election day, November 5, the sixteen women are at the polls at 7 A.M. When they vote, that big news goes by telegraph from Maine to California and from Washington to Florida.

Twenty-three days later, on Thanksgiving Day, a deputy marshal knocks on Susan B. Anthony's door. "Miss Anthony," he says, "I have come to arrest you." He has a warrant. It says she has broken an act of Congress. That day the other fifteen women voters are also arrested and brought to court. Anthony is asked if she went "into this matter for the purpose of testing the question." "Yes, sir; I had resolved for three years to vote," she answers. She is ordered to appear before a grand jury. The three men who registered the women are arrested for registering and accepting ballots unlawfully. The government decides to prosecute Susan B. Anthony alone—she will represent the sixteen women. The three men will all be tried. It is January. The trials are set for June. They have six months to prepare. Susan B. Anthony uses those six months well. She speaks in all of Rochester's districts on the Constitution and natural rights.

Rights are not something that governments own and give out to people, Anthony says. They belong to each of us. People are born with rights. Governments are formed to protect those rights. She uses Thomas Jefferson's word, *unalienable*. She calls them "God-given rights." She also talks about the "hateful oligarchy of sex." By which she means the rule of men over women. Half the people are ruled by the other half, she says. She keeps reminding people of the colonists' 1775 tea party cry: *No taxation without representation.* Women can be taxed but they can't vote. Women can be arrested, but they

Judge Ward Hunt

can't serve on a jury. Many in Rochester think she is making sense. When the June day comes, the courtroom is packed. The judge, Ward Hunt, won't let Susan Anthony speak for herself. He says she is "incompetent" to do so. Anthony's friend, lawyer Henry Selden, responds, "Every citizen has a right to take part upon equal terms with every other citizen.... Political bondage equals slavery." But Judge Hunt gets the final word. He turns to the jurors. "Under the Fifteenth Amendment … Miss Anthony was not protected in a right to vote," he says. "Therefore I direct you to find a verdict of guilty." No judge has a right to do that. Judges can tell a jury about the law. They cannot tell juries how to vote. The clerk of the court says to the jury, "You say you find the defendant guilty, so say you all?" No juror says a word.

Judge Hunt says, "Gentlemen of the jury [of course, there are no women], you are dismissed." The judge rules Anthony guilty. Not a juror has spoken. Most are outraged.

Now the issue is no longer the vote for women. It is an issue of a free trial in a free society. This trial has been a joke. Anthony and the three men are fined and sentenced to jail. The *New York Sun* writes of a "jury of twelve wooden [figures] moved by a string pulled by the hand of a judge." An Utica, New York, paper says Judge Hunt has "outraged the rights of Susan B. Anthony" (even though the editor doesn't think women should vote). Another paper says, "The right to a trial by jury includes the right to a free and impartial verdict."

Anthony refuses to pay her fine, and Judge Hunt, perhaps knowing he has gone too far, never demands it. She does not go

> "I came into this court to get justice. I have not only had no jury of my peers, I have had no jury at all."
> —Susan B. Anthony

Susan B. Anthony was a reformer in many areas besides women' suffrage: she worked for the temperance (anti-alcohol) movement, for girls' education, for abolition of slavery, for factory reform. She wore bloomers and short hair, too, but decided to drop such statements in the face of constant ridicule and sneering by political opponents—as in this cartoon, which caricatured her as a tough Auntie Sam.

> "We rejoice in the success of our experiment of self-government. But 'We, the people' does not mean 'We, the male citizens.' It is a mockery to talk to women of the blessings of liberty."
>
> —Susan B. Anthony

to jail. No appeal is ever heard by a higher court. The three male registrars spend five days in jail, where they eat fancy meals sent by the women they registered. Then President Ulysses S. Grant pardons them. At the next election, Rochester's male voters reelect them by a wide margin. But America's women have lost out. Winning that case in 1873 would have allowed women all over the nation to vote. The word *citizen* in the Fifteenth Amendment could have been reinterpreted to mean "men and women citizens." Judge Hunt decides otherwise.

Three years later, in 1876, the United States has a grand Fourth of July hundredth birthday with a big party and fair in Philadelphia. The focus of the celebration is American technology, ingenuity, and freedom. The Declaration of Independence is read aloud. That same day two uninvited guests appear at the centennial: Elizabeth Cady Stanton and Susan B. Anthony. They read their own Declaration:

> *While the nation is buoyant with patriotism, and all hearts are attuned to praise, it is with sorrow that we come to strike the one discordant note on this hundredth anniversary of our nation's birth. Yet we cannot forget that while men of every race have the full rights of citizenship, all women still suffer the degradation of disenfranchisement. We ask of our rulers no special favors. We ask that civil and political rights be guaranteed to us and our daughters forever.*

Anthony can hardly contain her fury. "The women of this nation in 1876 have greater cause for discontent, rebellion, and revolution than the men of 1776," she says. Why is she so angry? Because she and other women—Stanton, Lucy Stone, and Sojourner Truth are a few of them—worked hard to see slavery abolished. They believed that abolition went hand in hand with women's rights. But many male abolitionists have ignored them. "The best women I know do not want to vote," says Horace Greeley, an important abolitionist newspaperman. The women feel betrayed.

Lynching Means Killing by a Mob

"I was born in Holly Springs, Mississippi, before the close of the Civil War. My parents, who had been slaves and married as such, were married again after freedom came. My father had been taught the carpenter's trade, and my mother was a famous cook.... My father was the son of his master … and one of his slave women.... He was never whipped or put on the auction block, and he knew little of the cruelties of slavery.... My mother … was born in Virginia and was one of ten children. She and two sisters were sold to slave traders when young, and were taken to Mississippi and sold again."

Ida B. Wells, who wrote those words, was a newspaper writer (and a friend of Susan B. Anthony's). Holly Springs, where Ida grew up, was a small town with the kind of people—black and white—who, after the war, attempted to live together peacefully. "Our job was to go to school and learn all we could," she wrote. "The Freedmen's Aid had established one of its schools in our town.... My father was one of the trustees and my mother went along to school with us until she learned to read the Bible." Blacks and whites in Holly Springs rode streetcars and trains together. Ida's parents were community leaders. Mostly there was racial harmony.

Ida was the oldest of seven children, and a good student. She planned to go to college. But when she was sixteen, a yellow fever epidemic that was raging through the South reached Holly Springs and killed both her parents and her baby brother. Her childhood was over. Ida Wells got herself a job as a schoolteacher and became mother and father to her five brothers and sisters. She started to write. She began by sending letters to some black newspapers. Her letters made sense, and she soon had a regular newspaper column. Then, one day, she boarded a train for Memphis, Tennessee. Ida sat in the ladies' coach, as she had done before. But the South was changing. The conductor wouldn't take her ticket. He said blacks now had to sit in the smoking car. Ida Wells wouldn't budge.

As I was in the ladies' car I proposed to stay. He tried to drag me out of the seat, but the moment he caught hold of my arm I fastened my teeth in the back of his hand. I had braced my feet against the seat in front and was holding on to the back, and as he had already been badly bitten he didn't try it again by himself.

The conductor got two men to help him. They tore her dress and dragged her from the train. Wells hired a lawyer and sued the railroad. The judge said she was right and awarded her $500. But the Chesapeake and Ohio Railroad appealed the case to the Tennessee Supreme Court, which reversed the decision. Ida Wells had to pay a fine. She was devastated.

Wells had many friends in Memphis, but Thomas Moss and his wife were special friends. Moss was a postman who saved his money and, along with two partners, opened a grocery store. Their store was across the street from a white-owned grocery. The white grocer didn't like having competition. He threatened the new grocers. Then he and some other whites marched on the store—with guns. Moss and his friends had guns, too. Three white men were wounded. The three black grocers were taken to jail. But they weren't safe there. A mob invaded the prison, took the men, and filled their bodies with bullets. It was a lynching. It was murder by a mob.

Between 1882 and 1930, 4,761 people were lynched in the United States. It happened in the North and West as well as the South. Whites and Asians were lynched. But most lynchings were in the South, and most victims were black. In Mississippi, 545 people were murdered; in Texas, 492; in Louisiana, 388; Montana had ninety-three lynchings. In the West, it was called "vigilante" justice, but it was never just. It made laws and government irrelevant.

Still, there were myths that made many people accept the lynchings. Lynch mobs were said to be made up of poor, uneducated people. That was a myth. In every section of the country, the mob murderers had the consent and often active participation of community leaders. There were other myths. One said that the victims of the mobs were criminals who were raping women or committing horrendous crimes. Murder is never right, but if these men were really bad, maybe they were just getting what they deserved. At first, even Ida Wells believed that.

But Wells knew Tom Moss. She knew he was a decent citizen. He hadn't attacked any women. Could it be that some of the others who were lynched were also innocent victims? Ida Wells investigates. What she finds is that only a third of lynch victims have even been accused of attacking women. Women and children are among those who are lynched. Some of the dead are victims of mistaken identity. The major newspapers aren't covering the story; Wells does. She has become a skilled reporter and is now writing for a newspaper called *Free Speech*. Her frank, well-documented articles get her fired from her teaching job.

When the city refuses to even try to find Tom Moss's murderer, Ida Wells tells black people to leave Memphis: "There is only one thing we can do-leave a town which will neither protect our lives and property, nor give us a fair trial." Within two months, 6,000 black people leave the city. Then she organizes a boycott: her readers stay off the streetcars. When blacks stop riding the streetcars, white businesses begin to suffer.

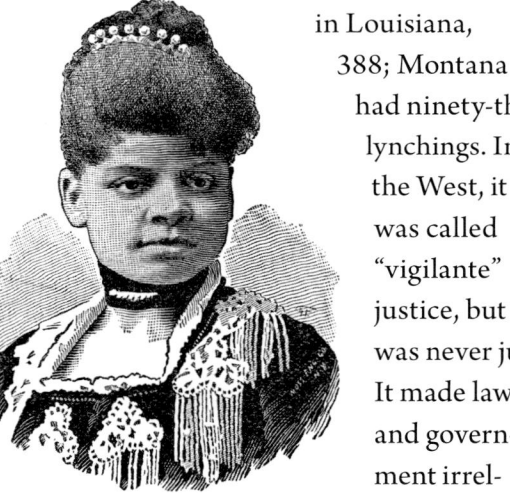

Ida B. Wells

"I had hoped such great things from my suit for my people generally. I have firmly believed all along that the law was on our side and would when we appealed to it, give us justice. I feel shorn of that belief and utterly discouraged."

—Ida B. Wells

> *The superintendent and the treasurer of the City Railway Company came into the office of the Free Speech and asked us to use our influence with the colored people to get them to ride on the streetcars again. When I asked why they said the colored people had been their best patrons. "So your own job then depends on Negro patronage?" I asked. And although their faces flushed over the question they made no direct reply.*

After one of her articles appeared, the *Free Speech* was attacked, its presses ruined. It happened while Wells was on her way to New York City. Editor Thomas Fortune met her at the ferry. "We've been a long time getting you to New York," he said. "But now I'm afraid you'll have to stay." Some people in Memphis were talking about lynching Ida B. Wells. It was thirty years before she could go south again.

An Attempt to Lynch the Court

Nevada Taylor—twenty-one, blonde, and pretty—is a bookkeeper at a grocery store on Market Street in Chattanooga, Tennessee. Her mother is dead and she and her brother live with their father in a cottage at the Forest Hills Cemetery, where Mr. Taylor works as groundskeeper.

On January 23, 1906, Nevada leaves work at 6 P.M. and rides the new electric streetcar home. The fare is three cents for the twenty-minute, three-mile trip. She chats with the conductor before getting off for the short walk to her house. It is winter dark and there are no streetlights. At the gate of the cemetery she hears footsteps, then something is around her neck and a man says, "If you scream, I will kill you." That's all she remembers. She never sees her assailant. A few minutes later, after she stumbles home, a doctor is called. Nevada Taylor has been raped.

Sheriff Joseph Franklin Shipp grew up in Georgia, served in the Confederate Army, and has three wounds to prove it. After the war Shipp married, moved to Chattanooga, built a water-pump manufacturing plant, then a furniture factory, became rich, and went into politics. One newspaper calls him "a natural-born leader." Shipp, who doesn't like losing anything, is up for reelection.

This awful crime enrages the community. It feeds racial tensions still unresolved after the failure of Reconstruction. It touches on issues of sex and women's place in society. Then there is the personal tragedy. A nineteenth-century woman raped is a woman forever shamed. Nevada's life is ruined (she dies within a year). People in Chattanooga are scared. There has been another rape and there are a few unsolved crimes. The *Chattanooga Times* (owned by

Adolph Ochs, who uses its profits to buy a struggling northern newspaper, the *New York Times*) runs a front-page editorial with this headline: DESPERADOES RUN RAMPANT IN CHAITANOOGA; NEGRO THUGS REACH CLIMAX OF BOLDNESS. A reward is offered for information leading to an arrest. Sheriff Shipp gets a phone call. "Is the reward money still available?" he is asked. The caller has a suspect, Ed Johnson, an illiterate young black drifter who does odd jobs. Johnson says he didn't do it, and sticks to that. He has witnesses to his whereabouts (at the Last Chance Saloon), but they are other blacks.

Johnson is arrested and a lynch mob attempts to storm the jail. Anticipating trouble, Sheriff Shipp has moved the prisoner to safety. On February 6, just fourteen days after the rape, Johnson is brought to trial. The defense lawyers request time to prepare; they ask to move the location of the trial. The judge, who makes his bias clear, turns down the requests. After a speedy verdict—guilty—Ed Johnson's lawyers tell him there is no point in appealing. Then two black lawyers appear: Noel Parden and Styles Hutchins. Neither is eager to get involved. They know it may be the end of their careers in Chattanooga. Somehow, something compels them to do it.

On March 17, Noel Parden climbs the ninety-five steps of the Supreme Court building, just seventy-two hours before Ed Johnson is scheduled to be hanged. Only once before has a black lawyer from the South taken a petition to the nation's highest court. With Parden is an attorney from Washington, one of only a handful of blacks admitted to practice before the court. They wait all day. Finally, toward evening, they are brought before a big, rumpled man. It is the justice they hoped to see: John Marshall Harlan. Because he often disagrees with his colleagues, he is accused of suffering from "dissent-ery." Harlan was the dissenting justice in *Plessy* v. *Ferguson,* the justice who said, "Our Constitution is color-blind and neither knows nor tolerates classes among citizens." Noah Parden knows something about the justice that few others know: Harlan has an older half-brother who, like Homer Plessy, is seven-eighths white. That brother was shut out of public school and never given equal opportunities.

Parden reviews the case for the justice. Harlan brushes him aside: "I'm not here to

> "Very few people understand the import of the Shipp case. It served as a foundation for many cases to come. At a time when racism and white supremacy ruled the day, the Shipp case demonstrated a real moment of courage by the Court, especially for Justice Harlan, who has always been one of the legal champions I have admired and studied."
> —Supreme Court Justice Thurgood Marshall, 1991, quoted in *Contempt of Court* by Mark Curriden and Leroy Phillips, Jr.

retry this case. A jury has already done that." But it is easy to see that Johnson's trial was a sham. Parden is asking the court to do something it has never done before-intervene in a state court criminal trial. He is asking the court to expand the Constitution, making the Bill of Rights and the other amendments pertain to the states. The Fourteenth Amendment, interpreted broadly, can do so. Parden knows that Harlan has been advocating that course and that the other justices have rejected the argument. Yet this case involves so many violations of basic rights, he hopes it will be hard to turn down.

The next day, a majority of the court meets and reads Parden's brief. It is clear: Johnson did not have a fair trial and now there is a rush to execute him. Justice Harlan wires the U.S. Circuit Judge in Chattanooga: HAVE ALLOWED APPEAL TO ACCUSED IN HABEAS CORPUS CASE OF ED JOHNSON. Johnson's execution is to be stayed; the case will be appealed and heard by the Supreme Court. Johnson is now a federal prisoner. In Chattanooga, the news spreads quickly. Much of the white community is outraged. This is their town, their crime, their prisoner—how dare a court in Washington get involved?

The next night, Sheriff Shipp gives his deputies an evening off, leaving just one guard in the jail. A mob appears. The deputy on duty hands over his keys. The trial judge, watching from a nearby window, does nothing. Johnson is hanged from a bridge, shot, and mutilated. The following day, the *Atlanta News*, while condemning the lynching, says, "The idea of the Supreme Court of the United States interfering in a case infamous as that of Chattanooga seems to us to be an outrage against justice."

Will the government respond? The Justice Department sends agents to investigate. As a result of that investigation, the Attorney General institutes contempt-of-court proceedings against Sheriff Shipp, several deputies, and some members of the lynch mob. The case is called *United States* v. *Shipp*. U.S. Solicitor General Henry Hoyt says, "This proceeding is about nothing less than establishing and protecting the rule of law." The court's decision is unanimous. It says, in part: "This was murder by a mob, and was an offense against the State as well as against the United States and this court; but the same act may be a crime both against the State and the United States, and the United States has complete power to punish, whether the State does or not." Sheriff Shipp and five other men are given jail sentences of a few weeks. When they come back to Chattanooga, 10,000 cheering people meet their train. Noah Parden and Styles Hutchins are never able to return to the city.

Law professor Thomas Baker has this to say about *United States* v. *Shipp*: "It could easily be argued that we have respect for the law today because of this case. What if the court had not punished the sheriff? What if cities and counties and states realized they didn't have to obey federal court orders or the U.S. Constitution?" In *Shipp* the Supreme Court affirmed the integrity of our federal system of government and the role of the court in seeing that its judgments are enforced. It broke ground that was not to be trodden again for half a century.

AN AGE OF EXTREMES

The Declaration of Independence celebrated self-government, equality, and the enigmatic "pursuit of happiness." But when the Constitution was written, the Declaration got elbowed into the background. It was Abraham Lincoln in his Gettysburg Address who knotted the Declaration's concept of freedom and the Constitution's plan of government together into an American testament.

He did more than that. For the Founders, happiness was a virtuous life in a free society. For those in the midst of an industrial revolution, happiness became the freedom to achieve and be prosperous. Lincoln defined the new happiness, tying it to freedom in a eulogy to his hero Henry Clay:

> [Clay] loved his country partly because it was his own country, but mostly because it was a free country; and he burned with a zeal for its advancement, prosperity, and glory, because he saw in such, the advancement, prosperity, and glory, of human liberty, human right and human nature. He desired the prosperity of his countrymen partly because they were his countrymen but chiefly to show to the world that freemen could be prosperous.

So American freedom headed off in a pragmatic direction, in what would be a continuing voyage. It often became a negative thing-an absence of restraints. (For those who cheered Sheriff Shipp, freedom meant keeping government out of state and local affairs.) In the West, that idea of unrestrained freedom encouraged shootouts, wide-open saloons, and horrific lawlessness, as well as the exhilaration of total independence. And American business? In much of the nineteenth century it was wholly without regulation. E. L. Godkin, the liberal editor of The Nation, defined freedom as "the liberty to buy and sell, and mend and make, where, when, and how we please." Which is the way it was for Mattie Silks, a Denver madam who carried a lace parasol and a gold cross and said, "I went into the sporting life for business reasons and no other. It was a way for a woman in those days to make money and I made it."

Mark Twain calls the era a "Gilded Age." For the very rich, and for a burgeoning middle class, life is good and will get even better. But for immigrants, minorities, the unlucky, and the unskilled there is often grinding poverty. By 1890, one percent of the population owns more property than all the rest of the nation's people combined.

The *New York Times* dubs Cornelius Vanderbilt a "robber baron," and the name sticks. He is smart, no question of that; he starts with one small boat and soon has a fleet. Then he sees the future of trains and becomes king of the railroads. He earns much of his money by getting favors from the government. As for living by rules, Vanderbilt is blunt. "Law! What do I care about law? H'ain't I got power?" He isn't the only one who feels that way. Andrew Carnegie, John D. Rockefeller, and other magnates hire police forces, shoot and intimidate workers, and make their own laws.

Early factory owners had worked alongside their employees. They knew and cared about their workers. The new form of business in America—the corporation—leads to behemoths. Merchant princes who make it to the top of the heap live like medieval sultans and have almost no contact with their workers. Monopolies exaggerate the extremes. But there are positives: the energy of it all helps turn the nation into an industrial giant.

Just how do the great tycoons of the Gilded Age make their money? For some, like Cornelius Vanderbilt and George Pullman, it is railroads. For others, like John D. Rockefeller, founder of Standard Oil—"the greatest, wisest and meanest monopoly known to history"—it is oil. For Thomas Edison, Henry Ford, and others, it is inventiveness. And then there is steel, an industry dominated by Scottish-born Andrew Carnegie.

At the age of twelve, in 1847, Carnegie is working from six in the morning until six at night as a bobbin boy in a Pennsylvania textile factory. A few years later, he is an

Three industrialists: Andrew Carnegie (top), who believed the ability to make money brought responsibilities; Cornelius Vanderbilt (right), for whom the only responsibility was to his own enrichment; and Thomas Edison (below), who wanted to be the best at everything he did.

At Andrew Carnegie's Homestead, Pennsylvania, steel mill, the strikers try to attack the Pinkerton detectives, who have been captured and are being escorted by union men carrying rifles.

> "It brutalizes you. You start in to be a man, but you become more and more a machine. It drags you down mentally and morally, just as it does physically. I wouldn't mind it so much if it weren't for the long hours. Twelve hours is too long."
>
> —a nineteenth-century steelworker

assistant to a railroad executive, learning about capital and how to use it. By the time he is thirty-three, Carnegie is very rich. Then he enters the steel business and becomes its lord, keeping wages low and profits high. Soon steel transforms the American landscape (and landscapes around the world). With steel for framing, tall buildings begin to scrape city skies. Steel cables help create the extraordinary Brooklyn Bridge linking Manhattan and Brooklyn. Across it walks a circus parade of elephants to show off and prove that it is safe.

There are no parades for steelworkers. The writer Hamlin Garland visits a Pennsylvania steel town. "The streets were horrible; the buildings poor; the sidewalks sunken and full of holes," he writes. "Everywhere the yellow mud of the streets lay kneaded into sticky masses through which groups of pale, lean men slouched in faded garments."

In 1889, the iron and steelworkers union wins a favorable three-year contract at Carnegie's Homestead Steel Works (located a few miles from Pittsburgh). Carnegie decides to break the union. In 1892, he stays at his palatial home in Scotland while his manager, Henry Clay Frick (whose Fifth Avenue mansion is now a superb museum), steps up production demands, locks workers out of the plant, and, when union officers protest, fires the union workers. Frick announces that all employees must sign individual contracts. The union responds by mobilizing the whole town of Homestead (about 12,000 people- mostly steelworkers and their families) in a strike that blocks access to the mill. Frick hires 300 Pinkerton detectives (they're called detectives, but they're just men with guns), who get into a fight with the strikers. Three Pinkerton agents and seven workers are killed before the Pinkertons surrender. The governor sends in 8,000 armed militiamen; that ends the strike. Union leaders are arrested, and strikebreakers replace many of the workers. Carnegie has won. He institutes longer hours and lower wages. Each side sees things differently. The strikers believe workers have a right to unionize and not be fired for doing so; Carnegie and Frick believe they have the right to do with their business what they see fit. It will be forty years before unions again organize workers in the Homestead steel mills.

THE RISE OF LABOR

Steelworkers work twelve hours a day, six days a week. Textile workers, many of them children, work sixty to eighty hours a week. Miners toil underground with explosives, but without safety regulations. In one year, 25,000 workers die on the job; many more are injured. If a worker loses an arm in a job accident—and many do to the machines—no one helps with doctor's bills. If workers complain, they are fired. Workers begin to demand their own power. They want higher wages, fewer work hours, and better conditions (owners want to keep labor costs low). "The labor question became the basic public issue of the late nineteenth and early twentieth centuries," says historian Eric Foner.

At the heart of the labor movement are the unions-groups of workers who band together to agitate for better conditions. These are people who want control of their destiny. It's in the unions that many Americans—especially new immigrants—learn about democracy and self-government. But many of the unions are loosely organized; some are led by socialists, who want the government to take over businesses that affect the public, like railroads, electrical power, and telephones; some unions are led by anarchists, who don't believe in government at all. On May

Thomas Anshutz's 1880 picture *The Ironworkers' Noontime* was highly realistic by the standards of his time. The workers he painted at a nail factory in Wheeling, West Virginia, were skilled "puddlers"—the men who poured the molten iron into molds.

Posters in German as well as English summoned workers to Chicago's Haymarket Square for the fateful rally on May 4, 1886. Samuel Fielden, a teamster, was speaking to the crowds when a cast-iron bomb filled with dynamite went off.

1, 1886, unions around the country start a strike for an eight-hour day. The strike is haphazard, but seems to be gaining momentum in Chicago.

On May 3, German-born journalist August Spies is in Chicago's Haymarket Square. There, 1,400 workers from the McCormick Harvester Company march in a peaceful strike focusing on the eight-hour issue (they are also asking for better pay). Cyrus McCormick, Jr., is so desperate for workers that he has hired substitute laborers-scabs-to take the strikers' places, and has agreed to let them work an eight-hour day. The strikers are angry. The police are testy. August Spies speaks, police move in, shots are fired, and at least two workers are dead.

Spies, an anarchist, prints a leaflet calling for "Revenge! Workingmen to Arms!" He compares the strike to the Revolution of 1776. "If you are men, if you are sons of those who shed their blood to free you," he writes, "then you will rise and destroy the hideous monster that seeks to destroy you. To arms, we call you to arms." The next day more than 3,000 protesters gather in Haymarket Square. But when it begins to rain, most of them leave. Only about 300 are

A Union Man

American labor laws lag far behind those of almost every other free nation. Working conditions are often unsafe, factory pay is rarely fair, and workers have few, if any, benefits. In 1900, only one American worker in twelve belongs to a union. Unions are feared by workers as well as managers; many labor leaders are radicals. Then a labor leader appears who is a conservative thinker. Samuel Gompers uses business methods to organize and negotiate for labor. He sticks to "pure and simple" unionism and tells workers to stay away from campaigns to overthrow capitalism.

Sam Gompers is a Dutch Jew who, at the age of ten, is apprenticed to a shoemaker. He decides he'd rather help his father, a cigar maker. But they can't keep the family fed. The Cigarmakers' Society, a union, comes to their rescue with an emigration fund that helps members go to America. A civil war is being fought there, but that doesn't stop the Gompers family. They head for the New World. Sam is thirteen when they move into a tenement apartment on New York City's Lower East Side. He and his father roll cigars at home. And Sam takes courses at New York's Cooper Union. Before long he's elected president of the Cigarmakers' Union. A good-humored, no-nonsense man, he has a vision and goes for it. The Cigarmakers is a craft union–all its members do the same kind of work. In 1886, Gompers persuades other craft unions to band together with the Cigarmakers and form the American Federation of Labor. For the next thirty-eight years Sam Gompers works for the AF of L, making it a major force in the American industrial world. He is convinced that if workers earn good pay it will make everyone prosperous. Besides, he believes a fair labor policy encourages a just society. "Show me the country in which there are no strikes and I will show you that country in which there is no liberty," he says.

Employers have almost unlimited power. They can lock employees in or out of the workplace. They can destroy unions by hiring armed guards or simply by buying unfavorable publicity. The courts almost always favor management. That begins to change as unions acquire power and respectability. It might not have happened without leaders like Samuel Gompers.

The long-hour men go home, throw themselves on a miserable apology for a bed, and dream of work. They eat to work, sleep to work, and dream to work, instead of working to live. The man who goes home early has time to see his children, to eat his supper, to read the newspaper. That reading the newspaper creates the desire to be alone for half an hour, and that starts a desire for an extra room, just a little extra room. That extra room is a milestone in the record of social progress. It means a carpet on the floor, a chair, an easy chair, a picture on the wall, a piano or organ.... Let the people demand an extra room with all that goes with it, and they will get wages enough to buy it. Time is the most valuable thing on earth: time to think, time to act, time to extend our fraternal relations, time to become better men, time to become better women, time to become better and more independent citizens.

—Samuel Gompers

still in the square when 180 policemen arrive. Suddenly a bomb is thrown; one policeman is killed instantly. Authorities disagree on how many others die—some from bomb injuries, some from bullets fired wildly by panicked officers. But several police as well as some strikers are killed, and perhaps a hundred injured. The bomb thrower is never identified.

The nation is outraged. Many of the workers are recent immigrants. Stories circulate about foreign conspiracies and plots to overthrow the government. The Chicago police make arrests without warrants to do so. Eight men are charged with conspiracy to commit murder. Four of those men had already left Haymarket Square when the bomb was thrown. One who was there says "there was not a syllable said about anarchism at the Haymarket meeting." It doesn't matter. The nation is now afraid of foreigners and socialists and anarchists and unionists. All eight men are found guilty. Four of them, including August Spies, are hanged. Another commits suicide. At the McCormick factory, the workers return to their old ten-hour day. In Paris, in 1890, the Socialist Second International adopts May Day (May 1) as its labor day. Three years later, the governor of Illinois pardons the three remaining survivors. He is not reelected.

Hard Times

Five years after August Spies is hanged and a year after the Homestead strike, the nation is hit by a depression. It begins with farmers; they are distressed and stop buying goods. The rest of the nation begins to hurt. The stock market falls. Banks take farms from farmers who can't make mortgage payments; but when they try to sell the farms, no one is buying. That puts banks in trouble. In the first half of 1893, 172 state banks, 177 private banks, and forty-seven savings-and-loan associations close. By the end of the year the total is 500 banks. More than 15,000 businesses fail. And that is just the beginning. Railroads begin closing, mines are shut down, steamers stay in port, factories shut their doors, and companies go bankrupt.

Unemployment in 1894 is said to have been higher, in relation to the country's population, than at any time in our history. The manufacturing states of Pennsylvania, New York, and Michigan are especially hard hit. One out of four people in Pennsylvania is reported out of work. In Michigan the figure is 43.6 percent. Nationally, one out of five workers is said to be idle. In Chicago, 100,000 men are sleeping on the streets. Even those who have jobs face cuts in pay. Eighteen ninety-three is an awful year; 1894 is worse.

Jacob Coxey is a Civil War veteran, a farmer, a quarry owner, and a devout

Wherever they went on their march from Ohio, the men of Coxey's Army were harassed by police and treated as dangerous vagrants.

Christian. He is also a reformer. He wants the government to help its out-of-work citizens find jobs. So, in 1894, when things are really bad, he assembles an army of unemployed men. They set off on a 400-mile freedom march from Massillon, Ohio, to Washington, D.C. They intend to ask the government to help the unemployed. But as Coxey's army tramps eastward, newspaper reports describe it as a bunch of ragged, hungry men out to terrorize the countryside. At the White House, extra guards are placed on duty. President Grover Cleveland makes it clear that he will not meet with the protesters. Thirty-five days after leaving Ohio, Coxey's army makes it to Washington. The men march down Pennsylvania Avenue to the steps of the

> "We need legislation which furnishes employment to every man able and willing to work; legislation which will emancipate our beloved country from financial bondage."
> —Jacob Coxey

Jacob Coxey

Capitol; there Coxey prepares to speak. But before he can even begin, National Guardsmen move in and arrest him. *Congress shall make no law ... abridging the freedom of speech,* says the First Amendment. "Freedom of speech is the safety valve of society; if it is obstructed there will be an explosion somewhere," says Coxey, who knows the Constitution well.

SOLIDARITY FOREVER

There is one union whose members hate Samuel Gompers's American Federation of Labor: the Wobblies. Yes, you read that right: Wobblies. Officially they were the Industrial Workers of the World, the IWW; but everyone called them "Wobblies." They complain that AFL members are skilled workers—aristocrats of the laboring world—and not everyone is welcome to join them. The Wobblies say the AFL should be called the American Separation of Labor. The IWW is democratic: any worker can sign up.

Utah's William "Big Bill" Haywood opens the Wobblies' founding convention in Chicago in 1905 when he takes a loose board, pounds on a table, and proclaims in his booming voice, "Fellow workers ... this is the Continental Congress of the Working Class." Lucy Parsons joins him on the platform. Her husband, Albert Parsons, was one of the men hanged after the Haymarket Square bombing. Lucy knows he had nothing to do with the bombing, so she takes her two children and goes off to speak at hundreds of meetings, until she sparks a worldwide protest movement. Finally, the governor of Illinois proclaims that Albert Parsons and the others were killed for their beliefs, not their actions.

The Wobblies' goal is to create one big union-all workers will belong to it—and then to have one big strike that will stop everything; then the workers can take over and make the country a better place. They are idealists, and mostly sincere, but they are rarely in agreement with one another about just how that ideal country will be organized. At first, most of the Wobblies are miners from the West. There is an abundance of writers among them, like the songwriter Joe Hill, and they write poems and songs about their problems and hopes. Just about every member has a copy of the little red IWW songbook; singing seems to come naturally to them. One of their songs, "Solidarity Forever," becomes a theme song for the whole labor movement. If a local union needs help, Wobblies hop train boxcars, arrive, march, climb on soapboxes, speak, get thrown in jail, and sing. Overthrowing capitalism is their long-range goal, but the IWW, like the AF of L, starts out by fighting for shorter hours, better pay, and safer conditions for workers. It is in Lawrence, Massachusetts, that they have their finest moment.

The state legislature has passed a law saying that women and children can't work more than fifty-four hours a week. But the owners of the textile mills in Lawrence aren't about to accept that. Women and children have been working fifty-six hours. The owners speed up their machinery so the workers will produce as much in fifty-four hours as they do in fifty-six (they're expected to work faster to keep up). Then,

Big Bill Haywood

"The working class and the employing class have nothing in common. There can be no peace as long as hunger and want are found among millions of working people and the few, who make up the employing class, have all the good things in life."

—Big Bill Haywood

in addition, they take two hours' pay out of each pay envelope. Mill profits are at an all-time high.

It is January of 1912, and bitter cold, when the Lawrence workers get those envelopes. There is less money than the week before and some women leave their looms. Soon 25,000 millworkers walk off the job. Most are foreign-born—between them they speak about forty-five different languages. Many of the workers have come to Lawrence because of advertisements in their native lands telling of opportunities in

> "To pay for fifty-four hours' work the wages of fifty-six would be equivalent to an increase in wages, and that the mills cannot afford to pay."
> —William Wood, president of the American Woolen Company

the mills. One poster showed a Lawrence workingman leaving the factory with a suitcase full of gold. When they get to Lawrence they find their pay barely keeps them from starvation. Their housing is terrible. Their children must work if the family is to survive. These immigrants dreamed of a free, abundant America; they believed in its promise; they feel betrayed. Their picket signs read, "We Want Bread and Roses, Too."

But they don't have a real leader, so they appeal to the IWW for help. Big Bill Haywood is soon on his way east. Elizabeth Gurley Flynn, a young, pretty Irish dynamo, comes too. Flynn chained herself to a lamppost in Spokane, Washington, after city officials began throwing Wobblies in jail (for having public meetings to protest job-hiring methods). But it is twenty-six-year-old Joe Ettor, a terrific organizer, who turns out to be the leader in Lawrence. The son of an Italian immigrant family, Ettor speaks Italian and English fluently, with enough Polish, Hungarian, and Yiddish to get by.

In Lawrence, leading citizens are calling the strikes "un-American" and blaming "foreign influences." They mean the immigrants. *The American Wool and Cotton Reporter* (the mill owners' magazine) warns of "anarchy" and "socialism" and challenges to "the fundamental idea of law and order." Ettor keeps the strikers calm. He says, "You can hope for no success on any policy of violence.... Violence ... means the loss of the strike." There is violence at Lawrence. Police violence. The mayor says, "We will either break this strike or break the strikers' heads." Militia, special policemen, and Pinkerton detectives are brought to the city. Dynamite is discovered, strikers are arrested, and newspaper headlines scream of anarchy. It is soon discovered that the dynamite is an attempt to frame the strikers; it has been planted by the son of a former mayor. Detectives, pretending to be striking workers, smash, destroy and grab headlines.

On the forty-third day of the strike, forty children and their parents gather at the Lawrence railroad station. Sympathetic families in Philadelphia have offered to take the children into their homes until the strike is over. But before the train arrives, the Lawrence police show up and begin clubbing women and children. "Police, acting under orders of the city marshal, choked and knocked down women and children, the innocent wives and babies of the strikers," says the *Boston Common*. An article in a major magazine says, "It is wrong to charge ... that the doctrine of the IWW ... at Lawrence ... was ... a doctrine of violence; fundamentally it was a doctrine of the brotherhood of man."

It is too much. A congressional investigation is ordered and the public learns details. Children sent to New York are "found to be suffering from malnutrition." Dr. Elizabeth Shapleigh says, "thirty-six of every 100 of all men and women who work in the mill die before or by the time they are twenty-five years of age." By the end of the hearings, the mill owners have agreed to raise wages, pay overtime, and rehire the strikers. The Bread and Roses strike is over! Lucy Parsons speaks for the union: "Our movement has but one infallible, unchangeable matter: 'Freedom'—freedom to discover any truth, freedom to develop, freedom to live naturally and fully."

"They cannot weave cloth with bayonets," said IWW organizer Joe Ettor to the demonstrators in Lawrence (below). "By all means make the strike as peaceful as possible." Left, Joe Hill—poet, song-writer, and martyr of the Wobbly movement.

PART 10

YEARNING TO BREATHE FREE

It is June of 1885, and workmen on New York's docks are preparing to unload 214 packing cases at the docks. The cases hold a remarkable cargo—the body of a handsome woman. This woman is big. Colossal, they call her. The biggest ever. Her nose alone is four feet long. Her weight almost sank the ship on the voyage from Europe. Now she is in New York harbor with no place to go. She is a gift from the people of France to the people of America, a monument in unassembled pieces. She is, of course, Lady Liberty—the Statue of Liberty—and she is about to become a metaphor: a metaphor for freedom.

She was conceived, in 1865, at a dinner party in France. Edouard de Laboulaye, the scholarly dinner host, is passionate about liberty, and, although he has never been to the United States, he is filled with enthusiasm for the young nation. Laboulaye sees America's Civil War, dreadful as it was, as a triumph for the forces of liberty. That terrible paradox—slavery in the land of the free—is no more. The dinner guests reminisce about the long friendship of America and France. As children, they heard their parents and grandparents talk of the time when Benjamin Franklin and Thomas Jefferson lived in France. Laboulaye is proud of the role France played in America's revolution, and of the French hero of that revolution, the Marquis de Lafayette. The guests want to do something

On the left, the Statue of Liberty in 1883, rising above the streets of Paris while under construction at the foundry. Several smaller models were made first to perfect the details; the final model was divided into many sections, each reproduced at four times the size. The result: a copper-and-steel lady 111 feet tall from heels to head (above, already in New York but still on the ground; her head is seventeen feet high, her mouth three feet wide). The seven rays of her crown symbolize the world's seven seas and continents.

The statue's sculptor, Bartholdi, began work on her in his studio, but she soon outgrew(right) that and towered over his Paris neighborhood. Above: for a while, the statue, 151 feet from ground to torch, could be viewed from top (her crown) to toe (her feet) on the same level-the ground.

to celebrate the triumph of freedom over slavery. They decide that a monument, symbolizing American freedom, would be appropriate and would speak to all the world (including the establishment in France).

Among the guests at the dinner party is a young sculptor named Frédéric Bartholdi; he is swept away by the conversation. He will design the monument.

Five years later, encouraged by Laboulaye, Bartholdi is in the United States visiting cities from Newport, Rhode Island, to San Francisco, California. "Everything is big here," he writes to Laboulaye, "even the green peas." When he sails to New York, Bartholdi is struck by the beauty and openness of its harbor. He finds a small spot of land named Bedloe's Island, and he knows almost at once that this is where his monument should stand. On Bedloe's Island one can see rivers, ocean, and land all at the same time. The island belongs to the government, writes Bartholdi to Laboulaye. "It is land common to all the states." By now he has a gigantic statue in mind; he will build a figure taller than the Colossus of Rhodes. That huge statue on a Mediterranean island was designed to show off the power of ancient Greece. Bartholdi's statue will be a symbol not of power but of freedom. "Trying to glorify the republic and liberty over there," he writes to Laboulaye, "I shall await the day when they may be found here [in France] with us."

Now an engineering genius is needed—someone who can figure out how to build a huge statue that will stand unprotected in an ocean harbor. France happens to have one: his name is Gustave Eiffel (he is soon to build a famous tower in Paris). Eiffel designs a skeleton of iron bars, elastic enough to bend with the wind, and strong enough to support the giant lady and the people who will climb inside her body. Her skin will be made of delicate sheets of copper. Piece by piece she is created. She is so large a full-size man can stand on her big toe and have room to spare. When her head and hand are completed, they are sent to the Centennial Fair in Philadelphia; nine million Americans come out to see them. But on that day in 1885 when the rest of the lady arrives in New York, she has no place to stand. Neither Congress nor American financiers are willing to provide a pedestal, and without one the statue cannot be erected.

What is to be done? A newspaper publisher, who is a promotional genius, decides he will tell the statue's story to the public. Joseph Pulitzer was seventeen when he came to the United States from Hungary without knowing a word of English. He was soon in the army, where he learned more than a few words fighting in the Civil War. After that, Pulitzer settled in St. Louis, Missouri, and became a newspaperman, creating the *St. Louis Post-Dispatch*. Then he headed for New York and his greatest success, which came when he bought the *New York World*. When Pulitzer learns that the wealthy citizens of New York will not build a pedestal for the statue, he decides to appeal to his readers.

> *The statue is not a gift from the millionaires of France to the millionaires of America, but a gift of the whole people of France to the whole people of America. Let us not wait for the millionaires to give the money. Let us hear from the people!*

Pulitzer announces that anyone who donates money—any amount—will have his or her name printed in the paper. All across America, people respond. Twelve public schools in Trenton, New Jersey, collect $105.07 from their students. A girl named Jane sends fifty cents. "I am only a poor sewing girl," she writes. A ten-year-old sends "my pocket-piece-20 cents in silver." A group of artists and writers give their work to be auctioned to raise money for the statue. Mark Twain contributes a pile of canceled checks featuring his famous signature. "Use them as freely as they are freely contributed," he writes. "Heaven knows there are a ton of them; I will send them all to you, for my heart is in the sublime work!"

"The $250,000 that the statue cost was paid by the masses of the French people … irrespective of class or condition…." wrote Joseph Pulitzer (above). He turned the *World* into a crusading publication that took up many good causes.

"Not like the brazen giant of Greek fame,
 With conquering limbs astride from land to land;
 Here at our sea-washed, sunset gates shall stand
 A mighty woman with a torch, whose flame
 Is the imprisoned lightning, and her name
 Mother of Exiles. From her beacon-hand
 Glows world-wide welcome; her mild eyes command
 The air-bridged harbor that twin cities frame.
 'Keep, ancient lands, your storied pomp!' cries she
 With silent lips. 'Give me your tired, your poor,
 Your huddled masses yearning to breathe free,
 The wretched refuse of your teeming shore.
 Send these, the homeless, tempest-tost to me.
 I lift my lamp beside the golden door!' "

—Emma Lazarus, "The New Colossus"

In 1886, with the help of millions of donors, the Statue of Liberty is finally installed on its new pedestal.

One of the writers who gives her work is a young woman named Emma Lazarus. Her ancestors came to the United States in the seventeenth century fleeing religious oppression in Europe. That was long before Emma Lazarus's birth. She has had a privileged childhood, but, beginning in 1879, she begins to hear about the pogroms, anti-Semitic mob attacks, that are sweeping Russia. Thousands of Jews are being killed; thousands more come to America. That touches the young poet, making her understand the importance of religious freedom. Emma Lazarus writes a sonnet about what the Statue of Liberty meant to her. She calls it "The New Colossus." What she doesn't know—and never learns during her short life (she dies at the age of thirty-eight)—is that her words will give the statue a second meaning. Lady Liberty becomes not only a symbol of freedom; she also becomes a symbol of America's policy of welcome—its golden door—its unusual decision to embrace people of all colors, races, and religions. The last five lines of Lazarus's poem are engraved on the pedestal of the statue. Millions of immigrants, sailing into New York harbor, will be welcomed by those words.

Telling It Like It Is

Mary Harris was born in Cork, Ireland, in 1837, and was still a girl when the potato famine came along. Facing starvation, her family headed for the New World. Later, she often claimed that her father had been active in the Irish resistance against England, and that political dissent came to her naturally. But she started with conventional careers, as a teacher and then a seamstress. She was living in Memphis, Tennessee, when she married George Jones; they had four boys and she seemed headed for a life of

Mother Jones (right) and the Great Fire of Chicago, which took her business, her home, and 18,000 other buildings in 1871. Much of the city was wooden and hastily built; and the heat was so strong that "fireproof" masonry and cast-iron structures melted away.

domesticity. Then the yellow fever epidemic hit Memphis (the same outbreak that killed Ida B. Wells's parents in 1867), and her husband and her four sons died.

Mary Harris Jones got her courage together, moved to Chicago, and opened a dressmaking shop. Mrs. Jones had style. She was becoming successful when, in 1871, a horrible fire swept through Chicago. Just about the whole city burned; Mary Jones's business went with it. She was left with nothing. That decided her. If she was going to start all over again—again—she wanted to do something important with her life. She wanted to help others. She knew that tens of thousands of children worked in American factories and mills and mines, many for twelve to fifteen hours a day in lives of near-slavery. Hardly anyone seemed to worry about them. Working children needed an advocate. Mary Jones had found her calling.

A fearless, pugnacious little woman, about five feet tall, with hair that turned white after her children died, she was called "mother" because she seemed like a nice old lady—until she opened her mouth. Then she swore like a trooper, spoke in ear-splitting tones, and said what she thought. "Whenever a fight is going on, I have to jump there," said Mother Jones. "My address is like my shoes—it travels with me wherever I go." Clarence Darrow, a well-known lawyer, wrote of her, "Mother Jones's ... fearless soul always drew her to seek the

Above, children in a Maryland packing factory. "Those too small to work are held in laps or closed away in boxes," said the photographer. Left, this newsboy had to pay for any papers he didn't sell.

> "The militant, not the meek, shall inherit the earth."
> —Mother Jones

spot where the fight was hottest and the danger greatest."

In Alabama, she spoke up on behalf of children in a cotton factory. "I have watched children all day long tending the dangerous machinery," she said. "And then, when they are of no more use to the master, I have seen them thrown out to die." She went on:

> *Little girls and boys, barefooted, walked up and down between the endless rows of spindles, reaching thin little hands into the machinery to repair threads. They crawled under machinery to oil it. They replaced spindles all day long; all night through … six-year-olds with faces of sixty did an eight-hour shift for ten cents a day: the machines, built in the North, were built low for the hands of little children…. At the lunch half-hour, the children would fall to sleep over their lunch of cornbread and fat pork. They would lie on the bare floor and sleep. Sleep was their recreation, their release, as play is to the free child.*

In 1902 Maria Jones gathered some working children together and marched them from Pennsylvania to New York, trying to raise money and make people aware. "The toil of these children makes others wealthy," she said. In Princeton, New Jersey, she introduced ten-year-old James Ashworth to a crowd that included college students and professors. James's back was bent from carrying heavy loads. "He gets three dollars a week working in a carpet factory ten hours a day. I shudder for the future of a nation that is building up an aristocracy out of the lifeblood of the children of the poor," said Mother Jones. Then she introduced Gussie Rangnew, whose tired face was like an old woman's, "a little girl from whom all the childhood has gone." She described how Gussie packed stockings all day long, day after day, summer, winter, spring, and fall. Mother Jones marched the underage textile workers to Theodore Roosevelt's home in Oyster Bay, on Long Island.

She also found time to support and organize miners, to help found the IWW, to aid Mexican revolutionaries in 1907, to help organize New York shirtwaist workers, and to speak out loudly and tell the story of the massacre of women and children in a miners' colony at Ludlow, Colorado (when almost everyone else was ignoring it). "Pray for the dead and fight like hell for the living," was one of her mottoes.

The police called Mother Jones a public nuisance. When a judge asked who gave her a permit to speak on the streets, she replied, "Patrick Henry, Thomas Jefferson, and John Adams!" Mother Jones was sent to jail—more than once. In jail she spoke of George Washington as a "gentleman agitator" who had fought the powerful British establishment. Each time Mother Jones got out of jail, she went right back to work. "I'm not a humanitarian," she said. "I'm a hell-raiser." But she was both. And very good at getting attention for herself and her causes. She was disorganized, she was mercurial, but she never wavered in her commitment to people she saw as oppressed. It was those, like Mother Jones—who shouted out on behalf of others—who laid the foundations for labor laws in this country.

THE PEOPLE'S PARTY

The place is Georgia. The time, 1892. A small, redheaded man—his name is Tom Watson—stands on a wooden platform under tall pines. Watson, a congressman, is running for reelection. He is a member of a new political party, the People's Party, also called the Populist Party. The Democrats have sent a brass band to his rally. They are playing loudly—very loudly. They are doing it on purpose. There is something unusual about this southern crowd. It is both black and white. The people are mostly poor whites and poor blacks. Watson believes they have something in common: their poverty.

If they stand together, perhaps they can do something about it. "You are kept apart that you may be separately fleeced," he tells them.

His listeners know that on election day they will be under pressure to vote for Democratic candidates. Voting is not private. The Democrats have become the only party with power in the South. They have been known to stuff ballot boxes with false votes to ensure victory. They have paid voters for their votes. Those who vote for any other party risk losing their jobs, or worse. Watson wants to change things. The People's Party is campaigning for secret ballots. A Democrat rides into Watson's crowd, inviting everyone to a free dinner. "These men are not going to be enticed away from free, fair discussion of great public questions by any amount of barbecued beef," shouts Watson. No one moves.

Watson and his Populists want to change other things, too. They see themselves as the party of the common man. They believe the government is working for the rich and powerful and taking advantage of the poor and weak. They believe that the people must take control of the government. These reformers speak for ordinary Americans who don't want to be left out of the good times that are being enjoyed by others. They demand rights. Some people call them communists; some call them hayseeds. But they are just people who want to take part in the governing process, and to have their ideas heard.

The farmers listening to Watson are angry. Farm prices are low. In 1865, cotton sold for a dollar a pound. It is 1892 and cotton is seven cents a pound. It costs more than seven cents to grow that pound! In the Midwest, wheat prices have tumbled from $2.50 a bushel in the 1860s to fifty cents a bushel in the 1890s. Farmers can't pay their bills. When they read the papers, they learn how good life is for America's millionaires. Railroad heir William Vanderbilt has just thrown a big party for his friends in ritzy Newport, Rhode Island. They sat on red damask chairs and dug with silver shovels in a play sandbox filled with rubies and diamonds. The society columns are full of that story. It's enough to make anyone angry, but especially farmers who can't

Populist Tom Watson was a lawyer and the largest landowner in Georgia; but he understood what it was to be in need. He got Congress to pass the first resolution to have rural mail delivered free. Until then, farmers had to pay the mailman for the letters he brought them.

"We believe that the powers of government should be expanded… to the end that oppression, injustice, and poverty shall eventually cease in the land."
—Populist Party platform

A cartoon that purported to show what the Supreme Court would look like if the Populists ran it; it sneered at them as a bunch of old fogeys and hayseeds. In the "waiting pen" in the left foreground, millionaires like the financier J.P. Morgan (second from left) and "gold bugs" (who believed in the gold standard) cool their heels

understand what is happening. They are working hard and helping to feed and clothe the world. Yet while some people are getting very rich, they are losing their farms. In Kansas, between 1889 and 1893, banks take back 11,122 farms.

Some Populist leaders tell the farmers that there is a conspiracy. They say the eastern bankers, the railroad magnates, and the grain-elevator owners are plotting against them, keeping the farmers poor so they can get richer. That isn't true—no one is plotting against the farmers on purpose.

The big-money powers care only about themselves. They are working *for* their own interests-not *against* the farmers'. But their interests often hurt the farmers. And their money gives them political power. Populism has arisen out of frustration. But it is no hick movement, as it is sometimes portrayed. The Populists are economic reformers who believe that money, and its political influence, is undermining the democratic process and throwing American society off balance. They initiate a lecturing system that sends speakers to some

40,000 "suballiances," providing farmers with economic insights that few other Americans have. But racists are attracted to Populism, and that will taint its reputation. Tom Watson, turned old and bitter, will get support from the Ku Klux Klan.

In its relatively brief career, the People's Party flashes across the nation like a comet, electing governors and congressmen. Some populist ideas that seem idealistic and unattainable later become law. It isn't long before there are secret ballots, women's suffrage and a graduated income tax and many other things that the Populists agitate for. And though the Populists themselves fade away (they merge with the Democrats and lose their identity), their ideas keep reappearing, in cycles, as comets do.

A Cross of Gold

President Grover Cleveland is worried about money. The dollar has been losing value. Cleveland thinks he knows what is causing the problem: the Silver Purchase Act of 1890. That act says the government has to buy so many million dollars of silver every year (which helps silver miners). Cleveland thinks the nation should be on a strict gold standard—that every dollar in circulation should be backed by its equivalent in gold in the government's vaults. So the Silver Purchase Act is repealed—but the gold reserves keep falling. The nation is in danger of going bankrupt. Cleveland goes to the country's leading financier, J. P. Morgan, and asks for help. Morgan, with other bankers, gives the government gold in return for government bonds. That

In the 1880s, a time of prosperity and good harvests, the U.S. Treasury had a huge surplus: it had more income than it spent. What was to be done with the surplus? President Benjamin Harrison gave most of it away in pensions to Civil War veterans; then the good times ended.

J.P. Morgan

helps stabilize the currency. But many Americans think it humiliating for the president of the United States to have to go to a private banker for help.

By 1894 and 1895, with the country in a depression, everyone is concerned about money. People argue about what is needed to bring back prosperity. Farmers and silver miners associate the bimetal (silver and gold) policy with good times. Farmers are earning less money because commodity prices are dropping; that really hurts those who have borrowed money to buy farm equipment. (Deflation-falling prices-is hard on people who borrow money. They have less income but they still have to pay back loans at interest rates based on the old, higher prices.) Those who believe in the gold standard think silver has brought the depression. Silver versus gold becomes the big political issue. (A stockpile in the treasury isn't the only thing that determines a country's wealth—its industry, resources, and people have much more to do with it-but you wouldn't have thought that in 1895.)

Populist leaders want more money in circulation. They support the bimetal standard—and go even further. They feel the supply of money should be controlled, not by private financiers like J. P. Morgan, but by an elected board. They are asking for a new monetary system to create money "in the name of the whole people." The financiers hate that idea. Most Americans don't understand it. (Decades later that Populist notion becomes law when a Federal Reserve System comes into being, with a board controlling the supply of money.)

Meanwhile, into this fray marches a silver-tongued orator from Lincoln, Nebraska. He is young, handsome, and very sincere. Farm boy William Jennings Bryan is a devout Protestant. Something else is central to his being: Bryan believes in the Constitution and American democracy with the same intensity he brings to his religion. He became a lawyer, moved to Lincoln, Nebraska, and impressed people with his honesty and sincerity. He is just thirty years old when, in 1890, he is elected

> "At the turn of the century, when it most needed to be said, when it took real courage, he spoke the meaning of America in words of fire. He kept insisting—and history will remember him for it—that America is not really America unless the lowliest man feels sure in his bones that he has free and equal opportunity to get ahead."
>
> —lawyer Clarence Darrow on William Jennings Bryan

Republicans saw William Jennings Bryan's audience as a bunch of hick farmers who wanted easy money—unlimited silver coins at a ratio of 16 to 1 with gold—and were totally taken in by Bryan, who was playing only the tunes they wanted to hear.

to Congress as a Democrat. It is money and its distribution that concern him and his farmer constituents. Why do some people who work hard have lots of money and others, who also work hard, have little? When Cleveland and the Democrats repeal the Silver Purchase Act, Bryan refuses to go along with his party. In 1896, at the age of thirty-six, he decides to run for president. He is unknown in most of the country, so he takes a job as editor of the *Omaha World-Herald*, which gives him a platform. Then he goes on a speaking tour.

Few of the delegates to the 1896 Democratic presidential convention in Chicago consider the young man from Nebraska a serious candidate—until he speaks about silver. He is clad in the armor of a righteous cause, he says. He leads them through the history of the struggle between silver and gold. On Bryan's tongue it becomes a struggle between good and evil. He divides the country between East and West. Between hardy pioneers and financial magnates. Between city and country. The convention is mesmerized. "Burn down your cities and leave our farms, and your cities will spring up again as if by magic," he said. "But destroy our farms and the grass will grow in the streets of every city in the country.... You shall not press down upon the brow of labor this crown of thorns; you shall not crucify mankind upon a cross of gold."

Novelist Willa Cather reported Bryan's campaign for a newspaper: "At Chicago, when Bryan stampeded a convention, appropriated a party, electrified a nation … one of those ragged farmers … leaned over the rail … and shouted, 'The sweet singer of Israel.'" But elsewhere he was hated. This cartoon suggested he was a rabble-rousing cousin of anarchists who exploited the Bible in his speeches.

The next day the Democratic Party nominates William Jennings Bryan for president of the United States. The Populists add their backing. The Republicans chose an Ohioan, William McKinley, as their candidate. He supports the gold standard and high tariffs. He sees no reason for government to try to impose controls on business and industry; if business prospers, he says, it will also benefit the poor and the farmers.

The election of 1896 is one of the most important in our history. American voters have tough issues to decide. Many want the reforms that the Populists are calling for. They want laws to improve working conditions. They want shorter working hours; they want laws to prevent employers from hiring children for adult jobs. They want the government to regulate the trusts and corporations in the public interest. Most want to see farmers helped. But all this demands active government, and Americans are ambivalent about that. And there are some things that are worrisome about Bryan and his supporters. They are dividing the country into warring groups. Bryan has picked a fight with the money interests. He romanticizes the yeoman farmer at a time when industrialization is the future.

The financial interests are alarmed. The Republicans spend $4 million on the campaign; the Democrats spend $300,000. A big, costly presidential campaign is something new. Maybe it is the money that made the difference—maybe not. But it is corporations that will dominate America in the twentieth century. Some say the American people made that choice in 1896.

AMERICA THE BEAUTIFUL

Thomas Jefferson thought America a land "with room enough for our descendants to the hundredth and thousandth generation." After 1890, most people know that is not so. That year, the U.S. Census Bureau says there is no more frontier. The great stretches of habitable empty land are gone. The country is filling up. The frontier has been a mixed blessing. It has made hard work, cooperation, and resourcefulness important American traits. On the frontier it is what you can do—not who you are—that people care about. The frontier made America more democratic, but it also made us wasteful—and it wasn't just land we wasted. By 1890 many indigenous birds (like the lovely passenger pigeon) are extinct; the endless herds of buffalo are being mowed down; millions of acres of towering, ancient trees are gone or

Below, *The Canyon of the Yellowstone*, by Thomas Moran; it took Moran eight years to finish another painting of the canyon, *The Grand Canyon of the Yellowstone* (1893–1901). It took Congress much less time, in 1872, to put a million acres of the Yellowstone area under federal control as parkland so settlers couldn't move in. There was much protest, but by 1916 there were thirty-seven national parks.

going; and mining is leaving mountainsides ravished and barren. For some Americans, freedom means the right to do with the land and its flora and fauna whatever they wish. A few see the land in its natural splendor as an irreplaceable common heritage. One of them is John Muir.

Mostly, when it comes to public land, the national policy has been to get it into private hands as quickly and cheaply as possible. Toward the end of the nineteenth century, things begin to change. Slowly, the idea of public preservation takes hold. The world's first national park, Yellowstone (mostly in Wyoming, it extends into Montana and Idaho), is established in 1872. Bigger than Rhode Island and Delaware combined, it is a place where nature puts on spectacular shows as water boils in natural pools and basins and steams erupts in plumes from earth fissures, especially at its Mecca: Old Faithful. In 1890, Yosemite National Park is created on the glorious western slope of the Sierra Nevada mountains in California. A slim, bearded fellow, who is an elegant writer, is among those making Americans aware of their natural heritage. He is known as a "pedestrian," which is the word used to describe long-distance walkers. That man, born in Scotland, is John Muir. President Theodore Roosevelt goes hiking with Muir at Yosemite: "John Muir met me there, and I spent three days and two nights with him," said the president. "There was a delightful innocence and good

John Muir

"I only went out for a walk and finally concluded to stay out till sundown, for going out, I found, was really going in."

—John Muir

will about the man. He was a dauntless soul, brimming over with friendliness and kindliness."

Muir is eleven when his family moves to Wisconsin. There his father uses his son as if he were an adult field hand, beating the boy when he falters. Muir is a hungry reader, but reading at night is prohibited. Muir has a talent for inventing, so he constructs an "early-rising machine," a

Steward of the People

Theodore Roosevelt was an avid naturalist before meeting Muir. His interest in nature began in childhood when he set up natural history museum in his house. When his mother threw a litter of field mice out of the icebox, the boy moaned "the loss to science." When young Roosevelt wanted to learn more about animals and how to stuff them, his parents gave him lessons with a taxidermist who had been taught by the great artist and naturalist John James Audubon. When the Roosevelts wanted to teach their children geography and art and history, they took the family on a year's trip to Europe. It would have been an idyllic childhood, except that Theodore had asthma and bad eyesight and stomach problems. "I was nervous and timid," he wrote. His father told him he needed to build his body to match his mind. At age eleven he began lifting weights and doing exercises. The weak, scrawny lad turned himself into a powerful, fearless man. He went to Harvard, published a paper on birds of the Adirondacks, began a book on naval affairs, and wrote a senior thesis in which he called for "absolute equality" of husband and wife in marriage. "See that girl," he remarked to a friend when he first saw Alice Hathaway, "I'm going to marry her." And he did. Then she, and his beloved mother, died on the same day in the same house (Valentine's Day, 1884)—his wife in childbirth, his mother of typhoid fever. Theodore is in his twenties; devastated, he goes west to the Dakota Badlands to try to forget his sorrows.

The cowboys chuckle when they see the young dude who has come to hunt and be a rancher. He is skinny, with a squeaky voice, thick glasses, and a big toothy grin—and he carries books under his arm. One day on the range, the cowboys figure, and the city slicker will hightail it back East. So the guide takes him buffalo hunting. They are gone seven days, riding the wildest, loneliest, most difficult trails in the Badlands. They are charged by a wounded buffalo, their food runs out, the dude falls into a bed of cactus, wolves frighten their horses, and they wake one morning to find themselves sleeping in four inches of water. The guide is close to collapse from exhaustion. But the worse things get, the more Roosevelt seems to enjoy himself. "By Godfrey, but this is fun!" is what he keeps saying. When he finally bags a buffalo he jumps, dances, and whoops. "There were all kinds of things of which I was afraid at first, ranging from grizzly bears to 'mean' horses and gunfighters," he writes. "But by acting as if I was not afraid I gradually ceased to be afraid."

When he gets back East, Roosevelt is ready to accept a new job: New York City police commissioner. Most of his peers look down their noses at politicians. But Roosevelt says he wants to be part of the governing—not the governed—class. He's soon walking the streets, talking to people, making sure the police are doing their job. No commissioner has done that before. Meanwhile, Congress, listening to Samuel Gompers, has passed a law prohibiting the manufacture of cigars in tenement sweatshops. The Supreme Court rules the law unconstitutional. Roosevelt visits sweatshops. In his autobiography he writes:

The judges who rendered this decision were well-meaning

men. They knew nothing whatever of tenement-house conditions; they knew legalism, not life. This decision completely blocked tenement-house reform legislation in New York for a score of years.

In 1898, Roosevelt, remarried and in the Navy department, resigns to fight in the Spanish-American War. The U.S. is on the side of the Cubans against a Spanish colonial government. In the same war, in the Pacific, the U.S. annexes the Philippines, Guam, and the Hawaiian Islands. Many native Filipinos and Hawaiians want to form their own governments. Carl Schurz says, "The question is not whether we can do such things, but whether we should do them." But this is an age of imperialism; most Americans cheer.

Roosevelt, in Cuba, leads his own cavalry unit, the Rough Riders and is catapulted to national fame. He becomes New York's governor, and so annoys established interests with his reforms that (to get rid of him) they promote him as a vice presidential candidate on the ticket with William McKinley. A few months after taking office in 1901, McKinley is assassinated. Republican insider Mark Hanna is dismayed. "That damned cowboy is president of the United States!" he laments. At forty-two, Roosevelt is the youngest man ever to assume the office. (That's still true.) He intends to be a voice of the people:

During the century that has elapsed since Thomas Jefferson, freedom of the individual has turned out to mean perfect freedom for the strong to wrong the weak. In the name of liberty, mighty industrial overlords now prey on the poor and helpless worker. My view is that the president is a steward of the people.

Roosevelt gets to work. He champions pure food and drug laws. He gets Congress to create a Bureau of Corporations to inspect corporate earnings. He promotes a bill to prohibit railroad discrimination against small shippers. Congress has passed the Sherman Antitrust Act, intended to curtail monopolies, but no one has enforced it. TR goes "trust-busting."

But he fails to turn his party into a serious agency of change. For the most part, its leaders side with corporate opponents of regulation. "There has been a curious revival of the doctrine of State rights ... by the people who know that the States cannot ... control the corporations," Roosevelt writes.

In 1902, the United Mine Workers union calls a strike of Pennsylvania coal miners to protest brutal conditions and low wages. The mine owners refuse to negotiate with workers. TR is outraged. He threatens federal seizure of the entire industry. The threat works. The owners agree to arbitration, and the miners go back to work. It is the first time in a labor dispute that the government is involved on the side of the workers. And it is a personal victory for the president, who often quotes an African proverb: "Speak softly and carry a big stick."

"We demand that big business give the people a square deal," said President Theodore Roosevelt.

wooden alarm clock that gets him up early enough to read before the chores begin. When Muir is in his twenties, he is working in a factory and a metal file flies into his eye. For a while he is blinded and believes he will never see again. When he recovers, he says he will waste no more time but will do what he loves most—live with nature. "God has to nearly kill us sometimes," he says, "to teach us lessons."

So, in 1867, at the age of twenty-nine, John Muir says, "I set forth ... joyful and free, on a thousand-mile walk to the Gulf of Mexico ... by the wildest, leafiest, and least-trodden way I could find." He is embarking on a life he wants to live: "I might have been a millionaire; I chose to become a tramp." Muir spends most of the rest of his life out of doors. He believes that it is in nature that one can best answer questions of life and its meaning.

Muir climbs mountains, slogs through swamps, faces bears, panthers, and snakes—but never carries a gun. To kill is to disturb nature, he believes. He walks through much of Alaska, the Grand Canyon, and the Yosemite Valley. Yosemite, carved by glaciers, has mountains, meadows, waterfalls, and cliffs. "God himself seems to be doing his best here," he says. After hiking with Muir, Teddy Roosevelt makes sure that Yosemite's forests are saved "for the people's children and children's children."

Using a scientist's eye and a poet's tongue, Muir begins to convince Americans that trees and birds and animals are too precious to destroy: "Thousands of tired, nerve-shaken, over-civilized people are beginning to find out that going to the mountains is going home; that wilderness is a necessity; and that mountain parks and reservations are useful not only as fountains of timber and irrigation ... but as fountains of life." Muir believes that all the world is interwoven. "When we try to pick out anything by itself," he writes, "we find it hitched to everything else in the universe."

RAKING MUCK

Samuel Sidney McClure, editor and publisher of *McClure's* magazine, notices that three of the articles in his January 1903 issue have the same theme. It wasn't planned. It just happened. One article is about a big corporation and its executives' contempt for the law; another is about a labor union committing and excusing crimes; the third tells of elected city officials knowingly breaking laws for personal profit.

In his introduction to that issue, McClure says of the disregard for the law, "We have to pay in the end, every one of us. And in the end the sum total of the debt will be our liberty."

If the Progressive era has a birthdate and place, it may be in that issue of McClure's. In response to an era of materialism and corruption, a spirit of reform manifests itself. Progressivism is diverse, but the basic idea is that life is on an upward path; progress means that things should get better over time, but without care and intervention a nation can get off track. It is a high-minded, moralistic, and socially responsible movement. *McClure's* crusading journalists target injustices. They go into slaughterhouses where meat is processed, see rats and dirt, and describe the scene. They write about city bosses and about how dishonest government cheats citizens of their rights and money. They write about industrial tycoons arrogantly manipulating and breaking the law for their own benefit. And they write that in a democracy wrongs can be righted by an informed voting citizenry.

These journalists have several things in common: they are eloquent, their research is thorough, they have courage, and they care—really care—about making this country a better place. They develop a new kind of journalism, investigative journalism, at a time when publishing techniques make it possible to produce a good magazine, distribute it widely, and sell it for ten cents. Theodore Roosevelt calls them "muckrakers," taking the name from John Bunyan's *Pilgrims Progress* (a book everyone knows), which describes a man who rakes filth (muck) rather than deal

S. S. McClure asked Ida Tarbell to write a book about the great success of Standard Oil. He didn't expect an expose of ruthless business practices, but that was what he got.

> "Mr. Rockefeller has systematically played with loaded dice, and it is doubtful if there has ever been a time since 1872 when he has run a race with a competitor and started fair. Business played in this way loses all its sportsmanlike qualities. It is fit only for tricksters."
>
> —Ida Tarbell

with nobler things. But if a nation is full of muck, someone has to do the raking. The muckrakers are willing to dig deep.

Ida Tarbell is the most famous of the muckrakers. Born in a log cabin in Hatch Hollow, Pennsylvania, she is living in Paris, barely making a living sending articles to

> "Men with the muckrake are often indispensable to the well-being of society, but only if they know when to stop raking the muck."
> —Theodore Roosevelt

America, when S. S. McClure offers her a job in New York. He publishes her biographies of Napoleon and Abraham Lincoln in installments, and *McClure's* circulation doubles. Then McClure encourages Tarbell to write about America's most powerful citizen, John D. Rockefeller, and his giant trust, Standard Oil. McClure has in mind a story of remarkable achievement. Tarbell finds something else. "As I saw it, it was not capitalism but an open disregard of decent ethical business practices that lay at the bottom of the story," she says, adding "a thing won by breaking the rules of the game is not worth winning." Read today, a hundred years after its publication, Tarbell's story of Standard Oil is still astonishing in its portrait of greed, secret dealings, and brazen contempt for the law. "I believe power to make money is a gift from God," Rockefeller declares. "I believe it is my duty to make money and still more money, and to use the money according to the dictates of my conscience."

For years it has been suspected that Standard Oil is taking unfair advantage of its competitors, driving many of them out of business in its effort to monopolize the industry. Tarbell wants to know if that is so. "I did not go to the Standard Oil Company for my information," she says. "They would have shut the door of their closet on their skeletons." She does four years of detailed research before publishing a series of articles in *McClure's*. Those articles show how Standard Oil's power affects the lives of virtually every American. Three years after the articles are turned into best-selling books, the Supreme Court dissolves the Standard Oil trust. "Miss Tarbell has done more to dethrone Rockefeller in public esteem than all the preachers in the land," says one newspaper editor. Rockefeller calls her "Miss Tar-barrel." Those around him are forbidden to mention her name.

Hull House

Jane Addams (who epitomized the best in Progressivism) might have had a life of parties and ease. Her father, an Illinois state senator and friend of Abraham Lincoln, is a wealthy man; well-to-do women of the Gilded Age are expected to stay home. Addams chooses a different path. She goes off to college, one of the first generation of American women to do so. Then, wanting to make her life count, she heads for Chicago's slums. There she buys a redbrick house, with white columns on its porch, right in the middle of the toughest part of the city. It was built by a Mr. Hull, so she names it Hull House. Chicago's inner city is crime-ridden and squalid. Most of her neighbors are immigrants; many don't speak English. Addams makes Hull House a place where people can take English lessons, get care for their children, study painting, go to a concert, exercise in a gym, or act on a stage. At Hull House various ethnic groups get together, celebrate their heritage, and also meet other Americans of different ethnic origins on equal turf.

Hull House is so successful that there are soon thirteen buildings and a staff of sixty-five. About fifty people are residents. At dinnertime, the dining room often includes political leaders, philosophers, and the homeless. Addams starts clubs for working-class boys and girls; she gets Chicago to build its first public playground; she helps get child-labor laws passed; she serves on the Chicago school board and sees that new schools are built. When nineteenth-century children commit crimes, they are treated as adults. Addams helps establish the first juvenile court in the United States. When she finds that the Hull House neighborhood is full of garbage, she gets herself appointed a city garbage inspector, rising every morning at six to ride a garbage truck.

She learns that reformers need to be involved in politics, so she gets involved. It isn't easy; women can't vote or hold

At Hull House, Jane Addams (above) learned of "the struggle for existence which is so much harsher among people near the edge of pauperism."

office. She writes about the problems facing women after she discovers that "59 percent of all the young women in the nation between the ages of sixteen and twenty are engaged in some gainful occupation." Women's salaries are appallingly low, and many young women, especially in cities, earn money as prostitutes. Addams's *A New Conscience and an Ancient Evil* is a shocker. She spreads her wings and becomes active in a world peace movement. In 1931, late in her long life, Jane Addams is awarded the Nobel Peace Prize—the first American woman to be so honored.

Part 11

Safe for Democracy?

The election of 1912 is an attention-grabber. Just four years earlier, Theodore Roosevelt decided not to run for a third term and blessed William Howard Taft as his successor. But Taft's phlegmatic presidency disappoints the energetic Roosevelt. So the Rough Rider comes back from an African safari to be a candidate on the Progressive Party ticket (it's actually known as the Bull Moose Party). Taft runs as a Republican. The Socialists field their perennial candidate, Eugene V. Debs. The Democrats pick a long-jawed, serious professor who is a friend of William Jennings Bryan. His name is Woodrow Wilson. Although Taft is supported by corporate interests, he and all the candidates are, in varying degrees, progressives. The Socialists poll almost one million votes, Taft three and a half million, Roosevelt four, and more than six million elect Wilson. It is a pinnacle for reform fervor in America.

Thomas Woodrow Wilson, who becomes the twenty-eighth president, is the son of a Presbyterian minister. One of his earliest memories is of Union soldiers marching

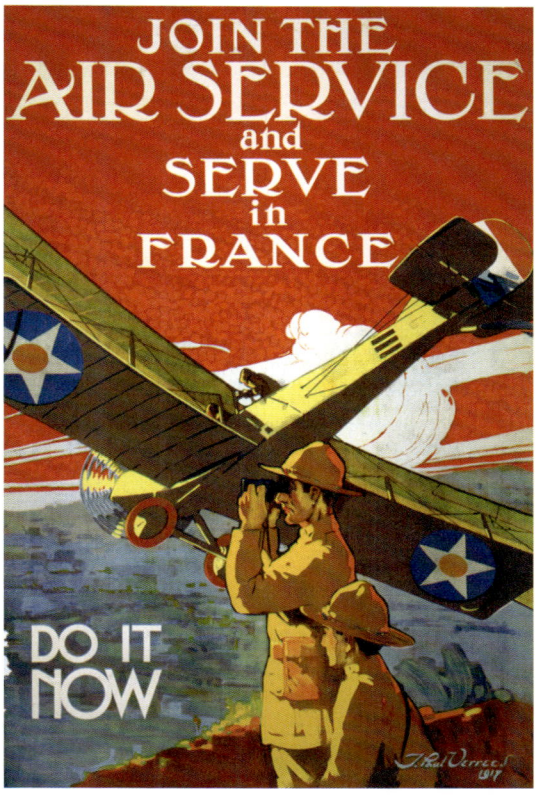

The American experience of the Great War: left, an artist's rendition of an American soldier strangling an enemy soldier at the Battle of Belleau Wood in France during June of 1918. The three weeks of desperate fighting cost the Americans 4,500 casualties. It did the job, though, repulsing the German army, only thirty miles from Paris, in its farthest advance since 1914. We pledged to have 5,000 pilots at the front by June 1918, and recruiting posters like the one at the right urged men to join up. The air force was slow to get off the ground (literally), but by mid-1918 US bombing had begun.

Woodrow Wilson was governor of New Jersey for only two years before he ran for president, but his efforts to protect the public from big trusts earned him fast recognition

through Georgia. His father preached that the Bible justified slavery. Woodrow Wilson's ideas on race and women's place reflect his traditional Southern upbringing. But his education, at Princeton and Johns Hopkins, makes him a liberal on most other issues. He becomes an extraordinary professor at Princeton; his specialty is government and politics. Not many experts on government get a chance to put their theories into practice—and even fewer of them turn out to be good at it—but Wilson did and was. He runs for governor of New Jersey at a time when the state government is a mess. New Jersey's citizens are disgusted with the corruption. Naturally, the political bosses don't want to change things—but they understand that people are demanding change. They want to back a governor who will look good but not do much. An egghead professor seems perfect as a figurehead. They pick Woodrow Wilson and soon regret their choice. Wilson not only has brains in his head, he has steel in his bones. He promises to clean up politics in New Jersey, and proceeds to do it. The bosses try to stop him; Wilson speaks out, explains the issues to New Jersey's citizens, and asks for their support. They give it. Most of the bosses are forced into retirement. New Jersey becomes a model state (for a while). People everywhere are talking about Wilson the politician.

When he is elected president, Wilson has a clear agenda: he wants to improve working conditions, help farmers, change the banking system, control monopolies, and lower tariffs. He calls his program the New Freedom and explains the issues so people understand what is involved. Soon there are lower tariffs, a Federal Reserve System, and controls on the giant trusts. Then Wilson begins to deal with the huge gap between rich and poor. He has preacher's genes, and Americans are ready to back a crusade. Wilson is making a difference. But foreign affairs keep intruding.

It begins with our neighbor, Mexico. That nation was ruled for thirty-some years by a powerful autocrat, Porfirio Diaz, who kept order with police and terror tactics. The Mexicans rebelled and overthrew Diaz.

Mexico's productivity was largely controlled by a small number of individuals and corporations. Americans (especially the Guggenheim, Rockefeller, and Aldrich families) held 43 percent of Mexico's wealth. These entrepreneurs were alarmed by the revolution. So was our president at the time, Taft. They were particularly disturbed when a dreamy-eyed intellectual, Francisco Madero, ran for office in Mexico's first free election, won, and promised reform. Taft's ambassador, Henry Lane Wilson, suggested that another "strongman," like Diaz, was needed. Then Ambassador Wilson conspired with a Mexican army general, Victoriano Huerta, who had Madero conveniently murdered. President Taft looked the other way.

Woodrow Wilson is horrified by all this. And when he becomes president the Mexico situation gets really complicated. The Mexicans rebel again, this time against murderous, drunken General Huerta, who is now in power; Wilson intervenes, intending to help them. But the Mexicans don't want U.S. help. A new president, Venustiano Carranza, ends the revolution; modem Mexico begins to emerge from the chaos. Relations between the two nations, though, are in tatters—and there's no time to mend them: things are happening in Europe that are claiming the world's attention.

Teenager Gavrilo Princip has done something that is about to help to end the optimistic Progressive era in America and lead some of the world's great powers from a democratic surge into totalitarian horrors. It all begins in tiny Bosnia-Herzegovina, in the Balkan mountains of southeastern Europe, which has been swallowed by the giant Austro-Hungarian Empire. Young Princip, a member of a terrorist organization, the Black Hand, is determined to set Bosnia free.

On sunny June 28 in 1914, Archduke Franz Ferdinand, heir to the throne of Austria-Hungary, and his wife, Sophie,

Some German-Americans felt ambivalent about fighting the motherland; this cartoon suggests that such "pacifist" (read: traitorous) attitudes helped the Kaiser keep an eye on the United States.

It's summer; this trench is dry and well sandbagged. In bad weather men drowned in mud or got trenchfoot from standing in water. Lice were constant companions.

arrive in Bosnia's capital, Sarajevo. Six Black Hand members are waiting. One of them throws a bomb at the official motorcade, wounding two soldiers. The police arrest the bomb thrower. Princip, disappointed, heads for a cafe. The archduke carries on with his ceremonial duties and then goes off to the hospital to check on the injured soldiers. It is an unplanned detour, and the driver makes a wrong turn; he is in a narrow street, where he stops before backing up. Princip, standing on the sidewalk in front of the cafe, can't believe his eyes. The archduke's open car is right in front of him. Princip fires two shots: Franz Ferdinand and Sophie bleed to death in the car.

Much of Europe has been arming for war since 1870, when Germany invaded and humiliated France in the Franco-Prussian War. Europeans have built up huge armies, stores of artillery, and fleets of warships. But the more the nations arm, the less secure they feel. Hatreds have festered and alliances formed. Europe is a tinderbox waiting for a match. Princip and the Black Hand provide it.

To avenge the archduke, Austria declares war on Serbia. That sets the alliances in motion. On one side are the Central Powers: Germany, Austria-Hungary, Italy, Bulgaria, and, later, Turkey (also known as the Ottoman Empire). Grouped around France are the Allies: Great Britain and Russia. On August 3, Germany's Kaiser Wilhelm II (who likes to be called "All Highest") sends his troops crashing through tiny Belgium on their way to Paris. The major powers, including Germany, have signed a treaty agreeing to respect Belgian neutrality. The Kaiser now calls it a "scrap of paper." England, honoring its commitment, dispatches an army to the aid of Belgium and France. "We'll be home for Christmas," soldiers tell their mothers and girlfriends as they march off to war. But on that sacred day, enormous armies are dug into dirt trenches that stretch uninterrupted for 500 miles from the Swiss border to the North Sea. For the next four years, millions of men will live and die in those hellish trenches in an insane war of attrition, with poison gas warfare added to make it macabre as well as lethal. "Humanity is mad! It must be mad to do what it is doing. What a massacre!" writes French officer Alfred Joubert before he dies at the battle of Verdun.

WAR

When the cannons begin firing in August 1914 no one anywhere has any idea where the "Great War," as it is called, will go. In America, Woodrow Wilson calls it "a distant event." He thinks it will soon be over—as do the young men in Europe who hurry to enlist, afraid the war will be won before they get a chance to fight. World War I turns out to be worse than anything nations knew before. It will change and chasten and embitter generations. What seemed a quarrel will become horrible, mindless, numbing slaughter.

> "The world itself seems gone mad and there was a sort of stern compulsion to keep sane amidst the general wreck and distemper."
> —Woodrow Wilson

President Wilson delivers his message before a joint session of the House and Senate on April 2, 1917: the United States will enter the Great War on the side of the Allies. Americans, he said, "have no selfish ends to serve. We desire no conquest, no dominion."

U.S. recruits on their way to basic training at Camp Upton. Some military chiefs and congressmen feared resistance to conscription, but on June 5, 1917, alone, 10 million men came forward to register for the draft.

During September, the first full month of war for the major participants, a million men are killed. New technology—tanks, long-range artillery, grenades, machine guns—provides new ways to mow down soldiers. The generals, trained in earlier wars, employ strategies suitable for riflemen. The airplane, only eleven years old when the war begins, is one of the new weapons. At first planes are just used to scout enemy territory. But some fliers lean out of cockpits and shoot their pistols at enemy pilots. Then bombs are brought aboard and dropped by hand over the side of the plane. After that, someone figures out how to synchronize machine-gun fire with propeller blades—and the air war takes off.

Yet the killing machines are not enough. It is still men, huge armies of men, who are needed. Armies dig themselves into the trenches and slay men in other trenches. Both sides fight on, stuck in the bloody mud. At least 10 million men will die.

The United States has always had the vast Atlantic Ocean as a moat to keep it isolated from Europe's troubles.

George Washington warned about "foreign entanglements." Woodrow Wilson believes America should stay out of the fray and remain neutral. Most Americans don't want to get involved. But technology is shrinking the globe, and America is now a world power; it is becoming harder and harder not to be involved. Wilson sees himself as a peacemaker. He campaigns for reelection in 1916 on a platform of neutrality. He tries talking to leaders on both sides; he hopes to end the war with open, honorable negotiations.

A new weapon is changing warfare. Great Britain has the world's greatest fleet, but the German submarine (called a U-boat) is not only a menace to warships, it is threatening passenger travel and shipping. The Germans are trying to strangle the capacity of the Allies to wage war. U-boats begin sinking ships without warning; Americans are horrified—and they are also victims. Germany announces that it will sink any ship going anywhere near England or France, even ships from neutral nations. Early in 1917, eight U.S. ships are sunk in the Atlantic. Then a decoded telegram from a German ambassador is made public. It details a plot to get Mexico to attack the United States. Germany has promised to give Texas, New Mexico, and Arizona to Mexico (once America is made to surrender) as a prize for entering the war.

On the night of March 31, 1917, Woodrow Wilson gets out of bed and takes his portable typewriter to the south veranda

> "Over there, over there,
> Send the word, send the word over there—
> That the Yanks are coming,
> The Yanks are coming,
> The drums rum-tumming
> Ev'rywhere.
> So prepare, say a pray'r,
> Send the word, send the word to beware.
> We'll be over, we're coming over,
> And we won't come back till it's over
> Over there."
>
> —"Over There," George M. Cohan, 1917

of the White House. Mrs. Wilson brings him a bowl of milk and crackers from the kitchen. In the quiet of early morning, the president types out a message that is to become famous.

> *The present German submarine warfare against commerce is a warfare against mankind. It is a war against all nations.... We are accepting the challenge.... The world must be made safe for democracy.*

Wilson says our nation has no selfish aims, and wants no territory—no gain for itself—and this president means what he says. On April 2, 1917, he goes before Congress. Without a microphone (they haven't been developed yet), and without shouting, Wilson makes his voice carry. *It is a fearful thing to lead this great, peaceful people into war,* he says:

> ... *into the most terrible and disastrous of all wars, civilization itself seeming to be in the balance. But the right is more*

Collier's put weapons of war on its cover in August 1917: planes, heavy artillery, and soldiers. The bitter fact was that much war strategy consisted of feeding men to the big guns.

A Letter Home

Harry Rennagel, U.S. Army, 101st Infantry, writes to his family from France on Armistice Day:

> Nothing quite so electrical in effect as the sudden stop that came at 11 A.M. has ever occurred to me. It was 10:60 precisely and—the roar stopped like a motor car hitting a wall. The resulting quiet was uncanny in comparison. From somewhere far below ground, Germans began to appear. They clambered to parapets and began to shout wildly. They threw their rifles, hats, bandoliers, bayonets, and trench knives toward us. They began to sing…. we kept the boys under restraint as long as we could. Finally the strain was too great. A big Yank ran out into no man's land and planted the Stars and Stripes at the lip of a shell hole. A bugler began playing "The Star-Spangled Banner." And they sang—Gee, how they sang!

> precious than peace, and we shall fight for the things we have always carried nearest our hearts—for democracy, for the right of those who submit to authority to have a voice in their own governments, for the rights and liberties of small nations, for a universal domination of right by such a concert of free peoples as shall bring peace and safety to all nations, and make the world itself at last free.

He makes it clear: the United States is not entering the war for personal gain. He finishes with emotion:

> The day has come when America is privileged to spend her blood … for the principles that gave her birth and happiness…. God helping her, she can do no other.

For a moment there is silence; then seventy-two-year-old Edward D. White, Chief Justice of the Supreme Court, sitting in the front row, tosses his hat in the air, leaps to his feet, and gives the Rebel yell. The congressmen, electrified, stomp, shout, and roar approval. Outside the Capitol a crowd gathered in the rain adds to the outburst. The president goes back to his office and looks at his aide. "Isn't it strange that men should cheer for war," he says. Then he puts his head on his desk and weeps.

Slim, frail, bookish Woodrow Wilson turns out to be a tough, effective war president. In amazingly fast order he makes a peaceful nation into a strong fighting force. The country's factories go from making corsets, bicycles, and brooms to production of guns, ships, and uniforms. The Germans believe it will take years for the United States to get ready to fight; but in a single year, beginning in April 1917, more than a million American men are drafted into the army, trained, and sent overseas. And just in time. In Europe both sides are near collapse. U.S. forces tip the balance in the Allies' favor; they make the difference.

Wilson has thought about the peace since the war began. He has written a peace plan based on fair play. He intends to change the way nations conduct their affairs. He wants no imperialist division of spoils after this war; the world's peoples are to determine their own fate. Wilson has organized his ideas into Fourteen Points; they're put into a pamphlet which is distributed around the globe. Many Germans, knowing the collapse of the Reich is imminent, are heartened by Wilson's generous proposals. The Kaiser is forced to abdicate.

After four years of almost uninterrupted cannon fire, the men in the trenches can hear each other without shouting. It is the eleventh hour of the eleventh day of the eleventh month, and the guns are silent. It has been a year and a half since Wilson gave his war speech to Congress; 112,432 Americans have been added to the death count. Finally, Germany has surrendered. At a hospital near Berlin, a twenty-nine-year-old corporal from Austria, who has been gassed in Belgium, hears the news and sobs into his pillow: Adolf Hitler vows to avenge his country.

It has been a horrible war. The modern weapons of killing have led to new kinds of slaughter. Burials were often just of arms and legs and bits and pieces rather than whole bodies. For the United States it has been ten times more costly, in monetary terms, than the Civil War. The idea that war is a kind of heroic game has been put to rest. "War," writes one soldier, "is nothing but murder."

In Washington, D.C., it is six o'clock in the morning, and President Wilson is at his desk. He writes these words on White House stationery:

Everything for which America has fought has been accomplished. It will now be our fortunate duty to assist by example, by sober, friendly counsel, and by material aid, in the establishment of just democracy throughout the world.

It is still dark, but on November 11, 1918, the news of war's end is too good to wait for daybreak. Whistles toot, church bells ring, and sirens blare. Before long the streets across the nation are filled with people cheering, shouting, hugging, and kissing. America has gone to war, and the world is going to be a better place because of it. President Wilson has called this "the war to end all war." And the war to "save democracy.' He believes that the awful sacrifice was ordained and that it will lead to a future of world harmony—and so do most Americans on that Armistice Day in 1918.

No Clear and Present Danger

In 1917, after the U.S. has entered the war, Congress passes an Espionage Act. In 1918 it passes a Sedition Act. They are meant to ban speech that might harm the war effort. But the First Amendment guarantees free speech. Are such laws unconstitutional? Or can the Constitution be overlooked in wartime?

Eugene V. Debs, antiwar activist, co-founder of the IWW union (the Wobblies), and head of the Socialist Party, says this after the passage of the Espionage and Sedition acts: *They tell us we live in a great, free republic; that our institutions are democratic, that we are a free and self-governing people. This was too much, even for a joke. Many of us have come to realize that it is extremely dangerous to exercise the constitutional right of free speech in a country fighting to make democracy safe in the world.*

The line between hard criticism of a war and espionage can be wavy. Charles Schenck sends out 15,000 leaflets urging men to resist the draft. He is convicted under the Espionage Act, but appeals the case as a violation of his First Amendment rights. In *Schenck* v. *United States*, the Supreme Court is unanimous in rejecting his plea. But Justice Oliver Wendell Holmes enunciates a doctrine of "clear and present danger" that is seen as placing a sensible line between the right of an individual to free expression and that of society to be protected.

The character of every act depends upon the circumstance in which it is done.... The most stringent protection of free speech would not protect a man in falsely shouting fire in a theater and causing a panic.... The question in every case is whether the words used are used in such circumstances and are of such a nature as to create a clear and present danger that they will bring about the substantive evils that Congress has a right to prevent. When a nation is at war many things that might be said in time of peace are such a hindrance to its effort that their utterance will not be endured so long as men fight and that no Court could regard them as being protected by any constitutional right. Holmes will refine that doctrine in a series of decisions that will become a standard of jurisprudence.

Eugene V. Debs

Oliver Wendell Holmes

The League of Nations

With the war over, Woodrow Wilson sets off for Europe, the first sitting American president ever to do so. He wants America to lead the world to a just peace, and he expects to be the peacemaker. People in Europe greet him with flowers and cheers and call him the savior of the world. Having grown up in the defeated South, Wilson knows of the hatreds that can follow war. He doesn't think an enemy needs to be shamed or impoverished. Wilson's Fourteen Points may be the most forgiving peace plan ever proposed. Under that plan, people all over the world are to determine their own fate. Self-determination is to end the old imperialist system that let winning nations grasp foreign colonies. The Fourteen Points call for free trade; an end to secret pacts between nations ("open covenants, openly arrived at"); freedom of the seas; arms reduction; and the creation of a world organization, the League of Nations. For Wilson the League is a legacy to the future; he intends that it will keep the peace. Some Europeans don't see it that way. The French are still smarting from their humiliating defeat in the Franco-Prussian War. (They've conveniently forgotten that they started it.) Georges Clemenceau, known as the "Tiger of France," was mayor of Montmartre when the Germans paraded down the Champs Elysees in 1871. A mustached, portly, cynical old man, unwilling to forgive, Clemenceau is president of the peace conference. He will plant anti-Wilson stories in the press and use police to spy on delegates. Openly contemptuous of the Fourteen Points, Clemenceau says, "God Almighty gave us only ten, and we broke those." David Lloyd George, recently elected on the slogan HANG THE KAISER! is Britain's representative. Like Clemenceau, he wants revenge.

The Germans surrendered in expectation of Wilson's generous peace. But their delegates to the conference are pointedly held in a hotel enclosed in barbed wire. The peace treaty is signed in the Hall of Mirrors at Versailles, a French royal palace near Paris. Everyone understands the significance of the site. It is where the Germans announced their victories and their new empire in 1871. The treaty demands that Germany admit guilt and pay for the cost of the war in reparations. The Germans feel betrayed. Most of Wilson's Fourteen Points have been thrown out the palace's windows. But the idea that means the most to Wilson—the League of Nations—is saved. Wilson believes the League will change the Old World way of doing things. He wants to bring democratic self-government to the world community.

According to the United States Constitution, treaties with foreign powers must be ratified by two-thirds of the members of the Senate. The Senate is dominated by strong Republican senators who loathe Wilson and his high-toned professorial ways. They believe a triumph for the president will hurt their party in the next election. And many Americans, Democrats as well as Republicans, are worried about the possibility that American will become more involved in Europe's problems. Wilson decides to do what he did in New Jersey, when he ignored the urban bosses and went directly to the people. It's a bad miscalculation. Congressmen are not like city bandits. And they don't take kindly to what they see as arrogant disdain.

Wilson crosses the country, giving three or four speeches a day, mostly explaining about the League. In Omaha, he says, "I can predict with absolute certainty that within another generation there will be another world war if the nations of the world do not concert the method by which to prevent it." His foes stalk him on the tour (they are financed by industrialists Andrew Mellon and Henry Clay Frick). The congressmen play on nativist fears of immigrants and foreign entanglements. They call for "isolation" as a national policy. They call for impeachment of the president.

It is all too much for Wilson's health; he has a stroke and is never the same again. The Senate accepts the Treaty of Versailles but rejects American participation in the League of Nations. Did Wilson achieve anything? Yes. The peace treaty, harsh as it turns out to be, is far more liberal than it would have been if Wilson hadn't been at Versailles. "Mr. Wilson's expression of American ideals was the only spiritual expression in the Conference," writes Herbert Hoover (in Paris heading an American-sponsored relief effort). "At every step he fought the forces of hate."

But Wilson is out of step with the times. After this terrible war, ideals no longer seem important; whether it is about progressive reforms at home, or Wilson's world-changing vision, the crusading spirit is gone. Most Americans just want to get on with their lives.

Votes for Women

A group of women is marching in front of the White House. It is 1917, and they carry a banner that says 20 MILLION WOMEN ARE NOT SELF-GOVERNED. In Europe, American soldiers are fighting for democracy; these women feel they should fight for it at home. They want to be able to vote. Without the vote, they say, they are not full citizens. Another of their banners includes President Wilson's own words: WE SHALL FIGHT FOR THE THINGS WHICH WE HAVE ALWAYS CARRIED NEAR OUR HEARTS—FOR DEMOCRACY. Day after day, month after month, the women march in front of the president's house. They are peaceful but persistent. Some people don't like it; they say the women, called

"This is what we are doing with our banners before the White House," says suffragette Anne Martin. "Petitioning the … president … for a redress of grievances; we are asking him to use his great power to secure the passage of the national suffrage amendment."

suffragettes, shouldn't annoy the president during wartime. The police order the women to leave. "Has the law been changed?" asks Alice Paul, the leader of the group. "No," says the police officer, "but you must stop."

"We have consulted our lawyers," says Alice Paul. "We have a legal right to picket." The next day two women, Lucy Burns and Katherine Morey, are arrested. Other arrests follow. On the Fourth of July, a congressman speaks to a large crowd gathered behind the White House. "Governments derive their just powers from the consent of the governed," he says. Police keep the crowd orderly and protect the man's right to free speech. In front of the White House a group of thirteen women silently hold a banner proclaiming those same words from the Declaration of Independence. Some are young women, some white-haired grandmothers; all are arrested. The women are taken to court and fined. They refuse to pay their fines—to do so would mean to admit they are guilty; and they do not believe themselves guilty of any crime. The police take them to jail. One of them, Anne Martin, speaks out in court.

Red Scare

Right in the middle of World War I, in 1917, the Russian people rebel against their autocratic czar. A new revolutionary government, under Alexander Kerensky, promises democracy and civil liberties. But Kerensky intends to keep fighting the war against Germany. The Russian people don't. They have had enough. Russia has lost a million men, and Russians have lost faith in their military leaders. A group of communist radicals, called Bolsheviks, promise to get Russia out of the war. One of them, Vladimir Dyich Lenin, calls the American embassy in Switzerland. The Americans are now the hope of many who long for a better world. In Paris, a young Vietnamese working as a photo finisher also tries to contact Woodrow Wilson or someone on his staff. He will become Ho Chi Minh; he will change the destiny both of his own country and of Wilson's. Neither Lenin nor Ho succeeds in reaching a U.S. official.

In Lenin, German authorities in Switzerland perceive an opportunity. Germany is eager to see Russia surrender and out of the war. So they put Lenin and some other Bolsheviks in a sealed train and speed them across Germany to Russia. After Lenin takes power, the Germans force the Russians to sign a very harsh peace treaty much worse than the treaty the Germans will sign at Versailles.

Lenin, now able to focus on Russian affairs, institutes a "dictatorship of the proletariat." He dissolves a governing assembly, embarks on state planning, redistributes land, nationalizes industry, and confiscates all Church property. Russia is under totalitarian rule. Most dedicated communists believe they are the wave of the future. (According to communist theory, most property and goods belong to the state to be shared equitably with the people. It sounds idealistic; it just never seems to work.) The radicalism of the Russian revolution terrifies Americans. Communism doesn't have much appeal in a country with traditions of individualism, freedom and concern for property rights. But fear of communism will become an American obsession.

The radical fringe in the United States does include some communists and a few anarchists, along with some crazies. Anarchism is associated with German intellectuals, and, during World War I, German Americans are mistrusted and often persecuted. A core of American intellectuals—mainly writers and philosophers—see communism as an answer to the corruption and immorality of most political systems. Some of the radicals and intellectuals are immigrants. At a time when immigration is under attack and new groups of immigrants are seen as degrading "pure American stock" (and competing with American workers), communists and immigrants are lumped together as undesirables. To further complicate things, a misinterpretation of Darwin's theories is leading some influential thinkers to believe there are indeed superior races. An immigration act passed in 1924 sets quotas favoring immigrants from northern Europe. (In the early 1930s, half a million Mexicans are deported.) Meanwhile, the few radicals who do have criminal intent become an excuse for widespread persecution of the innocent. Most Americans still haven't figured out how to deal with that phrase "all men are created equal." This is Jim Crow time; some blacks are hardly better off than they were in slavery, and, as for dealing with immigrants, here is what

A young Vietnamese, Ho Chi Minh, in Paris at the time of Versailles, pleads Indochina's case to the delegates.

A. Mitchell Palmer (first in his class at Swarthmore) has to say, believing he is fair and forward-thinking: "[Reform will] insure justice … to the lowest foreigner who comes to our free land as well as to the highborn American through whose veins course the blood of the Pilgrim fathers." It seems a reasonable, even progressive statement at a time when prejudice against immigrants is common. Palmer, a Pennsylvania Quaker, becomes a leader in the Democratic Party and a congressman. He introduces an enlightened child labor bill (it passes the House but is defeated in the Senate). Samuel Gompers's AFL lauds Palmer's voting record. In 1919 Woodrow Wilson names him attorney general. It isn't an easy assignment; times are tough, with runaway prices, major strikes, chaos in Europe, and worries about radicalism at home.

In June 1919, someone throws a bomb at Palmer's house. Palmer turns to a hotshot twenty-four-year-old, J. Edgar Hoover, and puts him in charge of the newly created Radical Division of the Justice Department. Hoover reports that radicals in the U.S. pose a serious danger and are part of a worldwide communist conspiracy. (In actuality, the radicals are disorganized and mostly unarmed.) Pressure grows for action. Palmer later says, "I was preached upon from every pulpit; I was urged … to do something and do it now." The president's stroke complicates things; Edith Wilson is keeping him isolated; she is making some executive decisions. So is Mitchell Palmer, who is already a candidate for the presidency. He agrees on a plan to deport alien radicals.

In two days of raids in major cities in 1920, agents invade homes, clubs, union halls, pool halls, and coffee shops, rounding up some 6,000 people, who are held in jail, not allowed to call anyone, and treated without regard to their constitutional rights. Those without citizenship papers are deported—to Russia. Some American citizens are held in prison for several months without being charged. Most aren't guilty of anything. Most arrests are made without warrants. Witnesses tell of beatings.

The United States was founded on the idea of the sanctity of the rule of law. These are government officials and institutions ignoring and abusing the law. It is more than a minor aberration. And it doesn't make the nation any safer. Thomas Jefferson wrote: *Truth is great and will prevail if left to herself, and errors cease to be dangerous when it is permitted freely to contradict them.* The ultimate test of a free nation may lie in its willingness to allow free expression of ideas that seem abhorrent (as long as they are not criminal). The Palmer raids were shameful; they were not unique.

Above: In September 1920, a bomb exploded on Wall Street, killing thirty-eight people and fueling fears that communism threatened American stability. Mitchell Palmer (right), a decent man, succumbed to pressure to arrest foreigners.

"Said Mr. Jones in Nineteen-Ten:
'Women, subject yourselves to men.'
Nineteen-Eleven heard him quote:
'They rule the world without the vote.'
By Nineteen-Thirteen, looking glum,
He said that it was bound to come.
This year I heard him say with pride:
'No reasons on the other side!'
By Nineteen-Fifteen, he'll insist
He's always been a suffragist.
And what is really stranger, too,
He'll think that what he says is true."

—Alice Duerr Miller, "Evolution," in *Are Women People? A Book of Rhymes for Suffrage Times*, 1915

As long as the government and the representatives of the government prefer to send women to jail on petty and technical charges we will go to jail. Prosecution has always advanced the cause of justice. The right of American women to work for democracy must be maintained.

More women go to jail. Prison conditions are awful. For seventeen days Ada Davenport Kendall is given nothing to eat but bread and water. Some women are held in solitary confinement. Some who go on hunger strikes are held down and force-fed. Now the women are interested in prison reform as well as women's suffrage. One woman writes that it is "necessary to make a stand for the ordinary rights of human beings for all the inmates." The suffragettes keep marching.

Mrs. John Rogers, Jr., is arrested. She is a descendant of Roger Sherman (a signer of the Declaration of Independence and originator of the "Connecticut Compromise," which created our bicameral Congress). Like her plain-speaking ancestor, Mrs. Rogers says what she thinks. She tells the judge:

We are not guilty of any offense ... we know full well that we stand here because the president of the United States refuses to give liberty to American women. We believe, your honor; that the wrong persons are before the bar in this court.... We believe the president is the guilty one and that we are innocent.

Mrs. Rogers's cause is just, but her comments aren't quite fair. It is Congress that is holding things up, not Woodrow Wilson. But the president hasn't helped. Finally, he does, urging Congress to pass the Nineteenth Amendment. It is known as the Susan B. Anthony amendment. The great crusader for women's suffrage died in 1906, her dream of equal rights for women still unfulfilled. The amendment reads: *The right of citizens of the United States to vote shall not be denied or abridged by the United States or by any state on account of sex.* Congress finally passes the amendment, but the battle isn't over. Three-fourths of the states need to ratify an amendment to the Constitution. The head of the National American Woman Suffrage Association, Carrie Chapman Catt, campaigns across the country. In Tennessee, Harry Burn, at twenty-four the youngest representative in the legislature, gets a letter from his mother. "Don't forget to be a good boy," his mom says, "and help Mrs. Catt put the 'Rat' in ratification." The Tennessee legislators are trying to decide whether to approve the Nineteenth Amendment or not. Half are for women's suffrage; half are not. Burn holds the deciding vote. He's a good boy; he follows his mother's advice. It is 1919, and Tennessee is the last state needed to ratify. The next year, 1920, America's women are free to go to the polls.

THE TWENTIES ROAR

What Americans want after that awful war is best expressed in a newly coined word: normalcy. For most, normalcy means enjoying freedom—especially the freedom to be left alone. But freedom is a hard-to-pin-down concept, and the freedom to try new ideas and new things is part of the American birthright. Innovation and inventiveness are in the nation's air. So, after the war, Americans have no hesitation in taking to the Wright brothers' airplane and Henry Ford's automobile. Ordinary people are free to go places and come back home, too. Thomas Edison's light bulb lengthens their day; his phonograph and moving pictures enliven it. It's the 1920s, and there's lots to do and see. So feel free to kick up your heels and enjoy yourself.

Some people call the new decade the "Roaring Twenties." Some call it the Jazz Age; some call it the Dance Age. Whichever you choose, it's a time to celebrate. More people in America have more money than ever before. And, mostly, they are intent on having a good time. Hardly anyone seems to worry that some people are being left out

"Together we'll show them
How the Charleston is done
We'll surprise everyone
Just think what heaven it's going to be
If you will Charleston, Charleston with me."
    —"Won't You Charleston With Me?" by Sandy Wilson

of the prosperity boom. In 1919, just before the Nineteenth Amendment is passed, girls' ankles can sometimes be glimpsed beneath long skirts. In the '20s, skirts start going up, and up, and up. Many young women are bobbing their hair-shedding those traditional long locks. Some daring girls wear bathing suits that actually leave their legs uncovered. (Police arrest women on the beaches for that.) And makeup! "Nice" women are wearing lipstick, rouge, and powder. The girls who bob their hair and wear short skirts and lipstick are called "flappers." They do other things, too. They drive cars, get jobs,

THE MONKEY TRIAL

It is 1925, and on the dusty streets of Dayton, Tennessee (pop. about 1,600), mule-drawn wagons compete with Model T Fords. Hotdog and soft-drink vendors are on most street corners. More than 100 reporters are here, along with photographers and motion-picture makers. A telegraph office is set up in a grocery store. Everywhere here are monkeys: monkey postcards, stuffed toy monkeys, and souvenir buttons that say YOUR OLD MAN IS A MONKEY. What's going on?

A sensational court case—the best-known trial of the decade. Newspapers are calling it "the monkey trial." A young teacher is in the dock because of what he is teaching in his classroom. Actually, it is modern science that is on trial. In Tennessee it is illegal to study evolution in public school. Most fundamentalist Christians don't agree with the scientific concept of evolution. They believe in the exact words of the Bible, and the Bible says that the world was created in six days and that Adam and Eve—humans—were part of the Creation from the start. In Tennessee, fundamentalists have gotten a law passed that says it is *unlawful for any teacher ... to teach any theory that denies the story of the divine creation of man as taught in the Bible, and to teach instead that man has descended from a lower order of animals.* Because of the law, Tennessee's citizens are not free to study evolution in public school. That state law is imposing a church doctrine on public schools. But most don't see it that way.

The issue is separation of church and state. The First Amendment to the Constitution protects that separation. It says *Congress shall make no law respecting an establishment of religion, or prohibiting the free exercise thereof.*

Many Tennessee schoolteachers ignore the law and keep teaching what is in their textbooks—evolutionary science. The American Civil Liberties Union believes the law is unconstitutional. The ACLU was founded in 1920 to protect civil rights in America. Its officers say the ACLU will pay the legal costs of anyone who wants to test the Tennessee law. In Dayton, twenty-four-year-old John Scopes, who teaches high school, comes forward. When William go to the movies, read romantic novels, play ping-pong, smoke cigarettes in public, and dance. My, do they dance! It's the big thing in the '20s. And the biggest dance is the Charleston. Doing the Charleston, you swing your arms, knock your knees together, and move as fast as you can.

It's a frantic age—and a materialistic one. The idealism of the Progressive era seems quaint. After the war, everything was going to be better, but anyone can see that isn't so. The Eighteenth Amendment, ratified in January 1919, made selling alcohol illegal, and that's supposed to make people

"Darrow [above] has lost this case. It was lost long before he came to Dayton," wrote journalist H. L. Mencken. "But … he has nevertheless performed a great public service by fighting it to a finish and in a perfectly serious way."

Jennings Bryan learns of the trial, he volunteers to prosecute in favor of the new law. Bryan, a fundamentalist, has run for president three times; everyone knows and likes him. Clarence Darrow volunteers to defend Scopes. He is a brilliant lawyer and an agnostic.

When the trial begins, it's hot; the judge moves everyone outdoors. Bryan accuses Darrow of wanting to "slur the Bible." Darrow says he wants "to prevent bigots and ignoramuses from controlling the educational system of the United States." Darrow puts Bryan on the witness stand and asks questions Bryan admits he hasn't thought much about. When Darrow forces Bryan to say the Bible's six days might not be six actual days, Bryan's fundamentalist friends are aghast. The great Populist orator looks foolish.

It is an angry trial, full of bad feeling, and it doesn't settle much. Bryan wins the case: the local court and the state supreme court agree that Scopes broke the law. The case is not appealed to the U.S. Supreme Court; the law stays on the books until 1967. Most people don't take it seriously—which is too bad. It is an issue that keeps popping up into the twenty-first century. In the 1980s, Arkansas and Louisiana pass laws that say that public schools teaching evolution must use "equal time" to teach creationism. In 1987, the Supreme Court finds those laws in conflict with the First Amendment's guarantee of religious freedom.

behave better. But if you read the newspapers you can see that criminals are making big money selling hooch. In many areas, Prohibition is making drinking fashionable.

Making money and spending it—it's the American thing to do. Successful businessmen are national heroes. There are growing numbers of unemployed; some city districts are havens for the desperately poor; and many farmers are in real trouble—but no one seems to be worried. For most Americans, the times are good. The stock market, like women's hemlines, keeps going up and up. Land values boom. In 1919 cars were a novelty. Ten years later, one family in five owns one. Before the war, life was slow-paced; now change is coming with cyclone speed. Everyone wants to own a radio; it keeps you up to date and entertained, too. People are flocking to movie theaters, and, in 1927, movies begin to talk. Talk about fun! The following year, in Hollywood, California, a young filmmaker named Walt Disney produces an animated sound film, *Steamboat Willie*, and introduces a little mouse named Mickey.

"The chief business of America is business," says the president, Vermonter Calvin Coolidge. Many agree without ever hearing the rest of his message. "The accumulation of wealth cannot be justified as the chief end of existence. So long as wealth is made the means and not the end, we need not greatly fear it." Then he adds, "I cannot repeat too often that America is a nation of idealists. That is the only motive to which they ever give any strong and lasting reaction."

All That Jazz

Can you hear the shrimp boats sing and the tankers growl? We're in New Orleans and music is in the air. On Lake Pontchartrain, lapping water beats its own tune. And on the broad Mississippi, riverboats hoot and moan. The warm climate brings people out of doors, so there are almost always people-on-the-street sounds—and sometimes animal sounds, too. In the early decades of the twentieth century, that meant the scratches and squeals of chickens and pigs, the clippety-clop of horses' hoofs, and the rolling cadence of wooden-wheeled wagons. That isn't all; the hoots of trains and the sad notes of riverboat foghorns add to the cacophony. Since there are no supermarkets, people buy ice, milk, bread, fresh fruit, vegetables, meat, and other things from the backs of wagons. The wagon drivers have to advertise what they're selling. Usually they sing their message. It's the same idea as a TV commercial jingle, but it may go like this: I got tomatoes big and fine, I got watermelons red to the rind. Or like this: My mule is white, the coal is black; I sell my

By the mid-1920s, dance halls and speakeasies, like this club-side street scene painted at the time by Archibald Motley, Jr., were booming in New York and Chicago. Musicians went north, and soon Chicago replaced New Orleans as the home of jazz and swing.

coal two bits a sack. Imagine street peddlers all singing their wares at the same time.

With all those sounds, perhaps New Orleans was ordained to produce a new kind of music. It was called jazz, and it was unlike anything heard in the world before. It combined the rhythm and drumbeat of Africa with the instruments and heritage of Europe. It added a dash from the spirituals of the black Protestant churches, and much from the talents of some black musical geniuses who could be heard in street bands and nightclubs. The first jazz was played by funeral bands wailing soulful music as they followed horse-drawn hearses down the streets of New Orleans. It was unique. Jazz is not African music, or European music. It is an American original. One of its greatest performers was a New Orleans boy named Louis Armstrong.

Louis was one of those boys who sold coal in New Orleans and sang his sales pitch. He was very poor. Then someone gave him a trumpet. It must have been a good angel, because Louis Armstrong was born to play the trumpet. People began calling him "satchelmouth" because his cheeks seemed to hold a suitcase full of air. "Satchmo" was soon playing on the riverboats that went up and down the Mississippi. Then he went to Chicago and began making history. Satchmo had a big grin, but when he played the trumpet he closed his eyes and blew clear, heavenly tones.

No two jazz performances are exactly alike. Talk about freedom! In jazz you do your own thing. It's called improvisation. Jazz musicians talk to each other with their instruments. It is something like African drum talk. One musician leads with a

Louis Armstrong

"There was one thing about good jazz. You don't always know what they are talking about, but when they pick up those instruments, we all speak the same language."

—Louis Armstrong

theme. Then someone answers that theme, playing in his own way. Soon the whole band is playing with it. It's wild. And not easy to do well. Jazz pioneers began popping up everywhere—in Chicago, in Kansas City and New York, and, thanks to radio, all over the country. People in the 1920s were crazy about jazz, and when the Jazz Age '20s ended—with a big thud called the Depression—jazz went right on growing. Duke Ellington, Billie Holiday, Joe "King" Oliver, Benny Goodman—those were just some of the great players' names. When someone asked Louis Armstrong once, "Just what exactly is jazz?" he answered, "If you gotta ask, you'll never know."

Lucky Lindy

In the 1920s, if an airplane went overhead, you'd probably stop what you were doing to look up in the sky. But, each year, there were more and more of them up there, competing with the birds. Right after the war, a wealthy hotel owner offered a prize of $25,000 to anyone who could fly across the Atlantic nonstop from New York to Paris. It was a lot of money. Several pilots tried and failed.

In May of 1927, three planes are being made ready. Each is going for the prize. Newspapers are full of their stories. One of them, a small single-engine craft called *Spirit of St. Louis*, can hold only one person. The pilot, Charles Lindbergh, is little known. He's delivered mail by plane, and he's been a barnstormer, a guy who does trick flying: circles and loops and daredevil showoff stuff; after the tricks, he takes people on plane rides for $5 a spin. No one really uses airplanes for transportation. Trains are for getting places. And no one is quite sure where the future of aviation lies. But if a plane can fly safely across the ocean, it may have an important future.

Lindbergh is a good pilot. He was the first man to fly from St. Louis to Chicago, and the first to survive four forced parachute jumps. There is a bold, daring side to him, and another side that is careful and methodical. In a crisis he won't panic.

It is 8 A.M. on May 20 when he takes off. The weather isn't good, but he's anxious to beat the competition, and he's used to flying the mail in all weathers. His little plane carries so much gasoline, some people are afraid it will never get into the air. But Lindbergh has planned carefully. There isn't an extra ounce of weight on the plane. He carries little besides the fuel: a quart of water, a paper bag of sandwiches, and a rubber raft. There is no radio. He will be on his own once he leaves the East Coast. He heads out to sea from Roosevelt Field on Long Island, New York; people around the world learn of his takeoff on their radios. And then there is nothing to hear. That evening, during a boxing match at Yankee Stadium, spectators rise and say a prayer for Charles Lindbergh, somewhere over the Atlantic. Lindbergh, meanwhile, is struggling to stay awake. Luckily, his frail plane bangs about in the wind, and, each time he starts to nod, it goes careening down toward the water. That keeps him awake. Then, miraculously, the fatigue is gone, he looks down, and there is Ireland. He is exactly where the charts he has drawn say he should be. He is spotted and the news is radioed to America and France. People cheer and weep with relief. He's seen over London, and then the English Channel. Thirty-three and a half hours after leaving the United States, he circles the Eiffel Tower in Paris. It has taken less time than he expected, so he is worried that no one will be at the airport to meet him. Then he looks at the ground and sees a mob of people. They are waving and screaming.

The young flier, who has brought nothing with him but the paper bag (which still has some sandwiches), is carried about on shoulders and hugged and kissed and cheered. He wants to stay in Europe and see the sights, but Calvin Coolidge has sent a naval cruiser to Europe just to carry "Lucky Lindy" and the *Spirit of St. Louis* back to America. He is the world's hero.

Right, Charles Lindbergh and the *Spirit of St. Louis*. At one time during the trip, he wrote, "sleet started to collect on the plane and I was forced to turn around and get back into clear air immediately and then fly around any clouds which I could not get over." Above, New York City greeted Lindbergh with a blizzard of confetti and ticker tape.

> "Twenty minutes after ten o'clock tonight suddenly and softly There slipped out of the darkness a gray-white plane as 25,000 pairs of eyes strained forward. At 10:24 the Spirit of St. Louis landed and lines of soldiers and policemen and stout steel fences went down before a mad rush as irresistible as the tide of the ocean. Not since the armistice of 1918 had Paris witnesses a demonstration of popular enthusiasm equal to that of the American flier, whose personality had captured the hearts of the multitude."
>
> —Edwin James, reporter; later managing editor of the *New York Times*

For the first time, the census of 1920 showed that more than half the nation was urban. In 1929 the payroll of full-time workers at U.S. Steel in Pennsylvania totaled 225,000; by April 1933 it was zero and the number of part-time workers was half as many as the 1929 full-time force. Many unemployed families lived without electricity or heat and stood in line to receive handouts of bread. In many cities, public employees such as teachers had to give up part of their already lean salaries to help pay for soup kitchens.

Part 12

Depression and War

Remember, this is the Roaring Twenties and it's easy to get rich. All you have to do is put a little money into stocks. Soon it will be big money. The stock market starts rising around 1924—slowly, at first. And then the bulls get frisky. By 1927, the bull market is jumping all the fences. Stocks are doubling and sometimes doubling again. Many experts are saying that something new is happening. This stock-market boom will just go on and on, they say. It isn't only business and political leaders who believe this. Professors from great universities are saying the same thing. So why not take your savings and buy all the stocks you can? If you're really smart, the experts say, you'll buy on margin that means you borrow most of the cost–and get lots of shares for little money. And that's what you do. Watch it go! That stock-market balloon is getting bigger and bigger. By 1929 you're rich. As President Calvin Coolidge leaves office (handing the reins to another Republican, Herbert Hoover), he gives the market his blessing: "It would seem perfectly plain from recent events that it is determined to go forward." Like many others, Coolidge seems to believe something new has been found: an economy that will just keep expanding.

That summer of 1929 people are eager to buy stock in anything–it doesn't matter if a company has any real worth or not. And then comes Thursday, October 24, 1929. Something is wrong. The stock-market balloon has been pierced; the air is rushing out. All at once everyone is trying to sell stocks—but no one wants to buy. Stock prices start falling and keep falling. The value of a share in Radio Corporation of America (RCA) goes from $505 on September 3, 1929, to $28 on November 13. "It came with a speed and ferocity that left men dazed," says the *New York Times*. "The market seemed like an insensate thing that was wreaking a wild and pitiless revenge upon those who had sought to master it." If you took the experts' advice and bought on margin, you not only lost your stocks, you owe money to the bank.

Most Americans aren't part of the stock-buying frenzy. Ordinary people usually keep their savings in banks. But the banks are in trouble, too. They've been lending money to stock-market speculators. The speculators can't pay their debts. Suddenly, lots of depositors want their cash, but the banks don't have it to give. Thousands of banks go bust and shut their doors. Factories close. Since people have no money, they stop buying cars. They stop buying houses. Which leads to layoffs in those industries. What's happening? We're having a depression. And it's spreading across the country. By 1932, at least 12 million people are out of work. That's one in four of all those who might normally be employed. Counting entire families, that makes nearly 50 million victims. This calamity will come to be called the Great Depression.

Down and Out

America has had depressions before. They are supposed to be a kind of self-regulating part of capitalism. The Great Depression is different. It hurts more people—rich and poor–than any previous depression. And it goes on, and on, and on.

This depression, shattering old patterns and expectations, reveals a new America. More than half the nation is now urban.

Most city people have nothing to fall back on when out of work. Those on farms have changed, too. The old, self-sufficient farm hardly exists anymore; the trend is to one- or two-crop farms. That makes sense when commodity prices are high. But while the rest of the country prospered in the 1920s, farm prices stayed low. America's farmers are in trouble. In 1929, few farms have electricity or indoor toilets. During the '30s, things get worse. The price of wheat falls so low that it is sometimes below what it costs to grow it. Dairy farmers dump thousands of gallons of milk onto the land to protest low prices. Other farmers destroy crops.

American farmers have abused the land for generations. They've cut down trees and dug up the sod. There seemed to be so much land that few worried about preserving it or practicing crop rotation. Now, with

> "The Depression is an embarrassing thing. The American Way had seemed so successful. All of a sudden, things broke down and didn't work. It's a difficult thing to understand today. To imagine this system, all of a sudden—for reasons having to do with paper, money, abstract things—breaking down."
>
> —Studs Terkel, *Hard Times: An Oral History of the Great Depression*

no more frontier and no place to move, no one is prepared for nature's tricks. Between 1934 and 1937, the normally low rainfall on the Great Plains is lower than ever. Droughts and windstorms dry up the land and turn it into desert. During the Great War, when grain prices were high, farmers on the plains plowed up thousands of acres of grassland to plant wheat. That left the light, dry soil without a grassy root system to hold it. Much of the Great Plains simply blows away.

The area that stretches from western Arkansas through the Oklahoma and Texas panhandles, to New Mexico, Kansas, Colorado, and Missouri is hardest hit. High winds pick up the topsoil, churning blizzards of dirt. Sailors at sea sweep Oklahoma dust from the decks of their ships. Cattle choke and people flee from what comes to be called the Dust Bowl. Thousands of poor farmers and sharecroppers head for cities in search of food and work.

But there are no jobs to be found in the cities. City people are moving in with relatives on family farms. This is a national calamity. Those who have no place to go build shacks out of old boxes and boards on public land, often near garbage dumps where they can scrounge for food. Hundreds of people camp in these unhealthy shantytowns; they spring up around the nation and are called Hoovervilles, after the president. Hoover says he is trying hard to solve the problem of the homeless and the hungry. But, by 1933, a million Americans are living in Hoovervilles.

President Hoover doesn't seem to know what to do. He announces that the economy is "fundamentally sound." In 1930, trying to be positive, he says, "We have passed the worst and with continuing unity of effort shall rapidly recover." In fact, the worst is yet to come. In the summer of 1932, the president announces that the Depression is over. But if he would only take a look at what's happening near the Capitol, he'd see that he is wrong.

At his inauguration in 1929, just months before the stock-market crash, Herbert Hoover says, "We in America today are nearer to the final triumph of poverty than ever before in the history of the land."

Thousands of World War I veterans and their families are camped in the center of Washington in a Hooverville of tents and shacks. Most are without jobs. Congress voted them a cash bonus for their war service, but it is not due to be paid until 1945. They need it now. They call themselves the Bonus Army, and they march through the streets carrying American flags and singing patriotic songs. When they won't leave, President Hoover asks the army to intervene. General Douglas MacArthur ignores the president's request not to use force, and sends in tanks and machine-gun units and soldiers with bayonets, billy clubs, and tear gas. The soldiers tear down the shacks and set them on fire. Some veterans are wounded. Two babies die from the tear gas. These are American veterans who just a few years earlier were cheered as heroes.

Hoover is a brilliant engineer, but he doesn't seem to understand. Each night he and Mrs. Hoover dress formally for dinner and are served seven-course dinners by the White House staff. Hoover has thought about cutting executive expenditures, but he decides that wouldn't be good for the country's morale. While many Americans are going to bed hungry, he says, "the lesson should be constantly enforced that though the people support the government, the government should not support the people." He means that no government money will be spent on relief programs. He says Americans can help themselves. If government money is spent, it should go to business. That will strengthen the economy, the president says, and business money will "trickle down" to the masses. Meanwhile people are starving in the land of plenty. Some Americans are talking revolution. The English poet Stephen Spender visits the United States and writes of his impressions:

> Despite its … amazing civilization, the social organization is right back in the Victorian Age…. She has no pensions for her old people; no medical benefits for her workers; no unemployment insurance for any trade.

When popular singing star Rudy Vallee visits the White House, the president suggests, "If you can sing a song that will make people forget the Depression, I'll give you a medal." Vallee comes up with a hit called "Brother, Can You Spare a Dime?" It isn't what the president hoped for.

In Washington, no one seems to know what to do. Then, in November 1932, the nation elects a new president. He has been New York's governor and he comes from a prominent family. Some people think he's a lightweight. His name is Franklin Delano Roosevelt.

A New Leader

Franklin Roosevelt grew up on a comfortable estate perched on the banks of the Hudson River at Hyde Park, New York. His was an astonishing childhood, something out of a Victorian picture book of the rich and privileged. His father, James Roosevelt, was a country gentleman who wore a silk top hat and was much older than his wife. James dabbled at work, but, steeped in the spirit of *noblesse oblige*, partook of civic and other do-good enterprises. Frank was an only child, adored by his parents. His doting mother kept her darling in long curls and dresses until he was nearly six. Franklin had Swiss tutors, his own pony, and just about every advantage a child could have—except for regular playmates his own age.

James Roosevelt was a friend of General George McClellan and had stories of Civil War politics to tell the boy. Franklin's formidable mother, Sara, was descended from Philippe de la Noye, who arrived at Plymouth colony in 1621 (missing the *Mayflower* by a year). Philippe married an Englishwoman, dropped the "ye" from his last name, and became Delano. A nineteenth-century Delano, Edward, profited handsomely from what he called "a fair, honorable and legitimate trade." He sold opium in China. The Delanos were a diverse lot. So were the Roosevelts, a Dutch family who landed in New York in 1650.

Most of the Roosevelts were Republicans, but James was a Democrat. When little Frank was five years old, in 1887, his father took him to meet President Grover Cleveland (James Roosevelt contributed money to help get him elected). Maybe the president was having a bad day. "My little man," said the huge president to the small boy in front of him, "I am making a strange wish for you. It is that you may never be president of the United States." You know how kids are. Just tell them what you don't want them to do, and that's what they'll go for. So perhaps it was that day that Franklin Delano Roosevelt first got the idea that he would like to be president.

When Franklin was ready to go to

Franklin Delano Roosevelt

school, at age fourteen, his parents sent him to prep school at Groton in a private railroad car. He had no experience making friends, and he wasn't much of an athlete, so he didn't fit in—but he had a sunny nature, he'd been taught not to complain, and he pretended that everything was fine. (He would go on pretending all his life.) Then he went to Harvard, as his parents expected him to do, and to Columbia Law School. His mother (always eager to run his affairs) intended him to lead the comfortable life of a country squire, like his father before him.

But there was another influence on his life. It was a man he admired more than anyone else he knew: the president of the United States, his distant cousin Theodore Roosevelt—a man who cared about people and wanted to leave the world better than

One of the two extant pictures of FDR in his wheelchair.

"He was brave, that Roosevelt. O Lordy he was brave.—A clear-cut nothing-from-the-waist-down case, and yet he forced himself to walk. With steel and fire he kept on pouring his will into what was left of his muscles, trying to walk that walk again."

—Lorenzo Milan, from *The Cripple Liberation Front Marching Band Blues*

he found it. Franklin, who had no need to concern himself with others, made TR a model. (Like his cousin, Franklin would use his initials to identify himself.) While he was still a student, FDR wrote to segregated southern colleges appealing to them to do as Harvard did and accept black students. He had already decided that he, too, would break the patrician mold and serve his country in elective office. At twenty-nine he was a New York state senator (as Teddy Roosevelt had been); then President Woodrow Wilson made him assistant secretary of the navy (a post TR had held). In 1920, Franklin Roosevelt ran for vice president with James M. Cox. They were trounced by Warren Harding and Calvin Coolidge, but people began to talk of handsome young Franklin as a politician to watch. By now he had a wife—Theodore's niece, Eleanor Roosevelt—and a daughter and four sons. He was an energetic father, full of good spirits, who loved to sail, ride horses, and hike; he was an expert marksman and birdwatcher. And he wanted to be president.

Then one night he went to bed, not feeling well; the next morning, he couldn't move. He was thirty-nine and had a dreaded disease: poliomyelitis. Usually it struck children; it was especially hard on adult victims. At first, Roosevelt couldn't move at all. Slowly, with painful therapy and concentration, he regained the use of his upper body. He would never move normally again. When he walked it was in heavy braces with agonizing steps, needing someone to lean on. Everyone was sure his political career was finished. But Franklin refused to be handicapped. His parents had trained him not to complain, and, even when he was in great pain, he didn't. As it turned out, he gained something from his terrible illness. His long struggle for mobility taught him patience, and it made him understand frustration. He—the boy who had everything—came to identify with the unfortunate. Seven years after polio crippled him, FDR reentered Democratic politics and, in 1928, was elected governor of New York (a post TR had also held). In 1932, some campaign buttons said ANYONE BUT HOOVER. It was an easy win for FDR.

A New Deal

In the months before Roosevelt takes office, the United States economy inches close to collapse. Each day more banks shut their doors. There is even a question as to whether the government has enough money to meet its payroll. A reporter describes Washington as like "a beleaguered capital in wartime." General MacArthur prepares his troops for a possible riot. Capitalism, say many experts, is too sick to recover. A group of prominent bankers is called to Washington to see what suggestions they can make for solving the banking crisis. They have none. President Hoover says, "We are at the end of our string. There is nothing more we can do."

On Inauguration Day, March 4, 1933, Franklin Delano Roosevelt stands, bareheaded, in front of the Capitol. He holds tightly to a lectern. Can this country gentleman provide the strong leadership that is needed? Some fear he is just a dilettante. But optimism is an American trait and most citizens are hopeful. Roosevelt has already done something never done before. He personally accepted his party's nomination at the Democratic National Convention, and electrified the delegates in doing so. It meant a valiant nine-hour flight in a tiny wind-tossed plane, but Roosevelt was determined to let people know that he intended to be a vigorous president. If anyone worried that his weak legs would slow him down, he would show them: they would not.

So he and Eleanor flew to Chicago, where he locked braces on his legs and stood before the delegates. "I pledge you, I pledge myself, to a new deal for the American people." To a nation that had suffered three years of devastating depression, the words *new deal* sounded very good. Herbert Hoover didn't have a chance.

On that Inauguration Day, people across America cluster around their radios. The new president speaks in a reassuring voice: "Let me assert my firm belief that the only thing we have to fear is fear itself." Then he gets to the meat of his talk. "I shall ask the Congress for the one remaining instrument to meet the crisis—broad executive power to wage a war against the emergency, as great as the power that would be given to me if we were invaded by a foreign foe. This nation is asking for action, and action now."

And that is exactly what Roosevelt delivers: action. The first hundred days of his presidency are famous for their accomplishments. New programs and laws begin pouring out of Washington. It is all labeled the New Deal. "It is common sense to take a method and try it," says Roosevelt. "If it fails, admit it frankly and try another. But above all, try something." They are the words of a man who exudes self-confidence; it is what the country needs.

Roosevelt puts together a group of advisers—to be known as "the brain trust." Many are college professors. They are new to government, but they have energy, intelligence, and a desire to help their country. They work hard. Washington becomes an exciting place for some tough, altruistic citizens who believe they are making a difference. And the president's handicap? It doesn't have anything to do with his ability to be chief executive; the press respects his privacy. Pictures are not printed of him in a

Eleanor

Eleanor Roosevelt had a dreadful childhood. Not an ordinary unhappy childhood; a horrible, awful, terribly lonely one. She adored her father, Elliott, Theodore Roosevelt's handsome, alcoholic brother, and lived for his visits. Sometimes he promised to see her and then, perhaps because he was drunk, he disappointed his child. Once he took her and his prize terriers for a walk. They stopped at his club; he left Eleanor and the dogs with the doorman while he went inside "for just a minute." Hours later he was carried out, drunk. The little girl—an ugly duckling whose beautiful mother was cold to her and called her "granny"—was sent home in a taxi. She never seemed to blame her father, who was the only person she believed really cared for her.

When she was eight, her mother died. When she was nine, her brother died. When she was ten, her father died. Eleanor and her younger brother, Hall, moved in with their grandmother, who lived in a big, spooky house and didn't know anything about bringing up children. The governess who looked after the children didn't like Eleanor and didn't hide her feelings. Finally, Eleanor was sent to school in England. The headmistress recognized the girl's intelligence and sweet nature. For three years she became the mother Eleanor never had, giving her praise and the confidence to face life on her own. When Eleanor came home from England, she'd grown up. She still thought she was ugly, but other people didn't especially her cousin Franklin. They fell deeply in love and were married. But, from the start, the marriage was rocky: he was an outgoing, secure man who thrived in a crowd and wanted to be president; she was thoughtful, insecure, and frightened of the public arena. Before long, Eleanor found herself with five children, three houses, a husband with a busy political career, and an interfering mother-in-law. When Franklin had an affair with her secretary, Eleanor was devastated and offered him a divorce. Sara Roosevelt made sure the divorce didn't happen. The couple stayed together in a marriage of respect, wheelchair, nor are there pictures of those who must lift him in and out of the special hand-controlled car he drives. The public never knows how physically crippled he is.

FDR changes America profoundly. He does away with most child labor, regulates the stock market, makes bank deposits safe, helps guarantee fair wages, encourages unions, limits work hours, helps farmers, brings electricity to rural areas, and gives Americans an old-age-pension policy called Social Security. The New Deal makes the

Eleanor traveled constantly; her Secret Service code name was "Rover."

partnership, even affection; but they did not share a bedroom again.

Then Franklin fell ill with polio. Eleanor had experience with tragedy; perhaps that was why she handled it so well. Her husband's legs would never carry him again. Eleanor said that needn't stop him. She could become his legs—and his eyes and ears, too. They became a team, one of the greatest political teams in history. He was president, but she was his link to the nation's citizens. He stayed in the White House; she went to mines and factories and workers' meetings. Then she told him what people were saying and what she'd learned.

The first time she spoke before an audience her knees shook. She conquered her fears. Soon she was one of the most successful speakers of her day. She wrote a newspaper column, a magazine column, and books. She was the first First Lady to hold regular press conferences. She served food to the needy, read to poor children, visited hospitals, spoke for minority rights when few did. When the Daughters of the American Revolution refused to let Marian Anderson, a famous black singer, use their auditorium, Mrs. Roosevelt resigned her membership. She encouraged Anderson to sing on the steps of the Lincoln Memorial in Washington. There, Marian Anderson sang "America"—and more people heard her than could have fit in any auditorium.

The purpose of many of FDR's New Deal programs was to find work or training for the unemployed while improving social services and infrastructure; above, Eleanor Roosevelt visits a WPA (Works Progress Administration) project to convert a city dump into a park in Des Moines, Iowa.

government an active participant in citizens' lives. Most of its concepts aren't really new. They are the old Progressive ideas in a new package. They have already been tried in Europe. America is behind the times when it comes to social welfare. (Later, many will see the pendulum swinging too far, but that will be in another time, with other problems.)

Roosevelt does something else that is new: he shares power with those who have never held it before. He rejects the idea of an aristocracy of birth and replaces it with the goal of an aristocracy of talent. There are those who hate him for doing it. He is called "a traitor to his class." Some who went to school with him refuse to speak his name. Some in the business world hate him, too. Business leaders were the heroes of the Roaring Twenties; now Roosevelt is a popular hero and the American people are demanding that the business world be regulated for the public good. Before the New Deal, the government was there to provide conditions that would help American business and industry grow and be profitable. During Roosevelt's presidency, government money and attention is also spent on the general public; laws are passed to help workers, farmers, and the needy.

Twentieth Century Monsters

On the very day of Franklin Delano Roosevelt's first inauguration in 1933, the day he tells America that "the only thing we have to fear is fear itself," something fearful is happening on the other side of the Atlantic. The Reichstag, Germany's congress, is bestowing absolute power on the German chancellor, Adolf Hitler. Imagine giving the worst people in a country the power of life and death. Imagine a nation that burns the books of its greatest writers because it fears ideas and truth. Imagine a nation that kills people because it doesn't like their religion or race or sexual identity. A nation that destroys its own freedom. That was Germany in the 1930s.

The German people were still angry over World War I. They believed that Germany was no more to blame for the Great War than any other nation; they believed the rest of the world had picked on them. They thought the Versailles treaty that ended the war was unfair. Germany, a nation that took pride in its military tradition, had been made to promise not to raise an army, navy, or air force; she was expected to make large cash reparations to the victors. On top of that, the German economy was a wreck. Inflation escalated until German money became almost worthless. About the time the inflation came under control, the Depression set in worldwide. There was large-scale unemployment. The German people looked for a strong leader; someone who could get them out of the economic mess and make Germany proud again. The United States, faced with the same depression, turned to Franklin Delano Roosevelt. Germany chose Adolf Hitler.

Hitler preaches the gospel of nationalism—that loving your country is more important than loving truth and right action. He isn't alone. Militant nationalism will become a twentieth-century disease. In Japan, in Spain, in Italy, and elsewhere, strong nationalist movements combine racism with militarism. Mussolini calls his political movement Fascism. Hitler names his Nazism (for National Socialism). In Russia, a totalitarian state expects world domination through communism.

Hitler invokes an old disease to explain Germany's problems. It is anti-Semitism, hatred of Jews. It's a form of cowardice and scapegoating that has been around a very long time. Whatever is wrong must be the fault of the Jews. Inflation? Depression? It is all because of the Jews, says Hitler. The Nazis paint the German word for "Jews," *Juden*, on Jewish shops and businesses to isolate and target them. One Nazi sign carries a skull and crossbones and says ATTENTION: JEWS! The Nazis will build factories for killing. They will hunt down the Jews of Europe and pack them into cattle cars to send them to be slaughtered. They won't kill just Jews. Hitler hates Slavs, gypsies, disabled people, homosexuals, and anyone who doesn't agree with him. The Nazis will kill as many of those people as they can, and enslave others.

Meanwhile, the rest of the world isn't paying attention. Despite the restrictions laid down at Versailles, Hitler builds and equips an army, navy, and air force. In 1938 he brings them out. First he conquers Austria; then Czechoslovakia. The European democracies let him do it. They're tired of war, and they hope that if they appease Hitler, letting him do a bit of conquering, he will be satisfied. They're wrong. When the Wehrmacht rolls into Poland on September 1, 1939, Britain and France realize a monster has been unleashed. They can appease no longer. Both nations declare war on Germany.

The Allies are now facing blitzkrieg—the German word for "lightning war." Germany speeds troops, tanks, and artillery across nations, obliterating them almost before they know what is happening. In 1940, Belgium is taken; then France is overwhelmed. German tanks enter Paris. Of the major European democracies, only England is left. And German bombers are pounding that small island. Everyone knows that Hitler's goal is world conquest and that the Nazis plan to invade England. In Asia, Japan also has world domination in mind. She has already occupied Manchuria, in 1931, some other parts of China, in 1937, and, in 1941, French Indochina (now Vietnam, Laos, and Cambodia). Japan is threatening Thailand, the Philippines, and other Pacific nations.

In the United States there are strong "isolationist" voices. They believe that the Pacific and the Atlantic oceans are buffers that isolate us from the world's problems. They believe we should mind our own

> "The victor will not be asked afterward whether or not he told the truth. Act brutally! The stronger is in the right."
>
> —Adolf Hitler

A Soviet caricature of Adolf Hitler.

business and not worry about what's going on elsewhere. Some, who are pacifists, don't think it right to fight any war. Still others believe our battleships can protect us. A few voices argue that air power is changing the usual rules of war and that we need to be prepared, but they are mostly ignored or mocked. In 1939, our military force is ranked behind that of Belgium (and Belgium quickly falls to the Nazis). FDR wants build up our military power, but Congress is reluctant. The president uses subterfuge. He begins by sending war supplies to England under a program called Lend-Lease. (Supposedly England is just "leasing" the supplies.) That gets our munitions factories going (and helps end the Depression).

In his State of the Union address early in 1941, Roosevelt says:

> In the future days, which we seek to make secure, we look forward to a world founded upon four essential freedoms. The first is freedom of speech and expression—everywhere in the world. The second is freedom of every person to worship God in his own way—everywhere in the world. The third is freedom from want.... The fourth is freedom from fear.

Later that year, in an Atlantic meeting with the British prime minister, Winston Churchill, those four freedoms (freedom of speech, freedom of religion, freedom from want, freedom from fear of armed aggression) are confirmed as joint goals.

Roosevelt promises America's "full support" for the Allied cause. But he doesn't ask the American people to go to war.

Meanwhile, the war news is beginning to resonate in the United States. In May 1941, a poll shows 73 percent of Americans in favor of fighting if that is the only way to help Britain. But Congress is not ready and FDR, castigated by interventionists and isolationists, is torn between the horror of war and the realization that England probably cannot survive Nazi power alone. In June, Hitler invades Russia. In July, the puppet French government turns control of French Vietnam over to the Japanese. The nation's editorial writers and citizens debate: does the United States, as the world's leading democracy, have a moral obligation to defend human rights elsewhere? At what cost? If the Nazis conquer Europe and the Japanese conquer the Pacific, will they stop there? In August 1941 President Roosevelt tells the American people they must be prepared "to defend freedom against forces which would enslave the world." But he doesn't go beyond that. That same month, at a meeting in the Imperial Palace in Tokyo, Emperor Hirohito, besieged by militarists who are winning control over the Japanese moderates, reads a poem written by his grandfather Emperor Meiji:

> Throughout the world
> Everywhere we are brothers,
> Why then do the winds and waves
> Rage so turbulently?

Pearl Harbor

It is sunny on the morning of December 7, 1941. At the White House, thirty-one guests are expected for lunch. On this same morning, Secretary of State Cordell Hull receives a call from the Japanese ambassador. He and an envoy from Japan, another ambassador, ask for an emergency meeting. Hull expects them to bring their government's answer to an American peace letter. The secretary has no idea what this day will bring.

After a cheery lunch, the president relaxes with his stamp collection. At about 2 p.m. Eastern Standard Time, the phone

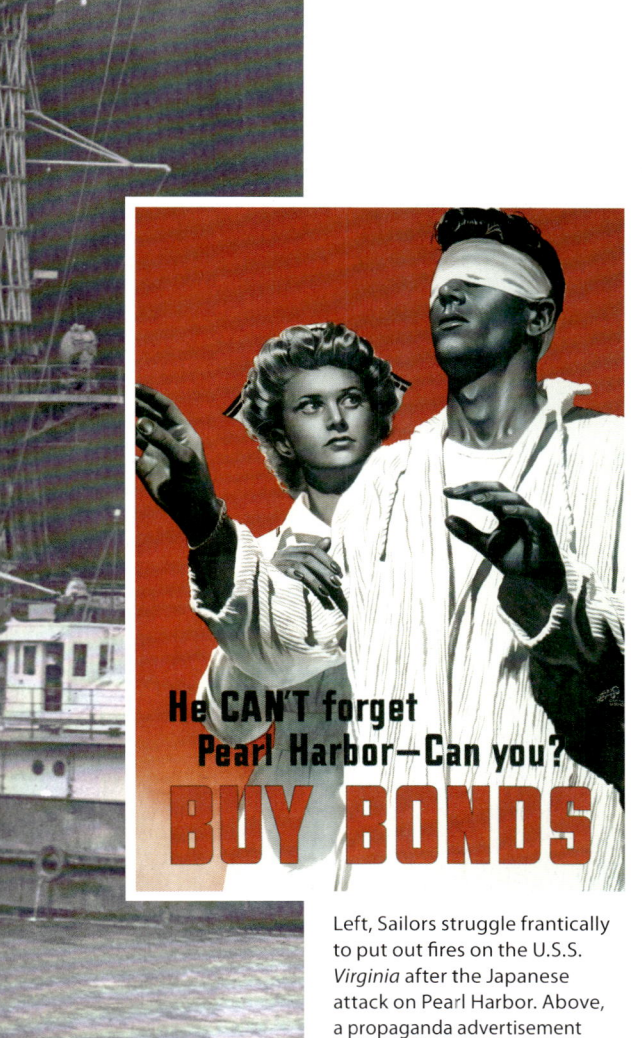

Left, Sailors struggle frantically to put out fires on the U.S.S. *Virginia* after the Japanese attack on Pearl Harbor. Above, a propaganda advertisement for U.S. defense bonds, through which the government raised money from the public to help finance the war effort.

rings. Secretary of the Navy Frank Knox is on the line relaying an urgent message from Hawaii: AIR RAID ON PEARL HARBOR—THIS IS NOT A DRILL.

The president knows the U.S. Pacific fleet is headquartered at Pearl Harbor in the Hawaiian Islands. He learns that at 7:55 A.M. Hawaiian time, Japanese planes dropped bombs on the harbor's Battleship Row. There, warships were docked in neat lines, midsections together, a come-and-get-me target. The battleship *Arizona* is among the first to go. It gives a tremendous roar, splits in two, and slips to the bottom of the harbor. That is just the beginning. Much of the fleet goes down; more than 2,000 people are dead.

Some officials in Washington were expecting a Japanese attack. (A decoded message suggested that something was being planned.) But one of this audacity and magnitude! It is beyond their imagination. On that same day, the Japanese hit American and British bases in the Pacific and in East Asia.

At 2:20 P.M. the two Japanese diplomats arrive at Cordell Hull's office and hand him a document. Glancing at it, Hull says, in icy Southern tones, "I have never seen a document that was more crowded with infamous falsehoods…. on a scale so huge that I never imagined … any government on this planet was capable of uttering them." He throws the Japanese out of his office, muttering about "scoundrels and pissants." The distraught ambassadors have

"Our national policy is not directed toward war. Its sole purpose is to keep war away from our country and away from our people."

—Franklin D. Roosevelt, December 29, 1940.

(In 1940 President Roosevelt has just been reelected to an unprecedented third term. He will be elected to a fourth term in 1944.)

not been informed by their government of the attack. Later that day, one of them attempts suicide.

In the United States, there are no more isolationists. And the critics of air power, who thought battleships were invincible, are silent too. The next day, the president goes before Congress. December 7, he says, is "a date which will live in infamy." He asks Congress to declare war on Japan. Three days later, Japan's allies—Germany and Italy—declare war on the United States.

A Fireside Chat

Franklin Delano Roosevelt knows how to explain complicated things in simple language. He enjoys speaking, and he is good at it. As soon as he takes office, he starts using radio to explain what the government is doing. This president, who understands that he is an elected representative of the American people, feels an obligation to inform his constituents. He calls his radio broadcasts "fireside chats." They become a regular thing. Here is part of what he says in a fireside chat on February 9, 1942:

We are now in this war. We are all in it—all the way. Every single man, woman, and child is a partner in the most tremendous undertaking of our American history.... On the road ahead there lies hard work—grueling work—day and night, every hour and every minute. I was about to add that ahead there lies sacrifice for all of us. But it is not correct to use that word. The United States does not consider it a sacrifice to do all that one can, to give one's best to our nation, when the nation is fighting for its existence and its future life.... There is no such thing as security for any nation—or any individual—in a world ruled by the principles of gangsterism. There is no such thing as impregnable defense against powerful aggressors who sneak up in the dark and strike without warning. We have learned that our ocean-girt hemisphere is not immune from severe attack—that we cannot measure our safety in terms of miles on any map anymore....

We are now in the midst of a war, not for conquest, not for vengeance, but for a world in which this nation, and all that this nation represents, will be safe for our children.... We are going to win the war and we are going to win the peace that follows.

FDR delivering his first fireside chat

This is a war on two fronts. In the Pacific, the Japanese move with astonishing speed. In a few months they capture Thailand, the Philippines, the Malay Peninsula, Java, Burma, Guam, Wake Island, the Gilbert Islands, Singapore, and Hong Kong. They control East Asia. People in India and Australia tremble–they believe they are next. In Europe, things are no better. Axis control extends from France in the west to Poland in the east and south into North Africa. The Russians,

African American soldiers at the Great Lakes Naval Training Center in Illinois, c. 1941–1945. African-Americans were a crucial part of the war effort, working as everything from (eventually) fighter pilots to munitions makers.

FORGETTING THE CONSTITUTION

Haruko Obata lives in Berkeley, California, where her father is a professor. Haruko is an American citizen of Japanese descent. She is proud of her Asian heritage; she is proud of her native land: the United States. Then, a few months after Pearl Harbor is bombed, her world changes. Haruko's father tells the family they are moving. They have just a few days to get ready, and they can take only what they can carry. They may never again see the things they are leaving behind. What have they done wrong? Nothing. But there is anti-Japanese hysteria in America, especially in California, where most Japanese-Americans live. Some of it is understandable—the war is terrible, and the Japanese government is our enemy. But the Japanese in America have nothing to do with that, any more than German-Americans have anything to do with the savagery in Nazi Germany. The real problem the Japanese face is racism. A racist law prevents Japanese immigrants from becoming citizens. Only the Nisei, like Haruko, who are born in America, are automatically citizens. Two-thirds of Japanese-Americans are Nisei. If these citizens are put behind barbed wire, their property will have to be sold, and quickly, for much less than it is worth. Some people will profit greatly from that.

The Sixth Amendment to the Constitution is supposed to protect citizens from unreasonable searches and seizures. The Fourteenth Amendment says, "nor shall any state deprive any person of life, liberty or property without the due process of law." But we are at war, and the War Department is worried about "national security." The right of habeas corpus has been shelved in wartime before. And so President Roosevelt issues Executive Order 9102. Without any notice, without due process, with only a few days to get ready, 120,000 Japanese-Americans and their families are arrested and sent to internment camps. This is the way Haruko remembers it:

When we arrived at Tanforan it was raining; it was so sad and depressing. The roadway was all mud, and our shoes would stick to the mud when we walked outside. They gave us a stable the size of our dining room—that was our sleeping quarters.

Most Japanese-Americans will remain in the camps for three years. Some work in war factories during the day. Some

young men become soldiers. A Nisei regiment fighting in Europe wins more commendations than any other single American fighting regiment. Not a single case of Japanese-American espionage is found. Forty years after war's end, the United States government apologizes to Japanese-Americans for the injustices done them during this time.

Right, the Japanese-American who owned this store put up the sign the day after Pearl Harbor. Like so many, he had to sell his business at a fire-sale price. Below, the mess line at Manzanar camp in the California desert.

Led by General Eisenhower (inset), more than 60,000 Allied troops—U.S., British, Canadian—assaulted the Normandy coast on D-Day; above, troops plunge off a landing barge ramp. "Our men … were pinned down right on the waters edge by an inhuman wall of fire," wrote reporter Ernie Pyle.

besieged, are taking astonishing losses. The Mediterranean is a Nazi sea. German U-boats, perfected since World War I, swim with arrogant dominance in the Atlantic. In the first four months of 1942, almost 200 U.S. ships are torpedoed and sunk.

The Allies—the United States, Britain, and Russia—are in disarray. Slowly things change. Believing they are invincible and that Americans are indulged weaklings, the Japanese get greedy. We have an advantage that the Axis powers don't grasp: free people setting their minds to something are a powerful force. The United States wins three big victories—in the Coral Sea, at Midway Island, and at Guadalcanal—and the Japanese learn some respect.

Meanwhile, at home, Americans throw themselves into the war effort. Factories turn out guns, ships, planes, and tanks faster than anyone believed possible. Women take factory jobs, plow wheat fields, deliver mail, drive buses, and do still more. They enter many domains that were previously all male. After the war, those women … well, that story is yet to come.

D-Day

In 1943 Britain's prime minister, Winston Churchill, says, "We have reached the end of the beginning." Churchill, like Roosevelt, has a gift of oratory. Much of London has been bombed to rubble. Churchill's eloquence helps his people survive. "Lift up your hearts; all will come right," he says in one speech. "Out of the depths of sorrow and of sacrifice will be born again the glory of mankind."

Finally, in 1943, the Allies begin to win important victories in Europe. In North Africa, U.S. General Dwight D. Eisenhower commands a joint force of British and American troops. Soon the Mediterranean no longer belongs to the Germans. From Africa, the Allies invade Italy. The Italians, dispirited, kick out their strutting dictator, Benito Mussolini, and, mostly, quit fighting. The Allies have a foothold on the European continent. Plans are made for Operation Overlord, the code name for the recapture of France. It will be the largest amphibious invasion in all of history. The Germans know an assault is planned, but they don't know where it will be. They have lined the beaches of northern France with mines and steel barriers; they have put heavy artillery in bunkers on high cliffs overlooking the English Channel. Now the question is: where and when will the invasion come?

On the first June weekend in 1944 the weather is poor, visibility terrible, and the possibility of invasion seems remote, even insane. Some key German officers stationed in France see that weekend as a chance to go on leave. General Eisenhower, now commander of all Allied forces in Europe, knowing there will be a brief window when the weather should hold, decides to go for it. It is June 6, 1944. It will forever be known as D-Day.

To his men he says:

You are about to embark on the great crusade. Good luck! And let us all beseech the blessing of almighty God upon this great and noble undertaking.

The first troops fall from the skies, parachuting at night with plans to detonate bridges and set up advance outposts. They are given toy clickers to signal one another. Some are successful; some parachute into lakes and are drowned. At daybreak the sky is filled with airplanes—9,000 of them. The largest naval fleet ever assembled appears off the French coast. The Allies have commandeered anything that can float: landing vehicles, minesweepers, attack transports, cruisers, battleships, hospital ships, and tugs. Engineers set up portable harbors. Some landing vehicles, deployed too soon, capsize and sink in the turbulent waters.

Soldiers who attempt to cross the mined beaches are blown away. The fierce guns on top of the bluffs are relentless.

Yet the men keep coming. Tanks unroll reels of steel matting to make roadways across the sand. Five thousand will die before there is a surge forward. But by nightfall, Allied troops—American, British, Canadian, French, and British soldiers—are holding French soil. The Allies have broken through the Nazi wall. For the Axis, it is the beginning of the end.

FREEDOM FROM FEAR

Roosevelt meets Stalin for the first time in Russian-occupied Teheran, the capital of Iran, in 1943. Roosevelt is impressed by Stalin's quiet confidence. With Churchill, he calls him "Uncle Joe." The president believes their mutual responsibilities give them common ground. "We talked like men and brothers," says the president. At Teheran, Stalin agrees to enter the war against Japan once Germany is defeated. There is also agreement about postwar global security that will lay the foundation for the future United Nations.

In January 1945, soon after his fourth inaugural, Roosevelt flies to Yalta, a resort city on Russia's Crimean peninsula. This time the leaders meet in an old palace that once belonged to Czar Nicholas II. Overlooking the Black Sea, the palace is short on toilets and long on bed vermin.

The Big Three at the Allied conference in Yalta in January 1945. Left to right, Churchill, Roosevelt, and Stalin. The exhaustion of the war years shows in FDR's face; he was a sick man.

The *Enola Gay*, the plane that dropped the atomic bomb "Little Boy" on Hiroshima, along with five of the plane's ground crew. In the center stands Paul Tibbets, the man in charge of the bombing mission.

But Roosevelt is concerned with important things, and getting along with Uncle Joe is a priority. He and Churchill disagree about Stalin. The Prime Minister, a hardheaded realist, believes that the best the Allies can do for now is to carve out future spheres of influence, keeping the Soviets as contained as possible. Roosevelt is focused on world harmony, going beyond the old imperialism. He thinks he can charm Joseph Stalin as he charms most men. The American ambassador, William Bullitt, warns him that Stalin is "a Caucasian bandit whose only thought when he gets something for nothing is that the other fellow is an ass." Roosevelt says (as Bullitt tells it): "I just have a hunch that Stalin is not that kind of man…. I think that if I give everything I possibly can and ask nothing in return … he won't try to annex anything and will work with me for a world of democracy and peace."

FDR and Uncle Joe disagree over the future of Poland; Stalin gets what he wants: control. The leaders agree that Germany will be divided into zones of occupation. Roosevelt asks for and gets Stalin's signature concurring in "free and unfettered elections" and "democratic institutions" in Eastern Europe. The Soviets will renege on those agreements, but the signature will haunt them. Plans for the United Nations are carried further. Yalta is controversial. Some believe that Roosevelt was bamboozled by the Soviet leader, others that he got as much as he could.

Meanwhile, there is still a war to be won. Russia's Red Army is just fifty miles east of Berlin; Allied forces turn back a powerful army in Belgium at the crucial but costly Battle of the Bulge. Soviet forces liberate a German concentration camp at Auschwitz, in Poland, and see horrific evidence of the inhuman acts committed by the Nazis. In the Pacific, U.S. General Douglas MacArthur recaptures the Philippines. Everywhere the Axis powers go on the defensive.

President Roosevelt is exhausted, and needs a few days' rest. In April he goes to his southern retreat in Warm Springs, Georgia. The natural baths there always make him feel good. He is writing a speech, thinking about the peace that is soon to come, when he raises a hand to his temple and says, "I have a terrific headache." They are the last words he speaks.

A military honor guard stands erect beside the flag-draped Georgia pine coffin in the last car of the train that carries the president on his final journey north. The lights in the car are turned on, and the blinds are up so those along the route can see and pay tribute to the man who led them for twelve years, longer than any other president. Eleanor, unable to sleep, gazes through the train window:

> *I lay in my berth, with the window shade up, looking out at the countryside he had loved and watching the faces of the people at stations, and even at the crossroads, who had come to pay their last tribute all through the night.... I was truly surprised by the people along the way; not only at the stops but at every crossing.*

Grief-stricken and silent, mourners stand at depots and crossings and everywhere the train passes. Near Gainsville, Georgia, black women working in a field fall to their knees, hands outstretched in prayer. As the train slows in Greenville, South Carolina, members of a Boy Scout troop begin singing "Onward, Christian Soldiers"; then others join in, and soon, according to one who was there, "eight or ten thousand voices were singing like an organ." Reporters, traveling in the train's press car, write of people who cluster respectfully, and of their tears. Nothing like this has touched the American people since the death of Abraham Lincoln. A few Roosevelt haters celebrate, but mostly there is a profound sense of loss. This patrician gentleman took the nation from depression through world war, with dignity, courage, and unfailing wit and confidence. Never pretending to be anything other than what he was, he made Americans everywhere feel that they were family.

In Washington, six white horses carry the caisson to the White House. From there it is taken to Hyde Park where the president is buried, as he wished, in his mother's rose garden. On April 30, during the memorial service, the whole nation comes to a halt. Airplanes sit on runways; radios are silent; telephone service is cut off; movie theaters close; 505 New York subway trains stop; stores shut their doors. Most Americans still can't believe it: Franklin Delano Roosevelt is gone.

Twenty days later Hitler is dead. He has killed himself. A week after that, Germany's military leaders surrender to General Eisenhower. The war in Europe is over. Eisenhower writes a victory statement in his usual to-the-point style: *The mission of this Allied force was fulfilled at 0241 local time May 7, 1945.*

In the Pacific, firebombs devastate Japanese cities. The Allied military plans to invade Japan; casualties are expected to be greater than any yet experienced. The Japanese seem to have no intention of surrendering. In Washington the new president, Harry S. Truman, is told of a super weapon. A letter from Albert Einstein to President Roosevelt led to its development. Einstein and others feared that Germany was working on something similar. The letter said, "it may be possible to set up a nuclear chain reaction in a large mass of uranium by which vast amounts of power … would be generated." Roosevelt turned to Alexander Sachs, who brought him the letter, "Alex, what you are after is to see that the Nazis don't blow us up." Then he called to an aide: "This requires action." He gave the go-ahead for research to begin.

Truman learns that some of the world's leading physicists have been developing the bomb in a remote enclave (a former boys' school) at Los Alamos, in New Mexico's wooded hill country. It has all been so secret that even the vice president didn't know about it. Now he does. It is a weapon that he believes will end the war:

Let there be no mistake-we shall completely destroy Japan's power to make war.

August 6, 1945, is a clear, beautiful day in the Japanese city of Hiroshima. The streets are filled with people on their way to work. And then, as one Japanese historian would write later, "everything was nothing." Seventy-five thousand Japanese are cremated instantly; tens of thousands more are burned or fatally poisoned by radiation and will die in the months and years to come. The center of the city is leveled. The atomic age has begun.

Three days later, a second bomb is dropped on Nagasaki. Emperor Hirohito asks his people to surrender and "accept the coming of peace." World War II is over.

After General Alfred Jodl signs the German surrender in a school in Rheims, France, the crowds pile out for a ticker-tape celebration on May 8, 1945—VE ("Victory in Europe") Day—in Ottowa, Canada.

PART 13

DEMOCRACY AND STRUGGLES

How do you follow a president like FDR? When most Americans looked at President Harry Truman, they winced. He was more like a next-door neighbor than a president. He didn't even try to be sophisticated. He hadn't gone to college. He was an avid reader, steeped in history—but hardly anyone knew that. He'd worked as a farmer, a bank clerk, a shopkeeper, and a county administrator—all in Missouri. His grandparents had come there from Kentucky in the 1840s, bringing slaves they got as wedding presents.

Truman was the surprising protégé of Missouri's less-than-pure political boss, Tom Pendergast. Maybe the boss wanted to back someone known for his honesty; maybe he just liked Harry. Anyway, when Truman ran for the Senate he won. At age fifty, he headed for Washington. "I am hoping to make a reputation," he wrote his wife, Bess, when he arrived in the capital in 1935. "But you'll have to put up with a lot if

I do because I won't sell influence." He was a quiet, hardworking senator who attracted some attention in the Democratic Party when he headed a committee that examined companies producing weapons of war. Truman's committee probably saved the government billions in military contracts. Still, he was mostly unknown when he was

The United States emerges from World War II as a superpower with a strong economy. In much of the rest of the world, especially areas where the war was fought, there is economic catastrophe and chaos. The winter of 1946 is especially hard in Europe. Fearing a repeat of what happened in Europe and Asia after the First World War, President Truman decides to try to help restore industry, agriculture, and trade. The Marshall Plan revives war ruined economies with billions in aid, from cash to tractors (left, a Marshall jeep on its way to southeast Asia).

asked to be vice president. Even President Roosevelt hardly knew Truman.

FDR had turned to advisers to pick a candidate. The other contenders were all controversial, and Truman didn't seem to have any enemies. The vice presidency wasn't much of a job then, unless the president made it so. And Roosevelt was too busy to do that. Harry had served four months in the office, mostly unnoticed, when, on April 12, 1945, with the war in Europe clearly nearing its end, he got a call from the president's press secretary. He was to come to the White House at once.

Truman headed through the underground passage from the Senate Office building—where Secret Service agents lost track of him. But a car was waiting. As they drove the fifteen long blocks to the White House, he guessed that the president, who was resting in Warm Springs, Georgia, had flown in and wanted him for something ceremonial. Upstairs at the White House, he learned differently. Eleanor Roosevelt put her hand on his shoulder and said softly, "Harry, the president is dead." For a moment he could say nothing. Then he asked if there was anything he could do for her. "Is there anything we can do for you?" she answered. "For you are the one in trouble now."

Most Americans have little confidence in this "accidental president." Cartoonists delight in ridiculing him; editorial writers

Truman is sworn in as president on April 12, 1945. The next day he tells a journalist, "There have been few men in all history the equivalent of the man into whose shoes I am stepping. I pray God I can measure up to the task." Assistant Secretary of State Dean Acheson said, "I think he will learn fast and will inspire confidence."

dismiss him as inadequate. Later, a historian will write of him, "With more fateful decisions than almost any president in our time, he made the fewest mistakes."

Harry Truman never expected to be president; he says it is as if a bull has fallen on top of him. But his wide reading and diligence have prepared him far better than he or most of his contemporaries realize. He puts two signs on his desk that seem to sum up his values. On the first are the words of another Missourian, Mark Twain: ALWAYS DO RIGHT, THIS WILL GRATIFY SOME PEOPLE & ASTONISH THE REST. The second sign (which is still in the Oval Office) says: THE BUCK STOPS HERE.

With quiet force, Harry Truman persuades Congress and the country to act generously to the nations defeated in World War II. As a student of history, Truman understands the bitterness of the vanquished. Like Woodrow Wilson, who tried to forge a compassionate peace after the First World War, Truman had Confederate ancestors who carried hate all their lives. He knows that Germany's anger after World War I, and the failure of Wilson's Fourteen Points, led to a second world war.

So he makes plans to send billions of dollars in aid both to our allies and our former enemies. The president says: *You can't be vindictive after a war. You have to be generous. You have to help people get back on their feet.*

People in Europe—in victorious as well as defeated nations—are starving (there is

> "The responsibility of a great state is to serve and not to dominate the world."
>
> —Harry S. Truman
> in his first presidential address to
> Congress, April 16, 1945

no food); they are freezing (there is little coal); they are sick (tuberculosis and other diseases are raging). In France and Italy there are food riots. We have food to spare; we have a democratic system of government that we believe can help bring freedom and prosperity elsewhere. The United States shares its wealth and its ideas. No winning nation has ever treated those on the losing side so big-heartedly.

Secretary of State George C. Marshall (the U.S. Army's chief of staff during the war) describes an aid program in a speech he gives at Harvard College; it reflects President Truman's thoughts. The Marshall Plan will be offered to every nation in Europe—including Germany and the Soviet Union. The Soviet nations refuse the aid, but sixteen others accept with enthusiasm. Marshall aid rebuilds steel mills in Belgium, ceramics factories in France, railroads in Germany, and bridges and buildings everywhere. The United States ships bulldozers, tractors and much other equipment needed to get Europe's infrastructure running again. American experts train Europeans in techniques of mass production. The Marshall Plan is devised to encourage Europeans to develop

On April 2, 1948, Congress passes the Foreign Assistance Act, making the Marshall Plan official. "We are the first great nation," writes Truman, "to feed and support the conquered."

> "Our policy is directed not against any country or doctrine, but against hunger, poverty, desperation and chaos. Its purpose should be the revival of a working economy in the world so as to permit the emergence of political and social conditions in which free institutions can exist."
>
> —Secretary of State George Marshall, in a speech at Harvard, June 5, 1947

their own talents and know-how. And it works. The plan helps revive economies and create customers.

America does more than send food and concrete aid to its former enemy, Germany; it helps reestablish a democratic German government that guarantees its citizens free speech and basic civil rights. In Japan, where there is no tradition of freedom and self-rule, Truman sends General Douglas MacArthur to lead a from-the-ground-up effort to create a democracy. A new Japanese constitution includes a bill of rights and an independent judiciary. Land is redistributed, providing a balance between large landowners and small farmers. Women are given the vote; thirty-nine are elected to the Diet (the legislative body). Secret political societies are prohibited; religious discrimination is ended. Japan, given freedom, democracy, and women's rights, is soon prosperous. Another Truman aid plan, Point Four, helps underdeveloped countries in Africa, Asia, and Latin America.

The world's quick recovery is the return the United States gets for its investment. But some people in the recipient countries think there must be a catch; there is no precedent for generosity on this scale. And some Americans protest the cost. But their opposition is nothing compared to what happens when President Truman decides to do something to help the less fortunate at home.

During World War II, African-Americans were allowed to die for their country—as long as they did it in segregated regiments. After the war, the army, navy, and air force remain segregated—blacks and whites are assigned to separate units, where blacks are almost always given inferior jobs. Things are about the same at home. In the South, black lynchings continue to be commonplace, and the perpetrators are rarely arrested. Because

In efforts to improve civil rights in America, Truman bypasses Congress, issuing executive orders to end discrimination in the armed forces and ensure fair employment in the civil service. Doing away with entrenched racism is harder; these NAACP members protest a lynching at Sikeston in Truman's home state, Missouri, in 1942.

of poll taxes, few blacks can vote; those who try are often intimidated. In Georgia, a black man is shot and killed trying to vote. In Mississippi, some black soldiers returning from the war are beaten viciously. President Truman hears of these outrages and is horrified.

"We cannot wait another decade or another generation to remedy these ills," he says. "We must work, as never before, to cure them now." Truman creates a commission on civil rights. He sends proposals to Congress to end lynchings, outlaw the poll tax, and do away with segregation in the armed services. On June 29, 1947, on the steps of the Lincoln Memorial, Truman gives the first speech a president has ever made to the National Association for the Advancement of Colored People. "Many of our people still suffer the indignity of

"We can't be leaders of the free world and draw a color line on opportunity.... We can't go before the world and try to maintain peace in the world when we ourselves, at home, discriminate against people on account of color or religion."

—President Harry S. Truman

insult, the narrowing fear of intimidation, and, I regret to say, the threat of physical and mob violence," he says to a crowd of 10,000 people. "Prejudice and intolerance in which these evils are rooted still exist. The conscience of our nation, and the legal machinery which enforces it, have not yet secured to each citizen full freedom from fear." Walter White, the head of the NAACP, stands next to Truman and thinks of Lincoln's Gettysburg Address. Later

In 1947, two years before the NAACP's fortieth anniversary, Truman becomes the first president ever to speak to the organization

he says, "I did not believe that Truman's speech possessed the literary quality of Lincoln's speech, but in some respects it had been a more courageous one in its specific condemnation of evils based upon race prejudice ... and its call for immediate action against them."

A Florida county commission calls the president's program "obnoxious, repugnant, odious, detestable, loathsome, repulsive, revolting and humiliating." A Mississippi congressman says that Truman has "run a political dagger into our backs and now he is trying to drink our blood." Then something happens on a playing field that makes just about every American, no matter his or her age, do some thinking about the cost of discrimination.

A Major Leaguer

In the South, schools, buses, restaurants, hotels, water fountains—just about everything—are segregated. If two people fall in love, and they happen to have different skin colors, they can't marry. Miscegenation laws make it a crime to do so. This is 1945, and we are a Jim Crow nation. The North and the West aren't as blatant about it, but separation and prejudice exist across the land. Even the national pastime—baseball—is segregated. There are major leagues, minor leagues, and separate Negro leagues. Major leaguers play in fine ballparks, travel first class, and sleep in decent hotels. Negro leaguers have no ballparks of their own (they rent what they can find), and they get lower pay (except for the amazing Satchel Paige). Their equipment is shabby and the travel brutal; black players almost always have trouble finding hotel rooms or restaurants.

Branch Rickey, general manager of the Brooklyn Dodgers, understands that it is not only wrong but stupid to keep baseball segregated. Rickey founded baseball's system of farm teams back in the 1920s, so he knows good ballplayers when he sees them. And he realizes that black ballplayers are a pool of untapped talent and that they play an exciting, hustling kind of baseball. Rickey believes African-American players could bring a huge new audience to the majors. He knows it is time for baseball to change, and he is willing to do what he can to make it happen. "I was convinced that there was timeliness about it," he said later. "After waiting a hundred years, these people [were] legally free, not spiritually free, never morally free. And I felt that if the right man … [with] an ability on the field and with control of himself off the field, if I could find that kind of man, the American public would accept him."

When he discovers Jack Roosevelt Robinson he has the man he's looking for. Jackie Robinson earned varsity letters in four sports as well as top grades at the University of California at Los Angeles (UCLA). He was an army officer when a driver asked him to sit at the back of the bus because he was African-American. Robinson refused to move. He faced a court martial for disobedience—but he fought the charges and the army dropped them.

Rickey is impressed. This is a man with courage. Rickey tells Robinson that the Dodgers are ready to try to break baseball's color line. Both men know that the first black ballplayer in the majors won't have it easy. Rickey asks Robinson to be that groundbreaker—but he must be willing to take abuse and hold his tongue. "Mr. Rickey," says Jackie Robinson, "do you want a ballplayer who's afraid to fight back?"

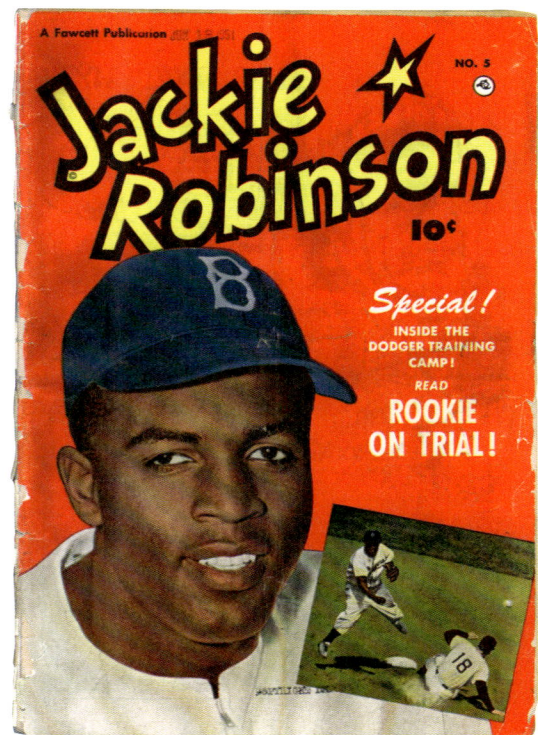

Branch Rickey signs Jackie Robinson (above) to the Dodgers on August 28, 1945. "It is the hardest thing in the world to get big-league baseball to change anything, " Rickey says later. Facing the haters isn't easy, either. Robinson says, "All I ask is that you respect me as a human being."

> "A life is not important except in the impact it has on other lives."
>
> —Jackie Robinson

"I want a player with guts enough not to fight back," says Rickey.

On April 15, 1947, Jackie Robinson goes to bat for the first time as a major leaguer. He makes four outs, and he doesn't do much better the rest of the week. Has Rickey made a mistake? When the Dodgers go to Philadelphia to play the Phillies, things turn ugly. Phillies' players spew hate language at Robinson. Runners slide into him spikes up; pitchers throw at his head. Robinson keeps his word, and his control. Even Rickey is stunned by the viciousness of some of the attacks: "No player in the history of baseball, I think, has ever been subjected to such vile baiting from opposing benches, such basely unkind criticisms in print. Jackie Robinson plays admirably in spite of it all. He is a credit to baseball, and to America."

By the end of the season, Jackie Robinson is first in the league in stolen bases and second in runs scored. He ties for the team lead in home runs. In September, the Dodgers win the National League pennant. Branch Rickey tells his star, "Jackie, you're on y   now. You can be yourself." Robinson   1 the affection and respect of his fellow ballplayers, and of the nation. "From my own personal experience on the baseball diamond," says Branch Rickey later, "the feeling of intolerance no longer exists. The brotherhood movement is gaining ground every day. It is slowly and surely becoming a fact, and not remaining just a theory."

Rickey and Robinson do much more than integrate baseball; they spotlight the stupidity of prejudice.

An Iron Curtain

American deaths in World War II totaled 234,874. Russia, America's ally, lost 7.7 million people. No nation fought harder against the Nazis than the Russians.

With the war over, everyone hopes for continued friendship between America and Russia. If Russia wants to be communist, and wants to be ruled by dictators in the name of the people, that seems all right to some Americans. But it isn't all right with Winston Churchill, England's great wartime leader. He knows that the goal of communism is world domination.

Right after the war, the victorious armies march into the vanquished lands and take control. In Germany, those in the American and British zones of occupation get aid, they get democracy, they get freedom. Those in the Russian zone have their factories taken over and their skilled workers exported. The Soviets rig elections, jail (or murder) opponents, and control the press. They seal borders, keeping people captive. Britain and the United States work to establish free governments in the lands they occupy; the Soviet army brings totalitarian control to nations they have promised to free. The Soviets also control the media; it's hard to know what is really happening in Russia.

Harry Truman believes Americans need to be informed. In 1946, he asks Winston Churchill if he will speak at tiny Westminster College in Fulton, Missouri. Churchill is eager to do so. He knows people will be listening to what he has to say. He warned the world of Adolf Hitler and Nazism long before most Britons or

Winston Churchill (left) and Harry Truman aboard their special train to Fulton, Missouri, where Churchill gives warning of the "iron curtain" that is separating the Soviet Union from the rest of the world.

Americans understood the danger they represented. Once again, Churchill wants to tell the world of a dangerous dictator and an odious form of government. "A shadow has fallen upon the scenes so lately lighted by the Allied victory," he says to the assembled students. "From Stettin in the Baltic to Trieste in the Adriatic an iron curtain has descended across the Continent."

That curtain is totalitarian rule; its shadow blocks out truth and freedom. The nations behind the curtain—from Bulgaria and Romania on the Black Sea, through Hungary and Czechoslovakia, to Poland and East Germany and the Baltic republics of Latvia, Lithuania, and Estonia in the north—have become prisoners of the Soviet Union. In the years to come, while the free nations of Europe flourish, they will stagnate and decay.

FDR dreamed of a world at peace. Like Woodrow Wilson, he thought a world government could maintain harmony. After World War II, the United Nations is established with the hope that it can be a force for peace. But no state is willing to hand over sovereignty to a world body. The major powers each insist on the power to veto U.N. legislation.

"I do not believe that Soviet Russia desires war. What they desire is the fruits of war and the indefinite expansion of their power and doctrines.... I am convinced that there is nothing they admire so much as strength and there is nothing for which they have less respect than weakness, especially military weakness."

—Winston Churchill

Meanwhile, Harry Truman has to deal with the reality of Soviet communism. While news from Russia is controlled and altered, disturbing rumors nonetheless leak out: stories about artists, writers, former soldiers, and political opponents who are being imprisoned in dreadful camps known as *gulags*, most never to return. Stalin seems to be on a killing spree. Statistics will later emerge suggesting that, in Russia and its satellite nations, as many as 20 million die because of repressive policies.

President Truman decides that the United States must act to stop Soviet Russia from expanding further. He announces that the U.S. will come to the aid of any nation endangered by communism. Here are the president's words to Congress describing the policy that will become known as the Truman Doctrine:

> *Communism is based upon the will of a minority forcibly imposed upon the majority. It relies upon terror and oppression, a controlled press and radio, fixed elections, and the suppression of personal freedoms. I believe that it must be the policy of the United States to support free peoples who are resisting attempted subjugation by armed minorities or by outside pressure.*

The president begins by sending $400 million in emergency aid to Greece and Turkey. The Soviet Union, at the same time, uses military might to intimidate and control Poland, Romania, and other eastern European satellite nations.

Instead of the postwar cooperation FDR hoped for, there is icy competition between Russia and the U.S (now the world's two superpowers). It will lead to a costly arms race and years of tension. It is wasteful of resources, energy, and good will. But, partly because of fear of nuclear devastation, there is no direct fighting between the two nations. The Cold War will last more than forty years.

TRUMAN VERSUS DEWEY

When a political candidate splits his own party he is in trouble—and, in 1948, Harry Truman and the Democratic Party are in triple trouble. Democrats have always been able to count on winning the South—it is known as the "solid South"; no southern state has voted Republican since before the Civil War. Now, because of Truman's civil rights proposals, many southern politicians can't abide their president. They aren't quite ready to turn Republican, but they're certainly against Harry. So they form another party, called the Dixiecrats. Other Democrats are unhappy with the president for other reasons. Some think Truman is too hard on communism—they want the United States to try to get along with Stalin and the Soviet-controlled countries. And they want more reforms at home. These people start a third party—the Progressive Party. This splitting up of Democrats is a recipe for political disaster. Clare Booth Luce, a prominent Republican, says what everyone is thinking: "Mr. Truman's time is short; his situation is hopeless. Frankly, he's a gone goose."

The Democrats have been in power since 1932; most people say it's time for a change. So everyone knows that Harry Truman doesn't have a chance to get elected in 1948. Some Democrats try to dump him. But Harry S. Truman is stubborn. He is head of the party and he is going to run.

The Republicans choose Thomas E. Dewey as their candidate. Dewey is governor of New York. He's a lot younger than Truman, but he acts old and wise. He's dignified. He doesn't say much. He doesn't campaign hard. He just begins to act as if he were president, because everyone is certain he's going to win—except for Harry Truman.

FDR used radio to talk to the American people. Truman isn't a very good speaker on the radio. But he is good in person, especially when he speaks without a prepared speech and just says what he thinks. So he gets on the presidential train, the *Ferdinand Magellan*, and crosses the country—twice. Standing on the train's back platform, the president speaks to anyone and everyone who comes to hear him. He's up and sometimes speaking before six in the morning; often he does ten or fifteen whistle stops in a day. Sometimes he leaves the train for a rally and a city hall luncheon or dinner speech. It's exhausting to everyone except Harry Truman, who gets more feisty and energetic as the campaign continues. He lashes out at the Republican-dominated Congress, which isn't passing the laws he wants, and he attacks those who ask for special government favors: he calls them "power lobbies" and "high hats." Supporters call out, "Give 'em hell, Harry!" And he does.

Still, it looks grim for the Democrats. *Newsweek* magazine asks fifty leading journalists—people whose business it is to know politics—who will win. All fifty predict that it won't be Truman. One of Truman's aides buys Newsweek and reads it on the campaign train; Truman spots it and checks the article. "Don't worry," he says to the aide. "I know every one of those fifty fellows, and not one of them has enough sense to pound sand into a rat hole." The *New York Times* conducts a survey, and concludes that twenty-nine states will go to Dewey, eleven to Truman, and four to the Dixiecrats. The

The *Chicago Daily Tribune* calls the election early, and is wrong.

remaining four (there are forty-eight states in 1948) are undecided. Every important poll shows a Dewey landslide.

On November 2, 1948, the American 306 people vote. That evening, Dewey's supporters crowd into the ballroom of New York's Hotel Roosevelt. They are there to celebrate. In Washington, the Democrats don't even rent their usual hotel ballroom. They're short of money, and there's no point in wasting it—they've got nothing to celebrate. Even before the returns start coming in, reporters file articles congratulating the new president: Tom Dewey. At the *Chicago Tribune*, the morning's headline is set in type: DEWEY DEFEATS TRUMAN. As night arrives, the counting begins. For the first time, results are broadcast on television. But few people have TV sets—even the president doesn't have one. He goes to bed early. When it's announced that he's won in Massachusetts, one of his Secret Service agents wakes him. "Stop worrying," says Truman, and goes back to sleep.

At midnight he wakes and listens to a deep-voiced NBC commentator named H. V Kaltenborn who is saying, "Well, the president is a million votes ahead in the popular vote … but we are very sure that when the country vote comes in Mr. Truman will be defeated by an overwhelming majority." Truman goes back to sleep.

At dawn the radio commentators are saying the election is very close—but they're still predicting a Dewey win. By mid-morning it is clear: the experts are all wrong! This time Truman is no accidental president. He has won the job on his own.

REDS SCARE US AGAIN

When it came to nuclear technology, we in the United States thought it was ours alone. But scientific knowledge doesn't work that way. You can't keep secrets for long. In 1949, Russia tests an atomic device.

Cold-blooded Joseph Stalin, murderer of millions, has the A-bomb. Scary? Terrifying? Yes. People have nightmares thinking about it. Meanwhile, in China, Mao Zedong, a Marxist scholar, soldier, and statesman, leads an army on a Long March across the land. In 1949 he comes to power and China turns communist. Newspapers carry angry letters blaming American foreign policy for the Chinese choice. Fear of communism turns politics and people nasty. Then North Korea, encouraged by communist China, sends an army into South Korea. Everyone knows that appeasement failed in Germany; President Truman, working with the United Nations, decides to stop the North Koreans. War is never officially declared (a disturbing precedent), but the Korean War is definitely a shooting war. The Cold War has developed a hot spot. Communism and democracy don't seem able to coexist on the same world stage. Dread of international communism gets mixed into domestic politics. Some citizens—the Roosevelt haters—are convinced that the New Deal was inspired by communism because its regulations put some limits on capitalism. Now Harry Truman, with his civil rights ideas and a program of liberal reform called the Fair Deal, wants to change society even more. Some people say that those who have the most money will foot the bills for his reforms. His critics say it sounds like communism.

Then communist spies are discovered at home. They have stolen secrets and sold them to Russia. Other shocking news comes from England—some top British intelligence officers turn out to be Soviet spies. And that's not all: in a case that fills newspaper headlines day after day, a former State Department adviser and president of an international peace organizations—a man named Alger Hiss, whom everyone trusted—is convicted of lying about his involvement with an admitted communist.

"Put that in your pipe and smoke it," says this cartoon to Stalin. It's the message of the Marshall Plan and the Truman Doctrine, which states "that we must assist free peoples to work out their own destinies in their own way."

When Hiss is found guilty of perjury, Americans are dismayed. It really does seem possible that the State Department is full of spies and traitors. A few people think communists are about to take over the United States. There's no good reason to believe that. But reason and hysteria are not often bedfellows. Hysteria elbows its adversary onto the floor. And Americans get involved in a witch hunt. It isn't pretty.

Senator Joseph McCarthy of Wisconsin wants people to notice him. He needs an issue, and communism captures headlines. At a speech in Wheeling, West Virginia, he waves a piece of paper and says it contains the names of 205 communists who work in the State Department. He's lying, but many people believe him; after all, he's a U.S. senator. Cameras and microphones make McCarthy an instant celebrity, and, once

The 1954 Army–McCarthy hearings.

he gets started, his stories get bigger and bigger. Before he is finished he will accuse many hundreds of people of communist activity. He never proves a single case. Given the fear of the time, that doesn't seem to matter. Whatever McCarthy says gets printed. And he knows how to use that new medium, television. He waves his arms and accuses. Those cited lose their jobs. Their friends desert them. Their lives are ruined. The few who speak against McCarthy are labeled communist sympathizers.

McCarthy isn't the only one who ignores the Bill of Rights and its protections. The House of Representatives has an Un-American Activities Committee. HUAC decides to investigate the movie industry. During World War II, when Russia was our ally, a number of Americans were attracted to communism. Its Marxist foundation seemed idealistic. Some filmmakers actually were members of the Communist Party; some attended communist meetings out of curiosity, or out of Depression-time fear that capitalism was doomed. Journalists at the time found good things to write about the Russian experiment. Few did anything more than study and dabble. Subversion was never a serious problem in America.

In the McCarthy era, past curiosity becomes enough to get your name put on a blacklist. Those on the blacklists—especially actors, producers, writers, and cameramen—are fired from their jobs. People called before the congressional committee are asked to name others who attended meetings of communist or liberal organizations. Some refuse to answer HUAC's questions; some are sent to jail. In a free country ideas are not criminal, actions can be. But government officials turn cowardly. McCarthy makes a list of 418 American authors who he says have disloyal ideas. His list includes writers like Ernest Hemingway and Henry Thoreau. Thirty-nine states pass anti-communist laws. Texas makes membership in the Communist Party a crime punishable by twenty years in prison. A Connecticut law makes it illegal to criticize the U.S. government or flag. Loyalty oaths are demanded of government workers, including many teachers. It is a time of overlapping fears. Some Americans hate communism so much, they don't seem to care if people's lives are destroyed. Many really do believe the government is full of communists. Two senators speak against McCarthy and are defeated. Eight senators McCarthy supports are elected. Then Senator Margaret Chase Smith of Maine stands up in Congress and says:

Margaret Chase Smith

> I think it is high time that we remembered that the Constitution speaks not only of the freedom of speech but also of trial by jury instead of trial by accusation…. I am not proud of the way we smear outsiders from the floor of the Senate and … place ourselves beyond criticism.

McCarthy keeps attacking. He holds hearings accusing the army and many of its officers and soldiers of being communist sympathizers. But he produces only an army dentist who may, at one time, have been a sympathizer. Television, a new feature in many homes, lets people see the Army–McCarthy hearings and the senator in action: bullying, shouting, and sneering. Finally a quiet, elderly man, respected in his home state of Vermont but little known elsewhere, speaks out in the Senate. His

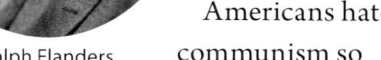
Ralph Flanders

name is Ralph Flanders. "He dons his war paint," he says of McCarthy. "He goes into his war dance. He emits war whoops. He goes forth to battle and proudly returns with the scalp of a pink dentist." Flanders asks the Senate to censure McCarthy. (One senator immediately says that Flanders must be on the side of the communists.) By this time most Americans have had enough of McCarthy. In 1954, the Senate votes to condemn him for "conduct contrary to the senatorial tradition." The man who has terrorized so wantonly now seems tragically silly.

Separate and Unequal

Some people call the decade "the nifty fifties." Elvis Presley—a white boy from Mississippi who sings black music with talent and energy—is dubbed king of rock and roll, and rock and roll is soon shaking, rattling, and rolling all over the world. Then there are hula hoops, a bombshell movie star named Marilyn Monroe, TV stars Lucille Ball and Ed Sullivan, and fast food (by 1955, McDonald's has sold one million hamburgers). A vaccine developed by Jonas Salk conquers polio, the disease that crippled Franklin Delano Roosevelt and usually targets children. Jobs are plentiful, and lots of people have money. The gross national product doubles between 1946 and 1956. The United States has 6 percent of the world's population, but it makes two-thirds of the world's manufactured goods (and consumes one-third of them). No nation has ever seen broad-based affluence like this. Americans are eating better (and more), life expectancies are stretching, and so is the young generation's measured height. A new middle class includes 60 percent of all Americans. Forty million babies are born in the fifties, in a baby boom that makes the country younger. Most Americans dream of owning their own home; now mass-produced suburbs

Elvis Presley

In 1952, Eisenhower (inset) is nominated as Republican presidential candidate at the first national convention covered on TV (shown above).

with affordable houses make the dream come true. And you can't live in the suburbs without a car. Cars get bigger, better, and fancier. Grandma and Grandpa remember horse-and-buggy days. Their children have two or sometimes three cars in the garage. Then there is television. In 1950 only 10 percent of American homes have a TV. Ten years later, 90 percent do!

In 1953, a wartime hero, General Dwight D. Eisenhower, becomes president. Ike ends the fighting in Korea. No one has

> "No State shall ... abridge the privileges ... of citizens of the United States ... nor deny to any person within its jurisdiction the equal protection of the laws."
>
> —from the Fourteenth Amendment to the Constitution

really won. Korea is still divided, as it was when the war began. The United States and the United Nations have proved what they set out to prove, though: they will stand up to communist aggression. (And Eisenhower has shown courage in getting out of a war.) Times are good.

But one suburban mom is conflicted. She is a labor journalist and aware that America's working women—often African-Americans, Latinas, or poor whites—are paid salaries way below their male peers. Betty Friedan is also aware that many nonworking, middle-class suburban women feel left out of the national excitement. Most high-level careers—in law firms, in the medical profession, in corporate America, and elsewhere—are closed to women. Friedan is writing about some of this in labor publications; later she will write a book that will influence and change most American women.

Besides the inequality of the sexes in the marketplace, something else is wrong in America. Back in 1896, the Supreme Court made a decision in the case of *Plessy* v. *Ferguson* that would change millions of lives-and not for the better. Homer Plessy, a man with white skin but some black ancestry, was arrested for sitting in a whites-only railroad car. The Fourteenth Amendment to the Constitution says:

> *All persons born or naturalized in the United States ... are citizens of the United States and of the State wherein they reside. No State shall make or enforce any law which shall abridge the privileges or immunities of citizens of the United States, nor shall any State deprive any person of life, liberty,*

> *or property, without due process of law; nor deny to any person within its jurisdiction the equal protection of the laws.*

In *Plessy*, the majority of the court says, in Justice Henry Billings Brown's words:

> *The absolute equality of the two races before the law ... could not have been intended to abolish distinctions based upon color, or to enforce social ... equality, or a commingling of the two races.*

That means that although the races are equal before the law, laws can prevent them from mingling. The *Plessy* v. *Ferguson* decision makes segregation legal. Jim Crow has the approval of the highest court. Justice John Marshall Harlan, who writes the only dissenting opinion in *Plessy* v. *Ferguson*, doesn't agree. "Our Constitution is color-blind, and neither knows nor tolerates classes among citizens."

By the 1940s, the hypocrisy of "separate but equal" is apparent to all fair-minded people. It is painfully unfair to those who have to live with it. One of them is Charles Hamilton Houston, a graduate of Amherst College and Harvard Law School who takes his education still further and gets a Ph.D. Even with all those degrees, Houston doesn't have a chance of getting a job with a mainstream law firm. His skin color makes it impossible. But Houston has no desire to be a corporate lawyer. He has studied law because he wants to effect changes. He believes Jim Crow should be tried, convicted, sentenced, and hanged—and that only the courts can do it. He becomes an expert in constitutional law and then, as dean of Howard University's law school, trains a generation of black lawyers to be experts, too. Houston is so tough his students call him "cement pants." "He made it clear to all of us that when we were done we were expected to go out and do something with our lives," says one of his students, Thurgood Marshall. Marshall, the great-grandson of a slave, will make his professor proud.

BROWN V. BOARD OF EDUCATION

Linda Carol Brown—who is seven years old and lives in Topeka, Kansas—has to walk across railroad tracks and take an old bus to get to school, even though there is a better school five blocks from her house. Linda can't go to that school because she is black, and the schools in Topeka are segregated. In 1951, Linda's father, the Reverend Oliver Brown, goes to court to try to do something about it. Their case becomes known as *Brown* v. *Board of Education of Topeka, Kansas*.

South Carolina's Clarendon County spends $43 a year on each of its black students. It spends $179 a year on each white student. The white children all have school desks; in two of the black schools there are no desks at all. Harry and Liza Briggs and twenty other black parents sue the Clarendon County school board. They want equal funding for the black schools. They sue in the name of ten-year-old Harry Briggs, Jr., and sixty-six other children. Right away, Liza Briggs is fired from her job. So are most of the other adults who sign the lawsuit that is titled *Briggs* v. *Clarendon County*.

Barbara Rose Johns, a junior at Moton High School in Farmville, Virginia, is angry about conditions at her school: it was built for 200 students, but holds 450. There is no cafeteria and no gym. The highest-paid teachers at Moton receive less than the lowest paid teachers at Farmville's white

The 1954 Supreme Court justices, led by Earl Warren (bottom center and inset), who handed down the historic *Brown* v. *Board of Education* ruling in an unusual unanimous decision.

schools. Barbara Johns gets the students at Moton to go on strike for a better school. They walk out of their classes. A member of the NAACP comes to Farmville to calm them down, but is so impressed with their determination that he helps 117 Moton students sue the state of Virginia. They demand that the state abolish segregated schools. Their case is called *Davis v. School Board of Prince Edward County*, because the first of the students listed is fourteen-year-old Dorothy E. Davis.

Each of these cases is defeated in court, but that doesn't stop the plaintiffs. They appeal their cases all the way to the United States Supreme Court. There they are grouped with two other cases dealing with school segregation. Together the five suits are called by the name of the first of them: *Brown v. Board of Education*. Thurgood Marshall, Charles Houston's star pupil, is the lawyer who reads the opening argument in the case. It is December 9, 1952. Does segregation contradict the ideas behind the Constitution? Marshall and the lawyers for the NAACP say it does. They say that the Fourteenth Amendment—which guarantees all citizens equal protection under the law—makes the doctrine of "separate but equal" unconstitutional. Moreover, says Marshall, segregated schools can never be truly equal, because separating people makes them feel unequal and inferior. "Like a cancer, segregation destroys the morale of our citizens and disfigures our country throughout the world," says Marshall.

A year passes. It looks as if the Supreme Court may be split. This issue is dividing the whole country. If the court splits, it will make those divisions worse. Then President Eisenhower names a new chief justice to the Supreme Court. He is Earl Warren, a former California governor and a mild-mannered man, not expected to be a dynamic chief justice. Some who know him well, though, realize he has a gift for leadership. On May 17, 1954, Chief Justice Warren reads the court's decision in *Brown v. Board of Education:*

> *Does segregation of children in public schools solely on the basis of race deprive children of the minority group of equal educational opportunities? We believe that it does. We conclude, unanimously, that the doctrine of "separate but equal" has no place. Separate educational facilities are inherently unequal.*

The new chief justice has convinced all the justices that, because of the importance of this decision, it should be unanimous. It is, as the *Washington Post* says the next day in an editorial, "a new birth of freedom."

But laws have to be enforced, and some people are determined not to enforce this one. Virginia's Prince Edward County closes all its public schools—for five years—rather than integrate the schools. White children are educated in "private" white academies, funded with public tax dollars. Black children are denied any schooling at all.

Outside the Supreme Court on May 18, 1954, the headline reads: HIGH COURT BANS SEGREGATION IN PUBLIC SCHOOLS. Nettie Hunt talks to her daughter Nikie about the decision affirming "the underlying American faith in the equality of all men and all children before the law."

It is a difficult time for moderate Southern whites. Those who speak against segregation often lose jobs and friends. Moderates go into hiding. McCarthy has helped make these conforming times. People keep silent while others are abused. In some places, when black children march into integrated schools, grownups insult them, or throw stones. Decent folks hide their heads in shame, or just pretend it isn't happening. *Brown* v. *Board of Education* may be a new birth of freedom, but the baby is having a hard time breathing on its own.

Young girls line up in an integrated classroom at Barnard School, Washington, D.C., in May of 1955. Behind them lounge the boys of the class.

PART 14

LET FREEDOM RING

It is 1954 (the very year that Congress votes to add the words "under God" to the Pledge of Allegiance). A young man named Martin Luther King, Jr., is on his way to the Dexter Avenue Baptist Church in Montgomery, Alabama, to take his first job as a minister. King will soon receive a doctorate in theology from Boston University; he is qualified to teach the subject at a college level, but he has decided he'd rather be a preacher than a teacher. His father—a sharecropper's son who has turned himself into one of the South's leading blacks—would like his son to join him as assistant pastor at his prestigious church in Atlanta. Martin Jr. wants to start his career on his own at a small church in a quiet city. What he doesn't know is that the city he has picked is about to make a big noise. Soon everyone in America will hear about Montgomery and its young minister.

BOYCOTT

Rosa Parks works as a tailor's assistant in a department store in Montgomery. She is a small, soft-voiced woman of forty-three who wears rimless glasses and pulls her brown hair back in a bun. Parks is a civil rights activist who has been secretary of the local chapter of the NAACP (National Association for the Advancement of Colored People). She is well known and well respected in the black community. But on the evening of December 1, 19 55, Mrs. Parks is just tired. She has put in a full day at her job as a seamstress, she doesn't feel well, and her neck and back hurt. She gets on a bus and heads home.

In 1955, buses in the southern states are segregated. Laws say that the seats in the front are for whites and, when the bus is full, whites get priority on all seats. On that December day, a white man boards Rosa Parks's bus

Rosa Parks—who cleaned class rooms to pay for her own junior high education—gets fingerprinted at the Montgomery police station.

> "This is what I wanted to know: when and how would we ever determine our rights as human beings?"
> —Rosa Parks

and the driver asks her to give her seat to him. Parks won't budge. She knows she will get in trouble, perhaps even end up in prison, but she keeps her seat. The bus driver calls the police. Rosa Parks is arrested and is soon on her way to jail. "Why do you push us around?" she asks the arresting officer. She knows that African-Americans are regularly beaten and abused in Montgomery's jail. It doesn't seem to matter to Parks. She's tired of riding on segregated buses. She's tired of being pushed around. She's ready to go to jail.

When people in Montgomery hear of Rosa Parks's arrest, they are stunned. Mild-mannered, dignified Mrs. Parks? E. D. Nixon, a former president of the Montgomery NAACP chapter, raises bond money to get her out of jail. But she will have to stand trial. He asks her if she will let the NAACP use her case to fight segregation. They both know that African-Americans who stand up for their rights are usually harassed and sometimes lynched. Her husband says, "The white folks will kill you, Rosa," but Parks thinks it over and says quietly, "I'll go along with you, Mr. Nixon."

Jo Ann Robinson is sick of the humiliation that comes with being sent to the back of a bus. As soon as she hears about Rosa Parks, Robinson begins organizing a boycott of the buses. She and some friends stay up most of the night printing leaflets asking everyone in the black community not to ride the buses on the following Monday, the day of Rosa Parks's trial. On Sunday, Montgomery's Negro ministers also urge their parishioners to stay off the buses on Monday. They know that won't be easy. Those who ride buses are mostly poor people. They need to get to work. Some are elderly. It is December; it is cold; many will have to walk miles. And they all fear white violence.

But something unexpected happens in Montgomery. Like Rosa Parks, black people no longer seem afraid. They have had enough. They stay off the buses on Monday. (Parks is convicted that day of violating Montgomery's segregation laws and is fined $14.) They stay off the buses on Tuesday. They

Martin Luther King, Jr.

After the bus boycott, Mrs. Parks gets to ride in the front of the bus. Her troubles aren't over. She loses her job as a seamstress, and her family is harassed and threatened.

stay off them all week. And all month. And on and on, in rain and cold and sleet and through the heat of the summer. They share rides; they work out carpools; they walk. "White zealots respond. Houses are burned, churches are bombed, shots are fired. Montgomery's jail fills with people whose crime is riding in a carpool. African-Americans keep walking. It is the twenty-six-year-old pastor of the Dexter Avenue Baptist Church, Martin Luther King, Jr., who has been heading the boycott. The black community looks to its ministers, and this man has an idea that is pointing him in a clear direction.

When King was a seminary student he learned about India's great leader Mohandas (Mahatma) Gandhi. Gandhi was inspired by America's Henry David

> "With understanding, good will and Christian love, we can integrate the buses with no difficulty.... I want Montgomery to prove to the world that we will refuse to hit back."
>
> —Reverend Dr. Martin Luther King Jr.

Thoreau, whose book *Civil Disobedience* describes the power of nonviolent protest. Thoreau believed that "one honest man" can create great change. Gandhi, a small squeaky-voiced lawyer, was the kind of man Thoreau envisioned. He led his countrymen in peaceful boycotts and marches attempting to end British colonial rule in India. British soldiers taunted, beat, and jailed Gandhi and his followers, who never lost their composure. The British were prepared for violence; they weren't prepared for passive resistance. They lost the moral high ground and were made to look like bullies. Gandhi's courage and calm dignity defeated the guns and cannons of a mighty empire. India became free.

King was moved by Gandhi's achievement. The Christian philosopher Reinhold Niebuhr, writing on morality in the modem world, convinces King that white society will respond only to pressure. And King's devotion to Christianity makes him believe in the power of love and brotherhood. For him, nonviolent protest is the righteous way to fight evil. But his followers soon discover that protesting peacefully takes far more courage than throwing rocks.

"We are not here advocating violence," says King to his flock in Montgomery. "The only weapon that we have … is the weapon of protest.... the great glory of American democracy is the right to protest for right." While the segregationists kick cars, set off bombs, and shout invective, Montgomery's black community protests with calm, unflinching courage. They maintain their dignity. They don't fight back. Television crews film what is happening. Soon people around the nation, and abroad, too, are watching the people of Montgomery march to work; march to carpool centers, get arrested, and march to jail.

"There are those who would try to make of this a hate campaign," Dr. King says to Montgomery's blacks. "This is not a war between the white and the Negro but a conflict between justice and injustice. If we are arrested every day, if we are exploited every day, don't ever let anyone pull you so low as to hate them. We must use the weapon of love." That weapon triumphs.

Thirteen months after Rosa Parks's arrest, the Supreme Court rules that segregation on Alabama buses is unconstitutional. The boycott is over. Martin Luther King, Jr., along with other leaders of the movement, black and white, climbs aboard Montgomery's first integrated bus—and they all sit up front. "We are glad to have you this morning," says the white driver. The people of Montgomery have not only changed their town, they have changed their times.

A Class Act

In the Supreme Court's 1954 decision *Brown v. Board of Education*, the justices said that integration of schools should take place with "all deliberate speed." But they didn't set the rate of speed. The southern states decide "deliberate speed" means with the speed of a snail. So, in 1957, there are still no classrooms in the Deep South where black kids and white kids sit together. Then a federal judge issues a court order: schools in Little Rock, Arkansas, are to be integrated.

Little Rock's Central High is one of the South's finest public schools. It has generous playing fields, modern facilities, and more than 2,000 students. But no black child has ever gone there. Melba Pattillo wants to go to Central High. Later, she wrote: "They had more equipment, they had five floors of opportunities. I understood education before I understood anything else. From the time I was two my mother said, 'You will go to college. Education is your key to survival,' and I understood that." Otherwise, Melba said, she had no "overwhelming desire to … integrate this school and change history." But fifteen-year-old Melba will change history. She becomes one of nine black children picked to go to Central High. At first, she doesn't expect problems; neither do most people. Little Rock's citizens believe their city has good race relations. But some people aren't ready for integration, and they are willing to use threats, insults, and even rocks to stop it.

The governor of Arkansas, Orval Faubus, calls in the state militia—not to protect the black students who are about to enter Central High, but to keep them out. He knows that he will lose white votes if he appears to back integration. Because of Jim Crow, most blacks can't vote so their needs don't matter to him. "The mission of the state militia is to maintain or restore order and to protect the lives and property of citizens," he says. "But I must state here in all sincerity that it is my conviction that it will not be possible to restore or maintain order if forcible integration is carried out in the schools of this community." The governor is making it clear: he will not enforce the law of the land.

Despite the governor, a federal court order says that desegregation must proceed in Little Rock. September 23 is to be the first day of integration. On that day the nine children get ready to enter Central High.

"The amazing thing about our movement is that it is a protest of the people. It is not a one-man show. It is not the preachers' show. It's the people. The masses of this town, who are tired of being trampled on, are responsible."

—Jo Ann Robinson, 1955

Elizabeth Eckford goes to school on her first day. Her family had no phone, so she didn't know that the nine kids were to meet in a different spot that morning.

One of them, slim, shy Elizabeth Eckford, hasn't gotten the message that the black students are to go into the school together. She is wearing a starched new black-and-white cotton dress for her first day at school, and she is alone at one end of the building. Elizabeth holds her head high and tries to walk up to the school door. Adults scream awful words. A woman spits. Some boys threaten to lynch her. The governor's militiamen stare at her, but make no move to help. Elizabeth runs back to the curb. There, a *New York Times* reporter puts his arm around her. "Don't let them see you cry," he whispers. A white woman (who is dismayed by what is happening) takes Elizabeth back home.

Melba Pattillo is with the seven others who are ready to enter the school. Before they do, four young blacks are seen heading toward Central High. A group of thugs is waiting for them. "Here come the niggers," they shout, and beat them up. They have mistaken four journalists for high school students. In the confusion, the eight enter the school through a side door. This is how Melba remembered that day:

The first day I was able to enter Central High School, what I felt inside was terrible, wrenching, awful fear. On the car radio I could hear that there was a mob. I knew what a mob meant and I knew that the sounds that came from the crowd were very angry. So we entered the side of the building, very, very fast. Even as we entered there were people running after us, people tripping other people.... There has never been in my life any stark terror or any fear akin to that.

In Washington, President Eisenhower doesn't want to take sides. He says he believes in persuasion. But there is no persuading the lawbreakers who stand vigil outside Central High. They are determined to keep black children out. Finally, the president acts. "Mob rule cannot be allowed to override the decisions of our courts," he says.

He orders federal troops sent to Little Rock. On September 25, under the protection of the U.S. military, the nine African-American students are escorted to Central High School. "The troops were wonderful," said Melba Pattillo. "I went in not through the side doors but up the front stairs, and there was a feeling of pride and hope that yes, this is the United States; yes, there is a reason I salute the flag; and it's going to be okay."

Ernest Green, another of the nine, remembered the convoy that took him to school. There was a jeep in front and a jeep behind.

> They both had machine gun mounts.... the whole school was ringed with paratroopers and helicopters hovering around. We marched up the steps ... with this circle of soldiers with bayonets drawn.... Walking up the steps that day was probably one of the biggest feelings I've ever had.

When Melba Pattillo got to her English class, "One boy jumped up to his feet and began to talk. He told the others to walk out with him because a 'nigger' was in their class. The teacher told him to leave the room." Melba went on, "The boy started for the door and shouted: 'Who's going with me?' No one did. So he said in disgust, 'Chicken!' and left. I had a real nice day." Nice days didn't come often. The students were harassed inside the school as well as out. But they stuck it out. At the end of that year, Ernest Green became the first black person to graduate from Central High. "I figured I was making a statement and

Governor Faubus refuses to obey federal orders. "It is time," says one senator, "for the South to face up to the fact that it belongs to the Union and comply with the Constitution."

> "A popular Government, without popular information, or the means of acquiring it, is but a prologue to a Farce or a Tragedy; or perhaps both. Knowledge will forever govern ignorance: And a people who mean to be their own Governors, must arm themselves with the power which knowledge gives."
> —James Madison, 1822

helping black people's existence in Little Rock," he said. "I kept telling myself, I just can't trip with all those cameras watching me. But I knew that once I got as far as that principal and received that diploma, I had cracked the wall."

Heeding the First Amendment

Amendment I: *Congress Shall Make No Law … abridging the Freedom of Speech, or of the Press*

On February 1, 1960, four college students enter F. W. Woolworth's in Greensboro, North Carolina, sit at the lunch counter, and order coffee. Because they are black, and because the store's policy is not to serve blacks, they are ignored. The four sit quietly until closing time. The next morning they are back, this time with five friends. They keep coming back. They are waiting, they say, for coffee. "Whites gather behind them taunting, poking, pouring ketchup on their heads, throwing cigarette butts, spewing nastiness. The sit-in, as it is labeled, spreads to other lunch counters in other places. Soon there are sleep-ins in segregated motel lobbies, read-ins in segregated public libraries, swim-ins on segregated public beaches, and watch-ins in segregated theaters. Then, in May, six Woolworth counters in Nashville, Tennessee, are integrated. In June, Virginia's Hot Shoppes decide to seat Negroes. In July, the Greensboro Woolworth's (where it all started) begins serving all customers. But the response is not widespread. In October, when Martin Luther King, Jr., leads a sit-in in Atlanta, he and fifty-one others are jailed. Dr. King is charged with tax irregularities in the first felony tax-evasion case in Alabama history.

In the midst of the sit-ins, the *New York Times* accepts a full-page ad from an organization called the Committee to Defend Martin Luther King and the Struggle for Freedom in the South. It is titled HEED THEIR VOICES; it is an appeal for funds. It says, "thousands of Southern Negro students are engaged in widespread nonviolent demonstrations in positive affirmation of the right to live in human dignity as guaranteed by the U.S. Constitution." The ad describes some of the sit-ins, along with the abusive treatment that they provoke. The ad also tells of attacks on Dr. King. "They have bombed his home almost killing his wife and child. They have assaulted him in person. They have arrested him seven times—for 'speeding,' 'loitering,' and similar 'offenses.' … They have charged him with perjury—a felony under which they could imprison him for ten years."

Sixty-four people, including Eleanor Roosevelt and Jackie Robinson, sign their names. While the ad speaks of "Southern violators of the Constitution," it does not criticize anyone by name. But in Montgomery, Alabama, City Commissioner L. B. Sullivan, who's in charge of the police, takes the ad personally. Sullivan sues the *Times* and four black clergymen for damages, claiming he has been libeled; he demands "a full and fair retraction."

Some of the facts in the ad are untrue. It says that students protesting segregation sang "My Country, 'Tis of Thee" on the steps of the Alabama Capitol. The truth is, they sang "The Star Spangled Banner." The ad says students were expelled from school for leading protests. They were actually expelled for participating in a sit-in. There are other, similar mistakes. A few of those whose names are on the ad did not see it in advance. The *New York Times* publishes corrections and an apology. The case goes to trial and the Alabama jury returns a judgment for

Sullivan amounting to half a million dollars from each of the defendants. And there's a problem that goes beyond the monetary damage. If papers are subject to libel when they don't get minute details exactly right, it will greatly inhibit news writing.

The *Times* appeals all the way to the U.S. Supreme Court. It is a tricky case, libel being fraught with ambiguities. In a brief supporting the *Times*, the *Washington Post* argues that papers are likely to hold back critical articles if they can only escape libel suits when stories are "absolutely confirmable in every detail."

Four years after the initial suit, the high court brings in a decision. It is 9 to 0. Justice William J. Brennan, writing for the court, says "erroneous statement is inevitable in free debate." Libel "must be measured by standards that satisfy the First Amendment." And: "we consider this case against the background of a profound national commitment to the principle that debate on public issues should be uninhibited, robust, and wide-open, and that it may well include vehement, caustic, and sometimes unpleasantly sharp attacks on government and public officials." What it means is that the First Amendment guarantee of a free press is to be broad and generous. Public officials cannot claim defamatory compensation for criticism of their official conduct, unless they can prove actual malice.

The *Times* has won far more than just a libel case. This decision revolutionizes libel law. Journalist Anthony Lewis, in a splendid book about the case, *Make No Law*, says "it treated free speech not just as an individual right, but as a political necessity." Legal historian Kermit L. Hall says it was "not only a triumph for free expression, it was a triumph for civil rights and racial equality as well." For those who argued that in a nation founded on the idea of citizen rule, free access to information is essential, the *Sullivan* decision was indeed a triumph. Philosopher Alexander Meiklejohn, who had long argued that the Constitution makes the people their own governors, said of the decision, "It is an occasion for dancing in the streets."

The *Sullivan* decision becomes a precedent in other cases. In *Cohen* v. *California*, a case dealing with offensive printed speech, Justice John Marshall Harlan (grandson of the dissenting judge in *Plessy* v. *Ferguson*) writes the majority opinion: "While the particular four-letter word being litigated here is perhaps more distasteful than most others of its genre, it is nevertheless often true that one man's vulgarity is another's lyric." Citing the First Amendment, Justice Harlan continues, "The constitutional right of free expression is powerful medicine in a society as diverse and populous as ours. It is designed and intended to remove governmental restraints from the arena of public discussion, putting the decision as to what views shall be voiced largely into the hands of each of us."

The sit-in at Woolworth's lunch counter in Greensboro, North Carolina.

Ask What You Can Do

It is bitterly cold and snow falls heavily in Washington, D.C. on January 19, 1961. That evening the army and navy are called and 3,000 servicemen, using 700 snowplows and trucks, work through the night. The next day the temperature stays below freezing and snow is piled high, but the streets and the sky are clear. At noon, some 20,000 guests fill wooden bleachers set up in front of the Capitol. The winter sun shines on the banks of new snow and wind nips at people's cheeks. It is Inauguration Day. America's favorite poet, Robert Frost, has written a special poem for the occasion.

> *Summoning artists to participate*
> *In the august occasions of the state*
> *Seems something for us all to celebrate.*

Most of the presidential party wears scarves and mittens with their top hats and formal clothes. But the president-elect seems to generate his own warmth. He takes off his overcoat before he speaks. Then John Fitzgerald Kennedy puts his hand on his grandfather's Bible and swears to uphold his mighty responsibilities. At forty-three, he is the youngest president since Theodore Roosevelt and the youngest man ever elected president. Harvard-educated JFK, the son of a wealthy businessman, has been given every advantage our society has to give. But the silver spoons that fed him have not sapped his ambition. He and the other members of the large Kennedy family have been trained to serve their country and to achieve.

The nation wants him to succeed. Not since the days of Franklin Roosevelt's New Deal have so many eager people clamored

John F. Kennedy

to join the political process. The new cabinet is going to be bipartisan, embracing people from both political parties. Some of Kennedy's college professors are leaving their classrooms to become government officials. Thousands of Americans hope to be part of the excitement that seems to be building. Kennedy has already suggested a "peace corps," a volunteer agency that will let Americans share their experience and knowledge with less fortunate nations. The young president, with his intense blue eyes, his thick head of hair, and his engaging smile, steps up to the lectern and begins to speak in strong, self-confident New England tones. He challenges his listeners:

> We observe today not a victory of party but a celebration of freedom.... Let the word go forth from this time and place, to friend and foe alike, that the torch has been passed to a new generation of Americans, born in this century, tempered by war, disciplined by a hard and bitter peace, proud of our ancient heritage, and unwilling to witness or permit the slow undoing of those human rights to which this nation has always been committed.... Let every nation know, whether it wishes us well or ill, that we shall pay any price, bear any burden, meet any hardship, support any friend, oppose any foe to assure the survival and success of liberty.... Let us begin anew ... remembering on both sides that civility is not a sign of weakness.... If a free society cannot help the many who are poor, it cannot save the few who are rich.... And so, my fellow Americans, ask not what your country can do for you, ask what you can do for your country. My fellow citizens of the world: ask not what America will do for you, but what together we can do for the freedom of man.

> "The United States is today the country that assumes the destiny of man.... For the first time, a country has become the world's leader without achieving this through conquest, and it is strange to think that for thousands of years one single country has found power while seeking only justice."
>
> —André Malraux, French politician and man of letters, on a visit to President Kennedy, 1962

On that bright January afternoon, hope vibrates in the air. When Kennedy notices that there are no black cadets among the Coast Guard marchers in the inaugural parade, his first act as president is to call an aide and ask him to do something about it. In September there is a black professor and several black cadets at the Coast Guard Academy. This president intends that the nation reach for greatness within itself. He surrounds himself with men and women who will be called "the best and the brightest." He expects to accomplish big things.

Cuba and the Cold War

It is just nineteen days after his inauguration and President Kennedy is relaxing next to the swimming pool at his father's home in Palm Beach, Florida. The head of the Central Intelligence Agency (CIA) spreads out some maps for him to see. That's when the president hears for the first time that plans have been made to invade the island of Cuba.

A year and a half before this, Cuba fell to a revolutionary government. At the time, many Cubans—and Americans—were hopeful. It seemed as if nothing could be worse than Cuba's old, corrupt government, which let a few make fortunes and kept most Cubans poor. The new leader, Fidel

the island the Cuban people will rise up and overthrow Castro. President Kennedy doesn't want to seem soft on communism; he agrees to go ahead with the CIA plan.

The CIA is sloppy, though, and Castro learns of the plans in advance. The operation, at a place on Cuba's coast called the Bay of Pigs, is one bungle after another. Castro is ready to meet the invasion; the Cuban people don't rise up; 114 Americans die; more than a thousand are captured. The president takes the blame. "This administration intends to be candid about its errors," he says. "For, as a wise man once said, 'An error doesn't become a mistake

Below, Fidel Castro and Nikita Khrushchev. On the right, a photograph taken by a U.S. U-2 spy plane of a nuclear missile site being built by the Soviets in Cuba.

until you refuse to correct it.'" The president's popularity ratings soar.

But the U.S. will pay a ransom of $53 million in food and medical supplies to get the captives released. The president is furious. He puts his brother, Bobby Kennedy, in charge of Operation Mongoose: American operatives sneak into Cuba by parachute and boat and plant bombs, set fires, and contaminate sugar fields. Their attempts to assassinate Castro fail. It's another fiasco. Meanwhile, people around the world wonder about Kennedy. Is this well-to-do young man strong enough to be president?

Russia's leader, Nikita Khrushchev, is sure he isn't. Khrushchev is angry at what he believes are U.S. efforts to intimidate Russia through the arms race. When it comes to nuclear warheads, the U.S. has a seventeen-to-one advantage over the U.S.S.R. U.S. missiles in Turkey point menacingly at Russia. The Cuban situation has added to the Soviets' outrage. Khrushchev decides to do something bold. Working with Castro, he makes plans to put nuclear missiles on Cuba and aim them at the United States' most important cities and military targets. In October 1962, American U-2 planes, flying thirteen miles high, take photographs of the island showing sixteen ballistic missiles in place. (The CIA doesn't know it, but there are more missiles than that-as well as 42,000 Russian soldiers and pilots.) Then a Russian submarine and twenty-three freighters, presumed to be carrying nuclear warheads

> "We had installed enough missiles already to destroy New York, Chicago, and the other huge industrial cities, not to mention a little village like Washington."
> —Nikita Khrushchev in his 1970 memoir, *Khrushchev Remembers*

Space Race

When Yuri Gagarin drops into a meadow on April 12, 1961, he scares a cow and startles two farm workers. Anya Taakhtarova asks the man in the orange flight suit if he's fallen from outer space. "Yes, would you believe it, I have," says the affable Soviet cosmonaut, who has a boyish grin and is an immediate world hero. Actually, he has orbited the earth in one hour and forty-eight minutes.

Many Americans feel chagrin. How did the Russians manage to do this? Why weren't we first? On May 25, President Kennedy goes before Congress and says, "I believe this nation should commit itself to achieving the goal, before this decade is out, of landing a man on the moon and returning him safely to earth." It sounds like pie-in-the-sky wishful thinking. But, five months before the end of the decade, American astronauts Neil Armstrong and Edwin "Buzz" Aldrin step out onto the moon. They take pictures, gather rocks, plant an American flag, and come home safely. It's an astonishing achievement.

In October 1962, Kennedy announces a blockade of all ships carrying offensive weapons to Cuba. Will Russia back down?

for the Cuban missiles, are sighted at sea. What should the president do? He knows that the wrong move could start World War III. The joint chiefs of staff want to bomb Cuba; Kennedy says he will not drop the first bomb. But he will react if attacked: "It shall be the policy of this nation," he says, "to regard any nuclear missile launched from Cuba against any nation in the western hemisphere as an attack by the Soviet Union on the United States requiring a full retaliation response upon the Soviet Union."

The president is firm. He tells the Russians the missiles must be removed. He gives Khrushchev time to make a decision. Secretly he agrees to remove the U.S. missiles threatening Russia from Turkey. American forces are put on high alert. More than fifty bombers, each carrying thermo-nuclear bombs, are in the air. For thirteen tense days, the world holds its breath. Some Americans ready fall-out shelters and stock up on supplies. Fear of nuclear war is widespread—and justified. Then the Russian ships, in mid-ocean, turn around. The missiles in Cuba are dismantled and removed. Secretary of State Dean Rusk says to an associate: "We were eyeball to eyeball and I think the other fellow just blinked."

Kennedy is now determined that both Russia and the United States sign a treaty agreeing to stop testing nuclear devices. He knows that no one can win a nuclear war. The Soviet Union keeps testing, and it seems as if the United States will be compelled to go on testing too. Then Kennedy makes a speech to his fellow citizens that is heard around the world.

> *Let us reexamine our attitude toward the Soviet Union.... The wave of the future is not the conquest of the world by a single creed but the liberation of the diverse energies of free nations and free men.*

Some Americans can't imagine getting along with Russia. Kennedy says there is no alternative:

> *Some say it is useless to speak of world peace. I realize that the pursuit of peace is not as dramatic as pursuit of war ... but we have no more urgent task.... we all inhabit this small planet. We all breathe the same air. We all cherish our children's future. And we all are mortal.*

A few weeks later, and a year after the Cuban missile crisis, Khrushchev accepts a U.S. proposal for a test-ban treaty. "This treaty … is particularly for our children and grandchildren," says Kennedy. "And they have no lobby in Washington."

Freedom Comes to Birmingham

In 1960, a *New York Times* reporter writing of life in Birmingham, Alabama, says: "Whites and blacks still walk the same streets. But the streets, the water supply, and the sewer system are about the only public facilities they share."

It is hot, very hot in Birmingham in the summer of 1962. But that doesn't seem to

One of the demonstrators picketing outside a segregated restaurant ("I solicit your business") carries a message board that says: I CAN COOK THE FOOD, BUT I CAN'T EAT IT.

Gideon Blows His Horn

Clarence Earl Gideon is arrested in Florida for breaking and entering a poolroom and stealing liquor and cash. Gideon, who has three children and a wife who is an alcoholic, has been in and out of jail much of his life. He says he isn't guilty, but he has no money to hire an attorney and asks the court to provide him with counsel. Gideon insists it is his constitutional right and he never wavers in that belief, or in his passion for justice.

But Gideon is wrong. According to a 1942 Supreme Court decision in a case called *Betts* v. *Brady*, state courts are required only to provide counsel to indigents in "special circumstances." There's nothing special about Clarence Gideon. Florida refuses to grant him a lawyer; he must defend himself

Gideon is convicted. From his jail cell he petitions the Supreme Court. He prints in bold letters using a pencil on prison stationery stamped ONLY 2 LETTERS EACH WEEK. Gideon's punctuation and spelling are unique, but his message is clear: he believes he has not had a fair trial. He says his conviction violates the due process clause of the Fourteenth Amendment. He has already appealed to the Florida Supreme Court for a writ of habeas corpus, asking to be freed on the ground that he was illegally imprisoned. He has been turned down.

Petitions to the Supreme Court follow a set procedure. To begin, forty copies must be filed. But the court shows concern for those without the means to comply. A federal law allows for a special category of cases, *in forma pauperis* (in the manner of a pauper), waiving many of the usual requirements.

In 1962, more than 10 million cases are tried in American courts. About 300,000 are appealed to higher courts. On January 8, the day Gideon's letter arrives in Washington, eight other *in forma pauperis* petitions come in the mail.

The Supreme Court is generous when it comes to *pauperis* cases. Gideon's plea meets the basic requirements and makes its way through the normal court winnowing procedure. But so do many other petitions. Now the question becomes, which will the nine black-robed justices (in 1962 all are white men) consider? The court is not concerned with Gideon's guilt or innocence. What they

matter to the white leaders. They have closed all the city's public recreational facilities rather than see them integrated. That means sixty-eight parks, thirty-eight playgrounds, six swimming pools, and four golf courses are locked up. No one in Birmingham—kindhearted or mean-spirited, young or old, white or black—can enter the parks or swim in the city pools. For rich people there are private pools and clubs, but for most people there's no escaping the heat.

Birmingham, Alabama's largest city, has moderate white citizens, but the South's moderates, white and black, are used to keeping quiet. Perhaps they fear mob action, or the disapproval of some of their friends, or the violence of the Ku Klux Klan. The Klan has helped elect Eugene want to know is: will this case test a question of substance? "The question is very simple," says Gideon in his petition, "I requested the court to appoint me an attorney and the court refused."

This case addresses issues of fair trials and the right to counsel. There is something else. Citizens of England or France or most other countries live with one set of legislative and judicial rules. In America we have dual legislation and a dual court system. The Sixth Amendment, which is about "the right to a speedy and public trial," says that the accused shall "have the assistance of counsel for his defense." But when the Constitution was written it dealt with federal, not state, jurisdictions. Does the Fourteenth Amendment's due process clause make the requirements of the Sixth Amendment apply in state cases? ("No State shall make or enforce any law which shall abridge the privileges or immunities of citizens of the United States, nor shall any State deprive any person of life, liberty, or property, without due process of law.") According to the *Betts* case it does not. But that decision has caused controversy. This is a question of substance.

The court decides to hear Gideon's case. For details, you can read Anthony Lewis's brilliant book *Gideon's Trumpet*. Lewis writes, "From time to time—with due solemnity, and after much searching of conscience—the Court has overruled its own decisions. Although he did not know it, Clarence Earl Gideon was calling for one of those great occasions in legal history. He was asking the Supreme Court to change its mind."

Prominent Washington lawyer (and later Supreme Court justice) Abe Fortas is assigned to argue the case before the court. The court overturns *Betts* and decides that indigent defendants charged with serious criminal offenses in state trials have the right to counsel. That unanimous decision changes American jurisprudence. Today more than two-thirds of the nation's population is served by public defenders. (Elsewhere, judges appoint private attorneys.) In Florida, Clarence Gideon, given a new trial, has a court appointed lawyer who uncovers new witnesses and discredits old ones. His client is acquitted.

"Bull" Connor as Birmingham's commissioner of public safety (which means he is chief of police). Connor is as big a bully as the South has ever produced. Besides that, he is an uncompromising racist.

Birmingham's black citizens have begun marching and protesting. They want to be able to eat in any restaurant, to go to any school. They want to vote. They want an end to segregation. They demonstrate peacefully.

In April 1963, Martin Luther King, Jr., who is now pastor of a church in Atlanta, joins the marchers. On Good Friday he and the Rev. Ralph Abernathy lead fifty hymn-singing African-Americans toward Birmingham's city hall, in direct violation of a court order. "Freedom has come to Birmingham," they sing. The police move

Martin Luther King, Jr., in jail in Birmingham, Alabama. Seven years earlier, when speaking at the 1956 annual NAACP convention, he said, "Where segregation exists we must be willing to rise up en masse and protest courageously against it. It might mean going to jail. If such is the case we must honorably fill up the jails of the South."

in to arrest them; Dr. King kneels and says a prayer. Then he and the others are taken to jail. A Southern jail is not a healthy place for a black civil rights leader. Eight local clergy—Christian ministers and a Jewish rabbi—criticize the civil rights demonstrators and ask why Dr. King has come to Birmingham. They counsel patience. Dr. King decides to write a letter from the jail in Birmingham, explaining the reasons behind the civil rights movement. He doesn't have any paper, so he writes on the margins of a newspaper and on toilet paper. He addresses the letter to the clergymen:

I am in Birmingham because injustice is here.... I cannot sit idly by in Atlanta and not be concerned about what happens in Birmingham. Injustice anywhere is a threat to justice everywhere.... What affects one directly affects all indirectly... I would be the first to advocate obeying just laws.... One who obeys an unjust law must do so openly, lovingly, and with a willingness to accept the penalty ... an individual who breaks a law that conscience tells him is unjust, and who willingly accepts the penalty of imprisonment in order to arouse the conscience of the community over its injustice, is in reality expressing the highest respect for law.

Many white Americans are asking blacks to "wait" and let racism continue for the present. King addresses that issue:

When you have seen hate-filled policemen curse, kick, brutalize and even kill your black brothers and sisters with impunity; when you see the vast majority of your twenty million Negro brothers smothering in an airtight cage of poverty in the midst of an affluent society; when you suddenly find your tongue twisted and your speech stammering as you seek to explain to your six-year-old daughter why she can't go to the public amusement park that has just been advertised on television, and see tears welling up in her little eyes when she is told that Funtown is closed to colored children.... When your first name becomes "nigger,"

African-American protestors jeer at policemen in a Birmingham civil rights demonstration. Shortly after this photograph was taken, police called in firemen to hose down the protestors. "Every channel of communication," says a reporter, "has been fragmented by the emotional dynamite of racism, reinforced by the whip, the razor, the gun, the bomb, the torch, the club, the knife, the mob, the police."

your middle name becomes "boy" (however old you are) ... then you will understand why we find it difficult to wait.

King makes it clear that his goal will enrich the whole nation:

We will reach the goal of freedom in Birmingham and all over the nation because the goal of America is freedom.

Meanwhile, President Kennedy comments, "The new way for Americans to stand up for their rights is to sit down." But, privately, JFK urges Dr. King to ease up on the confrontations. He, too, asks blacks to "be patient."

Dr. King and other civil rights leaders realize that something still more dramatic is needed to hold the nation's attention. Demonstrators are being sent to jail every day, yet the response is muted. Thousands of new demonstrators might do it. But where are the black thousands who can march and not worry about losing their jobs? Suddenly the solution seems obvious—they are in the schools.

"We started organizing the prom queens of the high schools, the basketball stars, the football stars," says the Reverend James Bevel of the Southern Christian Leadership Conference (SCLC). Those

Birmingham's Commissioner of Public Safety, Bull Connor. When a new mayor is elected in 1962, Connor refuses to leave office. So from then until May 1963, the city, one of the most segregated in the country, has been run by two governments.

student leaders attract others. "The first response was among the young women, about thirteen to eighteen. They're probably more responsive in terms of courage, confidence, and the ability to follow reasoning and logic. Nonviolence to them is logical.... The last to get involved were the high school guys, because the brunt of violence in the South was directed toward the black male."

Elementary school boys and girls are eager to march. Workshops are held to help them cope with what the leaders know will be danger and viciousness. Early in May, some 600 children march out of church singing songs of freedom. Bull Connor arrests them all. The next day another 1,000 children begin a peaceful march. One of them, a girl named Patricia King, remembers what happened: "Some of the times we marched, people would be out there and they would throw rocks and cans and different things at us," she says. "I was afraid of getting hurt, but I was still willing to march to see justice done."

Bull Connor calls out police attack dogs. "All you gotta do is tell them you're going to bring in the dogs," he explains to the press. "Look at 'em run.... I want to see the dogs work." Firemen turn on high-pressure hoses. The hoses are powerful enough to rip the bark off trees. Children hit by the blasts of water are thrown to the ground and roll screaming down the street. Police dogs bite three teenagers so badly they are taken to a hospital (a black hospital, naturally). Seventy-five children are squeezed into a cell built for eight prisoners. They sing freedom songs. A minister, thrown against a wall by the powerful hoses, is carried away in an ambulance. When he hears of it, Bull Connor says he's sorry it wasn't a hearse.

While all of this is going on, television cameras are taking pictures that are seen in living rooms across the nation. Brutalizing children? Few citizens have faced the realities of black life in the segregated South. Now they see it for themselves.

The March on Washington

In 1963, exactly a hundred years have passed since Abraham Lincoln signed the Emancipation Proclamation. For years, the venerable civil rights and labor activist A. Philip Randolph has talked of organizing a freedom rally in the nation's capital. Perhaps it can bring the diverse leaders of the African-American community—some of whom disagree on the best way to promote civil rights in America–closer. Perhaps it can help bring black and white people together. Perhaps it can influence Congress, to whom President Kennedy has submitted a civil rights bill. A march will show Congress and the president the importance of the civil rights movement. Many believe Kennedy is paying more attention to affairs abroad than to the problem of unfairness at home. When he gives a speech in West Berlin, Germany, on political freedom, Kennedy inspires cheers around the world. But some Americans are less than enthusiastic. They believe he needs to address the issue of freedom at home.

Philip Randolph is seventy-four. If he is ever to have his march, it has to be soon. And so it is decided: on August 28 there will be a march for freedom in Washington, D.C. Leaders hope that 100,000 people will participate. The marchers will demand four things: passage of the civil rights bill; integration of schools by year's end; an end to job discrimination; and a program of job training. Bayard Rustin, an organizational wizard, is in charge of planning. He sets up drinking fountains, first-aid stations, and portable toilets on Washington's grassy Mall. Workers make 80,000 cheese sandwiches. Movie stars, singers, high school bands, preachers, and politicians practice speeches and songs. The participants are to stand on the steps of the Lincoln Memorial and look toward the tall, slender Washington Monument and, beyond that, to the Capitol. Two thousand buses and twenty-one chartered trains head for Washington. A man with a freedom banner roller-skates from Chicago. An eighty-two-year-old man bicycles from Ohio. Sixty thousand white people come. Television crews, high in the Washington Monument, guess there are 250,000 people altogether. "My friends," says activist Roy Wilkins, "we are here today because we want the Congress of the United States to hear from us…. We want freedom now!" It is a day filled with song, and hope, and good will.

Finally, in the late afternoon, the last of the speakers stands on the steps of the Lincoln Memorial. It is Dr. Martin Luther King, Jr. He begins with a prepared speech, formal and dignified. Then something happens, and his training as a preacher takes over. He leaves his written speech and speaks from his heart. "I have a dream," he says.

I have a dream that one day down in Alabama … little black boys and black

Above, a crowd gathers on the Mall for the March on Washington. "We are not going to stop until the walls of segregation are crushed," says the chief speaker, Martin Luther King, Jr. "We've gone too far to turn back now." Right, protestors march for equal rights, integrated schools, decent housing, an end to bias, and freedom.

girls will be able to join hands with little white boys and white girls as sisters and brothers.... I have a dream that my four little children will one day live in a nation where they will not be judged by the color of their skin, but by the content of their character.... I have a dream that one day this nation will rise up and live out the true meaning of its creed—we hold these truths to be self-evident, that all men are created equal. I have a dream today.

He is speaking to the whole nation, not just those who have marched to Washington:

So let freedom ring from the prodigious hilltops of New Hampshire, let freedom ring from the mighty mountains of New York, let freedom ring from the heightening Alleghenies of Pennsylvania, let freedom ring from the snow-capped

"We shall overcome,
 We shall overcome,
 We shall overcome someday.
 Oh, deep in my heart,
 I do believe
 That we shall overcome someday."

—"We Shall Overcome,"
anthem of the civil rights movement, said to have originated in the 1940s at Tennessee's Highlander Folk School, a labor movement camp for black textile workers

Rockies of Colorado; let freedom ring from the curvaceous slopes of California. But not only that. Let freedom ring from Stone Mountain of Georgia; let freedom ring from Lookout Mountain of Tennessee; let freedom ring from every hill and molehill of Mississippi. From every mountainside, let freedom ring.

And when this happens and when we allow freedom to ring, when we let it ring from every village and every hamlet, from every state and every city, we will be able to speed up that day when all God's children, black men and white men, Jews and gentiles, Protestants and Catholics, will be able to join hands and sing in the words of the old Negro spiritual: "Free at last. Free at last. Thank God Almighty, we are free at last."

Less than three weeks after the March on Washington, on September 15, 1963, a bomb explodes during Sunday school at Birmingham's Sixteenth Street Baptist Church. Four schoolgirls are killed. Klanswoman Connie Lynch says the girls "weren't children. Children are little people, little human beings, and that means white people." (It will be thirty-nine years before one of the perpetrators is, finally, brought to trial and convicted.)

JOURNEY TO DALLAS

Despite his charm and popularity, Kennedy has a tough time as president. Congress is controlled by an alliance of northern Republicans and southern Democrats. They vote as a bloc—mostly against any kind of change.

Kennedy has a plan for social and economic reform meant to extend FDR's New Deal. He calls it the "New Frontier." It will enhance civil rights, cut taxes, improve health care, mandate equal pay for women, fund aid to the cities and poor rural areas, provide for workforce training, and raise the minimum wage. The public seems with him on those issues, but the chance of getting legislation passed is bleak. "When I was a congressman, I never realized how important Congress was. But now I do," moans the president. Then, in 1963, the political winds begin to shift. Kennedy expects to win a second term in the 1964 elections; he now sees votes in Congress to support his agenda.

But there is trouble in Texas—political trouble—and Texas will be important in the coming election. Vice President Lyndon Johnson asks Kennedy to go on a peacemaking mission. So, on a November day filled with sunshine, he and his wife, Jackie, wave goodbye to their two children and fly off to the Lone Star State.

Things start wonderfully well. The crowds in San Antonio and Houston are unusually warm and encouraging. At Fort

Former Vice President Lyndon Johnson, standing beside the First Lady in her bloodstained suit (on the left, her back is towards us), after being sworn in as thirty-sixth president aboard *Air Force One*.

Worth, unexpectedly, Kennedy goes out into a parking lot and shakes as many hands as he can. His fans are thrilled. When *Air Force One*, the presidential plane, touches down at Love Field in Dallas, Mrs. Kennedy, in a pink suit and her signature pillbox hat, is handed a bouquet of roses and asters. Thousands are there to greet the president and first lady. The weather is gorgeous, so the plastic bubble top is taken off the presidential limousine and the bulletproof side windows rolled down. Texas's governor, John Connally, and his wife sit in the front seat, the Kennedys are behind them. They take the busiest route through the city. Crowds line the streets, waving and cheering. When the car passes an old seven-story schoolbook warehouse, Mrs. Connally turns around and says to the president, "You can't say that Dallas isn't friendly to you today!" President Kennedy never answers.

For the rest of their lives, most Americans living then will remember exactly where they were on November 22, 1963, when they heard the news. Again and again, that day and for days to come, they will stare at their TV screens and see the motorcade, the president falling into his wife's lap, and Jacqueline Kennedy in her bloodstained suit.

At 1 P.M., John F. Kennedy is pronounced dead. At 2:30 P.M., Lyndon Baines Johnson is sworn in as chief executive on *Air Force One*. That plane carries him and the martyred president back to the nation's capital. And the world weeps.

PART 15

MARCHING TO FREEDOM LAND

Lyndon Baines Johnson is big. Taller than six feet three inches, he has big bones, big ears, a big nose, big hands, and big feet. His voice is big, his ego is big, and when it comes to ambition—his is bigger than big. It's colossal. He doesn't just want to be president; he wants to be a great president, right up there with Washington and Lincoln. No, he wants more than that. He says he wants to be "the greatest of them all, the whole bunch of them." And he has an idea how to do it.

Johnson's roots are in Texas, in the scruffy Hill Country near Austin, a region so isolated when he was a boy that no one had electricity at home, and few had running water or an indoor toilet. At the first school Lyndon went to all the grades were in one room, with just one teacher. Most of the kids went barefoot.

Lyndon was bright—everyone could see that—but he was a rebellious student. Sometimes he did well; often he didn't. A cousin said, "Lyndon would always have to be the leader." From the time he was a little boy it was politics that fascinated him. That wasn't surprising. His mother was the daughter of a Texas secretary of state; his father, Sam Ealy Johnson, served in the Texas legislature. Everyone knew Sam Ealy. He wore a six-shooter on his hip and a cowboy hat on his head. He was tall, loud, boastful, and sometimes mean. His son both feared and adored him. By the time Lyndon was six he was attending political rallies and handing out pamphlets. When he was ten he'd go with his father to the legislature and "sit in the gallery for hours watching all the activity on the floor." He knew just what he wanted to do with his life. "I want to wind up just like my daddy, gettin' pensions for old people," he told a friend.

But when he was ready to go to college, his father was in debt. The family farm had failed. Lyndon borrowed $75 to help pay his college expenses. After a year he had to drop out and teach in order to earn money to finish. He taught Mexican-American children that year and saw real poverty—worse than anything he knew.

On right, marching from Selma to Montgomery in 1965.

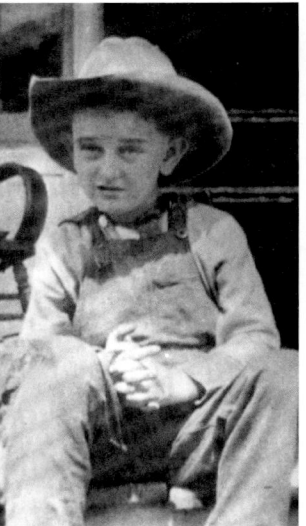

LBJ on the road to a career in politics: above, with the Mexican-American children he taught at school in Cotulla, Texas; left, with Texas governor James Allred (Allred was often airbrushed out of the picture later on to enhance Johnson's importance).

"When I was a young man I taught in a Mexican-American school, and there I got my real, deep first impressions of the prejudices that existed and the inequity of our school system between whites and browns."

—Lyndon Johnson

Back at college, he got a job carrying trash and sweeping floors. "He made speeches to the walls he wiped down, he told tales of the ancients to the doormats he was shaking the dust out of," a friend said. It was his energy everyone talked about. He never seemed to stop. If he was asked to do a job, he did double the job. "It pained him to loaf," said another friend. He ended up working as an assistant to the college president, who later laughed and told him, "You hadn't been in my office a month before I could hardly tell who was president of the school—you or me." When Lyndon Johnson graduated, the college president said the kind of thing college presidents always say: "I predict for him great things in the years ahead." He had no idea how prescient those words were.

Running a Race

Lyndon Johnson was born to be a politician. He was twenty-nine when he was first elected to Congress and he set out like a sprinter in a foot race. He worked sixteen-hour days, got a lot done, and impressed some Washington old-timers. "There was this first-term congressman who was so on his toes and so active and overwhelming that he was up and down our corridors all the time," recalled one of them. Another remembered, "This fellow was a great operator.... Besides the drive and the energy and the doing favors, which he did for everybody, there was a great deal of charm in this man." Johnson got the government to help finance slum-clearance projects and low-cost housing in the Texas state capital, Austin. Way ahead of his times, he insisted that Mexican-Americans and blacks have a fair share of the new houses. Money he got for the region helped farmers go from horse-and-plow farming to twentieth-century machinery. And he brought electricity to the Hill Country. "Of all the things I have ever done," he said twenty years later, "nothing has ever given me as much satisfaction as bringing power to the Hill Country of Texas." In 1948, Johnson won a race for the U.S. Senate. Just four years after that—unheard of for a freshman senator—he was elected leader of the Democratic Party in the Senate.

A cyclone in the Senate chamber might have been less noticed. When Lyndon Johnson let loose with his never-stop Texas energy, he usually got whatever it was he wanted. He knew how to manipulate; he also knew how to compromise. During Eisenhower's presidency he worked closely with the Republicans. He got their bills passed; they helped him get favors for Texas. "It was not merely the velocity of his rise within the institution that was unique," wrote his biographer Robert Caro. "He made the Senate work."

Under the three great mid-nineteenth-century orators, Henry Clay, Daniel Webster, and John Calhoun, the Senate functioned with the kind of spirited debates its founders envisioned. But after that it calcified. Johnson revived it single-handedly. "He was master of the Senate," said Caro, "master of an institution that had never before had a master, and that … has not had one since."

"He'd come on just like a tidal wave. He'd come through a door, and he'd take the whole room over. Just like that. He was not delicate. There was nothing delicate about him. He was a downfield blocker and a running fullback all the time."

—Democratic Senator and Vice President Hubert Humphrey

> "He [Johnson] was extraordinary; he did everything he could to be magnanimous, to be kind. I almost felt sorry for him, because I knew he felt sorry for me..."
>
> —Jacqueline Kennedy

When Massachusetts senator John F. Kennedy ran for the presidency, in 1960, he needed a Southerner on the ticket to pacify the conservative southern Democrats. He turned to Lyndon Johnson (who had hoped for the top spot himself). The most ambitious man in the Senate was asked to be vice president of the United States—a job that traditionally carried little clout. Johnson had never been second fiddle before. It was not a role he played easily. And Kennedy, mostly, ignored him.

ALL THE WAY WITH LBJ

To become president as it happened—through a horrendous stroke of fate rather than his own doing—and then to guide a country in mourning, is as difficult as anything Johnson has ever done. John Fitzgerald Kennedy was born wealthy, handsome, elegant—all the things his successor isn't. Johnson is both attracted by and disdainful of the icon he must follow. But he is where he has always wanted to be, and determined to honor the memory of the graceful young president. He will do what Kennedy couldn't quite manage. He intends to get a full plate of major legislation through Congress. He has spent a career preparing for this. Lyndon Johnson knows how to trade and maneuver and twist arms as few have. With his bulldog approach he mows down, or muzzles, his opposition. Soon Kennedy's program is sailing through Congress, with added ideas that are Johnson's. He calls the total package the Great Society.

Johnson envisions a land where poverty has no place; where all children are well schooled; where health care is a birthright; where jobs and job training are available to all. If he can make that happen, he knows he will be the greatest president ever. Being Lyndon Johnson, he wants no less. And he has a torrent of energy at his disposal.

I want to be the president who helped the poor find their own way, who helped to feed the hungry, and who protected the right of every citizen to vote in every election.

Nineteen sixty-four is one of those years that get labeled "pivotal." In the first ten months of the year, Johnson gets an astonishing ninety bills through Congress. Nothing in the century—not even the New Deal—can touch that accomplishment. Operation Headstart helps children prepare for kindergarten. The Job Corps finds work for school dropouts. Upward Bound helps needy kids go to college. The

Neighborhood Youth Corps trains unemployed teenagers. The Teacher Corps trains school teachers. VISTA funds volunteers. Medicare provides health insurance for old people. Medicaid helps those without resources afford a doctor. Elderly poverty, which has been a significant national problem, is no more. Economist Lester Thurow is given the job of making sure that none of the programs hands out cash to people. The emphasis is on self-help and personal responsibility.

This administration, here and now, declares unconditional war on poverty in America.... It will not be a short or easy struggle, no single weapon or strategy will suffice, but we shall not rest until that war is won.

Later critics will accuse the Great Society of profligacy, but close study shows something else. Johnson manages to cut taxes, balance the budget, and address human rights and social issues. In January, the Twenty-fourth Amendment is ratified, making it illegal to deny anyone the vote because of a poll tax. In July, Johnson signs a Civil Rights Act banning discrimination in public accommodation and in employment. African-Americans can now, legally, check into all hotels and sit down at all restaurants. Federal aid is extended in elementary and secondary schools, a liberalized immigration law is passed, and the National Endowment for the Humanities is established.

In 1964 Johnson runs for the presidency on his own. He doesn't just want to be elected; he wants the biggest popular vote in the history of the country. And he gets it. He also gets a Congress that is Democratic. But he loses in what has been the solidly Democratic South. Mississippi, Alabama, Louisiana, Georgia, and South Carolina vote Republican. Still, his support in the rest of the nation is awesome; he now has an opportunity few presidents have had. He has his vision of a Great Society; he has support from America's citizens, and he has the ability and energy to make his program happen. Tackling poverty, he says, "Our aim is not only to relieve the symptoms of poverty, but to cure it, and above all, to prevent it."

Lyndon and Lady Bird. As the young wife of a politician "Bird" was painfully shy; she changes with time. One aide said, "A modest, introspective girl gradually became a figure of steel cloaked in velvet."

The president and congress pass another bill that, by the century's end, will change the look of America. The Immigration and Nationality Act of 1965 makes for a new immigration policy. Previous quotas that favored northern Europeans are jettisoned; immigration is put on an equal basis for all nations. Asians, Latin Americans, and Africans will soon arrive in significant numbers and bring their religions, their foods, their music, and their ideas. The nation will be both challenged and enriched.

Johnson's budget puts the cost of his Great Society programs at $1 billion for fiscal 1964-1965. Actual expenditures are slightly more than $600 million. The deficit for that year is the lowest in five years. We are a rich nation. Congress and the president know that we can afford to pay for programs that will give a broad base to prosperity in America. That prosperous base will provide customers for America's astonishing productivity. Everyone, it seems, will be better off. "The pursuit of happiness" begins to take on concrete meaning. Then something gets in the way—and the big dream starts falling into disarray.

Way Down Yonder in Vietnam

When we put one foot (and then the other) into Vietnam, it is with the best of intentions. We are following the French—old-fashioned imperialists who colonized what they called Indochina (Vietnam, Laos, Cambodia) for their own benefit—but we want no colonies or loot for ourselves. What we do want is to keep the world stable.

The Vietnamese want to be free of foreign rule. Years earlier, Ho Chi Minh haunted the halls at Versailles, hoping to reach Woodrow Wilson and find support for Vietnamese freedom. It didn't happen. Ho backed the Allies during World War II and quoted America's Declaration of Independence when he announced Vietnamese independence at war's end, in 1945. Then he goes off to Moscow for training, when he finally gets help, it comes from communist China and Soviet Russia.

Crafty Ho is a communist, but he is also his own man and a fierce patriot. Most Americans believe that communists are braided together in a tight league and that Vietnam will soon be under Chinese control. We don't take into account the historic enmity between the Chinese and the Vietnamese. Experts say that if Vietnam

Ho Chi Minh

goes communist, all the other countries in the region will follow, like falling dominoes lined up in a row. And we believe it. In the United States, in the 1960s, seeming to be "soft on communism" is political suicide. In a world thought to be divided between two superpowers, any gain for one side is seen as a direct loss to the other. So this formerly insignificant bit of land becomes crucial to our future.

Meanwhile, the Vietnamese were trying to oust the hated French, who fled (or collaborated with the Japanese) during World War II, and then came back into power. Truman sent money and advisers to shore up the French regime. We had no intention of staying ourselves, and we asked the French to make plans for eventual self-rule for the Vietnamese. Truman focused on Europe, not wanting to antagonize the French and upset the region. The alternative—letting communist Ho take over—seemed unacceptable. Eisenhower ups the aid, eventually financing 80 percent of France's war costs. But the war goes badly. In a final, humiliating battle at Dien Bien Phu in 1954, the French are cut off, surrounded, held under siege, and forced to surrender. An international conference is held in Geneva to determine the fate of Vietnam. We aren't official participants, but our secretary of state, John Foster Dulles, is there—and pointedly refuses to shake the hand of Chinese premier Zhou Enlai, making his contempt clear. The conference divides Vietnam, as Korea has been divided, into north and south. Ho Chi Minh is leader in the north. The southern leaders have Western connections. What the diplomats in Geneva don't understand is that Vietnam is not Korea. The nation's rice bowl is in the south. Cut off from its food supply, Ho's North Vietnam will be forced to turn to Russia and China for food as well as military aid.

Under Truman and Eisenhower, and still more under Kennedy, we fund civil war in Vietnam. We back corrupt leaders, and we don't back the free elections called for in the Geneva agreement, because we know Ho Chi Minh will win them. With communism as a specter, we seem to have no faith in our own institutions. We are a nation where people are free to rule themselves, but he didn't trumpet that achievement.

When Lyndon Johnson becomes president, his military chiefs push him to enter the war with direct force. They believe this backward nation will fall easily to our massive power. Johnson is skeptical, but he doesn't want to appear to be soft on communism. So, in August 1964, when an American destroyer is involved in a minor incident in the Gulf of Tonkin, off North Vietnam, Johnson gets Congress to authorize the use of "all necessary measures to repel any armed attack against the armed forces of the United States and to prevent further aggression." This becomes the legal basis for all that will come later; there never is a declaration of war.

In 1965 we begin bombing North Vietnam. We will send more than half

A U.S. soldier motions to refugees to keep their heads down during an attempted Vietcong ambush.

a million Americans to do battle in this faraway land. More than 58,000 will be killed.

It is a war between the most powerful nation in the world—using bombers and rockets—and a small country of farmers, dependent on water buffalo and barefoot runners. How can guerrilla fighters who have their ammunition carried over jungle trails on the backs of old men and women beat a modern army supplied by helicopters? The military chiefs might have understood this—if they had thought about thirteen pesky colonies that once defeated the world's greatest military power. Our militarists keep telling the president that if we just send a few thousand more soldiers and bombs it will all be over. Before we finish we will drop more bombs on tiny Vietnam than we did on both Germany and Japan during all of World War II.

In 1966, George F. Kennan, an expert on Soviet affairs, is called before the Senate Foreign Relations Committee, holding hearings on the war in Vietnam. Kennan, who is a critic of the war, quotes John Quincy Adams to the senators. Adams, who may have had more foreign policy savvy than any other president, said, in 1821, that America's heart would always be with free people wherever they are; "but she goes not abroad in search of monsters to destroy." As to promoting freedom elsewhere, JQA said, "She will recommend the general cause [of freedom] by the countenance of her voice, and by the benignant sympathy of her example." Otherwise, the United States "would involve herself beyond the power of extrication." America could, he said, "become the dictatress of the world. She would no longer be the ruler of her own spirit."

It might have been an advisory text on Vietnam. But it comes late—and besides, who wants to pay attention to the words of a long-dead president?

We are involved in Vietnam for thirty years; we can't seem to extricate ourselves, and we never understand the Vietnamese.

President Johnson keeps saying we are winning the war—and it's true that we are winning battles. But for the first time in history, people can see war for themselves. The TV screens in their living rooms show dead American soldiers and dead Vietnamese and dead civilians. The war goes on and on. It becomes the longest war in United States history. It polarizes the nation as only the Civil War has done before. It makes Americans angry, cynical, and mistrustful of government. It takes money that might have gone to educate, beautify, and build, and uses it for grenades, rocket launchers, napalm, and chemicals, like "Agent Orange," that take the leaves off jungle trees. And we still can't beat the Vietnamese.

The war is about freedom—but not ours. The Vietnamese want to be free of foreign rule. They want to choose their own leaders. They even want the freedom to make wrong decisions.

A Different Kind of Fight

Back to 1964. The Reverend Dr. Martin Luther King, Jr. has just won the Nobel Peace Prize. At thirty-five, he is the youngest recipient ever. The chairman of the Norwegian parliament says Dr. King is "the first person in the Western world to have shown us that a struggle can be waged without violence." When Norwegian students sing "We Shall Overcome," King knows that his message has become part of a universal language of freedom. From Oslo he goes to England for another first. No non-Anglican has ever preached in St. Paul's Cathedral. King does so.

Soon after he returns to the United States, King is in jail again—for marching in a Southern city. He is trying to get the vote for black citizens. President Johnson's Civil Rights Act allows African-Americans to check into any hotel they desire, sit on buses wherever they wish, and eat in any restaurant. That it took congressional action to make that happen is appalling. Still, it is a powerful achievement. But it hasn't solved the voting problem. In most of the South, blacks still can't vote. Those who try are often beaten, or thrown out of their jobs, or even killed.

The Bill of Rights guarantees free speech, freedom of religion, and the right to bear arms. It says nothing about a right to vote. Few founders believed in universal suffrage. Initially the vote was reserved for white males—and not all of them. Usually

Tinkering with Freedom of Speech

Thirteen-year-old Mary Beth Tinker, her friend Christopher Eckerd, and her brother, John, arrive at their Des Moines school wearing black armbands. It is 1965, and this is their way of protesting American involvement in Vietnam. The principal (who, two days earlier, announced a ban on protest armbands) tells the three students to remove them. Mary Beth refuses. She believes her First Amendment rights are being violated and that the armbands are a form of speech—symbolic speech. She is suspended from school. Her parents go to court. The case, Tinker v. Des Moines Independent School District, makes it to the Supreme Court. Here is what the court says in its 1969 decision: School officials do not possess absolute authority over their students. Students—in school as well as out—are "persons" under the Constitution: "They are possessed of fundamental rights which the State must respect, just as they … must respect their obligations to the State."

The court's opinion is significant. The students who quietly wore the armbands caused no disruption and did not, says the court, intrude on the work of the school or the rights of others. There were no threats or acts of violence. The school officials feared the possibility of a disturbance that might be caused by unpopular views. The court says that protecting unpopular opinions is part of the price we pay for living in a free society.

These same school officials, the court notes, had allowed other political symbols in school, like campaign buttons and even the Iron Cross (a Nazi symbol). Only the black armbands protesting the action in Vietnam were singled out. Students and teachers do not "shed their constitutional rights to freedom of speech or expression at the schoolhouse gate," says the Supreme Court. "State-operated schools may not be enclaves of totalitarianism … students may not be regarded as closed-circuit recipients of only that which the State chooses to communicate." Justice Hugo Black dissents vigorously, asserting that school officials know better than federal judges how to run schools.

In a later case, *Bethel School District No 403* v. *Fraser*, in 1986, the court approves a school's curb of "indecent speech" as consistent with teaching moral values and civic virtues. Some see a tension and disconnect between these decisions. What role should schools play in teaching moral values? How much control should a school have over student expression, as in a school newspaper or assembly?

---

it meant those with property and education. The Fifteenth Amendment extended the vote to "citizens." That came to mean men. The Nineteenth Amendment brought suffrage to women. (In 1971, the Twenty-sixth will give the vote to eighteen-year-olds.) In the South, in 1964, it has been such a long time since blacks voted that few understand their constitutional rights. The newly ratified Twenty-fourth Amendment gives them the legal clout to protest the poll tax and other voting impediments; civil rights workers decide the time is right to get out the black vote.

The summer of 1964 is called Freedom Summer. College students are recruited to travel south to register African-Americans. Six hundred of them hit the road for Mississippi. African-Americans have not voted there since early in the century. The Congress for Racial Equality (CORE) opens an office in Meridian, and two young men head from there to Mount Zion Methodist Church, thirty-five miles away. At Mount Zion, the two speak about CORE's plans for black enfranchisement. One of them, cheerful, talkative Mickey Schwerner, is a twenty-three-year-old white social worker from New York City. His wife is teaching sewing classes as part of Freedom Summer. The other, James Chaney, a quiet, thoughtful black man from Meridian, is twenty. A few days later, Klansmen arrive at Mount Zion looking for Schwerner. One of them, Sam Bowers, the imperial wizard of a Klan spinoff, the White Knights, has Schwerner marked for "elimination." Frustrated at not finding Schwerner, the Klansmen beat up people attending a church service and burn the building to the ground.

A few days after that, Schwerner, Chaney, and another Freedom worker, twenty-year-old New York college student Andrew Goodman, drive back to find out what they can about the beatings and the church burning. Then they disappear. The

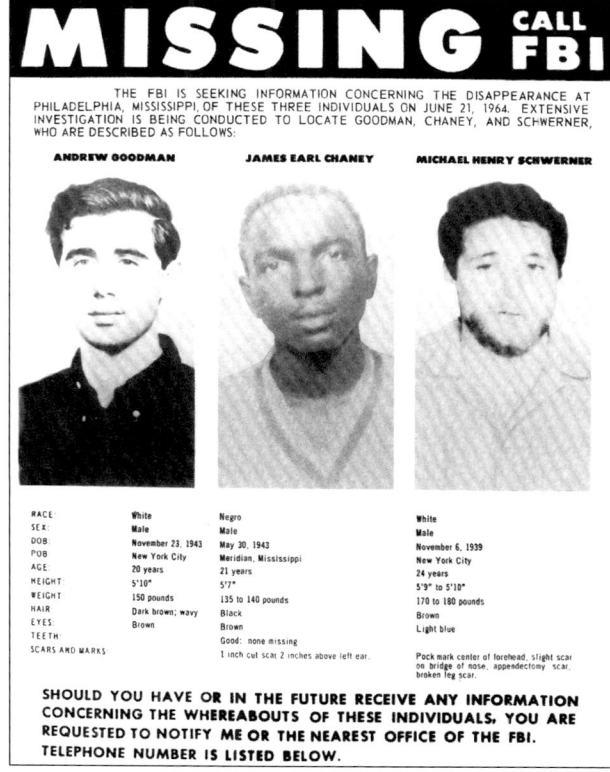

An FBI sheet describing James Chaney, Michael Schwerner, and Andrew Goodman, who disappeared on June 21, 1964.

national press headlines the story. Where are they? Mississippi's governor, Paul Johnson, says it is all a joke and there never were three boys. President Johnson sends the FBI. A large reward leads to three bodies dug from under a manmade dam.

Everyone knows the Klansmen who are guilty. In Mississippi, white people don't get punished for killing blacks, so the sheriff, his deputies, and some state patrolmen have been bragging about doing the deed. But the times are changing. Four years later, Sheriff Lawrence Rainey and eighteen others find themselves in court. In one photo, Rainey has what looks like a golf ball in his cheek. It is a wad of Red Man chewing tobacco. A hairy leg protrudes from the top of a cowboy boot across his lap. The men around him are grinning. Rainey is confident. Although he is known to be guilty, he has an alibi and he convinces the judge. Seven white men are convicted. Deputy Cecil Price and another Klansman get the stiffest sentence: six years. "They killed one nigger, one Jew, and a white man," says the judge. "I gave them what they deserved."

The Schwerners and the Goodmans ask that their sons be buried with James Chaney. But that is impossible; state law demands segregated cemeteries.

SELMA

The following year, 1965, the action moves to a town of 30,000 people: Selma, Alabama. It is an Old South cotton town on the banks of the Alabama River; more than half its residents are African-American. Mule-drawn carts still clatter down Selma's dusty streets, hauling cotton. Before the Civil War, one of the town's buildings was used to hold slaves—sometimes 500 of them—as they waited to be auctioned off. During the Civil War, Selma was a Confederate military depot. In the 1960s, the streets in the black section of town are made of red dirt; those in the white section are paved. Selma is Bull Connor's birthplace.

The leaders of Selma's black community invite Dr. King—and the organization he now leads, the Southern Christian Leadership Conference (SCLC)—to come to town. When they arrive, workers from SNCC ("SNICK," the Student Nonviolent Coordinating Committee) have already been in Selma for more than a year. SNCC has doubled the number of registered black voters—to 333. That's about one of every fifty who are eligible. A few SNCC members aren't happy about King's coming to Selma. They want to stay in charge. But SNCC's chairman, John Lewis, isn't one of them—he's thrilled. So are most of Selma's black citizens.

Dallas County Sheriff Jim Clark is not thrilled—he's angry. Clark is a crude, blustery white guy who wears a military jacket, carries a nightstick, hates Negroes, and says so. He's an embarrassment to Selma's leading white families, but he's been elected sheriff anyway. (If black citizens were voters, it wouldn't have happened.)

When a group marches to the courthouse to try to register, Sheriff Clark makes them stand in an alley. When SNCC workers try to bring them sandwiches and water,

"And I say segregation now, segregation tomorrow, and segregation forever!"

—Governor George Wallace of Alabama

Malcolm X

Coretta Scott King visits her husband, Martin Luther King, Jr., in jail. She brings a message from Malcolm X, who has come to Selma. Malcolm, who has been electrifying urban audiences with a spirit of militancy, has been invited to Selma by SNCC's leaders (some of whom resent the more conservative SCLC). While King is a child of relative privilege (his father is a distinguished minister), Malcolm is a product of the ghetto. He quit school before graduation, became a thief and drug dealer, and landed in jail. That's when his life changed direction.

Malcolm got a dictionary from the prison school and, starting on the first page, carefully copied every word onto a tablet. "With every succeeding page, I also learned of people and places and events from history." As his vocabulary grew, so did his control of language, and his confidence. He becomes a brilliant speaker and a leader of the Nation of Islam (the Black Muslims) and urges black people to

Malcolm X

be proud of their blackness and of their African roots. As to nonviolence, he has been critical of it and of King. But now Malcolm seems to be heading in a different direction. He tells Coretta, "I want Dr. King to know that I didn't come to Selma to make his job difficult." He adds, "If the white people realize what the alternative is, perhaps they will be more willing to hear Dr. King." Speaking to a crowd in Brown's Chapel, Malcolm says, "White people should thank Dr. King for holding people in check, for there are others who do not believe in these [nonviolent] measures."

Malcolm has been to the center of the Muslim world, Mecca, in Saudi Arabia, where he was converted to orthodox Islam. The experience moved him deeply and caused him to change some of his ideas. Malcolm has now broken with the Black Muslims—who believe that a fair integrated society cannot be. They want blacks and whites to each exist in their own spheres. It's the separate-and-equal idea, but this time on black terms. Malcolm no longer supports the hatred that provokes separation, and he is rethinking the use of violence. He tells a journalist about his change.

The sickness and madness of those early days. I'm glad to be free of them. It is a time for martyrs now. And if I'm to be one, it will be in the cause of brotherhood. That's the only thing that can save this country. I've learned it the hard way—but I've learned it.

Two and a half weeks after his trip to Selma, Malcolm X is indeed martyred—killed by Black Muslims—a victim of the violence he once tolerated.

the workers are hit with billy clubs. That gets more than a hundred black teachers marching. Teachers usually steer clear of controversy, but this time they don't—they want to vote. The teachers' march is the real turning point, says the Reverend Frederick Reese: "The undertakers got a group, and they marched. The beauticians got a group, and they marched. Everybody marches after the teachers march."

Dr. King speaks at Brown's Chapel. "Give us the ballot," he cries. Then Martin Luther King, Jr. leads 250 citizens to the courthouse; they want to register to vote. Instead they are thrown in jail. Five hundred children march in support. They are arrested and jailed. The evening television news covers it all. King writes a letter from jail. He says, "This is Selma, Alabama. There are more Negroes in jail with me than there are on the voting rolls." Fifteen congressmen come to Selma. They announce that "new legislation is going to be necessary." President Johnson holds a press conference and says, "All Americans should be indignant when one American is denied the right to vote."

In Selma the tension is palpable. Anyone connected with the march is likely to be roughed up and beaten. And it is the police, the state troopers, and Sheriff Clark who are doing most of the beating. When eighty-two-year-old Cager Lee marches, a state trooper whips him until he's bloody. Jimmy Lee Jackson, Cager's grandson, carries his grandfather into a cafe. But the troopers aren't finished; they storm into

Dallas County police attack protestors in hopes of preventing the march from Selma to Montgomery.

the cafe. One trooper hits Jimmy's mother; another shoots Jimmy in the stomach. He dies seven days later. It is too much. There is no stopping the civil right workers now. "We decided that we were going to get killed or we were going to be free," says one worker. The murder is also too much for some of Selma's white citizens. Seventy of them march in sympathy to the courthouse. One white minister says:

> We consider it a shocking injustice that there are still counties in Alabama where there are no Negroes registered to vote.... We are horrified at the brutal way in which the police ... have attempted to break up peaceful assemblies and demonstrations by American citizens.

On March 7, 1965, 600 people—men, women, and children—set out to walk the fifty-four miles from Selma to Alabama's capital, Montgomery. They intend to face Governor George Wallace and demand that all of Alabama's citizens be protected in their right to vote. Dr. King is not there. The president is worried about how Governor Wallace will respond, and hopes to tone down the action. He asks Dr. King to leave. Hosea Williams, a young firebrand, is in now charge.

The march begins with a prayer; then everyone starts walking, singing as they go. They march six blocks from Brown's Chapel to the Edmund Pettus Bridge, which crosses the Alabama River. Mounting the steep, sloping crest of the bridge, the marchers are stunned by what they see: George Wallace's state troopers are lined up, carrying bullwhips and billy clubs, many wearing gas masks, all in hard hats. The phalanx moves forward toward the marchers, releasing tear-gas bombs. A nine-year-old girl named Sheyann Webb is among the marchers:

> People were running and falling and ducking and you could hear the whips swishing and you'd hear them striking people. I tried to run home as fast as I could. Hosea Williams picked me up and I told him to put me down, he wasn't running fast enough.

But something new has come to this out-of-the-way southern town: television coverage. Camera crews film the action. On what will become known as Bloody Sunday, TV stations across the nation interrupt their regular programs to show scenes of policemen on horseback clubbing peaceful marchers. "It looked like war," says Selma's mayor. "The wrath of the nation came down on us."

Forty-eight hours later, Martin Luther King is back in Selma. He has sent telegrams to prominent clergymen asking them to join him for a ministers' march to Montgomery. They come from many places and many faiths: white-bearded Rabbi Abraham Herschel comes from the Jewish Theological Seminary and world leader Ralph Bunche from the United Nations. Unitarian minister James Reeb comes from Boston. He and some others eat dinner in a black café in Selma. As he leaves the restaurant, Reeb is clubbed to death. President Johnson and the nation react with shocked disbelief:

> At times, history and fate meet in a single place to shape a turning point in men's unending search for freedom. So it was at Lexington and Concord. So it was a century ago at Appomattox. So it was last week in Selma, Alabama.

The president announces that he is sending a voting rights bill to Congress and urges its passage. "The outraged conscience of a nation" demands it, he tells a joint session of Congress. "It is wrong—deadly wrong—to deny any of your fellow Americans the right to vote," he says to his former colleagues, pointedly to those from the South. Seventy million people hear him say on television:

> It's not just Negroes. It's really all of us who must overcome the crippling legacy of bigotry and injustice.

And he finishes with words from the civil rights theme song: *We shall overcome.*

Later someone remembered listening to the speech with Dr. King, and how it surprised him. "We were all sitting together, and Martin was very quietly sitting in the chair, and a tear ran down his cheek."

Six days after the president's speech, 4,000 people, black and white, march from the Edmund Pettus Bridge in Selma to Alabama's capital, Montgomery, camping

King is instructed by L.C. Crooker, a Dallas County deputy sheriff, on how his followers should line up to register to vote following a march. "We are on the move now," said King when speaking at Brown's Chapel in Selma, Alabama, in 1965. "Let us therefore continue our triumph and march … on ballot boxes until the Wallaces of our nation tremble away in silence."

"Ain't going to let no posse turn me 'round,
  Keep on walkin', keep on talkin',
  Marching up to Freedom Land."

—hymn sung by
Selma-to-Montgomery marchers

out at night and singing songs of freedom. This time National Guardsmen protect them. By the time they reach the capital, 25,000 people have joined the march. Rosa Parks is there, and so are many of those who, ten years earlier, walked through winter's bluster and summer's heat rather than ride Montgomery's segregated buses. Martin Luther King, Jr., then an unknown preacher, is now world famous. "We are on the move now," he says. "Let us therefore continue our triumph and march … on ballot boxes until the Wallaces of our nation tremble away in silence."

In August, the president signs the Voting Rights Act. In Mississippi, black registration goes from less than 10 percent in 1964 to almost 60 percent in 1968. Johnson, dedicated to civil rights, is also a consummate politician. He knows that his civil rights legislation will cost him white votes. He needs blacks on the voter rolls.

La Causa

It is 2 A.M. Lucia and Maria Mendoza, aged eighteen and seventeen, stumble out of bed, dress in the dark, make a lunch of tacos and soda pop in the kitchen of their adobe house, and fill a thermos with hot soup. Then they wake their dad and their younger brother. Soon the four of them are heading north, toward the border between Mexico and the United States. They're on their way to pick lettuce in California. Each of them expects to make $16 that Tuesday. It's not much, but it's more than they can earn at home. They will use short-handled hoes that keep them bent over all day. It's hot, dusty, back-breaking work.

These Mexican farm workers are entering the United States legally. They're wanted to help harvest crops to feed people across the nation. But some of them will stay in the United States illegally. Hundreds of thousands have already done it. Most of those illegal immigrants have little schooling and few marketable skills. They're crowded into cities in poor barrios. Their children go to school. Many need job training and other kinds of help. All that costs taxpayers money. Some Americans resent them. Many say the Mexicans take jobs from American citizens, but the growers want them because they work for less money than Americans.

Once they're across the border, the Mendozas park their car and walk to a place where workers are hired for agricultural jobs. By 3:30 A.M. they're settled just behind the driver in an old, rattletrap bus heading northward toward the lettuce fields. Most of the passengers try to sleep. They know they have a long ride ahead of them, and it's still dark. Later, one passenger remembers that they were going very fast when the driver missed a curve and they became airborne-crashing into the bank of a canal, bouncing off that bank into the other bank, and settling in the shallow waterway. All the seats in the old bus fly out of their sockets in a mess of arms, legs, twisted metal and broken glass. Nineteen passengers are trapped in the bottom of the bus; they drown in two and a half feet of water. The four Mendozas are among them.

César Chvez weeps for Lucia and Maria and the others who lie in silent caskets. Chávez is an American of Mexican heritage. Everyone knows him; he is the leader of the Farm Workers Association. They want to hear what he has to say. Speaking in Spanish, Chávez tells them:

> This tragedy happened because of the greed of the big growers who do not care about the safety of the workers and who expose them to grave dangers when they transport them in wheeled coffins to the field. The workers learned long ago that growers and labor contractors have too little regard for the value of any individual worker's life. The trucks and buses are old and unsafe. The fields are sprayed with poisons. The laws that do exist are not enforced. How long will it be before we take seriously the importance of the workers who harvest the food we eat?

Chávez knows all about harvesting food. He has been a migrant worker himself, traveling from bean fields to walnut groves to grape arbors, following the harvest of the seasons. That means living in a tent, or whatever room can be found. When he was a boy, it meant changing schools as often as he changed picking fields. It meant sometimes not having shoes or a bathroom to use. By the time César graduated from eighth grade he had attended thirty-eight different schools.

Left, labor organizer César Chávez. Migrant workers' children play marbles (above) while their parents work in the fields. Changing schools constantly as they move with the crops makes learning hard for them.

Chávez is a gentle man and doesn't call attention to himself, but when he has a job to do he does it carefully and well. He can be trusted; he is honest. People turn to him when they need help. Fred Ross, a welfare organizer who comes to California to try to help poor farm workers, hears about Chávez and gives him a job in the Community Service Organization (CSO). Chávez is soon helping farm workers find housing, medical care, food, and legal help. He gets them to register to vote. Then he begins to think about starting a labor union for farm workers. Organizing agricultural laborers is not easy. Unlike factory employees, they don't all work together in one place. In California they labor on thousands of farms that stretch the length of the state. Many growers take advantage of them, paying them little (and sometimes cheating them of that), ignoring unsafe conditions, and putting their children to work, although that's against the law.

César Chávez has a wife, eight children, and that steady job with the CSO. But when he tells his wife, Helen, that he wants to quit his job to start a union, she agrees. She knows that if La Causa—"the cause"—is successful, it will help millions. It's 1962, and Chávez starts going from farm to farm talking to the workers. Three years later, his Farm Workers Association votes to join with Filipino workers in a strike against grape growers. They refuse to pick grapes until they get better pay and working conditions. The growers get the Teamsters Union to bring scabs to replace them. Chávez

In the 1930s photographer Dorothea Lange took many pictures of California migrant workers like this family, forced to live in their car. Life for such workers was much the same in the 1960s, when César Chávez campaigned for better conditions.

convinces some of the scabs to strike with them. Grapes begin rotting because no one is picking them. The growers attack and beat union members; the police help the growers.

César Chávez, inspired by Gandhi, Martin Luther King, Jr., and his own devout Catholicism, insists that the farm workers fight with peaceful marches and prayers. Nonviolence, he tells them, takes more courage than violence. Like Dr. King, he believes in active Christianity. But he needs to draw national attention to La Causa. A 300-mile march across California might do it. He gets university students and religious leaders to march with the farm workers. La Causa and the farm workers' plight are shown on television nightly. A few growers sign contracts with the union (renamed the United Farm Workers, or UFW). Chávez asks people across the United States not to buy grapes grown in California. But boycotts work slowly, and some of his union members are impatient. Like Gandhi, Chávez decides to go on a fast. For twenty-five days he eats nothing. The media follow his fast. Finally, twenty-six growers sign contracts with the union. César Chávez starts eating.

LIBERATING HALF THE WORLD

Society works best if women are subservient to men. Come again? Did people actually believe that? Yes, they did. Search for women—doctors, lawyers, senators, presidents, scientists, professors—in the upper echelons of their professions before the nineteen seventies. You may find one or two, but almost none in positions of real power. The civil rights and anti-war struggles were revealing the shallowness of traditional concepts about race and the use of military power; could it be that traditional gender roles were based primarily on entrenched habit—and little else? When writer Betty Friedan publishes her groundbreaking book *The Feminine Mystique*, in 1963, the public is ready for it. The book sells more than a million copies.

Friedan's basic theme—that all people, including women, have a natural right to develop their potential—resonates. Besides, the demographics of the female world are changing. The suburban women who are Friedan's subject may not be working, but many other women are. During World War II, about 6.5 million women who never worked before took jobs. Men were fighting; women were needed on production lines. Many of those women found they liked working. Some had no choice. Some women have always worked. "By 1960," writes William H. Chafe, "both the husband and the wife worked in over 10 million homes (an increase of 333 percent over 1940)."

But attitudes don't change easily. Working women are paid much less than men. And they don't get prestigious jobs. Many are teachers, but women are not superintendents of schools. Many are

Betty Friedan

"I ask college students not born in 1963, 'How many of you have ever worn a girdle?' They laugh. So then I say: 'Well, it used to be, not so long ago, that every woman from about the age of twelve to ninety-two who left her house in the morning encased her flesh in rigid plastic casing.'"

—Betty Friedan

An equal rights amendment (first proposed in 1923) passes both houses of Congress in 1972, but intense opposition keeps it from state ratification. Not all women supported the amendment; here women and men both protest the ERA outside the White House in 1977.

nurses, but very few are doctors. Women aren't allowed to train as pilots, bus drivers, mechanics, or police officers. With only a few exceptions, professions like architecture, law, science, and engineering are closed to women. Those who do have jobs have to put up with prejudice against working women (and sometimes sexual harassment too). And if you have a job and get pregnant, that is cause for firing. An article in the *Atlantic Monthly* says, typically: "What [the] modern woman has to recapture is the wisdom that just being a woman is her central task and her greatest honor." But what the magazines and TV shows are saying is in conflict with what more and more women are beginning to believe: that they have minds and talents equal to men's. "Just being a woman" is no longer enough.

Women in the civil rights movement find that they are expected to make coffee, do the cleaning up, and not participate in major decisions. Isn't it all supposed to be about equal rights? Some women take the activism they learn as civil rights workers and bring it into the women's movement. Women begin reinventing themselves in two directions: label them "reformers" and "radicals" and you will have the idea.

Civil Rights for Native Americans

In the 1960s and '70s, many Native Americans pretend to be something else—because they are ashamed of their heritage. But that is changing. Just as it is inspiring women, the civil rights movement inspires Indian leaders. They, too, have faced centuries of discrimination and persecution.

In the state of Washington, tribes hold "fish-ins" to protest restrictions on their treaty-granted rights to harvest salmon. In Minneapolis, urban Indians create AIM (the American Indian Movement) and talk of Red Power. In San Francisco, like-minded Native Americans form Indians of All Tribes; when the Bureau of Indian Affairs refuses to listen to their grievances, they seize an abandoned federal prison on Alcatraz Island in San Francisco Bay and hold it for a year and a half, much of their tenure recorded for national viewing under the glare of TV klieg lights. Alcatraz is a pan-Indian action—tribes that have traditionally been enemies are now banding together, though it doesn't happen easily. The militant activists go from Alcatraz to the Bureau of Indian Affairs in Washington, where they stage a protest occupation in 1972. Next, they take over a trading post at Wounded Knee in South Dakota, where the final massacre of Plains Indian tribes took place in 1890.

The dramatic takeovers work: they make non-Indians aware of Indian grievances, and they made some Indians rediscover and take new pride in their heritage. Mohawk Richard Oakes says that Alcatraz is not "a movement to liberate the island, but to liberate ourselves." Life is still substandard, however, for many Native Americans.

In 1966, thirty women, including Betty Friedan, found the National Organization for Women (NOW), "to take action to bring American women into full participation in the mainstream of American society." Friedan and the reformers envision women as equal partners in an open, shared society.

Those who call themselves radical feminists don't think Friedan and her supporters are going far enough. They want to overthrow society as they know it. Many radicals see male-dominated institutions as hopeless. Their first national action is a protest of the Miss America contest, where they unfurl a banner that reads WOMEN'S LIBERATION. Here's Robin Morgan speaking for what is a diverse group:

> *I call myself a radical feminist.... I believe that sexism is the root oppression, the one which, until and unless we uproot it, will continue to put forth the branches of racism, war, class hatred, ageism, competition, ecological disaster; and economic exploitation.*

The radical feminists develop feminist publishing houses, health organizations, child-care centers, food cooperatives, and other women-run institutions. Some

Alcoholism devastates whole peoples, and unemployment is way above the national average, both on reservations and in urban areas.

The most tangible successes come to Native Americans through the courts. Again and again, lawsuits are decided in Indians' favor in disputes over rights granted in treaties—many of them signed a century or more earlier. In 1971, Aleuts, Eskimos, and other native Alaskans win 40 million acres of land and nearly $1 billion in settlements of long-standing claims. In Maine, Penobscot Indians received $81 million for claims based on a law passed in 1790. And some Native American entrepreneurs begin taking a new look at Indian reservations, which are nations within nations and thus not subject to most state restrictions. Their status allows for activities that are often illegal elsewhere in a state, like gambling. In the 1980s and '90s and beyond, casinos begin to bring in enormous wealth—and therefore jobs, better schools, and good housing—to some Indian reservations.

Besides these changes, other things are happening: in Washington, D.C., the Smithsonian Institution returns Indian skeletal remains and funeral objects to their rightful tribal owners. In Colorado, voters elect an American Indian, Ben Nighthorse Campbell, as a representative to the U.S. Congress (and as a senator in 1992). And in Oklahoma, Wilma Mankiller, the first female chief of the Cherokee nation, speaks of her "firm belief that 500 years from now there will be strong tribal communities of native people in the Americas where ancient languages, ceremonies, and songs will be heard."

say they hate all men. Some want to integrate everything, including bathrooms. Although their numbers aren't large, their ideas get a lot of publicity. NOW is strong on organization, marches, and specific actions; the women's liberation groups are effective theorists and writers. Susan Brownmiller details some of the radical issues:

> *The explosive creation of the antiviolence issues—rape, battery, incest and child molestations, sexual harassment—and, later on, the controversial development of antipornography theory, belonged to the domain of Women's Liberation, as did the early surge of lesbian feminism and the rise of a vital, alternative feminist press.*

By 1970, women activists are picketing and demonstrating for equal job opportunities and equal access to all-male clubs and schools. Feminists are making daily headlines in the newspaper—competing with the civil rights movement and the war in Vietnam. The demonstrations reflect a whole new attitude on the part of women. When one feminist leader is told, at a national political convention, to "calm down, little girl," she is anything but calm. The brouhaha begins making a difference. Some women are now getting good jobs in previously male-only fields. Women are becoming lawyers, bankers, newspaper editors, and TV commentators. But that is only part of the picture. Things do not go well for poor and minority women, as William Chafe writes:

> From 1955 to 1981, women's actual earnings fell from 64 percent of men's to 59 percent, and even in the late 1980s their earnings had climbed back only to 62 percent—still below the figure thirty years earlier.... Eighty percent of all women workers were employed in just 5 percent of all jobs—the lowest-paying 5 percent.... By the end of the 1980s, one in every four children in America was poor, and women comprised almost 70 percent of the adult poor.... Middle- and upper-class white women might be experiencing a new freedom, but almost none of the benefits they derived from women's new opportunities trickled down to the poor. For these women, race, class, and gender represented a triple whammy.

The women's rights movement has hit a class and race wall. It was unintended. Both NOW and the radicals have worked for racial as well as female equality. But it is the women who are educated and talented who are going places. If you are poor, it is difficult to get a really good education. For women who do, no matter what their race, there are jobs. Women without training or skills—who make up a majority—are usually stuck in dead-end, low-paying jobs and still suffering from sex discrimination.

Coming Apart

Lyndon Johnson is miserable. Vietnam aches like a raw scar on his body. "I feel like a hitchhiker caught in a hailstorm on a Texas highway," he says. "I can't run. I can't hide. And I can't make it stop." And the cost of it all ($150 billion between 1950 and 1975) means there is little left for domestic programs. Johnson knows he is losing his dream of a Great Society. He doesn't seem able to admit that he's made a mistake. He says, "We are not going to send American boys nine or ten thousand miles away from home to do what Asian boys ought to be doing for themselves." But he is doing just that. He says all the bombing is aimed at military targets—but newspapers tell of houses, schools, and stores flattened by bombs. Stories of the killing of innocent villagers—including women and children—begin to emerge.

In response, anti-war demonstrations explode across America. Soon thousands of young men, many of them on college campuses, are burning their draft cards.

Paul Potter, the president of the activist Students for a Democratic Society (SDS) voices their protests:

> *The president says we are defending freedom in Vietnam. Whose freedom? Not the freedom of the Vietnamese. And what has the war done for freedom in America?*

At first the demonstrations are mostly by students, but varied groups begin to join them. Martin Luther King, Jr., starts leading anti-war protests as well as civil rights marches. Ministers of many faiths are doing the same thing. Some of the college protests get ugly and violent. And then the cities, especially those in the north, start exploding. They have been neglected. The money being spent on the Vietnam War is derailing federal poverty programs; often there's no money for basic city maintenance. In many inner cities, schools are terrible, transportation poor, crime frightening, and unemployment devastating. In 1965, race riots in the Watts section of Los Angeles last six days and leave thirty-four dead. Newark, Chicago, and Cleveland erupt with riots of their own. LBJ's Kerner Commission warns that "our nation is moving toward two societies, one black, one white—separate and unequal." Some angry young black leaders are contesting Dr. King's doctrine of nonviolence. These leaders don't talk of brotherhood and love; they talk of power, separation, and sometimes hate and violence. "We have to show them that they have every right to be afraid," says black feminist Angela Davis. Martin Luther King says of one militant group, "In advocating violence it is imitating the worst, the most brutal, and the most uncivilized value of American life."

Yet by 1968 even King is becoming frustrated. When he marches near Chicago he meets white hatred more vicious than anything he encountered in Mississippi or Alabama. Many of the city's whites are poor and are competing with blacks for jobs. In the north, poor black and white people are growing farther and farther apart. Housing decisions keep them in separate enclaves. King decides to launch a new campaign, a campaign against poverty. His program is aimed at "all the poor, including the two-thirds of them who are white." Poverty is not just a black problem or a white problem—it is a national disgrace. He plans to bring poor people to Washington. This will not be a one-time march. They will stay; they will camp in the city; the government will have to pay attention.

Dr. King is preparing for the Poor People's Campaign when the garbage workers in Memphis, Tennessee, go on strike. They need help, and King agrees to lead a march on their behalf. It has hardly begun—King is in the front row—when teenagers at the back of the line begin smashing windows and looting stores.

"Hey, hey, LBJ!
 How many kids did you kill today?"
—Vietnam War protesters' chant

A protestor being carried away from an anti-war demonstration. Most demonstrations are peaceful, but in 1970 National Guardsmen fire on protesters at Kent State University in Ohio, killing four students.

King is upset. "I will never lead a violent march," he says. "Call it off." But the police and the rock-throwing youths aren't finished. By the time the violence is over, 155 stores are damaged, sixty people have been hurt, and a sixteen-year-old boy has been killed by police gunfire. It is the first time anyone has been killed in a march Dr. King has led. "It may be that those of us who [believe in] nonviolence should just step aside and let the violent forces run their course, which will be … very brief, because you can't conduct a violent campaign in this country." But he finds he can't step aside.

He is determined to lead a peaceful march in Memphis. "We must come back," he says. "Nonviolence … is now on trial." Some of Dr. King's aides disagree. They think Memphis is too dangerous. Dr. King is receiving death threats in the mail. J. Edgar Hoover, the head of the FBI, hates King and is tapping his phone illegally Secretly, Hoover is also starting rumors, planting false articles in the papers, and harassing him with direct threats. But King won't be stopped. He's going back to Memphis.

Meanwhile, the Vietnam War has gone from bad dream to nightmare. No one believes the president or the military chiefs who keep saying we are winning. A huge North Vietnamese offensive on Tet (the Vietnamese New Year) is worse than anything before. Casualties on both side are high, destruction is widespread. The heaviest battle is at Hué, where the Vietcong (the Northern army) brutally executes 3,000 Saigon sympathizers. In response, we level the ancient, historic city. An American officer makes the much quoted comment, "It was necessary to destroy the city to save it." The president calls the Tet offensive "a failure" for the North. Their losses are huge; ours are smaller, but Senator George D. Aiken of Vermont retorts, "If this is failure I hope the Vietcong never have a major success."

The administration is coming unglued. The war has become a costly killing machine with victory nowhere in sight. At home, anti-war protests are ugly. College campuses are in turmoil. Cities are erupting.

The night before his trip back to Memphis, King turns on the television. President Johnson is making an announcement. He is cutting back on the bombing and will try to get a settlement of the war. Then the president says something unexpected and stunning: "I shall not seek and I will not accept the nomination of my party for another term as your president." The man who wanted to be the greatest of all presidents, who wanted to end poverty, is giving up. The war has claimed yet another victim.

A Dream Deferred

The very next evening, on April 3, 1968, in Memphis, Dr. King talks to a huge crowd at a church rally. He doesn't have a written speech; he just speaks from his heart. "Only when it is dark enough," he says, "can you see the stars." He understands that he and others in the second half of the twentieth century have been given a great opportunity. They are grappling with problems of the first order: war and peace and human rights. Everywhere, people are rising up, saying "We want to be free." The only path to freedom King can tolerate is peaceful and forgiving; he will not condone the violence and hatred that seem to be gaining ground:

I would like to live a long life. But I'm not concerned about that now. I just want to

"This I do believe deeply. The dream of Martin Luther King, Jr., has not died with him. Men who are white, men who are black must and will now join together as never in the past to let all the forces of divisiveness know that America shall not be ruled by the bullet but only by the ballot of free and of just men."
—Lyndon Johnson

> do God's will. And He's allowed me to go up to the mountain. And I've looked over. And I've seen the Promised Land. And I may not get there with you. But I want you to know tonight that we as a people will get to the Promised Land.... I have a dream ... that the brotherhood of man will become a reality.

The following evening, on April 4, King steps out onto the balcony off his room at the Lorraine Motel. His friend Ralph Abernathy hears something that sounds like a firecracker. It is no firecracker. Martin Luther King, Jr., has been shot dead. He is thirty-nine years old.

Senator Robert Kennedy, younger brother of the assassinated president, is in Indianapolis campaigning for the Democratic nomination for the presidency when he hears the news. He is about to speak to an African-American crowd in a troubled section of the city. "Cancel the talk," the mayor urges. But Kennedy climbs onto the flatbed of a truck and tells the crowd of the tragedy in Memphis. He says:

> Martin Luther King dedicated his life to love and to justice for his fellow human beings, and he died because of that effort. In this difficult day, in this difficult time for the United States, it is perhaps well to ask what kind of a nation we are and what direction we want to move in. For those of you who are black—considering the evidence there evidently is that there were white people who were responsible—you can be filled with bitterness, with hatred, and a desire for revenge. We can move in that direction as a country ... black people amongst black, white people amongst white, filled with hatred toward one another.
>
> Or we can make an effort, as Martin Luther King did, to understand and to comprehend, and to replace that violence, that stain of bloodshed that has spread across our land, with an effort to understand with compassion and love.

Martin Luther King, Jr., is carried to his grave on a plain farm cart pulled by two mules. His casket is of polished African mahogany. Thousands come from across the country and around the world paying tribute to a man whose name will be forever linked to the message of love, brotherhood, peace, and freedom.

At the very time King is lowered into the ground, 130 cities around the nation are burning. Rioters—looting and shooting—are killing people and destroying homes and businesses; 65,000 troops called in to put down the riots. Almost all the victims are African-Americans. When the fires cool, thirty-nine people are dead. Meanwhile, King's assassin, a two-bit bank robber on the lam, is able to get to England and three other countries before finally being captured two months later—leaving unanswered the question of where he got the money and the savvy to do what he did.

Bobby Too

Brash Bobby Kennedy, the tough kid in his brother's administration, has been changed by his brother's murder and by the idealism at the core of many of the movements shaking the nation. He has gone himself into inner cities; he has marched with César Chávez. A long-shot candidate for president in 1968, Kennedy has a vibrant following, especially among the young and the disaffected. He is a product of affluent America. Can he reconcile the rich and powerful with aspiring America? Can he get the outs and the ins working together? Can he end the culture of governmental lying that is part of the Vietnam legacy? Robert Kennedy writes a book, *Toward A New World*, explaining his ideas. He begins with lines from Tennyson's "Ulysses":

*The lights begin to twinkle from
    the rocks:
The long day wanes: the slow moon
    climbs: the deep
Moans round with many voices.
    Come, my friends,
'Tis not too late to seek a newer world.*

Bobby Kennedy calls his campaign the "Impossible Dream," after a popular song. He is walking through a hotel kitchen, shaking hands, when a twenty-four-year-old Jordanian busboy, Sirhan Bishara Sirhan, angry about Kennedy's support of Israel, pulls out a gun and fires. For many, it is the end of a dream.

Robert Kennedy and Donald F. Benjamin (center) of Central Brooklyn Coordinating Council visiting with children outside the CBCC building in 1966. After Robert Kennedy's death, a historian wrote of him: "Born the son of wealth, he died a champion of outcasts of the world."

Part 16

BECOMING FREE

Soon after Franklin D. Roosevelt was inaugurated as president for the first time, in 1933, he paid a visit to the revered Supreme Court justice Oliver Wendell Holmes, Jr., then ninety-one. After Roosevelt had gone, Holmes was asked what he thought. "Second-class intellect," he said; "first-class temperament."

Richard Nixon, elected president in 1968, has a first-class intellect, but perhaps the most unfit temperament of any of those who have held the office. He sees demons everywhere and in everyone; but in the end it is his own demons that do him in.

The Nixon tale begins in the eighteenth century, when an Irish Quaker family named Milhous arrives in William Penn's colony. Hardworking, peace-loving folk, they eventually move to California and help found a Quaker town named Whittier. When the twentieth century begins, Frank Milhous is the prosperous owner of a plant nursery in Whittier and not at all impressed with Frank Nixon, the man his daughter Hannah chooses to wed. The Nixons, too, arrived in America in the eighteenth century, but prosperity has eluded them. It certainly eludes Frank Nixon, who is orphaned young. He and Hannah have five children and struggle to get by on Frank's modest income from a grocery store and odd jobs. They live in a small frame house Frank builds from an $800 kit (bought from Sears, Roebuck). Two of their sons die young, leaving the second son, Richard, feeling compelled to be three boys in one. A quiet, serious lad, Richard works hard in the grocery store and gets good grades at school. In high school he learns to debate and does some acting. California's Harvard Club picks him as its top choice the year he is ready for college. He is awarded a full tuition scholarship, but

Richard Nixon's journey to the presidency begins in California, where he was born in 1913 (right, Dick, far right, with his father, mother, and two of his brothers); it ends in disgrace sixty years later in Washington, D.C., with the break-in of the Democratic Party Headquarters at the Watergate Hotel (left).

> "I have never thought much of the notion that the presidency makes a man presidential. What has given the American presidency its vitality is that each man remains distinctive. His abilities become more obvious, and his faults become more glaring. The presidency is not a finishing school. It is a magnifying glass."
>
> —Richard M. Nixon, *Memoirs*

his parents can't afford to pay Harvard's costs for room and board. Maybe it is that disappointment that festers inside him; maybe it is something else. At any rate, he will harbor deep grudges. But, as a teenager, he has no choice but to stay home and go to Whittier College. There he is the skinny boy on the football squad, and learns "to come back after you have been knocked down or after you lose." He is elected president of the student council, gets a scholarship to law school at Duke University, and serves in the navy during World War II.

As a young, just-out-of-the-navy lawyer, Nixon sees a chance to run for Congress and grabs it. His opponent is one of the few congressmen who opposed the wartime internment of Japanese-Americans. Nixon calls him a communist—and wins. When he runs for Senate, someone on his staff forges a picture that shows his opponent with a well-known communist. Everyone does it, his supporters say of Nixon's mudslinging and dirty tricks. The idea is to get elected, so you can put your plans in place.

But there always seem to be two Nixons: one is highly capable, the other is combative and self-deceiving. When he becomes president, he brings his dual personalities with him. Nixon the statesman talks of law and order—and after months of riots in the cities, that's what most Americans want to hear. The other Nixon has little respect for law or truth when they don't suit him. Running for president, he claims he has a plan to end the war; but he keeps American soldiers fighting and dying in Vietnam for almost five more years (he's reelected in 1972). He expands the war into neighboring Cambodia and Laos without telling Congress he plans to do it. Nixon drops more bombs than any president in our history, although he says he wants to be a peacemaker. The anti-war demonstrations were bad when Lyndon Johnson was president; they're worse for Nixon. When protests erupt at Kent State University, National Guardsmen open fire and four students are killed. Given campus uprisings, turmoil in the African-American and feminist worlds, a war sending young men home in body bags, rising drug and crime problems, and three shocking assassinations, the nation is angry and polarized.

On June 13, 1971, the *New York Times* begins publication of the Pentagon Papers, a 7,000-page classified document commissioned by Johnson's secretary of defense, Robert McNamara. As his disenchantment with the war in Vietnam set in, McNamara got a team of experts to look at and analyze the process that took us into the mire. It turned out to be a story of secrecy and deception. At first, Nixon officials believe the documents are an embarrassment only to previous administrations—it's history, after all. But they quickly decide that publication of the Pentagon Papers will imperil their own policy of secrecy. Citing national security, the administration gets an injunction to stop further publication (the papers are being serialized in other papers, too). The *Times* appeals. The government argues that continued publication will endanger lives and inhibit the peace process. At issue is that wavy line between individual and societal rights. How much access should the media have? How many secrets should a democratic government keep from its electorate? Legally, what's at issue is prior restraint—preventing publication deemed harmful to the national interest. This is the first time the federal government has ever asked for prior restraint. The Supreme Court delays its summer recess to hear the arguments.

Three days later, nine separate opinions are handed down. No justice can command the support of a majority with his reasoning. But six of them reject the government's position that further publication constitutes "immediate and irreparable harm to the nation." Prior restraint, says Justice Hugo Black, is a "a flagrant, indefensible" violation of the First Amendment. "The press was protected so that it would bare the secrets of government and inform the people … and prominent among the responsibilities of a free press is the duty to prevent any part of the government from deceiving the people and sending them off to distant lands to die of foreign … shot and shell." Black says the "newspapers should be commended for serving the purposes the Founding Fathers saw so clearly."

In dissent, Chief Justice Warren Burger says he believes that publishers can be prosecuted for printing classified documents, but only after publication. The case was expected to produce a landmark decision on prior restraint. It doesn't. But it does end the injunction. Publication of the Pentagon Papers continues.

Secretary of State Henry Kissinger guesses that Daniel Ellsberg (one of the authors of the Pentagon Papers) is responsible for leaking them to the press; he feels personally betrayed. (He once hired Ellsberg as a consultant.) A Nixon aide writes in his diary, "Henry got Nixon cranked up and they started cranking each other up until they were both in a frenzy." In September the Beverly Hills office of

> "The basis of our government being the opinion of the people, the first object shall be to keep that right; and were it left for me to decide whether we should have a government without newspapers, or newspapers without government, I should not hesitate a moment to choose the latter."
>
> —Thomas Jefferson, 1787

Ellsberg's psychiatrist is broken into and rifled by White House operatives—later dubbed "plumbers." They're looking for derogatory information about Ellsberg. The executive branch is hiring thugs to get the goods on someone it doesn't like.

At about the same time, the Vietnam Veterans Against the War, men who fought in Vietnam, march in Washington protesting the war's atrocities. Nixon has the CIA and the District of Columbia police jail thousands of protesters without proper charges.

WATERGATE

Most Americans are weary of the continuing conflicts. Nixon, who has the ability to be decisive, doesn't seem capable of that in Vietnam. Eventually, he gets us out of the war much as we got in—one step at a time. It's called "phased withdrawal." When Saigon, the capital of South Vietnam, falls to northern forces, we agree to a truce. We have lost a war; lost it to a repressive regime; and we are confused and humbled and disillusioned. Vietnam was, as one of Nixon's advisers said, "an all-out limited war." We couldn't fight it all the way, because we didn't want to provoke World War III. And we couldn't win as participants in someone else's civil war.

Meanwhile, Nixon wants to go down in the history books as a great president—and foreign policy is where his interest lies. He's a pragmatist who understands that the world is changing and that dealing directly with communist nations makes more sense than existing at a continuing standoff. So the man who made his reputation as an uncompromising anti-communist goes to China and sets the stage for a working relationship between the two nations. Henry Kissinger precedes him on a secret trip where plans are laid. Kissinger, aware of John Foster Dulles's slight, makes a point of shaking hands openly with Zhou Enlai. Nixon and Kissinger may have seen the opening of relations with China as a way to get the upper hand with the U.S.S.R. Whatever their motives, the bipolar world now has a third important player.

Then Nixon goes to Moscow, the first American president to do so. A historic arms-control agreement comes of that initiative. But the solid accomplishments of this complex president will be made insignificant by his own actions. Richard Nixon has put our traditional freedoms in jeopardy as no president has done before.

On June 17, 1972, four Cubans and an ex-CIA man wearing sunglasses and surgical gloves break into Democratic Party headquarters at Washington's fancy Watergate apartment complex. They are employees of the Committee to Re-elect the President (CREEP) and they have been engaged in a crime—breaking, entering, and planting eavesdropping equipment. They are caught by the local police.

What are they doing? At first, it isn't clear. The administration is vague. Secret payments go to the burglars to buy their silence. But two *Washington Post* reporters have begun to investigate. And, as they say, one thing leads to another. And another. (For the astonishing details, read *All the President's Men* by Bob Woodward and Carl Bernstein.) The hijinks at the Watergate are the tip of an iceberg. This president has been out of control. Nixon and his aides have assembled a lengthy list of "enemies." It includes: senators Edward Kennedy and Walter Mondale, the economist J. K. Galbraith, actors Gregory Peck, Bill Cosby, Paul Newman, and Barbra Streisand, and the presidents of Yale University and Harvard Law School.

Telephone lines are tapped; government operatives listen to private conversations. Lies are planted in the media about people Nixon dislikes. The government's tax office is used against his personal enemies. The administration pressures corporate executives and labor leaders for campaign money in exchange for executive favors. It pays hush money to keep some people quiet and to have others lie in sworn

"Nixon wanted to become Richard the Great. He wanted nothing short of world peace and a prosperous, happy America. He was brought down by his own hubris, by his own actions, by his own character."

—Stephen Ambrose, *Nixon: Ruin and Recovery, 1973–1990*

"I am not a crook," Nixon tells reporters. But as Watergate unfolds it becomes clear that he has authorized wrongdoing. Sam Ervin says: "The president seems to extend executive privilege way out past the atmosphere. What he says is executive privilege is nothing but executive poppycock." By October 1973 Nixon's approval rating hits a low of 17 percent.

testimony to judges and juries. When some of the wrongdoing becomes known, the Nixon White House goes further. It attempts to hide the truth.

But there are surprises to come: records turn up. Nixon's chief of staff, H. R. "Bob" Haldeman has kept a diary. In it he writes, "He [Nixon] wants total discipline on the press, they're to be used as enemies, not played for help." And "He wants to be sure the IRS covers all major Democratic contributors and all backers of the new senators." Nixon has secretly taped conversations of everyone who comes into the Oval Office. Does a president have a right to privacy in the Oval Office? Are the tapes his? Nixon believes so. But now the nation wants to hear those tapes and, despite desperate legal maneuvering, they become public property. On March 22, 1973, speaking to his four top aides, Nixon says, "I don't give a shit what happens. I want you all to stonewall it. Let them plead the Fifth Amendment, cover-up or anything else, if it'll save it—save the plan. That's the whole point."

A month later, speaking of the presidency on television, he says, "The office is a sacred trust and I am determined to be worthy of that trust." But the *Washington Post* team, Woodward and Bernstein, have found an informant in the administration; they refer to him as "Deep Throat." He has some shocking revelations. Then a tape from June 1973 provides what is called the "smoking gun." On the tape, the president can be heard approving a plan to get the CIA to ask the FBI to halt its investigation into the source of the cash held by the Watergate burglars.

There have been more corrupt administrations: Ulysses S. Grant and Warren Harding presided over the worst. Their appointees took advantage of their positions to put money in their pockets. But once those presidents learned what was happening, they did all they could to stop it.

Nixon is different. He's the instigator of the malfeasance in his administration.

"This office is a sacred trust," says Richard Nixon in 1973. But almost all the senior White House staff is involved in the Watergate cover-up. Republican senator Barry Goldwater tells Nixon that if he is impeached in the House he will almost surely be convicted in the Senate. The president resigns on August 9, 1974.

It has little to do with greed for money (though there is some of that). It is about power, arrogance, vindictiveness and contempt for the democratic process. Richard Nixon has sworn to uphold the Constitution. Yet he seems to think that because he is president, and because he believes his goals are sound, that laws don't apply to him. But the whole point of the American experiment is that the same laws apply to everyone—even the president. North Carolina's Senator Sam Ervin, Jr., says of Nixon, "Divine right went out with the American revolution."

The president is not above the law. Nor are others in his administration. Vice President Spiro Agnew, in unrelated criminality, admits to filing a "false and fraudulent" tax return. He leaves office, is fined $110,000 and sentenced to three years' probation. Fifty-six men in the Nixon administration are convicted of crimes. Some go to jail. Officers of twenty large corporations are found guilty of making illegal contributions to Nixon's 1972 campaign. The writers of the Constitution prepared for this kind of emergency by giving Congress the power to impeach and try a president, as happened with Andrew Johnson after the Civil War—and as will happen again with President Bill Clinton, in different circumstances.

In the House of Representatives, articles of impeachment are prepared. Article I charges Nixon with "violation of his constitutional oath faithfully to execute the office of President." It cites obstruction of justice with specific reference to the Watergate break-in. Article II charges him with violating the constitutional rights of citizens by authorizing illegal wiretaps and by illegally using the FBI, the IRS, and the CIA. Article III charges him with violating the Constitution by failing to turn over materials subpoenaed by the Judiciary Committee. Most incriminating is the cover-up: the purposeful obstruction of justice. Representative Barbara Jordan, the first African-American woman elected to the Texas State Senate, is a member of the House Judiciary Committee considering the impeachment of the president. Her impassioned speech about the task facing the House is carried on national television:

Earlier today we heard the beginning of the Preamble to the Constitution of the United States, "We, the people." It is a very eloquent beginning. But when the document was completed, on the 17th of

"Truth is great and will prevail if left to herself ... she is the proper and sufficient antagonist to error, and has nothing to fear from the conflict, unless by human interposition disarmed of her natural weapons, free argument and debate, errors ceasing to be dangerous when it is permitted freely to contradict them."

—Thomas Jefferson, from the Virginia Statute for Religious Freedom, 1786

September in 1787, I was not included in that "We, the people." I felt somehow for many years that George Washington and Alexander Hamilton just left me out by mistake. But through the process of amendment, interpretation, and court decision, I have finally been included in "We, the people." Today, I am an inquisitor.... My faith in the Constitution is whole, it is complete, it is total. I am not going to sit here and be an idle spectator to the diminution, the subversion, the destruction of the Constitution.

Nixon chooses to leave the presidency rather than face almost certain impeachment in the House and then a trial (and probable conviction) in the Senate. He resigns the job, the only man ever to do so. Anthony Lewis, writing in the *New York Times*, says, "Those who manage the delicate institutions of government have a special responsibility to represent the law."

In England, the editor of the *Spectator* writes that the U.S. presidency has gone from George Washington, who could not tell a lie, to Richard Nixon, who could not tell the truth.

Barbara Jordan

There are positives in the calamity. Given a free press and some intrepid civil servants, our governmental structure works in a dignified manner to discover and remove those who have abused the public trust. Watergate shows, unequivocally, that in the United States everyone, even a president, is accountable to the law. Senator Sam Ervin, known for pithy comments, has a final word: "One of the great advantages of the three separate branches of government is that it is difficult to corrupt all three at the same time."

A Fourth Branch—and Some Twigs

The temptation to keep secrets—and keep the press on a leash—is hard for most politicians to resist. Watergate shouted out that a vibrant free press is essential in a democracy. It's through the courts that our guarantees of freedom of expression and of the press have evolved. Here are a few milestones.

During World War I, when some anarchists throw 5,000 anti-war leaflets from the windows of a New York City hat factory—pamphlets that call for a strike by weapons makers—they are arrested and convicted under the Espionage Act of 1917 (see part 11, page 259). The Supreme Court upholds the convictions, but two of its justices—Louis D. Brandeis and Oliver Wendell Holmes, Jr.—dissent. In this case, *Abrams v. United States*, Justice Holmes refines his doctrine of "clear and present

Guarantees of free speech include speech most find repugnant. Peaceful demonstrations, such as that lead by the Ku Klux Klan in 1926 down Pennsylvania Avenue in Washington, D.C., are protected.

danger." "Now nobody can suppose that the surreptitious publishing of a silly leaflet … would present any immediate danger," he writes in his opinion. Holmes makes it a First Amendment issue.

> The ultimate good desired is better reached by free trade in ideas—that the best test of truth is the power of the thought to get itself accepted in the competition of the market…. That at any rate is the theory of the Constitution. It is an experiment, as all life is an experiment.

In 1927, in *Whitney* v. *California*, the Supreme Court considers the California Syndicalism Act, which prohibits speech advocating illegal political activities. Charlotte Anita Whitney, dedicated to causes aiding the poor, has helped organize the Communist Labor Party in California. She is convicted as a "member of an organization, society, group and assemblage of persons organized and assembled to advocate, teach, aid and abet criminal syndicalism." Miss Whitney protests that at no time did she advocate acts of violence or terror.

Is she protected by the First Amendment, or is she guilty of criminal conspiracy—which would put her outside the protection of free speech? Justice Louis D. Brandeis writes, in an often-cited opinion:

> [Those who won our independence] believed that freedom to think as you

will and to speak as you think are means indispensable to the discovery and spread of political truth, that without free speech and assembly, discussion would be futile, that with them, discussion affords ordinarily adequate protection against the dissemination of noxious doctrine; that the greatest menace to freedom is an inert people, that public discussion is a political duty; and that this should be fundamental principle of the American government.

Despite Justice Brandeis's statement, he and the court side against Whitney with the state of California, deciding that dangerous speech or activities that have a "tendency" to encourage lawlessness, or that are part of a dangerous political movement (like communism), are illegal. But the issue is troublesome. In 1969, in *Brandenburg* v. *Ohio*, the court revisits it with the "clear and present danger" concept in mind.

Clarence Brandenburg has urged racial violence during a televised Ku Klux Klan rally and is convicted of violating an Ohio law (similar to the California act). This time the court says dangerous speech deserves protection unless "such advocacy is directed to inciting or producing imminent lawless action and is likely to incite or produce such action." In other words, law enforcement officers need to prove that speech is demonstrably dangerous. Whitney is overthrown. Brandenburg is free to advocate nastiness. Justice Hugo Black says, "The worst citizen no less than the best is entitled to equal protection of the laws of his state and of his nation." In Justice Felix Frankfurter's words, "It is a fair summary of history to say that safeguards of liberty have been forged in controversies involving not very nice people."

Does the press have a right to attend criminal trials? In 1980, the court answers this question in *Richmond Newspapers* v. *Virginia*. The defendant has been tried for murder four times; the previous trials have been reversed or declared mistrials. Because of the previous publicity, he now believes he cannot get a fair trial with the press present. Chief Justice Warren Burger says that the public and the press have a constitutional right to witness a criminal trial, a right "implicit in the guarantees of the First Amendment for freedom of speech, of the press, and of assembly" and in the Ninth Amendment's grant to "the people" of "certain rights" not enumerated elsewhere. And that, "absent an overriding interest to the contrary," criminal trials must be open to the public. Justice William Rehnquist is the lone dissenter.

In a ringing opinion written in 1941, Supreme Court Justice Hugo Black said,

"America's special commitment to free speech is based on … a collective bet that free speech will do us more good than harm over the long run."
—Ronald Dworkin, professor of law, Oxford and New York universities

"Freedom to speak and write about public questions is as important to the life of our government as is the heart to the human body."

Not a Lincoln but a Ford

Gerald Ford, a popular, hardworking Republican congressman from Michigan, was picked by President Nixon to replace Spiro Agnew when Agnew resigned as vice president. So when Nixon resigns in his turn, Ford finds himself president (although he has never been elected either president or vice president). He's a plain-spoken, sensible man untainted by controversy. That is what the nation needs. Ford grants Nixon an unconditional pardon for whatever wrongs he may have done the United States. (Those who carried out Nixon's instructions are in jail; but he will get the perks and pension of a former president.) Ford also pardons draft protesters who refused to fight in Vietnam. He orders the last U.S. troops and support workers evacuated from Vietnam. They leave in an inglorious frenzy.

Ford says that "the presidency and the vice presidency [are] not prizes to be won but a duty to be done." But that modest thought is not enough when he runs for the office himself, in 1976. James Earl "Jimmy" Carter becomes the thirty-ninth chief executive. A redheaded peanut farmer with a big toothy grin, Carter graduated from the U.S. Naval Academy at Annapolis, became a nuclear submarine officer, and then governor of Georgia. When he decides to run for the nation's top office he is hardly known outside his own state, and most people—including his own mother—laugh at the idea. But Carter is determined. Soft-spoken and deeply religious, he tells the American people, "I will not lie to you." And he never does.

Carter is a southern Democrat with progressive views on civil rights and moderate ideas on economics. But he's an outsider when it comes to dealing with Congress. He brings his friends from Georgia to the capital. They have good ideas, and Carter believes Congress will go along with them. But they don't know how to play the Washington game, and good ideas are not enough. Besides that, Carter is unlucky. While he is president, a worldwide energy crisis makes prices—especially the price of oil and gas—zoom up. Oil shortages cause long lines at gas stations. (For the first time since the internal combustion engine was introduced, Americans are forced to conserve energy and to buy smaller, more energy-efficient cars—though by the 1990s oversize "sport-utility vehicles" have made gas guzzling fashionable again.)

Even more unluckily for Carter, he must deal with serious problems in the Middle East. The roots of a crisis in Iran lie beyond the president's control—but, like

In 1976 Democrat Jimmy Carter (right) runs against President Gerald Ford (left) and wins. He is known for his honesty—"I will never lie to you," he tells the American people—and is untainted by scandal.

"I believe that truth is the glue that holds government together; not only our government but civilization itself.... As we bind up the internal wounds of Watergate, more painful and more poisonous than those of foreign wars, let us restore the golden rule to our political process, and let brotherly love purge our hearts of suspicion and of hate."

—Gerald Ford, in his inaugural address

much of the history of our engagement in the Middle East, they are linked to energy and oil. During Eisenhower's presidency, we helped return the hereditary ruler of Iran—the shah—to power through secret, and illegal, activities of the CIA. It was a move that undid Iran's democracy and left a legacy of bitterness toward the U.S.

During Carter's presidency, the shah is overthrown by a fundamentalist Muslim religious leader, the Ayatollah Khomeini, who, building on that bitterness, preaches hatred of the United States. At great political cost, Carter rejects intervention in the Iranian revolution. But when he allows the shah into the United States for medical treatment, militant Muslim students react by storming the U.S. embassy in Iran's capital, Teheran. They capture members of the embassy staff, holding them hostage for a harrowing 444 days. President Carter authorizes a daring rescue mission, but it fizzles into an embarrassing mess of poor planning and failed equipment. Carter continues to work hard to have the hostages returned. That will happen only hours after he leaves the presidency.

Jimmy Carter does achieve a major foreign policy success in the Middle East—succeeding in bringing the leaders of Israel and Egypt together to agree to a peace treaty. He also convinces Congress (again at political cost) to transfer control of the Panama Canal to the government of Panama and to stay out of a civil war in Nicaragua. A highly intelligent, compassionate man, he is nonetheless a poor communicator. He tries to solve problems of national debt and energy conservation by asking people to make sacrifices. Maybe he doesn't know how to ask—or maybe Americans aren't ready to make sacrifices. When he runs for reelection, Carter is defeated. As an ex-president he founds the Carter Center at Emory University, devoted to settling international disputes and solving health and poverty problems at home and abroad. Carter and his wife, Rosalynn, will work tirelessly for world peace.

A LEADING ROLE

The next president is a great communicator—in fact, that's what people start calling him. His name is Ronald Reagan, and, although he's sixty-nine when elected, few people think of him as a senior citizen. He's boyish, easygoing, and friendly. He has a great sense of humor and a hard-to-resist grin. He has been a Hollywood film star and he knows how to use television as no president before him. After the turmoil of the '60s and '70s, and the unsettled presidencies of Ford and Carter, many Americans think Reagan just right for the times. He calls himself "Mr. Normal," and doesn't seem to take himself too seriously.

A few months after he takes office, a would-be assassin takes aim at the president on a Washington street and puts a bullet into his lung. As Reagan is wheeled into the operating room, he says to his wife, Nancy. "Honey, I forgot to duck."

But he doesn't joke when it comes to ideas. He knows exactly what he believes, and he explains those beliefs clearly and simply. In a complex world that is harder and harder to understand, he seems reassuring and honest and old-fashioned. It is 1981, and Reagan is about to bring a radical change of direction to American politics—and be very

Ronald Reagan "believed in the magic of individual freedom," wrote biographer Lou Cannon. "He believed the appeal of free markets and personal freedoms ultimately would prove irresistible to all people everywhere."

"It remains true that nearly all of the world's richest countries are free (meaning, among other things, democratic) and nearly all of the poorest countries are not.... Across the world, in other words, the correlation between political freedom and prosperity is a close one."
—*The Economist*, August 1994

popular doing it. His partisans will adore him, his detractors will have apoplexy—but few presidents have been as effective.

Under Reagan, many of the ideas of an era, begun fifty years earlier with the New Deal, are overturned. "Welfare state" is the term used to describe programs designed to help the poor and needy. Although well intentioned, many welfare programs have become bureaucratic dead ends. Reagan not only attacks those New Deal/Great Society anti-poverty programs, he rejects the liberal philosophy that conceived them—the idea that the government has a responsibility to help those at the bottom of the ladder, using tax money to direct that effort, and taxing the rich at a higher rate than the poor. This is a central issue of government in our time, so it is worthy of consideration. To sum up the opposing views: liberals think government can actively solve social problems and make our society more fair; conservatives believe that doesn't work, and that (more or less) unrestricted capitalism leads to opportunity and prosperity—and that helps everyone.

Reagan is anti-tax, anti-union, and fiercely anti-communist. He wants to reduce the size of the government. He wants to cut spending on welfare programs, eliminate most government regulation of business, take the federal government out of the field of education, and balance the budget. He also wants to build up the armed forces and increase military spending. How do things actually turn out? Well, by the end of the 1980s, the United States is the world's greatest superpower, and very wealthy. But in most inner cities, schools, bridges, roads, and buildings are falling apart; urban crime is soaring; some education statistics are in a free fall; and access to good health care is not equal to that in most developed nations.

Balancing the budget is one of Reagan's key goals; he is strongly critical of the deficit, which, under Carter in 1979, seemed very high. He believes that if his administration cuts taxes and public welfare programs, and eliminates as much regulation of business as possible, it will stimulate the economy and tax revenues will increase—more than enough to pay for the huge increase in military spending that he believes necessary to continue to fight the Cold War. Under Reagan, Congress enacts the single largest tax cut in our history. That does stimulate the economy, which increases tax revenues and the total taxes paid by those in the higher income range. But people in the higher tax brackets (earning $50,000 and up) keep 35 percent of the revenue lost by the federal government. Before Reagan's tax reform, of each dollar the government collected in taxes, thirteen cents came from corporations; afterwards, the corporate share is eight cents. Programs directed at the poor and middle class are reduced by $41 billion. The gap between rich and poor grows from gully to chasm. "When income for the bottom 10 percent of the population fell by 10.5 percent from 1977 to 1987, that for the top 10 percent went up 24.4 percent—and that for the top 1 percent went up 74.2 percent," writes Garry Wills in *Reagan's America*.

At the same time, Congress embarks on a $1.6 trillion military expansion. (Both parties approve of this. Jimmy Carter's budget called for even greater military spending than Reagan's.) What happens to the national debt? It goes from $383 billion in 1980 to $2.3 trillion in 1988. Reagan's deficits total more than the deficits of all the presidents before him combined.

"Government is not the solution to our problem" says Reagan. "Government is the problem." Many agree. Too often, Americans dealing with the government face a frustrating, often arrogant, unresponsive bureaucracy. Bureaucracies—in big business, big schools, and big government—seem to define the twentieth century. What can be done? How do you conduct public business wisely without oppressive regulations? The Republican administration decides to cut or cut back the watchdog agencies that oversee business; it weakens already weak union power; where it can, it turns public land and agencies over to private interests, and it lifts restrictions on TV commercials on the public airwaves.

Some companies aren't prepared for the responsibilities that go with their new freedom. Savings-and-loan associations, created to lend money to ordinary people to buy houses, make speculative investments they don't understand, knowing that the government will guarantee their customers' deposits. Many of the mortgage banks go broke when the value of their investments falls; in the end the savings-and-loan bailout costs taxpayers an estimated $481 billion—more than the entire national debt under Nixon. (By comparison, in the 1980s we spend less than $2 billion a year on schoolbooks.) "If men were angels, no government would be necessary," said James Madison. But men aren't angels, and neither are women.

At the Department of Housing and Urban Affairs scandals cost the taxpayer more billions of dollars. One hundred and thirty-eight members of the administration

---

"Great as our tax burden is, it has not kept pace with public spending. For decades we have piled deficit upon deficit, mortgaging our future and our children's future for the temporary convenience of the present. To continue this long trend is to guarantee tremendous social, cultural, political, and economic upheavals."

—Ronald Reagan, first inaugural address, 1981

are investigated for criminal misconduct; many are convicted. All the money spent on military procurement is tempting for those who can't resist temptation. In 1985 alone, military contracts awarded to business total $163.7 billion. Arkansas senator David Pryor describes "an eight-year feeding frenzy at the Department of Defense." At the same time, libraries, public radio and television, museums, national parks, and other public institutions find themselves with less government aid. Spending on education drops 15 percent in real dollars. And with the federal government doing less, city and state government have to spend more. They grow enormously during the Reagan years.

Tear Down This Wall

Again and again, Ronald Reagan speaks out on the dangers of Russian communism. He calls the Soviet Union an "evil empire." Then something astonishing happens: President Reagan and Prime Minister Mikhail Gorbachev begin talking to each other. They meet at Geneva, in Switzerland, in 1985, and in Reykjavik, the capital of Iceland, in 1986. They talk about the dangers of nuclear war, and about grandchildren; and that leads to productive arms-control agreements. The following year, the president visits Berlin, Germany. That city has been divided in two since 1961. In West Berlin, people are free to come and go and practice democracy; in East Berlin, the communist government of the German Democratic Republic has fenced in its own people. There, a strong, well-guarded wall, built right through the middle of the city, keeps East Germans from visiting friends, family, and neighbors in the West. It is the symbol of the imprisonment of a whole people. Reagan stands before it and says bluntly, "Mr. Gorbachev, tear down this wall!"

Forces are at work in the eastern bloc nations that will indeed cause the wall to tumble. Gorbachev, who is a communist but also a realistic leader, is aware that Russia needs to change. Reagan the Cold Warrior is anxious to become a peacemaker; he is a passionate spokesman for freedom and democracy. In 1988, Reagan goes to Moscow, this time as a friend of the Russian premier (those grandchildren have helped). The two leaders realize they have a chance to change history; they can end the insane arms race that has been so costly to both nations and has affected the whole world. Reagan, speaking to students at Moscow State University, says:

> *Your generation is living in one of the most exciting, hopeful times in Soviet history. It is a time when the first breath of freedom stirs the air and the heart beats to the accelerated rhythm of hope, when the accumulated spiritual energies*

of a long silence yearn to break free.... We do not know what the conclusion of this journey will be, but we're hopeful that the promise of reform will be fulfilled. In this May 1988, we may be allowed that hope—that freedom, like the fresh green sapling planted over Tolstoy's grave, will blossom forth at last in the rich, fertile soil of your people and culture.

A year later, in 1989, the Soviet Union breaks into pieces. Yes, the Soviet Union, the U.S.S.R., the land we call Russia—a nation composed of many states—falls apart. The country doesn't collapse militarily, but, as a political system, communism has failed.

It began with high hopes as a visionary experiment. But the experiment turned Russia into an unfree, tyrannical, clumsy nation. Government ownership of land and products never brought the efficiency and productivity that the theorists promised. And the burden of ever-growing military expenditures wrecked Russia's economy. Television lets Soviet citizens, and others worldwide, see the success of free nations. The Russian people have had enough of communist repression; it hasn't worked. They throw communism out. It is stunning and it is peaceful. Everything has changed in world politics. The Cold War is over. It is hard to believe. Now that Russia is a free—and greatly weakened—nation, there is no giant for the United States to battle.

Ronald Reagan understands what is happening before most of America's Soviet experts figure it out. In an inspired speech in

In 1988, a few months after Mikhail Gorbachev visits President Reagan for a summit at the White House (below), Reagan travels to Russia and delivers a speech at Moscow State University celebrating life under freedom and democracy.

England to both houses of Parliament he says:
> Let us be shy no longer. Let us go to our strength. Let us offer hope. Let us tell the world that a new age is not only possible but probable.... For the sake of peace and justice, let us move toward a world in which all people are at last free to determine their own destiny.

The First President Bush

When Republican George Herbert Walker Bush, Ronald Reagan's vice president, is elected forty-first president in 1988, he inherits problems. All those costly years of cold war have been hard on the United States as well as on Russia. The country is in an economic slump; cities are in decay; school test scores don't match those of many other developed nations; crime is epidemic; and the huge national debt is making many Americans fearful of the future. After promising not to raise taxes, Bush, faced with reality, does it anyway—with the help of congressional Democrats. He may be laying the ground for prosperity to come, but his constituents feel betrayed.

Bush's foreign policy is more popular. Saddam Hussein, dictator of the Middle Eastern nation of Iraq, sends troops into neighboring Kuwait, a small, oil-rich kingdom, and the president quickly leads a forceful response in partnership with the United Nations. Talking to other world leaders directly, he gets hesitant Arab chiefs to agree to back sanctions against the aggressor. The brief Gulf War is labeled Operation Desert Storm. The next time Bush calls out U.S. forces, it is to help starving people in Somalia, where an ineffective government can't control marauding bands of thugs.

But we leave Somalia with many problems unsolved. In the former east European nation of Yugoslavia—now split into several different countries, some of them claiming the same land—Serbs and Croats, Christians and Muslims, Albanians and Bosnians are killing each other, partly (but only partly) because their religions are different.

> "How little do my countrymen know what precious blessings they are in possession of and which no other people on earth enjoy."
>
> —Thomas Jefferson

President George Bush in Saudi Arabia during the Gulf War (1990) with General Norman Schwarzkopf, commander-in-chief of U.S. Persian Gulf forces.

The Face of America

In 1889, the novelist Henry James, arriving home after twenty-five years in England, is amazed by polyglot New York City. When he sailed for Europe the city was primarily English-speaking. Returned and riding a streetcar (lit by Edison's lights) he hears Poles, Germans, Italians, and Swedes all speaking their own tongues. "The great fact … was that, foreign as they might be, newly inducted as they might be, they were really more at home … than they had ever been before."

As the twentieth century turns into the twenty-first, a new wave of immigrants is changing the look of America. Like those who came before them, they are quickly at home. Immigration laws, passed in 1965, prefer no nation, opening the door wider to Asians and Latin Americans. (The old laws had quotas that favored northern Europeans.) The number of immigrants admitted is raised to nearly a million every year. And that is only legal immigrants. Another 300,000 or more slip across the border from Mexico, or just stay in the country when their tourist or student visas expire. By 2000, nearly 10 percent of the U.S. population is foreign-born.

A high proportion of the newcomers are physicians, computer experts, professors, or entrepreneurs, given priority under immigration law as "members of the professions of exceptional ability." Others are willing to do the unskilled work that no one else seems to want to do. Their talents enrich the nation, to say nothing of their recipes for sushi, empanadas, or hummus. People talk of "minorities"—but there is no majority.

For decades we looked at turmoil—in places like Korea and Cuba and Vietnam—and saw the menace of international communism. Now we were beginning to understand that much conflict is indigenous. As the world's leading power, does the United States have a responsibility to try to solve the problems of other nations? Is it done best with armies or negotiators? Or should we concentrate on creating a just society at home and hope that the rest of the world will take notice?

From Hope to Despair

William Jefferson Clinton, at forty-six, becomes the third youngest president, and the first Democrat to hold the office in twelve years. Those who know him best are not surprised. His second-grade teacher predicted it, his mother believed in him, and so did many who met the gifted boy in the years that followed. Few have arrived at the presidency with a background to match Bill Clinton's. He's a graduate of Georgetown University's School of Foreign Service, he was a Rhodes Scholar at Oxford University in England, he has a law degree from Yale, and for twelve

Bill Clinton, standing between his wife Hillary and daughter Chelsea, taking the oath of office.

years he governed Arkansas. That a small-town boy from a place like Hope, Arkansas (one of the poorest of the states), can aspire to the opportunities Bill Clinton has had, and then make it to the nation's top job, is what America is all about. Everywhere he has left an impression of vigor, compassion, engaging friendliness, and dazzling ability—along with evidence of another side to his personality: stories abound of about-faces under pressure from wealthy interests, and other less than principled actions.

Bill Clinton turns out to be the most conservative Democratic president since Grover Cleveland. He cuts welfare, puts more police on the streets, builds prisons, steps up the war on drugs, expands the death penalty, and, after passage of a deficit-reduction bill (with no Republican support), balances the budget. All this helps bring about a stock-market surge, low unemployment, minimal inflation, and general prosperity. The 1990s are an era when business and big corporations are worshipped with almost religious fervor.

On the other hand, Clinton tries—and fails—to organize health insurance for all Americans; he doesn't succeed in changing the way we pay for political campaigns, or in doing much for public schools. The gap between the very rich and everyone else, which began to grow in the Reagan era, gets much wider. In foreign affairs, the Clinton administration brings warring parties from Serbia, Croatia, and Bosnia to Dayton, Ohio, where they sit down and agree to try to make peace. Former president Jimmy Carter is sent to Haiti, where he helps that impoverished island get its first fairly elected president, Jean-Bertrand Aristide. In the Middle East, Clinton helps negotiate agreements between Israel and its Arab neighbors in their long, agonizing struggle to coexist (unfortunately, as so often before, the gains won't last). Treaties that lower tariffs and bolster international free trade are negotiated. And Clinton journeys to China, where he charms the Chinese with his willingness to answer hard questions.

Yet Clinton's presidency, begun with promise, turns into a political and national disaster. He is investigated by a special prosecutor, he lies about his personal behavior, and, in 1998, is impeached in the House of Representatives and tried in the Senate, where he is found not guilty of "high crimes and misdemeanors." But the entire process—which focuses on his relationship with a young woman who worked as an intern in the White House—is intensely partisan, expensive, distracting, and humiliating for the entire country.

LIAR, LIAR, HOUSE ON FIRE

Are there times when a president needs to lie? The Cold War was raging when a U.S. spy plane was shot down over Russia in 1960. President Eisenhower couldn't bear to lie about it, so he got his secretary of state to do it for him. He said it was a weather research plane. The truth soon came out, and everyone knew they'd been told a flat-out fib. John F. Kennedy lied about the buildup of American military forces in South Vietnam. "National security" was the grounds for secrecy and deception; at least that was the reason given. Lyndon Johnson lied about an attack that didn't happen in the Tonkin Gulf off Vietnam. That led to the War Powers Act, which gave Johnson almost unlimited military control and got the Vietnam War going big time. Richard Nixon lied about the Watergate break-in and cover-up, and the resulting scandal forced him from office.

Administration officials under Ronald Reagan lied about illegal acts in Iran and Nicaragua—knowingly defying the will of Congress, breaking laws, and pretending innocence—all in the name of national security. Those officials secretly sold weapons to Iran and gave weapons to Nicaraguan forces fighting their country's left-wing "Contra" government—all while the president was saying he would never do such a thing. Congress held Iran-Contra hearings from 1984 to 1986. Lt. Col. Oliver North was called before the investigating committee and said, "I will tell you right now, counsel, and all the members here gathered, that I misled Congress." He was proud of it. Journalist Bill Moyers wrote, "Setting up White House operatives who secretly decide to fight dirty little wars is a direct assumption of war powers expressly forbidden by the Constitution."

Many of these lies were attempts to get around the Constitution. In most cases, the deceptive officials believed sincerely that they were doing the right thing for the country. None of them got away with it. And, mostly, they were wrong in their assumptions. Is there a need for secrecy and lies in government? Can a patriotic plan, intended in the public interest, be more important than the law? President Nixon thought so when he said, in a conversation taped in the Oval Office as the Watergate affair was unfolding: "I want you all to stonewall it, let them plead the Fifth Amendment, cover up, or anything else, if it'll save it—save the plan."

Lying is not illegal. It is often wicked, usually immoral, and sometimes cowardly. But it is not against the law. Perjury—lying under oath—is illegal. Most of us can forgive wrong actions; it's lying about them

> "The whole of government consists in the art of being honest."
> —Thomas Jefferson

that we find hard to accept. John Adams, the first president to live in the White House, had this inscription put over the fireplace in the State Dining Room: *May none but honest and wise men ever rule under this roof.*

Two hundred years after the founding generation of presidents, Bill Clinton went on television, looked the camera in the eye, and spoke a lie. His lie had nothing to do with national security. He was attempting to conceal personal behavior that was embarrassing and inappropriate. We are a forgiving people. It was the lie, even more than the action, that left Americans dismayed. In some other nations people laughed at our outrage over Clinton's personal actions. They said the president's private behavior should have nothing to do with his task as leader of the nation. But most Americans said it was more than that. We have set ourselves on a quest for civility and fair play. It is a national destination—liberty and justice for all—and you don't get there with untruthfulness.

Of Colleges and Courts

The Electoral College of the United States is not part of a university. It has no buildings. But when the members of the Electoral College vote, it is a weighty occasion. Those college members, called "electors," decide who will be president. Every four years, each state chooses its electors. The number of electors in a state equals its total number of representatives and senators in Congress. Electors never actually get together. What they do is send their votes for president and vice president to Washington, voting for the rest of us. The popular vote total determines which electors get to vote in each state. It's a winner-takes-all system. (Even if the vote is very close, the winning candidate usually gets all the votes in a state.) It means that if you're running for president, come in a close second in all the big states, win most of the small states, and have the largest total (popular) vote across the nation—you may still lose the election.

The decision to have electors came, in part, because of jealousies between North and South at the time the Constitution was written. A direct popular vote, with only free males voting, would have given the North the choice of president because it had a much greater free population. So the Founders came up with a system for picking electors similar to that for picking senators and representatives. That way the South was able to more than hold its own in selecting presidents. Having an electoral college had a lot to do with balancing power. The other, equally important, reason for the college was that the Founders did not trust the people to elect the president directly. "They expected the members of the Electoral College to be distinguished and independent citizens who would make up their own minds, after collective deliberation, about who the president and vice president should be," writes the legal historian Ronald Dworkin.

It hasn't worked that way. Electors don't make up their own minds. Republican electors vote for Republican candidates; Democratic electors vote for Democratic candidates. No one knows what would happen if we abolished the College and elected presidents by popular vote. The Electoral College has helped mold the American political system. It forces politicians to pay attention to small states.

In the presidential election in the year 2000, Clinton's vice president, Democrat Al Gore, wins the popular vote, nationwide, by about half a million votes out of 100 million cast. But the electoral vote is split, with Florida's twenty-five electors holding the key to the election. George Bush seems the winner by a slight majority, but Florida's votes are being disputed. Substantial numbers of voters—especially African-Americans—have been turned away from the polls for reasons that are later found to be invalid. Antiquated voting machines have failed in some places. The ballot in one county is so confusing that many people vote for a third-party candidate without meaning to do so. And thousands of absentee ballots have been treated in different ways in different parts of the state. TV coverage on election night is a disaster: the networks predict a winner before all the polls have closed, changing their minds, and changing them again.

The situation is a mess; no president has been elected—and both sides bring in armies of lawyers. When they fail to agree on how vote recounts should be conducted—and as days pass—the U.S. Supreme Court steps in. By a five-to-four vote, the cour hand recounts—and that decides tion. George W. Bush becomes th   hird president. A presidential election has been determined by the Supreme Court—and by one vote. Does the court have a sound legal basis for the decision? Or is it just voting on partisan lines? What began in Florida as an argument about who will be the next president has become something much larger and more lasting—an argument about the proper sources of government in this republic," writes columnist George F. Will.

COURTING CHANGE

If you drove along Southern highways during the 1950s and '60s, you often saw signs that read IMPEACH EARL WARREN.

The Supreme Court, with Warren as chief justice, was not only changing American jurisprudence; it was changing long-standing traditions—like the South's segregated schools. Opponents of the court used the words "liberal" and "activist" and meant them as insults. The court's decisions stemmed from ethical concerns and a focus on individual rights rather than on a literal interpretation of the language of the Constitution. *Brown* v. *Board of Education* (1954) was the most significant of the decisions, but in *Griswold* v. *Connecticut* (1965), the Warren court overturned a Connecticut statute banning the use of contraceptives. That ruling is based on a "right of privacy" the court found in the essence of the Constitution, if not in its text. In *Miranda* v. *Arizona* (1966) the Warren court said that the Fifth Amendment's protection against self-incrimination required police to warn suspects of their rights before they are interrogated. Finding a balance between freedom and order is the central challenge for a democracy. (Dictatorships don't worry about freedom.) The Warren court reflects the tenor of its times, making issues of individual freedom paramount.

A half-century later, the Supreme Court, with William Hubbs Rehnquist as chief justice, is equally activist, this time implementing a conservative agenda. It, too, reflects its times—with drugs, increases in crime, and terrorism augmenting concern for societal order and personal protection.

William Rehnquist was born in Wisconsin into a home where Herbert Hoover was a hero and Franklin Roosevelt was not. When an elementary schoolteacher asks him what he wants to do when he grows up, he says, "I'm going to change the government." And that's exactly what he proceeds to do. But not until he has taken advantage of Roosevelt's Servicemen's Readjustment Act of 1944 (better known as the G.I. Bill). It is a piece of social legislation that pays college fees for a generation of men (and a few women) who fought in World War II. They surprise some elitists, who don't believe ordinary people are meant to go to college, by enriching the nation with their fulfilled potential. Rehnquist, who served in North Africa during the war, goes to Stanford University (where he gets a B.A. and an M.A. in political science). He receives a second M.A. at Harvard and a law degree from Stanford, where he graduates first in his class in 1952. (The third-ranked student is Sandra Day, who will later become the first woman on the Supreme Court.)

Settling in Arizona, Rehnquist becomes a Republican Party official and an outspoken critic of the Warren decisions. Richard Nixon places him on the Supreme Court in 1972. In his first years there, Rehnquist is

Chief Justice William Rehnquist

Former Justice Sandra Day O'Connor, who usually voted with the conservatives.

an articulate lone dissenter—supporting states' rights and questioning the court's interpretation of the Fourteenth Amendment, aimed at expanding individual rights. In 1986, he is named chief justice, bringing an organized mind and a sense of humor to the job. He also reduces the number of cases the high court considers to about ninety each year.

When the first President Bush adds two conservative justices to the court, Rehnquist can begin writing for a 5–4 majority. In the court's 2002 session, that one-vote majority upholds the use of publicly financed vouchers for religious school tuition, challenging a tradition of strict separation of church and state. In the same term the court supports a decision allowing intercity bus passengers to be searched; it holds that students have no privacy rights protecting them from random drug testing. "For effectiveness in relation to an intended agenda, his has been a triumphant chief justiceship," says Kathleen M. Sullivan, dean of Stanford Law School.

The Rehnquist court's split decisions reflect the nation's liberal-conservative seesaw, with the shift of one justice's weight making a crucial difference. Justices Antonin Scalia and Stephen G. Breyer put the debate into words. For Scalia, "The Constitution that I interpret and apply is not living, but dead.... Our first responsibility is to not make sense of the law—our first responsibility is to follow the text of the law." For Breyer, the objective is to foster "participatory democratic self-government." He says: "An absolutist approach is unworkable."

"It is irresponsible to leave the law in such a state of utter indeterminacy," says Scalia. Linda Greenhouse of the *New York Times* calls it "a debate over text versus context. For Justice Scalia, who focuses on text, language is supreme, and the court's job is to derive and apply rules from the words chosen by the Constitution's framers or a statute's drafters. For Justice Breyer, who looks to context, language is only a starting point to an inquiry in which a law's purpose and a decision's likely consequence are the more important elements." It's a debate that affects all of us. Stay tuned.

Here are some words on the subject from Abraham Lincoln, who, living with the *Dred Scott*

Justice Ruth Bader Ginsburg, who usually votes with the liberals.

decision, had a few reservations about a too strong Supreme Court:

> *If the policy of the Government upon vital questions, affecting the whole people, is to be irrevocably fixed by decisions of the Supreme Court, the instant they are made, in ordinary litigation between parties in personal actions, the people will have ceased to be their rulers.*

The years following the Civil War show that Supreme Court decisions are rarely "irrevocably fixed." *Dred Scott* and *Plessy* are overturned (but not before they wreak devastation).

A New Century and a Catastrophe

As the United States enters the new millennium it is enjoying a breezy, confident, promising time of affluence and achievement. After a long and tortuous cold war, it seems as if the world's problems may be on the way to being solved and that democracy will soon be universal. How could there be a contest? How can oppression possibly triumph over freedom?

But we are underestimating the power of demons: of deprivation, anger, and jealousy. We are the world's superpower, and often so self-absorbed that we hardly pay attention to what is going on in the rest of the world. We know that a worldwide terrorist organization, al-Qaeda, is training a generation of young men to hate America, but we don't do much about it. Then, on September 11, 2001, something happens to jolt us out of our complacency, and we—and the whole world—shudder.

That day, nineteen terrorists hijack four airliners, ramming two of them into the World Trade Center's twin skyscrapers in New York City and one into the Pentagon in Washington, D.C.; the fourth crashes before it can reach its intended destination in Washington. Some 3,000 people die; many others are injured.

It is, as President Bush announces, a declaration of war by international terrorists based in the Muslim world. "The civilized world," says the president, is pitted against a network intent on "remaking the world—and imposing its radical beliefs on people everywhere." The terrorists blame us, and the world's free nations, for most of their problems of poverty, ignorance, and powerlessness. They hate us so much that their hijackers are willing to die themselves in order to kill our citizens. It is our deep beliefs—in freedom and pluralism and religious tolerance—that they especially abhor, as well as our material wealth. The terrorists preach that we are Satan's children; that only they and their followers know the truth about God; and that God will reward them for punishing us. Their message is a perversion of Islam, which rests on a foundation of peacefulness and respect for others.

New York City, September 11, 2001: flames and smoke spew from the World Trade Center after terrorists have flown two airliners into the buildings. Moments later the twin towers are gone, as are more than 3,000 humans, including hundreds of firefighters and police officers engaged in heroic rescue efforts.

(Around the world, religious leaders of every faith, including Muslims, recoil in horror.) The stridency and anger of the zealots creates a smokescreen that helps hide the real problems of a part of the world where people are hurting. Much of the Middle East, despite pockets of oil-based wealth, is in disarray. It is a region aching for answers.

The al-Qaeda hijackers are just another example in a parade of misguided humans willing to kill because their leaders tell them they are carrying out God's wishes. Middle East historian Bernard Lewis writes, "It is precisely the lack of freedom—freedom of the mind from constraint and indoctrination, to question and inquire and speak; freedom of the economy from corrupt and pervasive mismanagement; freedom of women from male oppression; freedom of citizens from tyranny—that underlies so many of the troubles of the Muslim world."

"What is dangerous about extremists is not that they are extreme, but that they are intolerant. The evil is not in what they say about their cause, but what they say about their opponents."

—Robert F. Kennedy

A 2001 collage piece by artist Jolanta Gora-Wita shows a portrait of Osama Bin Laden surrounded by references to the Mujahadeen and al-Qaeda, and terrorist attacks on the USS *Cole*, the U.S. embassies in Kenya and Tanzania, and the World Trade Center.

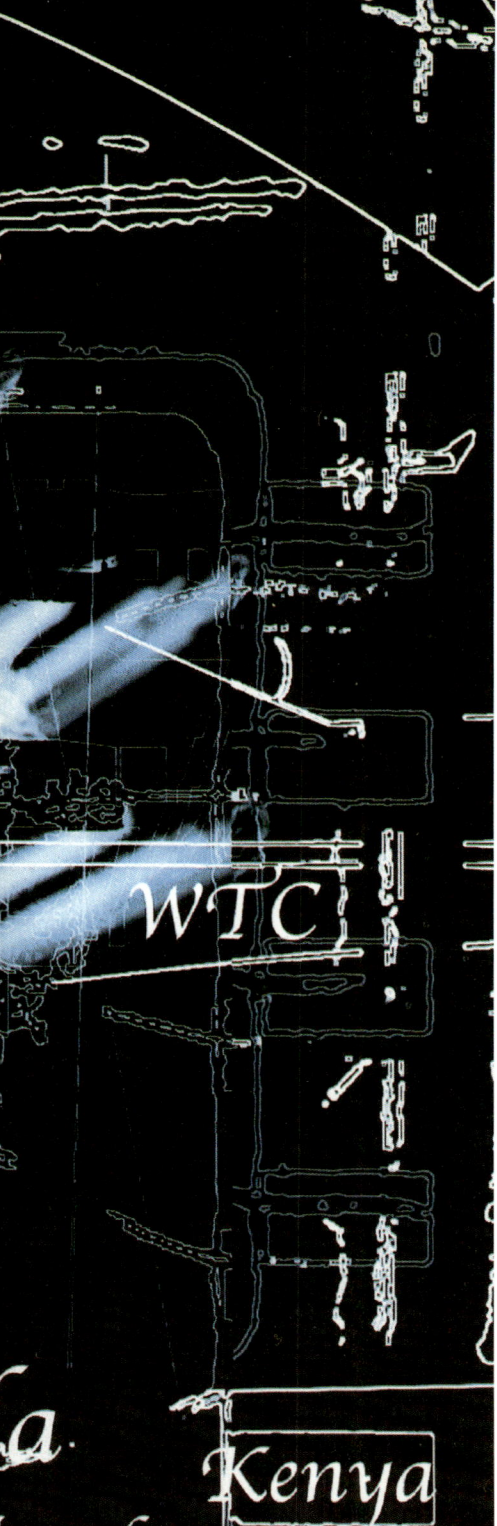

Part 17

War in Doubles

Less than a month after the horror of September 11th, the United States, the United Kingdom, and Australia send troops to Afghanistan; there they join forces with the Afghan Northern Alliance. All are determined to find the perpetrators of 9/11 who are hiding out in mountainous Afghanistan, bragging about the mass murder they have committed.

The joint "military action," which begins on October 7, 2001, is named: "Operation Enduring Freedom." In the United States, there is no official declaration of war, but President George W. Bush and a bipartisan Congress state their goals: the dismantling of al-Qaeda, the capture of Osama bin Laden, the removal of the abusive Taliban regime from power, and the creation of a democratic Islamic republic in Afghanistan.

With soldiers on the ground and massive air support, it is a matter of weeks until Taliban leaders are ousted from positions of official power; many flee to nearby Pakistan. By December 2001, troops from 42 United Nations countries have joined the fight; they establish an Islamic republic in Afghanistan.

However, Afghans have a long history of resisting foreign invaders, no matter how well-intentioned those foreigners. Operation Enduring Freedom was preceded by a Russian/Afghan war that lasted for nine years, until the Soviets pulled out in 1989. That war was actually a civil war centered on questions of

President George W. Bush (right) announces his $74.7 billion wartime supplemental budget request at the Pentagon as Secretary of Defense Donald H. Rumsfeld (left) looks on.

Declaration of Independence talks about "unalienable rights" to "Life, Liberty, and the pursuit of Happiness." That American doctrine has universal appeal, but the words that follow in the Declaration are often ignored: "That to secure these rights, Governments are instituted among men, deriving their just powers from the consent of the governed." Consent of the governed? Can democracy be imposed on others for their own good? Is that what the United States is trying to do in Afghanistan? This is a complicated issue.

The Taliban follows an ancient and uncompromising interpretation of Islamic tradition that is particularly onerous regarding women and has been rejected by many contemporary Islamic leaders. From 1996 to 2001, the Taliban rules a large portion of Afghanistan, including the important capital city of Kabul. Taliban forces massacre civilians, deny UN food relief to thousands of starving Afghans, burn large areas of fertile land, destroy tens of thousands of homes, and prevent girls from going to school—all in the name of religious belief. After the arrival of the joint forces, the Taliban turns to guerrilla tactics.

In the United States, the terrorism of 9/11 has left most citizens anxious. Congress passes the USA Patriot Act of 2001. Its title is a ten-letter acronym: Uniting and Strengthening America by Providing Appropriate Tools Required to Intercept and Obstruct Terrorism. The law, a response to fears of domestic terrorism, does what it suggests: it provides tools and

modernity, women's rights, and traditional religion, as well as political power. Russia's communists complicated the issues when they entered the fray on the side of those who wanted change; the United States got involved sending support to anti-communists who included Taliban forces. It all happened during the Cold War, which came to an end in 1991, but it is one reason that in the 21st century Americans are battling Taliban and al-Qaeda warriors, including Osama bin Laden, whom they once supplied with arms to fight the Russians. As for bin Laden, no one can find him.

In 2001, the allied forces find it harder to bring democratic government to Afghanistan than they expected. The permission that broaden the powers of law enforcement and immigration agencies; it also expands the reach of the Treasury Department, allowing it to search business records. How does the act play out?

Under the Patriot Act, immigrants can be held in detention indefinitely (challenging habeas corpus and due process guarantees); homes or businesses may be searched without the owner's or the occupant's permission or knowledge; searches of telephone, e-mail, and financial records can be made without a court order, and law enforcement agencies can get enhanced access to business, library, and financial accounts. All of that runs counter to the American tradition of minimal government surveillance and maximum individual liberty, so some Americans see the Patriot Act as an assault on traditional constitutional freedoms, much like the Sedition Act of John Adams's presidency. Others believe that modern terrorism brings unprecedented dangers and that new responses are essential.

Meanwhile, President George W. Bush is shifting his focus from Afghanistan to an oil-rich Islamic nation. The president seems determined to go to war in Iraq. His father was denounced for not sending troops to Baghdad during the First Gulf War when he might have unseated Iraq's murderous leader, Saddam Hussein. At that time, President George H. W. Bush said any attempt to overthrow the Iraqi government would come with "incalculable human and political costs."

After the First Gulf War, the United Nations prohibited Iraq from developing or possessing weapons of mass destruction (known as WMDs). UN Resolution 1441 calls for Iraq to cooperate with UN weapons inspectors, who are to make sure there are no WMDs. The UN inspectors, led by Hans Blix, find no evidence of any, but Blix says he needs "months" to finish the inspection. President

> "It [the Patriot Act] is also an example of the two parties coming together, and of the administration and the Congress coming together. In a sense, in this bill there is something for everyone to like and something for everyone to dislike, which may well show that it will end up in the right place.... When we are facing a war where it is more likely that more civilians will die than military personnel, the homefront is a warfront. The old high wall between foreign intelligence and domestic law enforcement has to be modified. The bill does a good job of that."
>
> —Senator Charles Schumer
> Congressional Record—Senate, October 25, 2001

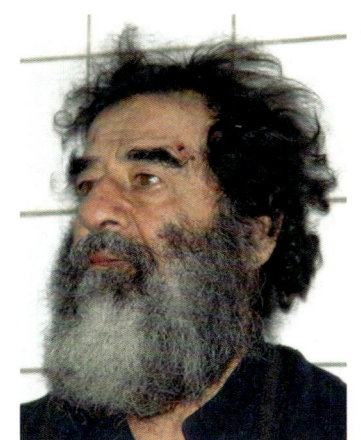

Saddam Hussein

Secretary of State Colin Powell

George W. Bush is in no mood to wait.

He knows that 12 years earlier, before the First Gulf War, Iraq had been stockpiling yellowcake uranium, which is used in producing nuclear arms. When rumors of further yellowcake purchases by Iraq in Africa surface in 2002, the CIA sends former Ambassador Joseph Wilson to Niger to see if they are true. Wilson reports that they are "unequivocally wrong." The administration then says that the Iraqis are buying high-strength aluminum tubes that could be used in the process of enriching uranium for nuclear bombs. A 2002 Institute for Science and International Security report says it is highly unlikely that the tubes can be used to enrich uranium. Rumors of weapons of biological warfare circulate, but turn out to be false. Saddam Hussein is accused of supporting al-Qaeda, which is all but impossible since the high-living Iraqi despot and the intensely religious radical leaders of al-Qaeda despise each other.

However, when U.S. Secretary of State Colin Powell addresses the UN Security Council, he stokes fears by citing both the aluminum tubes and biological weaponry as evidence of Iraqi malfeasance. Later, Powell will blame intelligence-gathering sources for evidence he says was "deliberately false." Powell has been misled by his own administration and has passed on fake information that alarms a world now obsessed with the threat of terrorism.

In October 2002, one year after the start of the war in Afghanistan, President Bush asks Congress for broad authority to use military force in Iraq. Massachusetts Senator Edward (Ted) Kennedy voices concern. He says, "The power to declare war is the most solemn responsibility given to Congress by the Constitution. We must not delegate that responsibility to the president in advance."

West Virginia's crusty Constitutional scholar, Senator Robert C. Byrd, attempts a filibuster to stop the vote, but he can't even get his fellow Democrats to support him. Byrd, who is the longest-serving senator in American history, voted for the Tonkin Gulf Resolution that led to the escalation of U.S. involvement in the Vietnam War. He says he isn't going to make that mistake again. In an article in the *New York Times*, the senator asks, "Why are we allowing the executive to rush our decision-making right before an election? Congress, under pressure from the executive branch, should not hand away its Constitutional powers … it is Congress that casts the vote, it is the American people who will pay for a war with the lives of their sons and daughters."

The Senate votes 77–23 and the House of Representatives 296–133 and gives the president a bipartisan mandate to defend the United States from the "continuing threat" posed by Baghdad. The Constitution gives Congress the power to declare war; this vote passes that power to the president.

In Illinois, a little-known state senator, Barack Obama, predicts that, "even a successful war against Iraq will require a U.S. occupation of undetermined length, at undetermined cost, with undetermined consequences."

On March 19, 2003, President Bush orders a military invasion of Iraq. The next day, at 5:34 A.M. Baghdad time, the invasion begins; its code name is "Operation Iraqi Freedom." Three weeks later, the U.S. Army's 3rd Infantry Division is in control of Baghdad. On May 1, in a speech broadcast worldwide, the president announces that the fighting is over. A banner behind him proclaims: "Mission Accomplished." He is wrong: Baghdad has fallen, but the war is just getting started.

Among the first casualties are irreplaceable treasures of art and history, lost to looters when Baghdad's National Museum of Antiquities is unprotected in the chaos of battle. The National Library burns and ancient texts go up in flame. At Baghdad's public zoo, 700 animals are lost when thieves steal them and hungry people in the food-starved city take some and eat them (a few are heroically saved). As the war expands, car bombings and other acts of violence erupt nationwide.

The United States and its allies are now engaged in two armed conflicts: one in Afghanistan, the other in Iraq. Jointly the president calls them a "war on terror." Neither will proceed as expected.

Four More Years

In 2004, President George W. Bush runs for a second term; this time he faces Massachusetts Senator John Kerry, a swift-boat commander during the Vietnam War. The morning after the election no one knows who has won, but when Ohio's votes are tabulated, Bush holds both popular and electoral majorities.

A year later, Hurricane Katrina devastates New Orleans and much of the Gulf Coast. Bush's response is slow; his popularity, eroding because of the two costly and indecisive wars, plummets. (Later, he will send substantial aid and assistance to the Gulf region.)

Senator John Kerry

Besides two wars and a natural disaster, there's another dominating issue in the president's second term: money. When he took office in 2000, Bush inherited an annual fiscal surplus of $237 billion, the largest in the nation's history. Some people say that surplus should be used to help pay off the nation's accumulated debt; the president says the surplus should be returned to the people, so the Bush administration cuts taxes. At the same time, the administration increases federal spending by more than a trillion dollars a year. But hardly anyone is paying attention. It is a time of optimism: technology is changing lifestyles and business practices; and real estate values, which have been going up, and up, keep rising. People who own property seem to be getting wealthier and wealthier.

An economic bubble bursts in 2000, but hardly anyone seems concerned. Known as the Dot-Com Bubble, it happens

In 2005, at least 1833 people died during Hurricane Katrina and the ensuing floods, making the storm one of the five deadliest hurricanes in U.S. history. It caused an estimated $81 billion worth of property damage. Left, at a Hurricane Katrina Supply staging area a member of the National Guard loads water for distribution. Below, a barber shop located in the Ninth Ward in New Orleans as it was left by the storm.

just after George Bush takes office. Prices of Internet and Information Technology stocks have been soaring, but in 2000 they plummet. Some investors lose a lot of money; some workers lose their jobs. Amazon stock plunges from $107 a share to $7. However, a decade later the stock far exceeds that high.

In February 2007, air begins to surge out of another bubble, this time it's an eight-trillion-dollar housing bubble. Banks have aggressively sold home mortgages to people without enough money to pay for them, and house prices have consequently soared; now most of those houses aren't worth what they cost. Many homeowners can't make their loan payments; banks foreclose on many of the houses and throw homeowners off their property. Overpriced property loses much of its paper worth. Economies slow worldwide, and international trade declines. None of that helps the real estate or construction industries, where people lose their jobs. Things get even worse.

Some banks have been selling securities tied to inflated U.S. real estate prices; now, with the air gone from the bubble, those securities aren't worth much.

A long-standing banking regulation, the Glass-Steagall Act, was eliminated during the Clinton administration. Glass-Steagall, a response to the Great Depression, put banks into two categories: commercial and investment. Commercial banks, the ones familiar to most Americans, hold money deposits, provide small loans, and

"What are the odds that people will make smart decisions about money if they don't need to make smart decisions—if they can get rich making dumb decisions? The incentives on Wall Street were all wrong; they're still all wrong."

—Michael Lewis,
The Big Short: Inside the Doomsday Machine

set up checking accounts. The government provides F.D.I.C. insurance to back these banks' transactions.

Investment banks are different. Their primary function is to raise capital to make investments for clients and themselves. That speculative activity carried no government insurance under the Glass-Steagall Act, but when the act gets axed, investment banks also get F.D.I.C. insurance. Big commercial banks can become investment banks and offer insured savings and checking accounts. Money deposited in those accounts can now be used to make risky investments (like credit default swaps). That means banks can invest—wisely or wildly—knowing that taxpayers will foot the bill when they make poor investments. And that is part of what happens when the whopping housing bubble ruptures, just as George Bush moves out of the White House.

Lehman Brothers, one of the largest financial institutions, goes bankrupt. Others like Merrill Lynch, AIG, Morgan Stanley, Citicorp, Bank of America, Freddie

CITIZENS UNITED V. CAMPAIGN FINANCE REFORM

John McCain, a Republican, and Russ Feingold, a Democrat, are united in their desire to do something about the massive spending necessary for politicians to win and stay in office. In 2002, they worked together to get the Bipartisan Campaign Reform Act passed. Known as BCRA or the McCain-Feingold Act, it outlaws "electioneering communications" within 60 days of a general election by corporations (whether they are nonprofit or for-profit) and by unions. Electioneering communications usually means TV advertising, which is very expensive. The idea is to keep corporate funding and big money out of political campaigns.

Six years after the passage of BCRA, a nonprofit corporation wants to air a film attacking Democratic primary candidate Hillary Clinton, but to do that would violate the McCain-Feingold Act. The corporation takes the matter to court; the case goes all the way to the Supreme Court.

In a 5-to-4 decision, that highest court decides portions of the McCain-Feingold Act violate the First Amendment's free-speech guarantees. It calls the act unconstitutional. The Court says corporations are associations of citizens with free speech rights. The justices' decision, in the case of *Citizens United* v. *Campaign Finance Reform*, changes the political game. Regulations limiting political spending by corporations are now eliminated. The impact of *Citizens United*, and the amount of money spent on future elections, will be enormous.

John McCain announcing his intention to run for president in April 2007.

Mac, and Fannie Mae get rescued with taxpayer funds.

Few experts saw the financial crisis coming. Early in 2007, Ben Bernanke, chairman of the Federal Reserve, proclaims, "the banking system is healthy." Within months, that "healthy" system will require a government bailout that costs taxpayers trillions of dollars.

By December 2007, the United States

is in a major recession; it will become the longest since the Great Depression. A Senate report blames the crisis on "high risk, complex financial products; undisclosed conflicts of interest; the failure of regulators, the credit rating agencies, and the market itself to rein in the excesses of Wall Street." (The report doesn't mention greed, but that is part of it too.)

In 2008, the U.S. loses a total of 2.6 million jobs—and the economic downturn is just getting started. The national debt (money borrowed by the government) reaches $11.3 trillion in 2008, a 100% increase from 2000 when the debt was $5.6 trillion. Mostly it is America's middle class that bears the burden of the economic downturn.

George W. Bush had campaigned on a theme of bringing people together; that hasn't worked out. As the Bush presidency comes to an end, the nation is engaged in two wars, the gap between rich and poor has become a gulf, politics is intensely partisan, jobs are disappearing; and the end of the financial crisis is nowhere in sight. Opinions on the Bush legacy vary widely. As he leaves office, most people agree on one thing: change is needed. In the 2008 presidential race, one of the candidates centers his campaign on the theme of change.

YES WE CAN

For a brief time after the 2008 election, many Americans enjoy a mood of optimism. Even those who dislike the results of the election understand the precedent-breaking importance of what has happened: The people of the United States have elected an African American to the presidency. If ever there is an affirmation of American ideals of justice, freedom, and equality, it comes in the 2008 election. The losing candidate, Senator John McCain, understands how significant this moment is and says so.

"America today is a world away from the cruel and prideful bigotry of [an earlier] time," says McCain, conceding defeat. "There is no better evidence of this than the election of an African American to the presidency of the United States. Let there be no reason now for any American to fail to cherish their citizenship in this, the greatest nation on earth."

The new president, Hawaiian-born Barack Hussein Obama, carries a name that sounds strange to many older Americans raised in a largely white culture. However, when they look around, it is obvious that the United States, always a land of diversity, has not only changed its complexion: it has changed some rules of the opportunity game.

Barack Obama, the son of a black African father and a white American mother, raised

"Change we can believe in" is one of the numerous slogans of the 2008 Obama campaign.

"If there is anyone out there who still doubts that America is a place where all things are possible; who still wonders if the dream of our founders is alive in our time; who still questions the power of our democracy, tonight is your answer."

—Barack Obama,
2008 election night victory speech

by grandparents and a single mother, has been superbly schooled. Describing his background, he says, "My parents shared not only an improbable love; they shared an abiding faith in the possibilities of this nation.... They imagined me going to the best schools in the land, even though they weren't rich, because in a generous America you don't have to be rich to achieve your potential."

Obama earns a law degree at Harvard University, graduating *magna cum laude* (with highest honors) also having served as president of the *Harvard Law Review* (a big-deal position). After that, he becomes a community organizer working in Chicago with those in need, a professor of constitutional law at the University of Chicago, and a U.S. senator from Illinois.

He writes, "my story is part of the larger American story … I owe a debt to those who came before me … in no other country on earth, is my story possible."

He owes a special debt to a lot of teachers who believed in him, to schools that gave him scholarships, and to his remarkable Kansas-born mother who takes him with her when she moves to Indonesia and wakes him early in the morning to do extra school lessons while at the same time she both works and pursues graduate studies.

His Kenyan father, a student who came to the United States to go to college and study economics, has returned to Africa, deserting his American wife and child. Later, he is killed in a traffic accident. Before that happens, he comes back to Hawaii for a month-long visit; Barack is ten, now living with his grandparents so he can attend Hawaii's prestigious Punahou School. That one month will be the only time the boy spends with his father.

Obama's first term as president brings major achievements (healthcare legislation, finding and killing Osama bin Laden, the end of government-backed torture of suspected terrorists, the creation of a National Commission on Fiscal Responsibility and Reform, an auto industry rescue plan), but those looking for a vigorous new version of the FDR-era response to a financial crisis are disappointed. There is no way it can happen. The Republican Party of the 1930s worked with the Democratic president to tackle problems. In 2008, the situation is very different.

Obama faces a Republican Party that seems determined not to support him no matter what—even if he is proposing something they agree with; as for the Democratic Party, like the Republican Party it is beholden to big-money interests. Articulate as a candidate, Obama as president seems unclear about his goals. Attempting to compromise, he often ends up powerless. The result is gridlock, frustration, and a level of partisanship that diminishes both Congress and the president, leaving much of the nation longing for clarity and guidance at a time when an interconnected world demands responsive government and sophisticated citizens.

AND THE WARS?

In December 2011, the American flag is lowered in Baghdad, American troops depart Iraq, and the war is declared officially over. Left behind is a destabilized region (with Iran having become stronger), suicide bombers, unleashed ethnic hatreds, a weakened infrastructure (transportation, electricity, water, police), and uncertainty about the future. On July 23, 2012, coordinated insurgent attacks around the country kill more than 100 Iraqi citizens. An article in the *Christian Science Monitor* comments,

The last U.S. convoy crosses over the border from Iraq into Kuwait, signaling the end of Operation New Dawn.

"the Iraq of 2012 is a country where a background level of violence has become a daily norm."

Meanwhile President Obama, at the urging of military advisers and congressional hawks, has expanded the war in Afghanistan by adding more U.S. troops. Antiwar protesters compare that decision to the expansion of the Vietnam War under the Johnson administration. The president says, "This continues to be a difficult endeavor."

The president and military leaders begin to change the way wars are fought: from troops on the ground to drones in the air. The idea is to find enemies and deal with them the way a surgeon attacks a cancerous growth—cutting it out precisely. Using GPS technology and unmanned aircraft, the administration searches out and targets enemies. Yet those who get hit by drones are often innocent. A Washington think tank, the Brookings Institution, suggests that the drone kill ratio of civilians to legitimate targets is probably 10:1 (ten innocents to one enemy). However, air strikes by piloted aircraft have much higher kill ratios. Is war ever anything but messy and destructive? Should civilized nations be doing any of this?

Newspapers and the Media in an Age of Information

Thomas Jefferson, a man often attacked by the press, understood the importance of information in a democracy. He realized that self-government, the experiment he and his peers were initiating, depends on educated, informed citizens. Writing to Richard Price, a feisty Welsh preacher, Jefferson said, "Whenever the people are informed, they can be trusted with their own government."

Informed? Where do citizens get information about civic issues? In Jefferson's day newspapers were *the* essential source. They came to be known as the fourth branch of government.

Jefferson said, "If I had to choose between government without newspapers, and newspapers without government, I wouldn't hesitate to choose the latter."

The new nation gets both. Some papers are sensationalistic and irresponsible,

> "For readers, the drastic diminishment of print raises an obvious question: if more people are reading newspapers and magazines, why should we care whether they are printed on paper? The answer is that paper is not just how news is delivered; it is how it is paid for."
>
> —David Carr, *New York Times*

but even those help provide a critical eye. Then, with the growth of the Industrial Revolution, huge presses begin rolling out multi-page newspapers and journalism gets more and more professional. By the end of the 19th century, muckraking reporters are doing sophisticated investigative journalism. Jefferson is proven right: newspapers become a vigorous fourth branch of government that often keeps politicians honest—and sometimes sends them to jail.

In the 20th century, technology changes the ways people receive information. It starts with radio, then TV, then the Internet, cell phones, Facebook, Twitter, and more.

The country's daily newspapers (some of them superb) have a hard time keeping up with the new technology and the speed with which it spreads information. The *Seattle Post-Intelligencer* goes online, the *Rocky Mountain News* closes its doors, and the *New Orleans Times-Picayune* changes from a daily newspaper to a three-times-a-week paper. Others cut way back on coverage. Many fold. What would Thomas Jefferson do?

Should journalism be subsidized by taxpayers? If so, will journalists still feel free to criticize the government? If not, who will support investigations of government bodies and officials? Who will be the Fourth Estate?

Before there are answers, along comes *WikiLeaks*, an international online organization that publishes classified information from anonymous news sources. In July of 2010, *WikiLeaks* releases more than 76,900 secret documents dealing with the war in Afghanistan. A few months later, it makes available almost 400,000 documents about deaths in Iraq. It then publishes secret files with information about prisoners held and sometimes tortured in a detention camp at Guantanamo Bay in Cuba—often without due process of the law.

WikiLeaks founder Australian Julian Assange says, "free speech is what regulates government and regulates law … the U.S. Constitution['s] Bill of Rights says that Congress is to make no such law abridging the freedom of the press.… Every constitution, every bit of legislation is derived from the flow of information. Similarly every government is elected as a result of people understanding things." Is he right? Would Jefferson have cheered, or, as a former president, would he feel this was going too far, that it was putting people at risk?

Issues of privacy and government security become high drama in November 2012, when General David Petraeus resigns as the head of the CIA (Central Intelligence

The WikiLeaks logo.

Agency). The much-decorated Petraeus, who led military forces in both Afghanistan and Iraq, is accused of an inappropriate personal relationship, which the FBI discovers by perusing his email. It is the fall of a giant, brought on by an indiscretion, but it highlights important questions about the conduct of the FBI, the breadth of the surveillance state, and the reach of the new technologies. The English newspaper *Manchester Guardian* comments, "What is most striking is how sweeping, probing and invasive the FBI's investigation … became, all without any evidence of any actual crime—or the need for any search warrant … This is a surveillance state run amok … the Obama administration has [been] aggressively seeking to expand that Surveillance State … to amend the Patriot Act to include Internet and browsing data among the records obtainable by the FBI without court approval and demanding legislation requiring that all Internet communications contain a government 'backdoor' of surveillance."

Can there be a balance between open government and official secrecy? Where will Americans in the next decades get most of their information? Can we use our technology to bring clarity to the information that surrounds us? The answer to those questions will help determine the vigor and future of our democracy.

Issues for Informed Debate

Mitt Romney speaks in Detroit in August 2012.

Michael Sandel, a political philosopher who teaches a popular online Harvard course titled "Justice," says, "If American politics is to recover its civic voice, it must find a way to debate questions we have forgotten to ask."

We've done it before. In 1858, Abraham Lincoln and Stephen Douglas, pitted against each other for an Illinois Senate seat, engaged in a series of debates that tackled the big issue of the day: slavery. Clarifying and explaining their differences, they gave voters a clear choice. (The voters picked Douglas, but later, after the debates were published, they helped Lincoln become president.)

A half century earlier, Alexander Hamilton and Thomas Jefferson articulated the conservative and liberal issues of their day with eloquence, but no less passion than today's partisan politicians. Hamilton, holding a pessimistic view of human nature, felt citizens needed strong leadership. Jefferson believed that citizens, left unfettered by the government, could be trusted.

In the presidential election of 1912, Woodrow Wilson and Theodore Roosevelt argued similar themes. Roosevelt championed the federal government as the regulator of big business. Wilson disagreed, saying that, "the history of liberty is a history of limited governmental power, not the increase of it." Today, the divide remains between those who see the need for active government as a provider of basic rights, and those who want limited government.

The question about the proper role of government is one of big ones facing the nation in 2012, when Republican businessman and former Massachusetts governor Mitt Romney squares off against the Democratic president, Barack Obama. How do the candidates address this question? Unfortunately, they respond mainly with shallow slogans and negative TV commercials. While many Americans seem ready for a Lincoln/Douglas-type debate that will bring clarity to the candidates' differences, it doesn't happen in what is the costliest campaign in American history.

Here are a few of the questions that might have been debated:

The One World Trade Center, previously known as the "Freedom Tower," under construction in New York City in August 2012.

Should the religious freedom guarantee of the First Amendment (and of Jefferson's Statute for Religious Freedom) remain fundamental to American society, or do new times demand new interpretations? The "Freedom Tower" under construction where the World Trade Center once stood is just blocks away from where an Islamic

> "This is a matter of vital importance to the public safety.... While we recognize that assault-weapon legislation will not stop all assault-weapon crime, statistics prove that we can dry up the supply of these guns, making them less accessible to criminals."
> —President Ronald Reagan

group wants to build a community center. Should they have the freedom to do so in a wounded neighborhood?

In the United States, much of the cost of elections reflects charges for television commercials. However, the airwaves belong to the people. Is this a solvable problem?

When you shrink government what should get cut? Who will pay a price for smaller government? Who will benefit? Can we have leaner government in an increasingly complex urban world? What are legitimate governmental responsibilities?

Should public services be privatized? Is government shirking its responsibility when it turns prisons over to for-profit companies that are traded on the stock market, or is it becoming more efficient?

How do we retain our privacy in cyberspace and maintain an interconnected world?

Is health care a human right? Is my personal freedom compromised if I'm penalized for not having health insurance, or is the greater freedom and welfare of our country advanced if everyone can have medical care?

What role should the federal government play in education? Is education a basic right that taxpayers should finance? Should education be funded through college, as it is in many other Western nations? What about for-profit schools? Should they be regulated? Tying school funding to local tax revenue means rich communities have lots of money for their schools and poor ones have hardly any. Should that funding method be examined?

Is there a need for a broad discussion of gun control in a nation where almost anyone—even the mentally deranged—can get access to high-powered automatic weaponry designed for military use?

In an increasingly fluid world, questions of terrorism, asylum, immigration, and citizenry have a large impact on many nations. Can the United States bring clarity to these issues? Do asylum seekers—or even suspected terrorists—have basic rights like *habeas corpus* that have been America's pride?

At the Constitutional Convention, when Pierce Butler of South Carolina suggested that the president be given the power to declare war, his proposal was overwhelmingly rejected. Elbridge Gerry of Massachusetts said he, "never expected to hear in a republic a motion to empower the Executive to declare war." The Constitution says in Article I, Section 8, that "Congress shall have the power to declare war." Why has that article been ignored? Should it be?

President Harry Truman bypassed Congress, sending troops to Korea in the early 1950s while declaring that it wasn't really a war. (Actually, it was a United Nations Police Action in response to an invasion.) Vietnam, another not-really-a-war followed. Then came the two Iraq Wars. (In the First Gulf War, a coalition of nations responded to an invasion.)

The United States has not declared a war since World War II. Who should have the power to declare war in our democracy, the president or Congress? The Constitution is clear about this: it is Congress. This is a subject that needs a national discussion.

REELECTION

On Tuesday, November 6, 2012, the American people peacefully go to the polls and pick a leader: Barack Obama wins a second term. It's an election that reflects a new America: Hispanic voters, along with African Americans and other minorities, make a difference. Political pundits write of the opportunity for the president to bring the nation together, noting that strong leadership is called for. In a stirring second inaugural speech, President Obama says,

> *We, the people, still believe that our obligations a Americans are not just to ourselves, but to all posterity.... We the people, declare today that the most evident of truths—that all of us are created equal is the star that guides us still; just as it guided our forebears through Seneca Falls, and Selma, and Stonewall; just as it guided all those men and women, sung and unsung, who left footprints along this great Mall ... to hear a King proclaim that our individual freedom is inextricably bound to the freedom of every soul on Earth....*
>
> *That is our generation's task—to make these words, these rights, these values—of life, liberty, and the Pursuit of Happiness—real for every American."*

BEING FREE

So here we are, well into the twenty-first century, the richest people the world has ever known. Opportunities abound. Freedom reigns. That old bear, Russian communism, is dead and buried. A majority of the world's peoples now live in at least nominal democracies. The concept of "liberty and justice for all" articulated by our founders has spread throughout the world. So why aren't we cheering? One reason: we've come to realize that government by the people isn't easy. You have to work at it—and keep working. There are no guarantees. The odds were we wouldn't make it as a nation. The Founders themselves were skeptical. Thomas Jefferson, in a letter to his friend Lafayette was blunt, "We are not to expect to be translated from despotism to liberty in a featherbed."

It was given to us to try something that hadn't been done by any government before. We are expected to make our own decisions, but that only works with an educated citizenry. In addition, the proliferation of information in the Internet Age means there's more and more to know.

One of the astonishing things about American democracy is the number of elections we have—from local school boards to governors to presidents. Power is widely dispersed in this country. Our government is not some unresponsive "them"; it is us. If it doesn't work as well as it should, we the people have the power to change things.

We Americans are often accused of hubris, of believing that we are special. However, most of us realize that it isn't that we are special; it's our place in world history that is unique. We are heirs of that simple idea: people can govern themselves. We don't need kings, shahs, mullahs, or czars to tell us how to live. We can figure that out for ourselves, but running our own government not only takes participation and cooperation, it takes oversight. If those in power abuse their trust, we need to vote them out. To do that, we need to be informed. Given the information devices at our fingertips, that should be increasingly possible, yet many of us let media advertising and sound bites—not solid information—sway us.

I Can't Resist: a Bit More History

In 1901, there were fears that our democracy was finished. Business corruption and greed stood at appalling levels, and dazzling innovations from Thomas Edison and his fellow inventors were speeding up the pace of society. It was hard to imagine how a slow, deliberate form of government like democracy could keep up.

Mark Twain, who once proposed creating an "Anti-Doughnut Party" that would make sure the Democrats and Republicans put forth their best possible candidates, was seriously worried about America's future. In his *Autobiography*, he wrote, "Look at the tyranny of party—at what is called party allegiance, party loyalty—a snare invented by designing men for selfish purposes—and which turns voters into chattels, slaves, rabbits, and all the while their masters, and they themselves are shouting rubbish about liberty, independence, freedom of opinion, freedom of speech, honestly unconscious of the fantastic contradiction."

Twain's contemporary, Henry Adams, a fine historian and great grandson of the second president, said in a political novel titled *Democracy*, "At the rate of increase of speed and momentum the present society must break its damn neck in a definite, but remote time, not exceeding fifty years or more."

Twain should have stuck to humor and Adams to history. During their lifetimes, we Americans had an average life expectancy of about 47 years. In 2010, it had risen to 78.3 years.

By the mid-20th century, having survived a Great Depression and some horrific wars, America's democracy was thriving: the middle class was prosperous, our schools and universities were among the best in the world, and our politics were productively bipartisan. A string of puny colonies had become the greatest power the world has ever known. As for science and technology, we were on a roll, with triumphs changing not only the length of our lives but the way people live and think.

Now here we are, well into the twenty-first century, and democracy seems to be in trouble again. The pundits are sounding as discouraged as Henry Adams and Mark Twain were a hundred or so years earlier. I even have a book on my desk that's subtitled, "The Subversion of American Democracy.'

Meanwhile, there are important issues to be decided. As usual, Thomas Jefferson had thoughts on this. In a letter to James Madison, he wrote, "Above all things I hope the education of the common people will be attended to: convinced that on their good sense we may rely with the most security for the preservation of a due degree of liberty." We can also look at his words to the Rev Richard Price, which bear repeating: "Whenever the people are informed, they can be trusted with their own government."

Informed? It shouldn't be hard, given the technology of our time, to find ways to make civic information widely available. Big issues need deciding. Those who don't participate in the governing process—who don't read, think, and play their part—are missing the whole point of democracy; others will make decisions for them. The nation's future rests with those who participate. The more informed they are, the more likely they are to understand America's meaning to the world. The founding generation gave us a responsibility and a challenge, as well as a legacy. Here's how Tom Paine put it in *Common Sense* back in 1776, "The cause of America is in great measure the cause of all mankind."

The Declaration of Independence

When in the Course of human Events, it becomes necessary for one People to dissolve the Political Bands which have connected them with one another, and to assume among the Powers of the Earth, the separate and equal Station to which the Laws of Nature and of Nature's God entitle them, a decent Respect to the Opinions of Mankind requires that they should declare the causes which impel them to the Separation.

We hold these Truths to be self-evident, that all Men are created equal, that they are endowed by their Creator with certain unalienable Rights, that among these are Life, Liberty and the Pursuit of Happiness—that to secure these Rights, Governments are instituted among Men, deriving their just Powers from the Consent of the Governed, that whenever any Form of Government becomes destructive of these Ends, it is the Right of the People to alter or to abolish it, and to institute new Government, laying its Foundation on such Principles, and organizing its Powers in such Form, as to them shall seem most likely to effect their Safety and Happiness. Prudence, indeed, will dictate that Governments long established should not be changed for light and transient Causes; and accordingly all Experience hath shewn, that Mankind are more disposed to suffer, while Evils are sufferable, than to right themselves by abolishing the Forms to which they are accustomed. But when a long Train of Abuses and Usurpations, pursuing inevitably the same Object, evinces a Design to reduce them under absolute Despotism, it is their Right, it is their Duty, to throw off such Government, and to provide new Guards for their future Security. Such has been the patient Sufferance of these Colonies; and such is now the Necessity which constrains them to alter their former Systems of Government.

The History of the present King of Great-Britain is a History of repeated Injuries and Usurpations, all having in direct Object the Establishment of an absolute Tyranny over these States. To prove this, let Facts be submitted to a candid World.

He has refused his Assent to Laws, the most wholesome and necessary for the public Good.

He has forbidden his Government to pass Laws of immediate and pressing Importance, unless suspended in their Operation till his Assent should be obtained; and when so suspended, he has utterly neglected to attend to them.

He has refused to pass other Laws for the Accommodation of large Districts of People, unless those People would relinquish the Right of Representation in the Legislature, a Right inestimable to them, and formidable to Tyrants only.

He has called together Legislative Bodies at Places unusual, uncomfortable, and distant from the Depository of their public Records, for the sole Purpose of fatiguing them into Compliance with his Measures.

He has dissolved Representative Houses repeatedly, for opposing with manly Firmness his Invasions of the Rights of the People.

He has refused for a long Time, after such Dissolutions, to cause others to be elected; whereby the Legislative Powers, incapable of Annihilation, have returned to the People at large for their exercise; the State remaining in the meantime exposed to all the Dangers of Invasion from without, and Convulsions within.

He has endeavoured to prevent the Population of these States; for that Purpose obstructing the Laws for Naturalization of Foreigners; refusing to pass others to encourage their Migrations hither, and raising the Conditions of new Appropriations of Lands.

He has obstructed the Administration of Justice, by refusing his Assent to Laws for establishing Judiciary Powers.

He has made Judges dependent on his Will alone, for the Tenure of their Offices, and the Amount and Payment of their Salaries.

He has erected a Multitude of new Offices, and sent hither Swarms of Officers to harass our People, and eat out of their Substance.

He has kept among us, in Times of Peace, Standing Armies, without the consent of our Legislatures.

He has affected to render the Military independent of and superior to the Civil Power.

He has combined with others to subject us to a Jurisdiction foreign to our Constitution, and unacknowledged by our Laws; giving his Assent to their Acts of pretended Legislation:

For cutting off our Trade with all Parts of the World:

For imposing Taxes on us without our Consent:

For depriving us, in many Cases, of the Benefits of Trial by Jury:

For transporting us beyond Seas to be tried for pretended Offences:

For abolishing the free System of English Laws in a neighbouring Province, establishing therein an arbitrary Government, and enlarging its Boundaries, so as to render it at once an Example and fit Instrument for introducing the same absolute Rule into these Colonies:

For taking away our Charters, abolishing our most valuable Laws, and altering Fundamentally the Forms of our Governments:

For suspending our own Legislatures, and declaring themselves invested with Power to legislate for us in all Cases whatsoever.

He has abdicated Government here, by declaring us out of his Protection and waging War against us.

He has plundered our Seas, ravaged our Coasts, burnt our Towns, and destroyed the Lives of our People.

He is, at this Time, transporting large Armies of foreign Mercenaries to compleat the works of Death, Desolation, and Tyranny, already begun with circumstances of Cruelty and Perfidy, scarcely paralleled in the most barbarous Ages, and totally unworthy of the Head of a civilized Nation.

He has constrained our fellow Citizens taken Captive on the high Seas to bear Arms against their Country, to become the Executioners of their Friends and Brethren, or to fall themselves by their Hands.

He has excited domestic Insurrections amongst us, and has endeavoured to bring on the Inhabitants of our Frontiers, the merciless Indian Savages, whose known Rule of Warfare, is an undistinguished Destruction, of all Ages, Sexes and Conditions.

In every stage of these Oppressions we have Petitioned for Redress in the most humble Terms: Our repeated Petitions have been answered only by repeated Injury. A Prince, whose Character is thus marked by every act which may define a Tyrant, is unfit to the the Ruler of a Free People.

Nor have we been wanting in Attentions to our British Brethren. We have warned them from Time to Time of Attempts by their Legislature to extend an unwarrantable Jurisdiction over us. We have reminded them of the Circumstances of our Emigration and Settlement here. We have appealed to their native Justice and Magnanimity, and we have conjured them by the Ties of our common Kindred to disavow these Usurpations, which would inevitably interrupt our Connections and Correspondence. They too have been deaf to the Voice of Justice and of Consanguinity. We must, therefore, acquiesce in the Necessity, which denounces our Separation, and hold them, as we hold the rest of Mankind, Enemies in War, in Peace, Friends.

We, therefore, the Representatives of the UNITED STATES OF AMERICA, in GENERAL CONGRESS Assembled, appealing to the Supreme Judge of the World for the Rectitude of our Intentions, do, in the Name, and by the Authority of the good People of these Colonies, solemnly Publish and Declare, That these United Colonies are, and by Right ought to be, FREE AND INDEPENDENT STATES; that they are absolved from all Allegiance to the British Crown, and that all political Connection between them and the State of Great-Britain, is and ought to be totally dissolved; and that as FREE AND INDEPENDENT STATES, they have full Power to levy War, conclude Peace, contract Alliances, establish Commerce, and to do all other Acts and Things which INDEPENDENT STATES may of right do. And for the support of this Declaration, with a firm Reliance on the Protection of divine Providence, we mutually pledge to each other our Lives, our Fortunes, and our sacred Honor.

Signed by ORDER and in BEHALF of this CONGRESS,

John Hancock, PRESIDENT.

Freedom in the Constitution

The following selection of material from the Constitution of the United States was made by Henry J. Abraham and Barbara A. Perry and is presented in their excellent book Freedom and the Court *(sixth edition, 1994; reprinted by permission).*

Provisions from the original Constitution

Article I
Section 9....
2. The privilege of the writ of habeas corpus shall not be suspended, unless when in cases of rebellion or invasion the public safety may require it.
3. No bill of attainder or ex post facto law shall be passed.

Section 10.
1. No State shall … pass any bill of attainder, ex post facto law, or law impairing the obligation of contracts....

Article III
Section 2....
3. The trial of all crimes, except in cases of impeachment, shall be by jury …

Section 3.
1. Treason against the United States shall consist only in levying war against them, or in adhering to their enemies, giving them aid and comfort. No Person shall be convicted of treason unless on the testimony of two witnesses to the same overt act, or on confession in open court.

Article IV
Section 2.
1. The citizens of each state shall be entitled to all privileges and immunities of citizens in the several States.

Article VI
3. … no religious test shall ever be required as a qualification to any office or public trust under the United States.

The First Ten Amendments (adopted in 1791)

Amendment I
Congress shall make no law respecting an establishment of religion, or prohibiting the free exercise thereof; or abridging the freedom of speech, or of the press, or the right of the people peaceably to assemble and to petition the Government for a redress of grievances.

Amendment II
A well-regulated militia being necessary to the security of a free State, the right of the people to keep and bear arms, shall not be infringed.

Amendment III
No soldier shall, in time of peace, be quartered in any house without the consent of the owner, nor in time of war but in a manner to be prescribed by law.

Amendment IV

The right of the people to be secure in their persons, houses, papers, and effects, against unreasonable searches and seizures, shall not be violated, and no warrants shall issue but upon probable cause, supported by oath or affirmation, and particularly describing the place to be searched, and the persons or things to be seized.

Amendment V

No person shall be held to answer for a capital, or otherwise infamous crime, unless on a presentment or indictment of a Grand Jury, except in cases arising in the land or naval forces, or in the militia, when in actual service in time of war or public danger; nor shall any person be subject for the same offense to be twice in jeopardy of life or limb; nor shall be compelled in any criminal case to be a witness against himself, nor be deprived of life, liberty or property, without due process of law; not shall private property be taken for public use, without just compensation.

Amendment VI

In all criminal prosecutions, the accused shall enjoy the right to a speedy and public trial, by an impartial jury of the State and district wherein the crime shall have been committed, which districts shall have been previously ascertained by law, and to be informed of the nature and cause of the accusation; to be confronted with the witnesses against him; to have compulsory process for obtaining witnesses in his favor, and to have the assistance of counsel for his defense.

Amendment VII

In suits at common law, where the value in controversy shall exceed twenty dollars, the right of trial by jury shall be preserved, and no fact tried by a jury, shall be otherwise reexamined in any court of the United States, than according to the rules of the common law.

Amendment VIII

Excessive bail shall not be required, nor excessive fines imposed, nor cruel and unusual punishments inflicted.

Amendment IX

The enumeration in the Constitution of certain rights shall not be construed to deny or disparage others retained by the people.

Amendment X

The powers not delegated to the United States by the Constitution, nor prohibited by it to the States, are reserved to the States respectively, or to the people.

OTHER AMENDMENTS

AMENDMENT XIII (ratified in 1865)
SECTION 1. Neither slavery nor involuntary servitude, except as a punishment for crime whereof the party shall have been duly convicted, shall exist within the United States, or any place subject to their jurisdiction.
SECTION 2. Congress shall have power to enforce this article by appropriate legislation.

AMENDMENT XIV (ratified in 1868)
SECTION 1. All persons born or naturalized in the United States, and subject to the jurisdiction thereof, are citizens of the United States and of the State wherein they reside. No State shall make or enforce any law which shall abridge the privileges or immunities of citizens of the United States; nor shall any State deprive any person of life, liberty, or property, without due process of law; nor deny to any person within its jurisdiction the equal protection of the laws....
SECTION 5. The Congress shall have power to enforce by appropriate legislation the provisions of this article.

AMENDMENT XV (ratified in 1870)
SECTION 1. The right of citizens of the United States to vote shall not be denied or abridged by the United States or by any State on account of race, color, or previous condition of servitude.
SECTION 2. The Congress shall have power to enforce this article by appropriate legislation.

AMENDMENT XIX (ratified in 1920)
SECTION 1. The right of citizens of the United States to vote shall not be denied or abridged by the United States or by any State on account of sex.
SECTION 2. The Congress shall have power to enforce this article by appropriate legislation.

AMENDMENT XXIV (ratified in 1964)
SECTION 1. The right of citizens of the United States to vote in any primary or other election for President or Vice-President, for electors for President or Vice-President, or for Senator or Representative in Congress, shall not be denied or abridged by the United States or any State by reason of failure to pay any poll tax or other tax.
SECTION 2. The Congress shall have power to enforce this article by appropriate legislation.

AMENDMENT XXVI (ratified in 1971)
SECTION 1. The right of citizens of the United States, who are 18 years of age or older, to vote shall not be denied or abridged by the United States of any State on account of age.
SECTION 2. The Congress shall have power to enforce this article by appropriate legislation.

President Obama's Second Inaugural Address

January 21, 2013

Thank you. Thank you. Thank you so much.

Vice President Biden, Mr. Chief Justice, members of the United States Congress, distinguished guests, and fellow citizens, each time we gather to inaugurate a president, we bear witness to the enduring strength of our Constitution. We affirm the promise of our democracy. We recall that what binds this nation together is not the colors of our skin or the tenets of our faith or the origins of our names.

What makes us exceptional, what makes us America is our allegiance to an idea articulated in a declaration made more than two centuries ago. We hold these truths to be self-evident, that all men are created equal.

That they are endowed by their creator with certain unalienable rights, and among these are life, liberty, and the pursuit of happiness. Today we continue a never ending journey to bridge the meaning of those words with the realities of our time. For history tells us that while these truths may be self-evident, they've never been self-executing. That while freedom is a gift from God, it must be secured by his people here on earth.

The patriots of 1776 did not fight to replace the tyranny of a king with the privileges of a few, or the rule of a mob. They gave to us a republic, a government of, and by, and for the people. Entrusting each generation to keep safe our founding creed. And for more than 200 years we have. Through blood drawn by lash, and blood drawn by sword, we noted that no union founded on the principles of liberty and equality could survive half slave, and half free.

We made ourselves anew, and vowed to move forward together.

Together we determined that a modern economy requires railroads and highways to speed travel and commerce, schools and colleges to train our workers. Together we discovered that a free market only thrives when there are rules to ensure competition and fair play. Together we resolve that a great nation must care for the vulnerable and protect its people from life's worst hazards and misfortune.

Through it all, we have never relinquished our skepticism of central authority, nor have we succumbed to the fiction that all society's ills can be cured through government alone. Our celebration of initiative and enterprise, our insistence on hard work and personal responsibility, these are constants in our character.

For we have always understood that when times change, so must we, that fidelity to our founding principles requires new responses to new challenges, that preserving our individual freedoms ultimately requires collective action.

For the American people can no more meet the demands of today's world by acting alone than American soldiers could have met the forces of fascism or communism with muskets and militias. No single person can train all the math and science teachers we'll need to equip our children for the future. Or build the roads and networks and research labs that will bring new jobs and businesses to our shores.

Now, more than ever, we must do these things together, as one nation, and one people.

This generation of Americans has been tested by crises that steeled our resolve and proved our resilience. A decade of war is now ending.

And economic recovery has begun.

America's possibilities are limitless, for we possess all the qualities that this world without boundaries demands: youth and drive, diversity and openness, of endless capacity for risk and a gift for reinvention.

My fellow Americans, we are made for this moment and we will seize it, so long as we seize it together.

For we, the people, understand that our country cannot succeed when a shrinking few do very well and a growing many barely make it.

We believe that America's prosperity must rest upon the broad shoulders of a rising middle class. We know that America thrives when every person can find independence and pride in their work, when the wages of honest labor will liberate families from the brink of hardship.

We are true to our creed when a little girl born into the bleakest poverty knows that she has the same chance to succeed as anybody else because she is an American, she is free, and she is equal not just in the eyes of God but also in our own.

We understand that outworn programs are inadequate to the needs of our time. So we must harness new ideas and technology to remake our government, revamp our tax code, reform our schools, and empower our citizens with the skills they need to work hard or learn more, reach higher.

But while the means will change, our purpose endures. A nation that rewards the effort and determination of every single American, that is what this moment requires. That is what will give real meaning to our creed.

We, the people, still believe that every citizen deserves a basic measure of security and dignity. We must make the hard choices to reduce the cost of health care and the size of our deficit.

But we reject the belief that America must choose between caring for the generation that built this country and investing in the generation that will build its future.

For we remember the lessons of our past, when twilight years were spent in poverty and parents of a child with a disability had nowhere to turn. We do not believe that in this country freedom is reserved for the lucky or happiness for the few. We recognize that no matter how responsibly we live our lives, any one of us at any time may face a job loss or a sudden illness or a home swept away in a terrible storm. The commitments we make to each other through Medicare and Medicaid and Social Security, these things do not sap our initiative.

They strengthen us.

They do not make us a nation of takers. They free us to take the risks that make this country great.

We, the people, still believe that our obligations as Americans are not just to ourselves, but to all posterity. We will respond to the threat of climate change, knowing that the failure to do so would betray our children and future generations.

Some may still deny the overwhelming judgment of science, but none can avoid the devastating impact of raging fires, and crippling drought, and more powerful storms. The path towards sustainable energy sources will be long and sometimes difficult. But American cannot resist this transition. We must lead it.

We cannot cede to other nations the technology that will power new jobs and new industries. We must claim its promise. That's how we will maintain our economic vitality and our national treasure, our forests and waterways, our crop lands and snow capped peaks. That is how we will preserve our planet, commanded to our care by God. That's what will lend meaning to the creed our fathers once declared.

We, the people, still believe that enduring security and lasting peace do not require perpetual war.

Our brave men and women in uniform tempered by the flames of battle are unmatched in skill and courage.

Our citizens seared by the memory of those we have lost, know too well the price that is paid for liberty. The knowledge of their sacrifice will keep us forever vigilant against those who would do us harm. But we are also heirs to those who won the peace, and not just the war. Who turn sworn enemies into the surest of friends. And we must carry those lessons into this time as well. We will defend our people, and uphold our values through strength of arms, and the rule of law.

We will show the courage to try and resolve our differences with other nations peacefully. Not because we are naive about the dangers we face, but because engagement can more durably lift suspicion and fear.

America will remain the anchor of strong alliances in every corner of the globe. And we will renew those institutions that extend our capacity to manage crisis abroad. For no one has a greater stake in a peaceful world than its most powerful nation. We will support democracy from Asia to Africa, from the Americas to the Middle East, because our interests and our conscience compel us to act on behalf of those who long for freedom. And we must be a source of hope to the poor, the sick, the marginalized, the victims of prejudice.

Not out of mere charity, but because peace in our time requires the constant advance of those principles that our common creed describes; tolerance and opportunity, human dignity and justice. We the people declare today that the most evident of truth that all of us are created equal—is the star that guides us still; just as it guided our forebears through Seneca Falls and Selma and Stonewall; just as it guided all those men and women, sung and unsung, who left footprints along this great mall, to hear a preacher say that we cannot walk alone; to hear a King proclaim that our individual freedom is inextricably bound to the freedom of every soul on Earth.

It is now our generation's task to carry on what those pioneers began, for our journey is not complete until our wives, our mothers and daughters can earn a living equal to their efforts.

Our journey is not complete until our gay brothers and sisters are treated like anyone else under the law, for if we are truly created equal, then surely the love we commit to one another must be equal, as well.

Our journey is not complete until no citizen is forced to wait for hours to exercise the right to vote.

Our journey is not complete until we find a better way to welcome the striving, hopeful immigrants who still see America as a land of opportunity, until bright young students and engineers are enlisted in our workforce rather than expelled from our country.

Our journey is not complete until all our children, from the streets of Detroit to the hills of Appalachia to the quiet lanes of Newtown, know that they are cared for and cherished and always safe from harm.

That is our generation's task, to make these works, these rights, these values of life and liberty and the pursuit of happiness real for every American.

Being true to our founding documents does not require us to agree on every contour of life. It does not mean we all define liberty in exactly the same way or follow the same precise path to happiness.

Progress does not compel us to settle century's long debates about the role of government for all time, but it does require us to act in our time.

For now, decisions are upon us and we cannot afford delay. We cannot mistake absolutism for principle or substitute spectacle for politics, or treat name-calling as reasoned debate.

We must act. We must act knowing that our work will be imperfect. We must act knowing that today's victories will be only partial, and that it will be up to those who stand here in four years and 40 years and 400 years hence to advance the timeless spirit once conferred to us in a spare Philadelphia hall.

My fellow Americans, the oath I have sworn before you today, like the one recited by others who serve in this Capitol, was an oath to God and country, not party or faction.

And we must faithfully execute that pledge during the duration of our service. But the words I spoke today are not so different from the oath that is taken each time a soldier signs up for duty, or an immigrant realizes her dream.

My oath is not so different from the pledge we all make to the flag that waves above and that fills our hearts with pride. They are the words of citizens, and they represent our greatest hope. You and I, as citizens, have the power to set this country's course. You and I, as citizens, have the obligation to shape the debates of our time, not only with the votes we cast, but the voices we lift in defense of our most ancient values and enduring ideas.

Let us each of us now embrace with solemn duty, and awesome joy, what is our lasting birthright. With common effort and common purpose, with passion and dedication, let us answer the call of history and carry into an uncertain future that precious light of freedom.

Thank you.

God bless you.

And may He forever bless these United States of America.

INDEX

A
Abernathy, Reverend Ralph, 337
abolition, 102, 105–107, 113, 119, 125, 157, 208
Abrams v. *United States*, 384
Acheson, Dean, 300
Adams, Abigail, 13, 15, 17, 19
Adams, Henry, 44, 423–424
Adams, President John, vi–vii, x, 12, 14, 17, 20, 32, 42–45, 97, 171, 233
Adams, President John Quincy, 63–64, 354–355
Adams, Samuel, 7–9, 12
Addams, Jane, 246–247
Afghanistan, 405, 407, 409, 417
Afghan Northern Alliance, 405
African Methodist Church, 21
Alabama, 66, 78, 95, 120
Alamo, battle of the, 69
Albany, New York, 18, 24–25, 82–84
Alien Act of 1798, 42–45
Allied Powers, 252
al-Qaeda, 402–403, 404, 405–406, 408
amendments to the Constitution, *see* Bill of Rights; constitutional amendments
American Civil Liberties Union (ACLU), 266–267
American Federation of Labor (AFL), 219, 222–223, 263
American Indian Movement (AIM), 368–369
American Party; *see* Know-Nothings
American Revolution, *see* Revolutionary War
Anaconda Plan, 131, 133
Anderson, Marian, 281
Anglicans, 9, 57, 59; *see also* Church of England
Annapolis, Maryland, 8
Anthony, Susan B., ix, 90, 92–93, 205–209, 264
Antietam, the battle of, 123, 135–136, 138
Antin, Mary, 202–203
Appalachian Mountains, 64, 66–67, 183, 186
Appomattox Court House, 152–153
Arizona, 193
Arkansas, 120, 131, 179
Arkwright, Richard, 75
Armistice Day, 256–257
Armstrong, Louis, 269–270
Army-McCarthy hearings, 312–313
Arnold, General Benedict, 23
Arthur, President Chester, 199
Articles of Confederation, 29, 31, 33–34, 64
Assange, Julian, 417
Atlanta, Georgia, capture of, 149
Atlantic Ocean, 254
atomic bomb, 295
Auschwitz, 295
Austin, Stephen, 68
Austin, Texas, 347
Australia, 405
Austria-Hungary, 251–252
Axis powers, 292, 295

B
Baghdad, Iraq, 409, 415
Barron v. *Baltimore*, 164
Bernanke, Ben, 412
Bill of Rights, 6–7, 37–38, 43–44, 51–52, 60–61, 417–418
bin Laden, Osama, 404–406, 415
Bipartisan Campaign Reform Act, *see* McCain-Feingold Act
black codes, 102, 104, 162, 164, 177
Black Hand, 251–252
Black, Hugo, Supreme Court justice, 379, 386
Blair, Reverend James, 59
Blix, Hans, 407
Bloomer, Amelia, 91
Bonus Army, 275–276
Boone, Daniel, 61
Booth, John Wilkes, 157–158
Bosnia-Herzegovina, 251
Boston, Massachusetts, 202
Boston Tea Party, 3, 5, 5–7
Bradford, William, of Plymouth settlers, 52
Brandeis, Louis D., Supreme Court justice, 384–386
Brandenburg v. *Ohio*, 386
Brennan, William J., Supreme Court justice, 329
Breyer, Stephen G., Supreme Court justice, 401
Briggs v. *Clarendon County*, 317
Britain, vii, 12, 70, 284, 306, 405; *see also* England
Brookings Institution, 416
Brooklyn Bridge, 73, 216
Brooklyn Dodgers, 304
Brown, Henry B., Supreme Court justice, 316
Brown, John, 118–120
Brown, Linda Carol, 317
Brown, Reverend Oliver, ix, 317
Brown v. *Board of Education*, 317–319, 325, 400
Bruce, Blanche K. Bruce, 165
Bryan, William Jennings, 237–238

Buchanan, President James, 110–113
Buffalo, New York, 81–83
Buford, General John, 142
Bulgaria, 252
Bulge, Battle of the, 295
Bull Moose Party, 249
Bull Run, first battle of, 126–128
Burger, Warren, Supreme Court chief justice, 379, 386
Burgoyne, General John, 24–25
Burn, Harry, 265
Burns, Anthony, 116
Burnside, General, 135
Bush, President George H. W., 394, 399, 401–402, 407
Bush, President George W., 399, 402, 405–411, 413
business, government regulation of, 214, 239, 243, 244–246, 250, 281–282, 390–391
Butler, Benjamin, senator, 175
Byrd, Robert C., senator, 408

C

Calhoun, John C., senator, 108–109, 126, 130
California, 108, 193, 199, 201
Cambodia, 352
Campbell, Ben Nighthorse, senator, 369
Cardozo, Francis Louis, 167
Carlisle Indian School, Pennsylvania, 190
Carnegie, Andrew, 215–216
Carter, President James Earl "Jimmy", 387–389
Castro, Fidel, 332–333
Cather, Willa, 113, 239
Catlin, George, 182
Catt, Carrie Chapman, 264
Catton, Bruce, 127
Cazeau, Jane, 70
Central High School, Little Rock, Arkansas, 325–327

Central Intelligence Agency (CIA), 332, 417
Central Powers, 252
Chamberlain, Daniel Henry, 168
Chancellorsville, Virginia, battle of, 134
Chaney, James, 358–359
Charles II, king of England, 58
Charles I, king of England, 53
Charleston, South Carolina, 27, 121, 156, 158
Charlottesville, Virginia, 62
Chattanooga, battle of, 122
Chattanooga, Tennessee, 211
Chavez, Cesar, ix
Cherokee tribe, 68
Cheyenne tribe, 188
Chicago, Illinois, 158, 218, 371
Chickasaw tribe, 69
Chief Joseph, 191–192
China, 161, 199–202
Chinese Exclusion Act, 199–200
Chiricahua Apache tribe, 193
Chivington, Colonel John, 188
Choctaw tribe, 69
Churchill, Winston, prime minister of Britian, 285, 293–295, 306–308
Cincinnati, Ohio, 113, 137
Citizens United v. *Campaign Finance Reform*, 412
City Point, Virginia, 150
Civil Rights Act, 1866, 163
Civil Rights Act, 1964, 351, 355
civil rights movement, 321–329, 338, 341–344, 355–363
Civil War, (1861–1865), 121, 122–153
Clark, Sheriff Jim, 358
Clark, William, 45, 49, 190
Clay, Henry, senator, 104–105, 109, 111, 214, 349
Clemenceau, Prime Minister Georges, of France, 259

Cleveland, President Grover, 221, 236, 238, 277
Clinton, Governor DeWitt, 82
Clinton, Hillary, senator, secretary of state, 396, 412
Clinton, President William Jefferson, 383, 395–396, 398–399, 411
Coffin, Catherine and Levi, 113
Cohen v. *California*, 329
Cold War, 406
College of William and Mary, 59
Colonel Robert Gould Shaw, 140
Columbia, South Carolina, 159
Columbus, Ohio, 82
committees of correspondence, 9
Common Sense, Tom Paine, 10, 423
communism, 234, 262–263, 283, 306, 310–314, 332–333, 352–354, 380, 386, 390, 392–393, 395, 421
Community Service Organization (CSO), 365
Compromise of 1850, 108
Concord, Massachusetts, battle of, 10–11, 12, 362
Confederacy, 120, 123, 133, 135–136, 152, 161
Confederate army, 123, 133, 136, 147
Confederate States of America, 120
Confederation, Articles of, 29, 31, 33, 131
Congress, vii, 29, 31, 34, 42, 44, 66, 408
Congress for Racial Equality (CORE), 357
Connally, John, governor of Texas, 345
Connecticut, 33
Connecticut Compromise, 264
Connor, Eugene "Bull", 337, 340, 358

constitutional amendments, 152
Constitutional Convention, 33, 420
Constitution of the United States, vii, 14–17, 34–39, 97–100, 163–164, 174–176, 180, 181, 264, 318, 383
Continental Army, 12–13
Continental Congress, First, 12, 15
Continental Congress, Second, 13, 23, 30
Coolidge, President Calvin, 268, 271, 273, 278
Cooper, James Fenimore, 73–74, 84
Cooper, Peter, 83–84
Cooper Union, 83, 219
Copperhead Democrats, 141
Corbin, Molly, 19
Cornwallis, Lord Charles, 27–29
Cosby, William governor, 38
Cotton, Reverend John, 53, 55
Coxey, Jacob, 220–221
Coxey's Army, 221
Crafts, Tom, 17
Crandall, Prudence, 106
Crazy Horse, Sioux chief, 188
Creek, tribe, 69
Crèvecœur, Hector St. John, 2–3
Crockett, Davy, 69
Cuba, 332–335
Cuban missile crisis, 335
Currier, Nathaniel, 3, 121
Custer, Lt.-Col. George Armstrong, 153, 188–189

D

Dallas, Texas, 344
Darrow, Clarence, 231, 237, 267
Davenport, Iowa, 85
Davis, Jefferson, 107, 120, 130, 151, 155, 165
Davis, Joseph, 130
Davis v. School Board of Prince Edward County, 318

Day O'Connor, Sandra, Supreme Court justice, 401
Dayton, Tennessee, 266
D-Day, 292–293
Debs, Eugene V., 249, 258
Declaration of Independence, x, 19, 20, 35, 90, 97, 117, 126, 208, 214, 261, 264, 352
Deere, John, 85, 184–185
Delaware, 33
Delaware River, 23
democracy, 423
Democratic Party, 63, 239, 299, 308
Democrats, 422
Depression, the Great, 270, 273–275, 283, 285, 312, 411, 423
Dewey, Thomas E., 308–310
Diaz, Porfirio, 250–251
Dickinson, Emily, 88
Dickinson, John, 33–34
Disney, Walt, 268
Dixiecrat Party, 309
Dot-Com Bubble, 410
Douglass, Frederick, ix, 113, 138, 149, 181
Douglas, Stephen A., U.S. senator, 109–110, 116–119, 418–419
draft riots, 139
Dred Scott v. Sandford, 111–112, 180
Dulles, John Foster, secretary of state, 353, 380
Dust Bowl, 275

E

Eastern Europe, under Soviet Union, 295
East India Company, 5
Eckford, Elizabeth, 326
Edison, Thomas, 215–216, 265, 422
education, v, ix, 30, 57, 74, 86–88, 202–203, 391–392

Eiffel, Gustave, 229, 271
Eighteenth Amendment of the Constitution, 267
Eisenhower, Dwight D., general and president, 293, 296, 315–316, 318, 326
Ellington, Duke, 270
Elliott, Robert Brown, 166–167
Ellis Island, 196–197
Ellsberg, Daniel, 379–380
Emancipation Proclamation, 136, 138, 163
Emerson, Irene, 111
Emerson, Ralph Waldo, 11–12, 79
England, vii, 1, 4, 7–9, 14, 19, 23, 27, 29, 42, 51, 56, 58, 70, 74
equality, 1, 20, 22, 29, 47
Erie Canal, 73, 81–82
Ervin, Sam Jr., senator, 381, 383–384
Espionage Act, 258, 384
Ettor, Joe, 224–225
Everett, Edward, 145

F

Farm Workers Association, 364
Farragut, Admiral David, 124
Faubus, Orval, governor of Arkansas, 325, 327
F.D.I.C. (Federal Deposit Insurance Corporation), 411
Federal Bureau of Investigation (FBI), 418
Federalist Papers, The, 38
Federalist Party, 41–42, 44, 64
Federal Reserve, 237, 250, 412
Feingold, Russ, 412
Feminine Mystique, The, 366
Fifteenth Amendment to the Constitution, 173, 176, 205–207, 356
Fifth Amendment to the Constitution, 382, 397, 400

First Amendment to the Constitution, 379, 385–386, 419
Five Forks, Virginia, battle of, 150
Flanders, Ralph, senator, 313–314
Florida, 120
Flynn, Elizabeth Gurley, 224
Ford, Henry, 215, 265
Ford, President Gerald, 387, 389
Forrest, Colonel Nathan, 132
Fortas, Abe Suplreme Court justice, 337
Forten, James, 21
Fort Sumter, battle of, 121, 156
Fort Wagner, battle of, 139–141
Fourteenth Amendment to the Constitution, 163, 164, 169, 180, 202–203, 401
Fourth Amendment to the Constitution, 37
France, 9, 42, 59
Frankfort, Kentucky, 177
Frankfurter, Felix, Supreme Court justice, 386
Franklin, Benjamin, v, vi, 6, 13, 15, 32, 36, 39, 61
Franklin, Missouri, 62
Franz, Ferdinand, Archduke, 251–252
Freedmen's Bureau, 161–162, 209
Freedom Summer murders, 357
French and Indian War, 2, 4, 13, 81
French Indochina, 284
Frick, Henry Clay, 216, 260
Friedan, Betty, 316, 366, 368
Fugitive Slave Law, 98, 113–114
Fulton, Robert, 83

G

Gagarin, Yuri, 333
Gandhi, Mohandas (Mahatma), 323–324, 365
Garrison, William Lloyd, 105, 157
Gates, General Horatio, 25

George III, king of England, 1, 4–5, 12, 17, 64, 91
Georgia, v, 12–13, 32, 67–68, 76, 120
Germany, 9, 25, 66
Geronimo, Apache chief, 193–194
Gerry, Elbridge, 17, 99, 420
Gettysburg Address, 147, 214, 303
Gettysburg, Pennyslvania, battle of, 142, 144, 150, 151
Gibbs, Jonathan C., 169
G.I. Bill, 400
Gideon, Clarence L., 336–337
Ginsburg, Ruth Bader, Supreme Court justice, 401
Glass-Steagall Act, 411
Glidden, Joseph, 185
Glorious Revolution, 7
gold standard, 236–237, 239
Gompers, Samuel, 219, 222, 242, 263
Goodman, Andrew, 357–358
Gorbachev, Mikhail, prime minister of Russia, 392–393
Gore, Al, vice president, 399
Grant, General Ulysses S., 144, 147, 150, 152–153, 155, 177–178, 382
Grasse, de, Admiral, 27–28
Great Fire of Chicago, 231
Great War, *see* World War I
Greene, Nathanael, 26–27
Green, Ernest, 327
Greensboro, North Carolina, 328–329
Gregg, Josiah, 61, 66
Grimké, Angelina and Sarah, 87, 90
Griswold v. *Connecticut*, 400
Guantanamo Bay, Cuba, 417
Gulf of Tonkin, 353, 408
Gulf War, first (1990–91), 394, 407–408

H

Hamilton, Alexander, vii, 33, 41, 384, 419
Hamilton, Andrew, 38
Hammond, James Henry, 107
Hammond, M. B., senator, 133
Hancock, John, 13, 16, 426
Hanna, Mark, 243
Harding, President Warren, 278, 382
Harding, Rebecca, 78, 80
Harlan, John Marshall, Supreme Court justice, 180, 212–213, 316
Harpers Ferry, Virginia, 119, 158
Harris, Mary, *see* Mother Jones
Harrison, Benjamin, 16, 236
Hawaiian Islands, 243, 287, 415
Hayes, President Rutherford B., 178, 195, 200
Hay, John, 146
Haymarket Square, Chicago, 218, 222
Haywood, Big Bill, 222, 224
Hebrew, Newport, congregation of, vii, 60
Henry, Patrick, 129
Hewes, George, 4
Hicks, Edward, 2, 58
Hill Country, Texas, 347
Hill, Joe, 223, 225
Hirohito, emperor of Japan, 285, 297
Hiroshima, Japan, 295, 297
Hiss, Alger, 311
Hitler, Adolf, 257, 283–285, 296, 306
Ho Chi Minh, 262, 352–353
Holiday, Billie, 270
Holly Springs, Mississippi, 208
Hollywood, California, 268
Holmes, Oliver Wendell, Jr., Supreme Court justice, 377, 384
Homestead Act, 184
Homestead, Pennsylvania, 216

Hong Kong, 289
Hoover, J. Edgar, 263, 372
Hoover, President Herbert, 260, 275, 279
Hoovervilles, 275
Hope, Arkansas, 396
Hopkins, Stephen, 13
House of Burgesses (Virginia), 8, 55, 59
House of Representatives, 33–34, 167, 172, 409
Houston, Charles Mamilton, 316–317
Houston, Sam, 68–69
Howe, Elias, 76, 86
Howe, General Sir William, 23–24
Howe, Timothy, senator, 165
Hudson River, 24, 28, 82
Huerta, General Victoriano, 251
Hull, Cordell, secretary of state, 286
Hull House, 246–247
Humphrey, Hubert, senator and vice president, 349
Hunkpapa Sioux tribe, 194
Hunt Judge Ward, 207
Hurricane Katrina, 409–410
Hussein, Saddam, 407–408
Hutchins, Styles, 212, 213

I
Idaho, 241
immigrants, 1, 66, 71, 139, 184, 194–203, 217, 220, 224, 230, 262, 352, 395, 420
Indian lands, 183
Indian Removal Act, 66
Indian reservations, 369
Indians, 35, 368
Indian wars, 183, 194
Industrial Workers of the World (IWW); see Wobblies (IWW)
Internet, 411, 417, 422

internment of Japanese-Americans, 378
Intolerable Acts; see Restraining Acts
Iowa, 85, 201
Iran, 294, 387–388, 397, 415
Iran-Contra hearings, 397
Iraq, 394, 407–408, 409, 415–418
Ireland, 66, 71, 139, 158, 196
Iroquois, 49, 50, 153

J
Jackson, Andrew, 63–64, 65, 69, 70
Jackson, General Thomas "Stonewall", 128, 134
Jackson, Jimmy Lee, 360
James I, king of England, 52
Jamestown, Virginia, 1, 29
Japan, 199, 200, 283, 284–285, 288, 294, 297, 302
J. Edgar Hoover, 263
Jefferson, President Thomas, 416, 419, 421, 423
Jefferson, Thomas, 206, 227, 233, 240
Jews, 56, 196, 230, 283–284
Jim Crow laws, 179, 180–181, 304, 316–317, 325
Job Corps, 350
John, king of England, 6
Johnson, Andrew, 157, 160, 164, 170, 172, 174, 383
Johnson, Dr. Samuel, 64
Johnson, Ed, 212–213
Johnson, Lady Bird, 351
Johnson, President Lyndon B., 347–349, 351, 353, 370, 373, 378, 397, 416
Johnson, Sam Ealy, 347
Jones, "Mother" (Mary Harris), 230–233
Jordan, Barbara, 383–384

K
Kabul, Afghanistan, 406
Kansas, 109, 118
Kansas City, Missouri, 270
Kansas-Nebraska Act, 111
Kennan, George F., 354
Kennedy, Edward (Ted), senator, 408
Kennedy, Jacqueline, 345, 350
Kennedy, President John F., 350, 353, 397
Kennedy, Robert F. (Bobby), senator, 374–375
Kent State University, Ohio, 372
Kentucky, 61, 66, 113, 114, 116, 120, 130, 136, 177
Kerry, John, senator, 409
Khrushchev, Nikita, 332–335
King Coretta Scott, 359
King, Dr. Martin Luther, Jr., 321, 323–324, 328, 337–338, 341
King, Patricia, 340
Kissinger, Henry, secretary of state, 379–380
Know-Nothing Party, 198
Korea, 311, 315, 353, 395, 420
Korean War, 311
Kosciuszko, Colonel Tadeusz, 25
Ku Klux Klan, 162, 177, 198
Kuwait, 415

L
Laboulaye, Edouard de, 227–228
La Causa, 363, 365–366
Lafayette, Marquis de, 28, 227, 422
Lake Erie, 82
Lawrence, Massachusetts, 223–225
Lazarus, Emma, 230
League of Nations, 259–260
Lee, "Light Horse" Harry, 129
Lee, Robert E., 129, 134, 142–148, 150, 152–160

Lend-Lease program, 285
Leni-Lenape tribe, 58
Lenin, Vladimir Dyich, 262
Leutze, Emanuel Gottlieb, 26
Lewis, Meriwether, 45–47, 49
Lexington, Massachusetts, 11–13
Liberator, The, 105
Liberty Trees, 8
Lincoln, Brigadier-General Benjamin, 28
Lincoln-Douglas debates, 117–118
Lincoln, Nebraska, 237
Lincoln, President Abraham, ix, 85, 110–111, 116–118, 120–121, 123, 125–126, 130, 133, 135–136, 138, 141–142, 145, 418
Lindbergh, Charles, 270–271
Litchfield Female Academy, 87
Little Bighorn, Montana, battle of, 153
Little Rock, Arkansas, 325, 327
Livingston, Robert, x
Lloyd George, David, prime minister of England, 259
Locke, John, vi
Longfellow, Henry Wadsworth, 11
Los Alamos, New Mexico, 297
Louisiana, 120, 130, 135, 156, 178, 180
Louisiana Purchase, 45, 105
Lowell, Massachusetts, 80
Loyalists, 20, 23, 27
Lynch, Connie, 344
lynching, 177, 179, 210–211, 213, 302
Lyon, Mary, 87
Lyon, Mathew, 43

M

MacArthur, General Douglas, 275, 279, 295, 302
Madero, Francisco, 251
Madison, James, 327, 391, 423
Magna Carta, 6
Maine, 369
Malcolm, John, 4
Malcolm X, 359
Malraux, André, 331
Manassas, battle of, 126, 153; *see also* Bull Run
Manchuria, 284
manifest destiny, 70
Mankiller, Wilma, 369
Mao Zedong, 310
Marbury v. *Madison*, 44
March on Washington, 341, 344
Marshall, George C., secretary of state, 301–302
Marshall, John, Chief Justice of Supreme Court, 212
Marshall Plan, 299, 301
Marshall, Thurgood, Supreme Court justice, 212, 317–318
Martin, Anne, 261
Maryland, 64, 97, 136–137, 186
Mary, Queen of England, 7
Mason, George, 30, 36
Mason, James M., senator, 126
Massachusetts, Commonwealth of, v, 5, 9, 55–56, 63, 104, *and* Bay Colony
Massillon, Ohio, 221
Mayflower, 52–53, 277
Mayflower Compact, 53
McCain-Feingold Act, 412
McCain, John, senator, 412, 413
McCarthy, Joseph, senator, 311
McClellan, General George, 277
McClure's, 244
McClure, S. S., 244
McCormick, Cyrus, 86, 184–185, 218
McCormick Harvester, 218
McLean, Wilmer, 153, 156, 160
McNamara, Robert, 378
Meade, General George, 142

Medicaid, 351
Medicare, 351
Mellon, Andrew, 260
Melville, Herman, 77
Memphis, Tennessee, 209–211, 371–373
Methodists, 57
Mexican Revolution, 233
Mexican War, 128, 130, 133, 147, 193
Mexico, 107, 162
Michigan, 132, 205, 220
Mickey Mouse, 268
middle class, 423
Middle East, 387–388, 396, 403
Miranda v. *Arizona*, 400
Mississippi, 351, 357, 363, 371
Mississippi River, 64, 85, 144, 145
Missouri, 66, 68, 78
Missouri Compromise, 69, 105, 110, 112
Missouri River, 46
Monmouth, New Jersey, battle of, 18
Monroe, Colonel James later president, 26, 59, 63
Monroe Doctrine, 63
Montgomery, Alabama, 321–323
Morgan, J. P., 236–237
Morgan, Robin, 368
Morris, Gouverneur, 34
Morris Island, 139
Morse, Samuel F. B., 79, 83, 86
Mosby's Raiders, 160
Moss, Thomas, 209–210
Mott, Lucretia, 90
Mount Holyoke College, Massachusetts, 87
Mount Vernon, Virginia, 40, 42
muckrakers, 245
Muir, John, 241, 244
Mujahadeen, 404
Mussolini, Benito, 283, 293

N

Narragansett tribe, 56
National American Woman Suffrage Association, 264
National Association for the Advancement of Colored People (NAACP), 303, 318, 321–322
National Commission on Fiscal Responsibility and Reform, 415
National Endowment for the Humanities, 351
National Guard, 410
National Organization for Women (NOW), 368–370
National Road, 81–82
Nation of Islam, 359
Native Americans, 3, 35, 46, 56, 368
Nazism, 283, 306
"New Colossus, The", 230
New Deal, 279, 282, 311, 330, 344
New England, 17, 20, 53, 55, 75, 81, 331
New England Anti-Slavery Society, 106
New Jersey, 201, 229, 233
New Orleans, Louisiana, 268, 409, 410
Newport, Rhode Island, viii, 60
Newton, Sir Isaac, v
New York City, 17, 23, 38, 73, 81, 86, 419
New York, colony of, 16
New York State, 2
Nez Perce tribe, 190–192
Nineteenth Amendment to the Constitution, 264–265, 356
Ninth Amendment to the Constitution, 386
Nixon, E.D., 322
Nixon, Frank, 377
Nixon, President Richard, 377, 380, 382–385, 391, 397, 400
Nobel Peace Prize, 247, 355
North Carolina, 61, 101, 120, 124, 150, 167, 186, 328
North, Lt. Col. Oliver, 397
North Star, The, 102
North Vietnam, 353
Northwest Ordinance, 65

O

Obama, President Barack, 409, 413–415, 419, 421
Oberlin, Ohio, 113–114
O'Hara, Brigadier Charles, 28
Ohio, 64, 78, 82, 88
Ohio River, 113, 137
Olive Branch Petition, 14
Oliver, Joe "King", 270
One World Trade Center, 419
Operation Enduring Freedom, 405
Operation Headstart, 350
Operation Iraqi Freedom, 409
Operation New Dawn, 415
Operation Overlord, 293
Oregon territory, 70, 190
Oregon Trail, 62
O'Sullivan, John L., 70

P

Paine, Tom, 9–10, 12
Pakistan, 405
Palmer, A. Mitchell, 263–264
Panama Canal, 388
Parden, Noel, 212, 213
Parker, Captain John, 11
Parker, Colonel Ely, 153
Parks, Rosa, 321–324
Parliament, English, 394
Parsons, Lucy, 222–223
Patriot Act, *see* USA Patriot Act
Patriots, 13, 27; *see also* Continental army
Pattillo, Melba, 325–327
Paul, Alice, 261
Pawtucket, Rhode Island, 74
Peace Corps, 331
Peake, Mary, 161
Peale, Charles Willson, 40
Pearl Harbor, attack on, 286–287, 290–291
Pendergast, Tom, 299
Peninsula campaign, Virginia, 133
Pennsylvania, 13, 23, 32, 34, 36, 58–59
Pennsylvania, colony of, 58
Penn, William, 58–59, 377
Pentagon Papers, 378
Petersburg, Virginia, 150–151
Petersburg, Virginia, siege of, 123, 148
Petraeus, David, general, 417
Philadelphia, Pennsylvania, 208, 224, 229, 305
Philippine Islands, 243, 284, 289, 295
Pickett, General George, 143–144, 150
Pierce, Franklin, 110, 420
Pierce, Sarah, 87
Pierce, William, 32
Pilgrims, 52
Pinkerton men, 217, 224
Pitcher, Molly (Hays), 19
Plains, American, 184
Pledge of Allegiance, 321
Plessy, Homer, 212
Plessy v. Ferguson, 212
Plymouth, Massachusetts, 1, 53
Point Four, 302
Poland, German invasion of, 284
Polk, James K., 70
poll taxes, 177–178, 303, 351, 357, 429
Pony Express, 78
Poor People's Campaign, 371
Pope, General John, 187

popular sovereignty, 110, 117
Populist Party, 233–239
Post Office, U.S., 78
Potomac River, 119
Powel, Elizabeth, 39
Powell, Colin, secretary of state, 408
Presley, Elvis, 314
Price, John, 113, 115
Price, Rev. Richard, 416, 423
Princeton, battle of, 23
Princip, Gavrilo, 251
Progressive Party, 309; *see also* Bull Moose Party
Progressivism, 245–246
Prohibition, 268
Providence, Rhode Island, 56
Pulitzer, Joseph, 229
Pullman railcar strike, 204
Puritans, 52, 54–55

Q

Quakers, 54, 56, 58
Quartering Act, 5

R

Radical Republicans, 155, 163, 174
Rainey, Sheriff Lawrence, 357
Randolph, A. Philip, 341
Randolph, Peyton, 13
Reagan, President Ronald, 389–390, 392, 394, 397, 420
Rebels, 120; *see also* Confederate army, the South
Reconstruction, 155–156, 160, 164, 169, 171, 174, 176–179
Reconstruction Act, 1867, 165
Red Jacket (Sagoyewatha), 49–50
red scares, 262, 310–314
Reeb, Reverend James, 362
Rehnquist, William, Supreme Court chief justice, 386, 400–401
republicanism, 14–15, 35–36, 39

Republican Party, 400, 415
Restraining Acts, 5
Revels, Hiram R., 165
Revere, Paul, 10–11
Revolutionary War, 22, 49, 64
Rhode Island, viii, 13, 20, 27, 56, 60, 75, 80
Richmond, Virginia, 44, 127, 131, 133–134, 148–149, 151–152
Rickey, Branch, 304–305
Riis, Jacob, 196
Rio Grande River, 70
Robinson, Jackie, 305–306
Robinson, Jo Ann, 323
Rochambeau, Comte de, 27
Rochester, New York, 83, 92, 205–207
Rockefeller, John D., 215–216, 246, 250
Rock Island Line, 85
Rocky Mountains, 45–46, 61
Rogers, Mrs. John, Jr., 264
Romney, Mitt, governor, 418–419
Roosevelt, Eleanor, 280, 282, 328
Roosevelt, President Franklin Delano, ix, 276–279, 276–283, 285, 288, 294–297, 300, 377
Roosevelt, President Theodore "Teddy", 233, 241, 244–245, 278, 419
Ross, Edmund, senator, 174
Rothermel, Peter, 9
Rough Riders, 243
Rush, Benjamin, 13
Russia, 183, 196, 202
Russian Revolution, 262
Rustin, Bayard, 341
Rutledge, John, 32–33, 36

S

Sagoyewatha (Red Jacket), 49
Saigon, Vietnam, 373, 380
Salem, Massachusetts, 55
Sampson, Deborah, 19

Sandel, Michael, 418
San Francisco, California, 200–201, 228
Santa Anna, Antonio López de, 68
Santa Fe, New Mexico, 61
Santa Fe Trail, 61, 63, 66
Santo Domingo, 100
Sarajevo, 252
Saratoga, battle of, 23–25, 27
Scalia, Antonin, Supreme Court justice, 401
Schenck v. *United States*, 258
Schumer, Charles, senator, 407
Schurz, Carl, 194, 243
Schwerner, Mickey, 357–358
Scopes trial, 266–267
Scott, Dred, 112, 401
Scott, General Winfield, 124, 131
Scott, Thomas, 99
secession, 109, 121, 126, 160; *see also* the South
Second Amendment to the Constitution, 37
Sedition Act of 1798, 42, 44
Sedition Act of 1918, 258
segregation, 179, 303, 316, 318–319, 323–324, 337; *see also* Jim Crow laws
Selden, Henry, 205
Selma, Alabama, 358, 360, 362
Selma-Montgomery march, 324, 362
Senate, U.S., 33–34
Seneca Falls, 91
Seneca Falls Declaration, 91
Seneca tribe, 49
separate but equal, doctrine of, 180
Separatists (Saints), 52
September 11, events of, 402, 405
Sequoyah, 51, 67
settlers, 49, 52–53, 64–65, 66, 70, 183–184, 186–187

Seven Days, battle of, 134
Seward, William, secretary of state, 157
Sharpsburg, Maryland, 135
Shaw, Colonel Robert Gould, 140
Shawnee tribe, 50, 58
Shenandoah River, 119
Shenandoah Valley, Virginia, 128
Sheridan, General Philip, 162, 187
Sherman Antitrust Act, 243
Sherman, General William Tecumseh, 148–150, 187
Sherman, Roger, x, 13, 33, 264
Shipp, Sheriff Joseph Franklin, 211
Sierra Nevada mountains, 241
Silver Purchase Act, 1890, 236, 238
Singapore, 289
Sioux tribe, 187
Sirhan Bishara Sirhan, 375
Six Iroquois Nations, 18
Sixth Amendment, 290, 337
Slater, Samuel, 75
slavery, 1–2, 16, 20, 30, 33, 35, 36, 47, 76, 90, 93, 95–121, 137
Smalls, Robert, 167
Smith, Gerrit, 106
Smith, Margaret Chase, senator, 313
Social Security, 281
Somalia, 394
Sons of Liberty, 8
South Carolina, 27, 63, 73, 97, 120, 121, 420
Southern Christian Leadership Conference (SCLC), 339, 358
South, the, 20, 27, 36, 76, 108–109, 120–121, 123, 126, 128–129, 131, 135, 156–157, 159, 161–162, 169, 176–177, 234, 302–303, 319, 351

Soviets, 405
Soviet Union, 301, 307, 334
Spanish-American War, 243
Spanish colonies, 68
Spies, August, 218
Spirit of St. Louis, 270
Springfield, Illinois, 112
Stalin, Joseph, 294–295, 308–310
Stamp Tax (Stamp Act), 32
Standard Oil, 215, 245–246
Stanton, Edwin, 133
Stanton, Elizabeth Cady, 90–92, 205, 208
states' rights, 81, 120, 129, 164, 169, 401
Statue of Liberty, 227–229
Stephens, Alexander, 120
Steuben, Baron von, 25
Stevens, Thaddeus, 169, 171
St. Joseph, Missouri, 78
Stowe, Harriet Beecher, 87
Stuart, General J. E. B., 123
Student Nonviolent Coordinating Committee (SNCC), 358
suffrage movement, viii, 236, 260–261, 264–265; *see also* women, rights of
Sullivan, L.B., 328
Sumner, Charles, senator, 175
Supreme Court of the United States, 111, 172, 180, 201, 412
Susquehannock tribe, 58
Sutter's Mill, California, 78

T

Taft, President William Howard, 249, 251
Taliban, 405–406
Taney, Roger chief justice of Supreme Court, 111
Tarbell, Ida, 245
Taylor, Nevada, 211
Teacher Corps, 351

Tennessee, 63, 120, 161, 211, 265, 371
Tenth Amendment to the Constitution, 38
Tenure of Office Act, 1867, 172
Tet offensive, 373
Texas, 68–70, 120, 210, 255, 275, 313, 347, 383
Thailand, 284, 289
Third Amendment to the Constitution, 37
Thirteenth Amendment to the Constitution, 163
Thomson, Charles, 16
Thoreau, Henry David, ix
Tilden, Samuel, 178
Tinker, Mary Beth, 356
Tinker v. *Des Moines Independent School District*, 356
Tocqueville, Alexis de, 47, 62
Topeka, Kansas, 317
Toussaint L'Ouverture, 100, 102
Townshend, Lord Charles, 5
Trail of Tears, 66, 69
Truman, Bess, 299
Truman Doctrine, 308, 311
Truman, President Harry S., ix, 297, 299–304, 306, 308–311, 353, 420
Trumbull, John, artist, x, 22
trust-busting; *see* business, government regulation of
Truth, Sojourner, 88, 208
Tubman, Harriet, 114–115
Turner, Nat, 100
Twain, Mark, 214, 301, 422–423
Twenty-fourth Amendment of the Constitution, 351, 357
Twenty-sixth Amendment of the Constitution, 356

U

Un-American Activities Committee (HUAC), 312
Uncle Tom's Cabin, 137

Underground Railroad, 113–114
Union army, 107, 122, 135
United Mine Workers, 243
United Nations, 294–295, 307, 311, 405, 421
United States, 29, 31, 34
United States v. *Shipp*, 213
UN Resolution 1441, 407
UN Security Council, 408
Upward Bound, 350
USA Patriot Act (Uniting and Strengthening America by Providing Appropriate Tools Required to Intercept and Obstruct Terrorism), 406–407
U.S. military, 128, 327

V

Vallandigham, Clement Laird, 141
Vallee, Rudy, 276
Valley Forge, Pennsylvania, 23
Vandalia, Illinois, 82
Vanderbilt, Cornelius, 215
Vermont, 43, 105, 173, 268, 313, 373
Versailles, treaty of, 259–260, 283–284
Vicksburg, Mississippi, siege of, 144
Vietnam, 421
Vietnam War, 371, 372, 397, 408, 416
Virginia, 120
Virginia, colony of, 8
VISTA, 351
Voting Rights Act, 1965, 363

W

Wallace, George, governor of Alabama, 361
Wall Street Crash, 273–274
War on Poverty, 351
Warren, Earl, Supreme Court chief justice, 399

Washington, D.C., 79, 369, 377, 402
Washington, Martha, 25
Washington Post, 381
Washington, President George, vi, ix, 13–14, 20, 21, 23, 26, 28, 31–34, 36–37, 40–42, 59, 60, 86–87, 255
Watergate, 376, 381–382, 384, 397
Watson, Tom, 233
Watts riots, Los Angeles, 371
Webb, Sheyann, 361
Webster, Daniel, U.S. senator, 108, 349
Wells, Ida B., 209
"We Shall Overcome", 343
Westminster College, 306
West Point, U.S. military academy at, 128, 130, 147
West, the, 61, 64, 70, 210, 392
Wheeling, West Virginia, 78
White House, 45, 65
White, Walter, 303
Whitney, Eli, 185
Whitney v. *California*, 385
WikiLeaks, 417
Wilderness Road, 61
Wilhelm II, emperor of Germany, 252
Wilkins, Roy, 341
William III (of Orange), king of England, 7
Williamsburg, Virginia, 8
Williams, Hosea, 361
Williams, Roger, 55
Wilson, James, 32, 36
Wilson, President Thomas Woodrow, 63, 249–251, 253, 255–257, 259–260, 262–263, 301, 419
Winthrop, John, governor of Plymouth colony, 53
Wisconsin, 64, 83, 400

Witherspoon, Rev. John, 57
WMDs (weapons of mass destruction), 407–408
Wobblies (IWW), 204, 222, 258
women, rights of, 2, 13, 19–20, 21, 35, 87–93, 205–208, 236, 247, 260–261, 264–265, 316, 366–370, 406
Worcester, Samuel, 67
Worcester v. *Georgia*, 68
working conditions, 239, 365
Workingmen's Party, 198
World Trade Center, 402, 404, 419
"World Turned Upside Down", 27
World War I, 249, 251–257, 275, 283, 299, 301, 384
World War II, 283–297, 299, 301, 306, 312, 352
Wounded Knee, South Dakota, 368
Wright brothers, 265

Y

Yalta, Crimea, 294
Yankees; *see* Union army
Yellowstone Park, 241
Yick, Lee, 201
Yick Wo v. *Hopkins*, 201
Yorktown, Virginia, battle of, 27–29
Yosemite, 241, 244
Yugoslavia, former, 394

Z

Zenger, Peter, 38
Zhou, Enlai, 353, 380